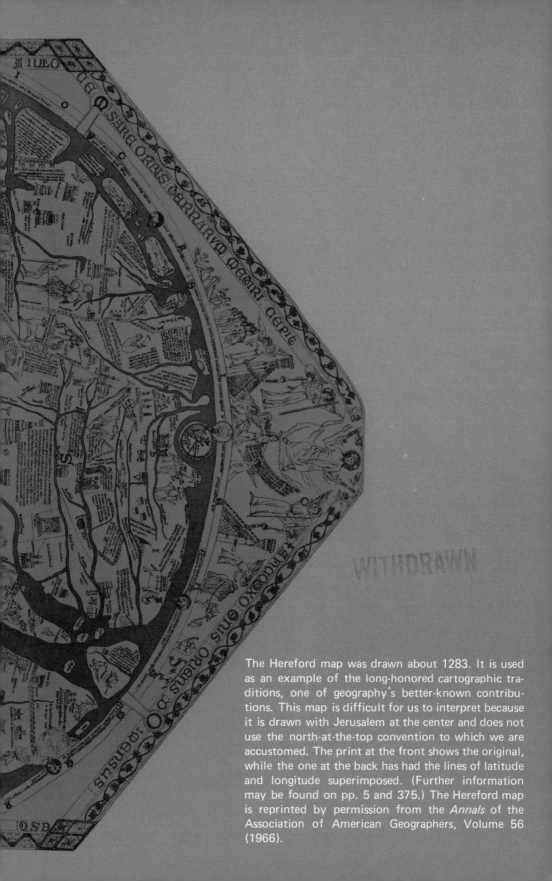

The Hereford map was drawn about 1283. It is used as an example of the long-honored cartographic traditions, one of geography's better-known contributions. This map is difficult for us to interpret because it is drawn with Jerusalem at the center and does not use the north-at-the-top convention to which we are accustomed. The print at the front shows the original, while the one at the back has had the lines of latitude and longitude superimposed. (Further information may be found on pp. 5 and 375.) The Hereford map is reprinted by permission from the *Annals* of the Association of American Geographers, Volume 56 (1966).

HERBERT G. KARIEL The University of Calgary
PATRICIA E. KARIEL

EXPLORATIONS IN SOCIAL GEOGRAPHY

ADDISON-WESLEY PUBLISHING COMPANY
Reading, Massachusetts
Menlo Park, California • London • Don Mills, Ontario

Artwork appearing in this text were reproduced from camera-ready copy supplied by the authors.

To our parents and teachers

PREFACE

This book is designed as a text for introductory courses in human, cultural, or social geography* and can be covered in a fast-moving quarter or semester course. It would also be useful as background reading for advanced undergraduate and graduate students who are unfamiliar with the concepts and methods used. The references and additional readings accompanying each chapter suggest sources for exploring the topics and techniques in greater depth. This text is topically organized, beginning with empirical observation and gradually introducing abstract concepts and developing theory, with the intention of helping students to move easily between the two. Most textbooks in this field are organized regionally rather than topically. Those which are topically organized tend to be either empirical, almost ignoring the more abstract and theoretical elements of geography, or extremely abstract and theoretical, and therefore difficult for beginning students.

It represents our attempt to deal with social geography using a scientific approach. This approach provides a methodology by which diverse observations may be related to each other and to patterns discerned among these relationships which transcend the immediate context. Within this context, we have presented a number of topics in the field of social geography, trying not to emphasize facts but rather to stress ways in which they may be used in deriving generalizations and developing laws and theory. We have also tried to relate these topics to each other and to develop a systems model incorporating the interrelationships. We have proceeded on the assumption that

---

*A logical distinction can be made among these three types of geographic study, although such a distinction is rarely made in practice. Human geography can be defined as the study of the spatial aspects of the set of phenomena involving man in which the dependent variables include population and human activities: economic, political, and social. Strictly speaking, social geography would include only that subset of variables dealing with the spatial aspects of organizations, social institutions, individuals, and groups, whereas cultural geography would deal with another subset of variables related to the spatial aspects of both material and non-material elements of culture.

For purposes of simplicity, however, we shall use the term social geography to mean study of the spatial aspects of characteristics of the population, social organization, and elements of culture and society.

scientists do not expect in the short run to find the ultimate answers to their questions, recognizing that often, for each question answered, a number of new ones arise. Knowledge acquired is gradually fitted into a theoretical framework in which there are ever high levels of abstraction and generality, with the result that a large number of observations can be explained by a single law, and several laws by a theory. Because geographic study of human phenomena is in the early phase of this process of developing theory, much work remains to be done.

We have chosen to concentrate upon a single approach, that of spatial analysis. Both parts of this term are important: first, the notion that geography is distinctive because it concentrates on *spatial* aspects of phenomena, and second, the idea that geographic study should be based on *analysis* of these spatial aspects, within the general framework of the scientific method. There are several reasons for this decision. A review of the geographic literature over the past ten years reveals an increasing number of articles based on this approach and employing a variety of analytical techniques, such as statistical tests and mathematical models. Whatever his own ideas, a student who is seriously interested in geography should be able to read and analyze such articles intelligently, and students not intending to major in the field should be aware of the newer trends. It is believed that concentration on one approach will give students a solid foundation in it, rather than diffusing their efforts in a number of directions within a single course. Finally, but perhaps most important, is our faith that taking a scientific approach to the building of knowledge about the world in which man lives and his relationships to it will prove most productive in the long run—a belief which can be tested only by time.

Since the overall aim is to help students acquire both knowledge about their world and analytical techniques for understanding it, the two themes of substantive knowledge and methodology are developed concurrently. The substantive chapters illustrate applications of the scientific approach to the study of a number of topics. No claim is made that the particular ones considered include all those studied by social geographers, although they are representative and of more than casual interest and importance. For each topic we have attempted to compile the results of numerous studies, provide an overview of what has already been learned and what is being studied, and suggest directions for further exploration. The sophistication with which each topic is treated depends upon the material available. Topics are arranged in order of increasing complexity with respect to methodology and degree of abstractness and generality, so that knowledge of relatively elementary notions of spatial analysis and simple means of testing hypotheses explained and illustrated in the early chapters is assumed in subsequent ones, as is familiarity with the subject matter. The methodology is presented both explicitly and implicitly, with emphasis on the logic underlying each technique and on the purpose for which it is used rather than on the manner of carrying it out.

In keeping with the newer practice in many disciplines, much of the material is presented inductively, so that students, beginning with observations, learn to formulate and answer questions in a way which may be fruitful. They are helped to identify geographic problems, to define and delimit topics for study, and to investigate the problems thus delineated. Each topic is considered at more than one scale, and similarities and differences among the findings are analyzed with the aim of formulating generalizations which are applicable at different levels of areal analysis. Our aim is to help students learn to make spatial predictions based upon the generalizations developed so that, even though specific items of information become outdated, students will be able to apply their knowledge to new situations.

In Chapter 1 the notion of geography as spatial analysis is presented in an everyday context, and the general plan of the book is given. Chapters 2 and 3, the first substantive ones, explore two topics and acquaint the student with the approach used throughout. Chapter 4 then presents this approach explicitly. It should be read several times, carefully, since it contains the ideas of scientific analysis upon which the entire book is based. The student is advised to return to this chapter from time to time when reading the remainder of the book, because the discussion will become increasingly meaningful as his experience with application of these techniques to the analysis of geographic problems grows. In spite of their apparent simplicity, the early chapters are extremely important, since they introduce both substantive knowledge and method-ology which are used in the later, more sophisticated chapters. Whereas Chapters 1 through 9 emphasize analysis, in Chapters 10 through 12 focus is upon synthesis and dynamic aspects of the process of change. In Chapter 13 we shall look back at the explorations, relating them to some of the questions raised in Chapter 1 and considering the role of values in scientific study.

Readers may find that this text appears deceptively simple, because we have made an effort to avoid jargon and to explain even difficult concepts in ordinary English, using a minimum of technical terms and defining or otherwise explaining those unfamiliar to the average student. The greatest benefit will be gained if each chapter is read according to the method generally suggested in how-to-study texts. Look it over once to get a general overview of the material covered and pose questions which you hope to answer by more careful readings. Then read it all the way through. On the next reading, try to understand the major points covered and fill in the details. Taking notes or outlining are more helpful for this purpose than underlining. Finally, review the list of key concepts at the end of the chapter to make sure you understand each one. After completing this process, work through some of the suggested activities to improve your ability to apply knowledge to new situations. These activities are primarily ideas for longer-range individual or group projects, suitable for use in connection with discussion sections or tutorial groups.

We have set ambitious goals for ourselves in writing this text. As we proceeded, we felt more and more that we were indeed exploring ways in which the scientific approach might help to open up new areas of knowledge in geographic study. We were often frustrated by the lack of systematic studies which could be reviewed and the lack of comparability from one study to another. We realized how incomplete the discussion of each topic was, often because we had reached the end of the available knowledge about it. New questions constantly arose which we were unable to answer.

Sometimes we conducted our own research to fill in the gaps, as in the discussion of world dietary patterns and the work on the systems model of technology and related factors. As the manuscript neared completion, we recognized that these could only be called explorations in social geography, and that we were more aware than ever not only of gaps in knowledge but also of our own shortcomings and inability to compile and collate the work of many specialists, as well as to cover all the major developments within the compass of a single text. We hope that the result, imperfect and exploratory as it is, may serve to stimulate future geographers to use this framework and add their bit to knowledge, so that some day a more definitive book may be written.

We recognize that no one book will satisfy everyone. Some geographers may feel that our work is too cold and uninteresting because geography is considered as a science rather than an art. Others may think it is too unsophisticated, and fails to deal with the newer developments on a sufficiently abstract and mathematical level. Our aim has been to steer a course between the two extremes, and we hope we have succeeded sufficiently that the results will pave the way for future, perhaps more successful attempts.

We are indebted to the many people who helped to make this book a reality. We were introduced to philosophy of science and use of the scientific method in geography by many of the faculty at the University of Iowa, especially Harold H. McCarty, Clyde F. Kohn, and Gustav Bergman. Comments and evaluation have been received from more people than can be mentioned by name. We are especially grateful to all the students and graduate assistants who have given us the students' viewpoint. Bill McCormack provided expert assistance with Chapter 6, and Bob Stoddard gave most careful consideration to the entire manuscript at different stages of its development. My colleagues Ron Bolin, Al Gonzalez, Lynn Rosenvall, and Maurice Scarlett made helpful suggestions throughout, and Ron Bolin suggested the use of the Hereford map. Several reviewers have also made valuable criticisms. All comments were carefully considered, but any shortcomings or inaccuracies in the final product remain our responsibility. Appreciation is expressed to the Canada Council for assistance which made possible much of the material contained in Chapter 10, Technology. Editorial assistance and typing were provided by Mrs. Elise Wittig and the staff of the Stenographic Services at the University of Calgary, as well as by many persons at California State College at Hayward and Western Washington State College. Marilyn Boucher helped to prepare many of the maps and diagrams; Nick Babey, Hank Liphuysen, Minnie Medwid and the secretarial staff, all of the Department of Geography at the University of Calgary, provided additional technical assistance.

Calgary, Alberta   H. G. K.
January 1972   P. E. K.

CONTENTS

*Since content and methodology are emphasized throughout the text, both are included in the table of contents. To aid in distinguishing between the two, items given in italics refer to sections in which methodology is discussed explicitly.

Chapter 5   Food

Chapter 6   Language

Chapter 8   Land Use

CHAPTER 1
INTRODUCTION

1.1 IDEAS ABOUT SPACE, LOCATION, WORLD PROBLEMS, AND GEOGRAPHY

How do you react to questions like these? Do you prefer the wide open spaces, or do you feel more comfortable in a city, surrounded by other people? When talking to another person, how far from him do you like to be? Would you rather be closer to some people than to others? Do you find conversation difficult when you are too far away, or when there are so many others around that you cannot hear the person with whom you are talking? When speaking with someone of a higher status than you, do you feel more comfortable when there is a barrier, such as a table or a desk, between you? Where do you go when you want to concentrate—do you try to get away from others, behind a closed door, where less is going on?

We try to organize our personal space—the area immediately surrounding our bodies—in a way which makes us most comfortable and facilitates our activities. Sometimes we are aware of our preferences and prejudices about this space, but at other times we take our feelings for granted, possibly not realizing that they may differ from those of others. Yet these beliefs influence our daily behavior in many ways.

On a larger scale, the use of space and the location of different things in relation to each other are matters of concern. Most of us have thought about questions such as these: Where do you want to live and work? Do you imagine yourself in a 60-story office building in a large city, looking out of a window at the homes of millions of other people? Or do you dream of life in a small town, where you know almost everyone? What kind of work will you do? Will you teach in a country school, be an engineer on a heavy construction project, or argue cases in court? How will your work influence your way of life? Will you commute to the city from the suburbs, or will your home be close to your work? In what kind of a neighborhood will you raise a family? Will you have your own home with a yard and garden, or live in an apartment?

Where do you go to ski, surf, dance, or listen to music? What facilities are available nearby, and how many miles do you travel on weekends or vacations?

1

Do you take for granted the ease with which you can board an airplane and within hours be carried to almost any place in the world? Or, if you cannot go, do you accept the rapidity with which news travels from any part of the globe to your television set or radio, and with which pictures are transmitted from the moon? Have you become accustomed to new sights and sounds and smells and tastes? Never before in history have men and women had so many choices. Formerly, what they would be and where and how they would live were almost completely determined at birth. Their perspective on the world was limited by their knowledge about it, and often their travels were restricted to within a few miles of their birthplace. Few people journeyed far from home, and most of those that left never returned.

Although much of the world's population is still limited in this manner, more and more people are moving from the country to the city, breaking ties with their families, and learning to survive in a new urban setting. In the world's cities live the urban poor, some sleeping on the street, others erecting makeshift shelters or paying exorbitant rents for rundown, unsanitary slum housing. Their children may be forced to beg, steal, forage in garbage cans for food, or make what little money they can shining shoes or diving for money thrown into the water by tourists. There is no question of education for them, as their families need their help to survive.

And what about those who are fortunate enough to have the security of a job, a comfortable home, and adequate food, medical care, and education for their children? Are they also threatened by other problems such as impure air, polluted water, and unabated noise? Will their children and grandchildren have enough room to live on the earth, enough food to eat, enough natural resources to guarantee them the comfortable existence so many of us take for granted? Will mankind learn to control the technological forces at its disposal, using them to enrich the quality of human life rather than to destroy it?

Questions such as these frequently evoke strong emotional responses, and discussions about them often create more heat than light, as each participant promotes his or her cherished point of view. Although their ultimate solutions are complex, simplistic answers are often advocated. These are usually ineffective, however, since trial-and-error answers are often costly of time, effort, and resources, and solutions aimed at only a single problem may create new ones or make the existing ones worse. For example, the large-scale public housing projects of the 1950's provided low-rent housing for many families, but created new and bigger ghettos where crime and delinquency flourished. Schools and recreation facilities were inadequate, since planners had not considered the total environment in their eagerness to provide shelter alone. The advantages of the new physical setting were soon more than offset by the unhealthy social climate, so that by the end of the 1960's many buildings had to be abandoned as unlivable. The problems of poverty, unemployment, poor education, and inadequate housing became increasingly concentrated in the cities as many of the more affluent urban dwellers moved to the suburbs in search of privacy, quiet, better air, less noise, good schools, and recreation facilities. Roads became clogged as suburbanites drove to and from work. New roads were built: first expressways, then four-, eight-, and twelve-lane freeways. More cars drove on them, traffic congestion increased, and the smog worsened. Productive agricultural land was covered by homes, shopping centers, and roads. People began to wonder whether, in spite of the fact that they had more and better possessions than ever before, the overall quality of life might not be deteriorating.

Young people, and older ones as well, who are concerned about the quality of life can drop out, accept things as they are and try to get as much as possible for themselves without worrying about anyone else, or attempt to make some contribution, however small, to bettering the situation. Accepting the fact that change is a reality of modern life, they can work to see that it moves in a desirable rather than an undesirable direction. Public pressure can help to make industries and municipalities stop polluting air, water, and the land, and can direct research toward finding better ways of disposing of society's wastes and utilizing resources. It can suggest locations for new parks and better ways of designing urban areas if enough concerned individuals act.

How can this goal come about? How can people learn enough to act intelligently in our complex world of today? Although there are no quick and easy answers, forming habits of observation and analysis is essential. Being aware of what goes on about us, both in the immediate environment and at greater distances, asking questions about what we see and hear and read, trying to explain these observations, and drawing conclusions from them will all help.

You may well be wondering how all the questions we have raised relate to geography. In studying geography, you have probably learned how people live in different parts of the world, how climate, resources, and topography vary from place to place, and how products from one area are shipped to others where they would otherwise be unavailable. Like our questions, these topics are concerned in part with man's use of space and his natural environment. Geographers focus not so much on the particular questions or topics they are studying, but rather upon their spatial aspects. The main questions which they ask are these: Where are these phenomena located? Why are they there? What other phenomena are often found in association with them? How does this distribution change over time? Are there certain spatial laws and processes which seem to apply to many different phenomena in different places and at different times? When some of these questions can be answered, we shall have the beginnings of a general theory of location.

Consequently, in thinking about some of the issues we have raised, we can consider what their geographic aspects might be. We have for example, raised general questions about housing; geographers would ask more specific ones such as: Where is substandard housing found? What other social phenomena might also be found in areas of substandard housing? What changes take place over time in such areas—how do areas of substandard housing increase, in what directions are they most likely to spread, and what factors might bring about reversals in the amount of substandard housing in an area? Or, if you were thinking about where you might want to live, some knowledge of the general land use pattern might be helpful. You would probably wish to select a location reasonably accessible to your work, in which there were adequate shopping, educational, and recreational facilities for your family, and which was free from annoyances such as excessive air, water, and noise pollution.

In our technological age, you might be concerned about the relationship of technology to many of the other factors in your environment, and possibly even throughout the world. What general conclusions can be drawn about relationships between technology and other phenomena such as the kinds of houses people live in, type and amount of food consumed, and the amount of education which people have?

Finally, as we think about movement among areas, we might wonder how far people travel for an evening's entertainment, a weekend, or a summer vacation, or to attend meetings or enroll at a college or university. Do these distances vary from place to place and from time to time, and to what other factors might they be related? How do ideas spread from place to place?

These are the kinds of questions which we shall be exploring throughout this book. We shall look at a number of different phenomena, in different places and at different time periods, and try to discern some regularities among our findings.

1.2 A GEOGRAPHIC MATRIX

Since as geographers we shall be dealing with the location and areal arrangement of different phenomena on the face of the earth at any given time or over a period of time, it is helpful to organize data according to these three elements of area, topic, and time. We can visualize a three-dimensional matrix with each axis representing one dimension: the X-axis area, the Y-axis topics, and the Z-axis time (Fig. 1.1). If data were organized and stored in this manner, as Berry (1964) has suggested, all the phenomena for a given place at a given time would be found in a single column; the distribution of a particular phenomenon among areas would be found in a row, and the variations over time would be found along the Z-axis. Thus, the data for any phenomenon i, at any place j, at any time k, would be located in cell ijk of such a matrix. For example, port activities in Hamburg in 1905 could be located by specifying three coordinates. The activities of the port of New York at the same time would be located at the same points on the Y- and Z- axes, but at a different point on the X-axis. If we then wished to study the activities of the port of New York from 1850 to 1950, we would include all the cells along the X-axis from 1850 to 1950 bounded by the values of x and y assigned to ports and New York, respectively.

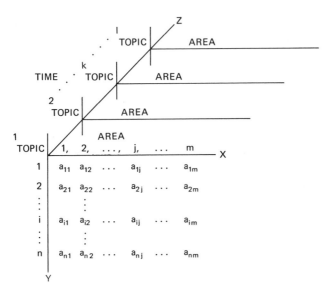

Fig. 1.1. Three-dimensional matrix for ordering geographic data. Adapted from Berry, 1964. Reproduced by permission from the *Annals* of the Association of American Geographers, Volume 54 (1964).

1.3 CHANGES IN PERSPECTIVE

Even though we may try to understand our observations and to develop generalizations, we must recognize that we are bound by our own conceptions of time and space. As man's knowledge increases, his view of the world and his relationship to it changes. This changing perspective on and knowledge about the world may be illustrated by the map on the front and back endpapers, which is known as the Hereford map because the original is located in the cathedral at Hereford, England. Drawn during the late Middle Ages, about 1283 A.D., it represents the contemporary view of the world. Jerusalem is in the center because of its religious significance, and all other places are located with respect to it. The map looks distorted to us because the conventions of latitude and longitude have not been observed. Tobler (1966)* explained how a number of places were identified and their locations used as a basis for drawing in the lines of latitude and longitude, as shown on the back endpapers. Translating this map to our own frame of reference should help us to recognize that our geographic perspective and concepts are equally limited by our own knowledge and viewpoint, and that they may look as outdated to scholars even a decade or two from now as this map looks to us.

---

*The Hereford map is reprinted by permission from the *Annals* of the Association of American Geographers, Volume 56 (1966).

1.4 FOCUS OF OUR EXPLORATIONS IN SOCIAL GEOGRAPHY

In the present explorations in social geography our concern will be with only a small portion of the discipline of geography. We shall examine spatial aspects of certain phenomena of interest to social geographers, and learn how cartographic and quantitative methods can be applied to geographic study of these phenomena. Since we are concerned that knowledge be cumulative, so that persons can build upon the work of others and integrate their findings into what is already known, we shall review some of what has been learned not only by geographers but also by persons in other disciplines whose findings are relevant for geographic study. We can then point out some of what remains to be learned, and possible directions which might be taken in further research.

We shall concentrate on definition, location, and explanation of the observed distribution of each phenomenon which we explore. In the early chapters the identification of the phenomenon and the particular aspects of it to be studied will be considered first, and it will be defined as precisely as possible. Its location within a given area or areas will then be discussed. Certain spatial aspects of the phenomenon will be examined on different scales and within different universes, or study areas, such as countries, states, or cities. The knowledge of the spatial distribution of a given phenomenon over a given area will then be used in accounting for the way in which it is distributed.

As our explorations continue, we hope to discover some generalizations which apply to the spatial distribution of several phenomena; in other words, we shall be working towards developing a general, if rudimentary theory of the location of human phenomena. We shall consider some of the theoretical formulations and models which have been constructed and learn how they are used by geographers. Our last major area of concern will be with the processes by which changes in the spatial aspect of phenomena, especially their distributions, occur over time.

REVIEW YOUR UNDERSTANDING OF THESE CONCEPTS

geographic matrix
ordering geographic data
relationship between (1) ideas about space and location and (2) geography

REFERENCES

Berry, Brian J. L. (1964), "Approaches to regional analysis: a synthesis," *Annals* of the Association of American Geographers **54**, 2–11.

Tobler, Waldo R. (1966), "Medieval distortions: the projections of ancient maps," *Annals* of the Association of American Geographers **56**, 351–360.

Additional Readings

Ackerman, Edward, A. (1958), *Geography as a Fundamental Research Discipline*, Department of Geography Research Paper No. 53, Chicago: University of Chicago Press.

Ad hoc Committee on Geography (1965), *The Science of Geography*, Publication No. 1277, Washington, D.C.: National Academy of Sciences—National Research Council.

James, Preston E. and Clarence F. Jones, eds. (1954), *American Geography: Inventory and Prospect*. Syracuse: Syracuse University Press.

McCarty, Harold H. (1963), "The geographer and his intellectual environment," *New Zealand Geographer* **19**, 1–6.

Pattison, William D. (1964), "The four traditions of geography," *The Journal of Geography* **63**, 211–216.

Warntz, William (1964), *Geographers and What They Do*. New York: Watts.

CHAPTER 2
ARCHITECTURE
AND HOUSING

2.1 INTRODUCTION

Our first exploration in social geography will be concerned with elements of architecture and housing. We shall first organize our observations about architectural style and study them on a world-wide basis; then we shall study housing in smaller areas.

Shelter is one of the basic needs of human beings. In many places in the world, men would be unable to survive without it; in most places they would be, at best, extremely uncomfortable. Men have responded to this need in a wide variety of ways by constructing many different types of shelter and using many different materials. They have constructed not only simple homes as shelter from the elements, but also more elaborate structures such as temples, palaces, and governmental buildings. Since shelter is a basic need of mankind which is fulfilled by the erection of visible structures, it is an excellent topic for our first exploration.

Many questions can be posed which a geographer might seek to answer. What spatial variations are found in the use of building materials? Does the spatial distribution of a particular building material coincide with that of other phenomena? Turning our attention to architectural style, we might ask about the origin and spread of a particular house type. Why do we find one kind of home in one place and a different kind in another? Are there any patterns in the spatial distribution of various elements related to housing? Are these similar to the distributional patterns of other phenomena? Can they be expressed quantitatively? Can we discern any general principles, or laws, which would explain the distributions we observe? These are but a few of the questions geographers have asked and are still trying to answer.

From our general knowledge, we know that men satisfy their basic need for shelter in many ways. In various parts of the world, men live in such diverse structures as snow houses, tents, shacks, ranch-style homes, and high-rise apartments. Although all these shelters serve the same primary purpose of protection from the elements, they differ in many ways. Walking down the street of a North American city we can see many variations. Structures are of varying age, size, color, and overall condition. Some houses are large, others small. Paint comes in many colors and degrees of wear. In certain sections of town most of the houses are well kept, whereas in others, many structures are in various stages of dilapidation. Houses are made of different materials: brick, wood, and stone, and have a variety of structural features: bay windows, balconies, or porches, while others do not.

If we were to extend our observation to an around-the-world trip, we would note an even greater variety in the buildings from place to place. We would find people living in grass shacks, mud huts, castles, and manor houses, to mention but a few possibilities. By the time we returned home, we might well feel overwhelmed by the task of organizing our observations. Making sense out of these observations and organizing them in some meaningful manner would appear to be difficult, if not impossible.

Organization of our observations is, nevertheless, an essential step in our attempt to understand and explain the spatial distribution of any phenomenon. Bearing in mind, then, the many differences we noted in our brief observational around-the-world tour, let us consider the various possibilities. What elements might serve as criteria upon which a classificatory scheme could be based?

2.2 SOME POSSIBLE WAYS OF CLASSIFYING SHELTER

Beginning with a relatively simple, common-sense approach, we might first try to organize our observations according to descriptive elements such as size, shape, or floor plan. Classification on the basis of size alone—either floor area or volume—would be relatively simple and would result in an easily determinable quantitative measure susceptible to statistical analysis. Unfortunately, however, size alone would be of little value for our purposes. Classification according to either shape or floor plan would likewise be of limited usefulness to us.

On a more technical level, we could consider in combination the materials and type of construction used. Both of these elements have been employed in historical and anthropological analyses of housing as an element of culture. They are interrelated, since each material places limitations upon the type of building which can be constructed with it. Larger buildings with longer unsupported spans can be built of wood than of stone; in turn, the use of steel and reinforced concrete has made possible the construction of buildings with even longer spans between the load-bearing members. Technological developments often extend the use of an existing material; for example, the development of prefabricated laminated wood beams has opened new possibilities in the building of churches and larger structures. A person concerned with designing or building structures might well find a classification based on construction materials and methods to be a useful one.

Another possibility would be to consider the functions of different structures. On farms we see that some buildings house animals or equipment, others people. In cities we find not only residential structures but also banks, office buildings, factories, churches, schools, and public buildings such as post offices and libraries, to name but a few. Such a classification based on function is frequently useful to the geographer or planner concerned with land use.

A sociologist or social worker, on the other hand, might be particularly interested in determining the adequacy of housing. He might look at such features as the general condition of a structure; the presence or absence of plumbing, heat, or hot water, and the number of persons living in a room. He would find families of two or three people living in twelve- or twenty-room homes, and other families of twelve or more crowded into single rooms. A geographer would be concerned with studying the spatial variations in such housing conditions, seeking to find social, economic, or other phenomena associated with them. He would be likely to discover, for example, that laborers with limited incomes were often crowded into rundown urban housing with little or no plumbing, while a bank president enjoyed the comfort of a large house in the country with many baths and a swimming pool. A classification based on adequacy of housing would be useful for many purposes. Hartman and Hook (1956) have carried out a study of substandard housing, which we shall discuss later.

A commonly used basis for a classificatory scheme is architectural style. Such names as Gothic, Romanesque, Greek, and Byzantine bring to mind specific styles of building. Similarly, Indian and Chinese architecture are easily distinguished, if not identified, even by an untrained observer. The name of a well-known architect, such as Christopher Wren, LeCorbusier, or Frank Lloyd Wright, conveys both a time period and a distinctive artistic concept. Although helpful for architects, classification on the basis of architectural style has the disadvantage for the social geographer of being restricted as to both time and space.

2.2.1 Style as a Continuum

When we attempt to span both time and space with a classification scheme equally applicable to teepees, ranch houses, and Gothic cathedrals, we are faced with what appears to be an almost insuperable task. Because it is so difficult to establish a classificatory scheme with a number of well-defined classes for the entire world, we shall combine several of the criteria suggested to develop a continuum along which we can place structures. We shall attempt to identify only its two extremes and the broad middle range. Although several criteria are considered in deciding where structures may be placed, the major one is the extent to which a structure is the product of conscious artistic considerations in design and construction. For want of better terms, we shall designate one extreme as *primitive* architecture and the other as *conscious*. The wide intermediate range we shall call *folk* architecture.

2.3 A WORLD-WIDE SURVEY OF THE ARCHITECTURAL CONTINUUM

2.3.1 Primitive Architecture

According to our designation, primitive structures are those built with little or no conscious architectural design. They are further characterized by direct use of materials; that is, use of materials found in the immediate environment, with a minimum of processing requiring only simple tools. The Pygmy in the African bush is not in a position to purchase prefabricated wall panels or prehung doors for building his shelter. Little specialization of labor is required for building primitive structures; an Eskimo does not call in an architect, contractor, plumber, or electrician when he wishes to construct a home. Finally, there is relative uniformity among structures of a given type; all snow-houses, teepees, or log cabins, for example, are much the same. In summary, four characteristics are present in varying degrees in structures designated as primitive: (1) lack of conscious architectural style, (2) direct use of materials available in the locality, (3) little specialization of labor required for construction, and (4) relative uniformity among the structures of the same type in a given area. With these criteria in mind, let us look at some primitive structures and their locations.

Like many animals, prehistoric men took shelter from the elements wherever it was available. Some men were fortunate enough to find caves; others may have piled up rude shelters of tree boughs to protect themselves from wind and rain. Some groups of people still depend upon such shelters. Of the African Pygmies, Wagner (1960) says,

> The dwelling is a simple affair, seldom more than a temporary lean-to of brush, covered with boughs, skins or bark . . . Some few groups . . . lived in caves during the course of their wanderings . . . (pp. 162–163)

Trees and saplings available in the natural environment may be used in a variety of ways to provide the framework of such a shelter. They may be covered by many different materials, depending upon what is available as well as upon the climatic conditions against which shelter must be provided. The spaces between the supporting framework of poles are filled with reeds, grasses, or leaves and may be plastered with mud, clay, or dung.

Some of these pole-frame structures are round, others rectangular in shape. In the Ethiopian highlands, for example, the houses, cylindrical in shape, are made of a framework of withes (branches) covered with clay. They have conical thatched roofs. Other African tribes, such as the BaVenda, Bantus, and Zulus, also build round huts that have straw or grass roofs which overhang the walls. Hogans of the Navajos are similarly constructed. The typical Navajo dwelling is a dome-shaped framework of logs or sticks covered with brush, bark, or grass and earth.

In various islands in the Pacific, many variations on the theme of rectangular houses of pole construction are found. The supporting framework is lashed together with lianas and covered by palm leaf matting or thatch made of whatever material is at hand. In Tonga, coconut leaves are used for walls and thatch; in Samoa, roofs are thatched with leaves from a special variety of sugar cane. The Fijian bures and the Samoan fales are examples of this type of construction. Similar homes may be built on pilings, as is done in frequently flooded areas of Indonesia and the Philippines.

Pole construction is also used by people who migrate from place to place. Their portable homes usually consist of a framework of wooden poles covered with whatever material is available. The Plains Indians, for example, covered their homes with animal skins, while the Indians of north central and north-eastern North America used birch bark. In other areas, where woven cloth was available, it was used as an outer covering. Even today, people in some parts of the world still live in movable homes. The wooden framework of the Mongolian yurt is covered with an inner layer of felt and an outer layer of canvas. The nomadic Bedouins of Arabia and the Berbers of North Africa live in cloth tents, the interiors of which are often elaborately furnished with oriental carpets.

Not only is mud used as plaster in homes of pole construction, but also earth is used as a building material in its own right. In China, men have for centuries lived in caves hollowed out of loess, a soft soil of wind deposited origin; today their houses are built into the cliffs, and have doors and windows. At some un-determined time in prehistory, men learned to make bricks out of mud, and dried them in the sun. These adobe bricks were used in areas where no wood was avail-able: in the southwestern United States, and in parts of Africa, the Near East, and northern India. Skole (1962) has described the distribution of adobe in Africa:

> The use of adobe in Africa is as widespread as it is varied, and by no means con-fined to arid regions. Beyond the Sahara, with such extremes as the area around Lake Chad where no rain falls for years on end, adobe is prevalent as a building material from the humid coastal belt of West Africa to the lowlying inland country where annual precipitation ranges from 30 to 170 inches, throughout the equatorial regions to the highlands of Kenya, and from the grasslands, swamps and forests of Tanganyika [Tanzania] to the semi-arid tip of southern Africa.*

When we think of adobe houses, we usually visualize the square homes of the Pueblo Indians. In Africa, however,

> The house-types range from the predominantly Islamic styles of North Africa and northern Nigeria to the square houses of Central Africa and the round beehive huts of the eastern and southern parts of the continent. In some areas, as along the banks of the upper Niger, the indigenous African villages consist of round huts while the ancient towns, such as Gas, are composed of square houses, possibly due to Arab influence.

---

*This and the following excerpt are reprinted by permission from *Landscape*, Volume 12 (1962).

The firing of clay into bricks was a later discovery which enabled people to build more durable homes. Many thousands of years ago they were used for construction in China and Mesopotamia. Since then they have been used in almost every part of the world, especially in areas where clay is available but wood is scarce.

In forested areas homes are often built entirely of wood. Building a log cabin served two purposes for the American pioneer: at the same time he was procuring shelter, he was clearing forested land for cultivation. Indians of the Pacific Northwest coastal area had built similar wooden structures before the coming of the white man. The long houses of the Indians were constructed with a pole framework covered with wooden planks, all of which had been hand-dressed with stone tools. The Maori of New Zealand built similar wooden structures, many of them elaborately decorated.

Simple shelters may be constructed from blocks of various materials occurring in the natural environment. Even without tools, a man may pile up rocks, and chink the crevices with mud, moss, or sod. In the Outer Hebrides, where no wood other than driftwood is found, many people live in so-called "black houses," Hance (1951) says of them:

> The "black houses" are built of undressed stone gathered from every available source. The rock of the islands is hard to work and much of it is covered by a layer of peat. Often two or three years are spent by a young man in collecting stones to build his house.

> Because of the absence of material for mortar, the walls are erected dry. They are built double, the space between being filled with turf or sand—this weatherproofs as well as insulates the walls—washed up logs and lumber and other bits of driftwood are carefully collected for the roofs.*

Even though the national government has been granting aid for new houses, many people prefer the black houses, especially during the winter, because they provide greater warmth during the cold, windy, winter months.

The domed snow-house of the Eskimo is built of blocks of snow cut from the most abundant material in the environment with simple tools. It is easy to heat, the warmth from the bodies of the persons dwelling in it often being sufficient, even during the intensely cold winter months. It is, however, rapidly being replaced by more modern dwellings which are in many respects less well adapted to the climate. Probably less than ten percent of the Eskimos today know how to build a snow-house; igloos are used only for emergency shelter when traveling during the winter.

Instead of living in snow-houses, many Eskimos today construct shacks using

---

*Reprinted by permission from the *Annals* of the Association of American Geographers, Volume 41 (1951).

whalebone or driftwood for the framework and pieces of cardboard, discarded plywood, gasoline tins, or corrugated iron for siding. Similar shacks are to be found in the slums of urban areas, whether in Hong Kong, Recife, or Johannesburg.

2.3.2 Conscious Architecture

What we have termed conscious architecture lies at the opposite extreme of the continuum from the primitive architecture discussed in the preceding section. The main distinguishing characteristic of a structure in this category is that it is not simply utilitarian, but is the product of conscious artistic creation. In explaining his work, Basil Spence (Seth, 1964), the architect who designed the rebuilt Coventry Cathedral after the original was destroyed during a bombing raid in World War II, said that he was a "traditionalist in doing what the builders of cathedrals throughout history had done, designing in a style relevant and meaningful for their day, and drawing upon the finest materials, craftsmanship, and technical facilities available to them."

As suggested in this quotation, structures at this end of the continuum are made of materials and by methods which are technologically advanced for the time and place in which they are built. Specialization of labor is required for their construction. Four major characteristics in conscious architecture contrast with those given above for primitive architecture. These are: (1) the presence of an architectural style which is the result of conscious artistic creation, (2) the use of technologically advanced materials, often obtained from distant areas and considerably processed before being used, (3) specialization of labor and construction, and (4) wide variations in appearance among the same category of structures.

As with primitive architecture, conscious architecture has existed over time and space. Many of the earliest structures which still stand are temples erected in honor of gods, tombs, or monuments to the dead; the common everyday structures of wood, reeds, and clay have long since disintegrated. Thus, conscious architecture can be traced at least as far back as the third millenium B.C. in Egypt when the great pyramids were built as royal tombs. Ruins of tombs and temple pyramids can be found not only in Egypt, but throughout the Near East. Structures such as the Parthenon, built at the height of Athenian glory, and temples to the many gods of Rome are representative of the highest artistic conception, workmanship, and technological achievement of their times.

The great cathedrals of Europe embody the major architectural styles of the Christian world: the Byzantine church of Santa Sophia in Constantinople, the Gothic churches of Amiens (Fig. 2.1), Chartres, and Notre Dame de Paris, and St. Peter's church in the Vatican. Each was conceived and designed by the finest architects of the time, and built by master craftsmen in the various arts. St. Peter's, for example, was designed by many architects working together—Bramante and Michelangelo are among the best-known. It was decorated by Raphael and Michelangelo, whose works still stand as among the most famous in the world.

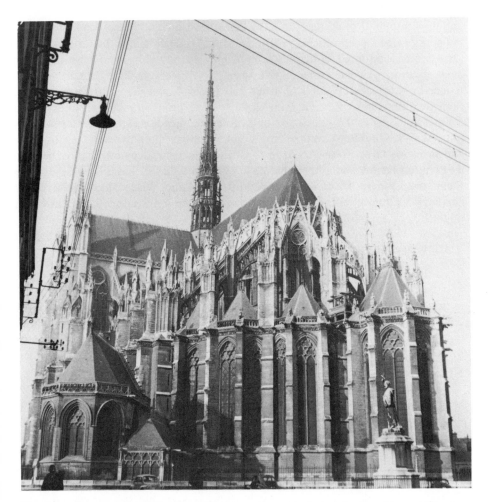

Fig. 2.1. An example of Gothic architecture: the cathedral at Amiens, France. Courtesy of French Embassy, Ottawa.

Throughout Asia, Buddhist and Hindu temples and Muslim mosques represent architectural styles prevailing in different countries at different times. One of the best-known memorial structures is the famed Taj Mahal, built by an Emperor to honor the memory of his favorite wife.

Many secular buildings may also be included in this category. Commercial and governmental structures such as the Roman Forum, the medieval guild halls, and many castles, palaces, and manor houses of the nobility reflected the artistic tastes of the eras in which they were built. One of the most grandiose is the Palace at Versailles, a half-mile long, with the Hall of Mirrors as its climax.

In the twentieth century, architects have striven to make not only churches and governmental buildings, but also factories, office buildings, and large-scale housing projects both efficient and beautiful. To do this, new materials—structural steel, reinforced concrete, lightweight metals, glass, and plastics—have been used in new and imaginative ways. Architects such as Miehs van der Rohe, Le Corbusier, Walter Gropius and Frank Lloyd Wright have developed their own personal styles, each making use of a variety of materials to express a distinctive concept. Hospitals, schools, colleges, museums, churches, apartment houses, office buildings, and private homes demonstrate the results of this lively and inspiring effort to use modern construction to produce new kinds of beauty. The United Nations building in New York City, the United States Embassy in New Delhi, the Johnson Wax Company building in Racine, Wisconsin, and the rebuilt Coventry Cathedral in England, are but a few of the multitude of examples which might be chosen.

2.3.3 Folk Architecture

Even this brief and hasty tour through time and space conveys some idea of the vast scope and variety of conscious architecture. We find coexisting with it the majority of structures representing what we shall call folk architecture—the common, everyday architecture of the less pretentious homes, banks, schools, factories, hotels, motels, public buildings, and churches. No clear line can be drawn between the two categories; it is rather a gradual merging from the largest and finest to the more commonplace and routine.

Styles used in folk architecture are often derived from styles in conscious architecture. For example, although many secular buildings in France erected during the period of the Gothic cathedrals did not imitate their structural forms, decorative details such as the pointed arch, traceries, and the general type of ornament current in churches were employed. In pre-twentieth century eclecticism, American architecture passed from imitation classical Greek and Roman to the ornate turrets and gingerbread of the Victorian era, sometimes called carpenter Gothic. As functionalism of design in conscious architecture increased, these styles gave way to the square bungalows common in the 1920's and 1930's. Since World War II, houses in the United States and Canada have become larger and more elaborate, with two or three bathrooms rather than one. In private homes, as in public buildings, there is increasing use of prefabricated wall panels, aluminum, and large areas of glass. From north to south and east to west, many square miles of the United States and Canada are covered with suburban sprawl, consisting of almost identical mass-designed and produced homes, the folk architecture of our day.

2.3.4 Synthesis

Although the classification scheme we have suggested is more useful for descriptive than explanatory purposes, we can suggest some simple hypotheses which would help to account for the spatial distributions of each kind of architecture. We have observed that buildings which are examples of conscious architecture tend to be found in major urban centers of various types. In ancient times, works of conscious architecture were usually religious buildings such as the Parthenon in Athens, governmental buildings such as the Forum in Rome, or monuments to the dead such as the Pyramids in Egypt. Beginning with the Renaissance, many commercial buildings which were the product of conscious artistic creation have also been erected. Only a small proportion of residential buildings, however, have come within this category. From these observations we can make the generalization that works of conscious architecture tend to be concentrated in important cities which were political, religious, or commercial centers, or metropolitan areas which were combinations of any of these, and in areas where there was greater wealth.

We have also observed that at any given time and place buildings representing conscious architecture tend to be constructed by technological methods which are advanced for the time. Egyptian obelisks and pyramids, Gothic cathedrals, and a few contemporary office and university buildings are illustrations. Many of these methods, including new materials and ways of using them, gradually diffuse into folk architecture and are superseded by new ones. They tend to diffuse spatially from major centers in the form of folk architecture rather than conscious architecture. If this line of reasoning from our observations is valid, and if we are willing to extend our conclusions, we would also expect to find that the number or proportion of buildings representing conscious architecture decreases with distance from such major centers and areas of wealth.

2.4 STUDIES OF HOUSING IN SMALLER AREAS

In the world-wide survey of housing we considered only the highlights; details were of necessity obscured. In order to observe the details of a phenomenon, it is necessary to study it over an area smaller than the entire world, and possibly also to restrict the study of a particular type of structure. It is then often possible to obtain greater fineness in a classificatory scheme.

Some geographers have made studies of housing for relatively restricted areas such as cities or parts of a state, or of one type of house within an area. Although most of these studies are primarily descriptive, in a few the attempt has been made to account for observed variations in the spatial distribution of different elements: style, size, shape, building materials, or condition.

There are two main reasons for reviewing the findings of studies. First, we wish to see the kind of studies which have been done, and to assess the present state of knowledge about the topic. Second, we are interested in the methodology used in different studies: what the objectives were, how the study was carried out, and what conclusions were reached. We are interested not in the substantive conclusions themselves—the particular house types defined or building materials used—but rather in the kind of conclusions which can be generalized beyond the immediate study. Although many of the studies reviewed in the early chapters are concrete and specific, concentrating on a particular topic, area, and time, the findings of some of them can be generalized beyond their immediate temporal and spatial matrices.

2.4.1 Log Houses in Georgia

Zelinsky (1953) was interested in the rapidly vanishing log houses of Georgia, most of which had been built by the early pioneers. He defined the log house by its material, method of construction, and function. He found all except recently-built ones to be of one story with only a few basic floor plans. From samples taken in all counties of the state, he was able to estimate the number of log houses in each county and to map their distribution. Through historical research, he determined that log houses had first been built in the United States by German settlers in Pennsylvania. This type of construction was quickly adopted by English settlers, and log houses were soon found all along the frontier. In Georgia, log houses were first built in the northern interior and later spread south and coastward. They are not found along the coastal plain which was settled earlier by English people who did not know of log construction. He concluded,

> All these distributional facts point to a major conclusion concerning the cultural evolution of that preponderant part of Georgia in which the log house has appeared. North Georgia, with its more recent house types, its square-hewn timbers, and the dominance of relatively skilled techniques for scaling walls, would seem to to lie closer in time and space to the center of dispersion for log-house traits (and presumably others) than South Georgia, with its greater proportion of archaic or degenerate house types, round logs, and cruder treatment of walls. (p. 192)*

2.4.2 Louisiana House Types

Kniffen (1936) carried out an extensive study of house types in rural Louisiana. He attempted to identify a number of house types small enough to be useful and meaningful for purposes of analysis. With much effort, he reduced his fifty original types to nine basic ones. House form was the essential element considered. Most of the houses were found to have sideward-facing gables; that is, the front door was on one long side, with the gables at each end. Several subtypes were found, characterized by having: (1) a built-in porch, (2) an attached porch, (3) no porch, (4) an open passage, with the steep roof projecting on either side to form porches both front and back, and (5) two stories, called the midwestern style. Two types had front-facing gables: (6) shotgun, a folk-term commonly used in Louis-

---

*Reprinted by permission from the *Geographical Review*, Volume 43, 1953. Copyrighted by the American Geographical Society of New York.

iana to designate a long, narrow house, and (7) bungalow, a house two or more rooms deep. Two other types were identified: (1) trapper, a square, one-room house with a shed roof, used by trappers, and (2) oysterman, which rests on a pile-supported platform and is usually of a single-room shotgun type.

The percentage distribution of each house type was computed and mapped. Finally, a combined map was made showing areas of dominance of a single type and areas of mixture. Certain generalizations could then be drawn about the distribution of the different types. Kniffen says,

> The type distinguished by the built-in porch is rather closely confined to the flood plain of the Mississippi. . . . Its absence in the pine hills and prairies is noteworthy. . . . The type with the attached porch also attains its greatest prominence in the flood plains, but it is by no means so confined. . . . The Midwestern type is strikingly and sharply confined to the heart of the Prairie region of southwestern Louisiana, whither it was imported from the Corn Belt about forty years ago. . . . The open-passage type is restricted to the three pine hill areas of Louisiana. . . . The porchless type is very localized, reaching mappable significance in only one section. . . . The trapper and the oysterman types are very specialized, and are entirely restricted to the navigable waterways of the immediate coastal region. The Shotgun house is strikingly associated with the state's waterways. . . . The island in the western part of the state may represent a case of mistaken identity, but more likely it marks a migrant group of people. (pp. 166–168)*

On the basis of these generalizations, four culturo-geographic regions of the state were defined and mapped: (1) coastal marsh, (2) prairie, (3) pine hills and flatwoods, and (4) flood plains and blufflands. In each of these a distinctive house type or mixture of types was found.

2.4.3 House Types in Australia

Three studies were carried out in Australia with a similar aim of defining the boundaries of regions within which a certain house type was found. Rose (1955) investigated the distribution of the Queensland house type, built on stilts and surrounded by a veranda, which was well suited to the tropical climate. He found that, in general, the borderline for this type coincided with the boundary between the states of Queensland and New South Wales, but the departures from this were of interest. In New South Wales, the Queensland house is found on alluvial flats of frequently flooded areas, where the stilts mitigate flood damage. It is also found in higher elevations of Queensland, even though it is less suited to the cooler climate. Rose suggests that the Queenslanders settling in this area brought their house style with them.

In another study, Rose (1962) was concerned with establishing regional

---

*Reprinted by permission from the *Annals* of the Association of American Geographers, Volume 26 (1936).

boundaries in the use of building materials in southeastern Australia. He found that timber is widely used throughout the eastern part of the area from Queensland south to Tasmania, while stone is prevalent in the west, essentially in South Australia. Brick is used primarily in urban areas. Asbestos siding is being used increasingly in newer houses.

He suggests several factors which might explain this pattern. Of primary importance is the economic factor: "people build their houses of the cheapest, most readily available materials of acceptable standard (p. 256)." Illustrating this principle, timber is used where it is widely available—stone is substituted in other areas. Bricks are used primarily in urban areas located relatively close to brickworks, where transportation cost is not an overwhelming factor. Asbestos siding is inexpensive and lightweight; it costs relatively less to transport than stone or brick, and involves less labor cost in erection. Although these economic considerations are primary, social factors also enter in. For example, in many cities, certain higher-class residential districts are designated as brick areas, where homes may be built only of brick. He also notes the tendency for people in an area to continue using familiar materials, with the result that change occurs slowly.

In a study of building materials used in Hobart, Tasmania, Scott (1959) found that wooden walls prevailed in five of the seven regions of the city, and brick was dominant in the other two. Corrugated iron roofs predominated throughout the entire city. He concluded that the material used was related primarily to the time at which a house had been built, and secondarily to the socio-economic status of the owner.

2.4.4 The Distribution of Substandard Housing

Pownall (1960) studied low-value housing in two New Zealand cities: Christchurch and Dunedin. He was concerned about the many older houses in these cities which were rapidly deteriorating and which should be replaced in the near future. As an index of deterioration the valuation per square foot, based on assessed valuation, was computed and this value expressed as a percentage of the standard replacement cost. Houses depreciated 80 percent or more of their replacement cost were rated as "of extremely low value;" those depreciated 90 percent or more as "of extremely poor quality." The distributions of three categories of houses were mapped: those depreciated 70 percent or more, 80 percent or more and 90 percent or more respectively. Compared with Christchurch, Dunedin had only about one-third the percentage of houses in the category of 80 percent or more depreciated. These houses were concentrated in one area of Dunedin, but were more widely scattered in Christchurch. Some of them had become depreciated primarily because of age, others had been shoddily built in the first place and had rapidly deteriorated. Projection of the dates at which these houses would be 100 percent depreciated and would have to be replaced indicated urgent need of extensive planning for urban renewal.

Hartmann and Hook (1956) were also concerned with substandard housing. They asked three questions: (1) How does the proportion of substandard housing vary among the 1,262 cities of the United States with populations of 10,000 or more (1950 census)? (2) What is its spatial distribution? and (3) What other phenomena are areally associated with it?

1.   Variation in the proportion of substandard housing:

Housing is defined as substandard in the 1950 United States Census of Housing if it is either dilapidated—structurally unsound, unsafe, or otherwise unsuitable for human occupancy—or lacks basic sanitary amenities—hot running water, a flush toilet, or bathing facilities inside the structure. Housing with one or more of these characteristics is considered to be below the generally accepted minimum standards for housing in the United States, but such minimum standards would vary from country to country, and would change over time. It is recognized that any such definition is to some extent arbitrary. The percentage of such dwelling units in each of the cities was obtained from the Census of Housing. The figures ranged from 0.2 percent in University Heights, Ohio, to 73.6 per cent in Helena, Arkansas. The median was 22.2 percent.

2.   Spatial distribution of substandard housing:

Their next objective was to investigate areal variations in the proportion of substandard housing. They wished to construct an isopleth map* (Fig. 2.2) such that each region would contain cities with approximately the same percentage of substandard housing; that is, each region would be relatively homogeneous with respect to the proportion of substandard housing in the cities located in it. In attempting to determine the class intervals for such a map, they found certain cutting points in the distribution which seemed reasonable. Not all of these, however, were suitable as dividing points for isoplething; for example, they found that cities with less than 13 percent substandard housing were not concentrated in any region, but were scattered over the entire country as dependent urban places of large cities. Therefore it was not possible to delineate a contiguous region of cities with 13 percent or less substandardness. The class intervals finally chosen as suitable for mapping were these: less than 28 percent, 28 to 44 percent, and 44 percent and over.

As can be seen by examining the map (Fig. 2.2) and Table 2.1, the West, Northeast, and Peninsular Florida were in the class with the lowest percentage of

---

*An isopleth map is one which involves an indication of quantity as well as spatial distribution. The lines on the map join places (points) having the same quantity or amount of a given phenomenon. The contour map is perhaps the most common example of an isopleth map.

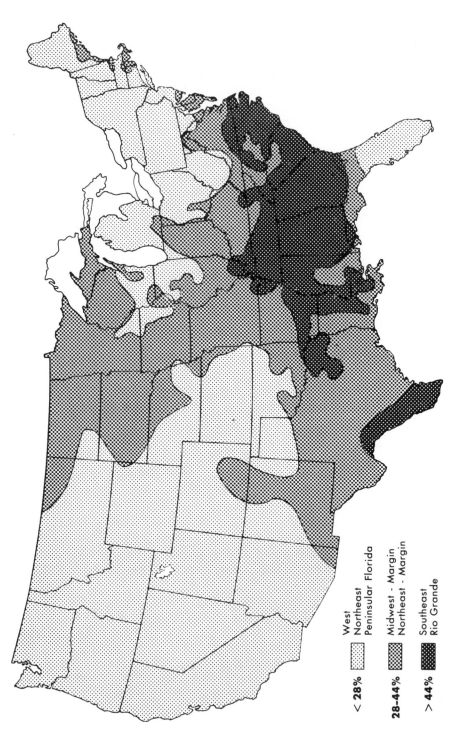

Fig. 2.2. Regions of substandardness in urban housing in 1950. Source: Hartman and Hook, 1956. Reprinted by permission from the authors and *Economic Geography*, Volume 32 (1956).

West
Northeast
Peninsular Florida

Midwest - Margin
Northeast - Margin

Southeast
Rio Grande

< 28%

28–44%

> 44%

Table 2.1   Regions of substandard urban housing

Region	No. of cities	Substandardness value	
		Regional limits (Percent)	Mean (Percent)
West	228	Less than 28	14.9
Northeast	552	Less than 28	16.5
Peninsular Florida	23	Less than 28	25.6
Midwest-Marginal	302	28 to 44	33.0
Marginal New England	25	28 to 44	37.4
Southeast	121	More than 44	49.5
Rio Grande	11	More than 44	55.8

Source: Hartman and Hook (1956). Reprinted by permission from the authors and *Economic Geography*.

substandard housing; the Middle West, including most of Texas and New Mexico in the middle group; and the Gulf coast of Texas and most of the Deep South in the group with the highest percentage.

3. *Other phenomena associated with substandard housing:*

Their third objective was to find other phenomena which might be areally associated with the percentage of substandard housing. They reasoned that such factors as low income, the proportion of non-whites in the population, and home ownership might be significantly related. In order to minimize the labor required for this phase of the study, they selected a random sample of 100 cities from the universe of 1,262. Correlation coefficients were then computed to determine the degree of relationship between the percentage of substandard housing and each of sixteen variables. Those variables found to be most closely related to the percentage of substandard housing were: percent of families with family income less than $2,500, median family income (an inverse relationship) and percent of families with overcrowding and no mechanical refrigerator. Other, less closely related variables were: percent of non-white families, renter families, foreign-born population (an inverse relationship) and no central heat. Data for all variables were drawn from the 1950 Census of population of the 1950 Census of Housing.

Further statistical analysis indicated that the percentage of substandardness could be predicted from the variables more accurately from separate analyses made for each region. The regions they delineated were found to be relatively homogeneous; that is, there was more variation in the proportion of substandard housing among regions than within them.

2.4.5 Synthesis

As stated in Chapter 1, we are interested in exploring spatial aspects of many phenomena. These spatial aspects include their location and spatial distribution. As we consider each topic, we wish to identify what it is we are studying, and to define it as precisely as possible; to describe where it is located; and to attempt to account for some of its spatial aspects, especially its spatial distribution.

The researchers who reported these studies of housing in smaller areas focussed on different aspects of the phenomenon, including house types, building materials used in construction, and substandard housing. These geographers studying house types found that, because of wide variations in style and the lack of clear-cut distinctions among them, it was virtually impossible to delineate definite house types. Kniffen resorted to a quasi-intuitive set of house types based on combinations of features. Other researchers, not reviewed here, used typologies similarly constructed to fit a particular situation. Unfortunately, however, each classification scheme is usable only in the area for which it is designed; there is no overall scheme for classifying house types. This difficulty was circumvented in those studies in which the researchers were not concerned with style. In grouping their observations, they used criteria such as building methods and materials (Zelinsky), percentage of depreciation (Pownall) or substandardness (Hartman and Hook) which are more precisely defined and have wider applicability.

Location of the phenomenon was depicted on one or more maps, by the types or classes defined in the study. In addition, certain of the investigators established regions within which the different classes or groups were located.

Many studies ended at this stage; in others, suggestions were made as to why the distribution was as it was. Zelinsky, for example, proposed an historical explanation of the distribution of log houses in Georgia. Scott also found historical factors to be of primary importance in the use of different building materials. Rose, on the other hand, suggested that economic factors were of primary importance in deciding what building materials were used, but that social factors also played a secondary role. Hartman and Hook formally tested sixteen hypothesized relationships between the distributions of various economic or social factors and substandard housing.

2.5 CONCLUSION

We have suggested several criteria which can be used to classify houses, including size, shape, building size, shape, building materials, and architectural style. We have illustrated the use of these criteria for both the entire world and smaller areas, and pointed out the many difficulties involved in establishing a generally applicable system of classifying house types. Comparison of our world-wide overview with more detailed studies of smaller areas points up some of the problems involved in studying a phenomenon on different scales. It is neither feasible nor desirable to achieve the same degree of detail in a world-wide study that might be attempted in studying a single city, as the myriad of detail might well obscure the overall pattern.

Consideration of both the world-wide overview and the findings of the studies of smaller areas suggests hypotheses which might explain the spatial distribution of different elements of housing. The amount of technology in an area is an important factor, as it limits the building materials available and the construction methods used. At a given time and place, both economic and non-economic factors affect the choice made from among these possibilities. Although economic factors appear to be more important, certain building materials and types of houses are used partly because of their association with higher or lower wealth or social position.

We have also noted the diffusion of architectural styles and house types: Roman architecture was found throughout the former Roman Empire, and the building of log houses was carried from Germany to Pennsylvania, where it was adopted by English settlers and carried along the frontier. Many of the styles and techniques of building introduced by architects are spread by imitation to folk architecture and are then spread spatially. The generalizations suggested to account for the location and spread of these architectural styles are too broad to be tested rigorously. Although it would be necessary to state them more specifically and to define the variables more precisely before this could be done, our observations appear to support them.

REVIEW YOUR UNDERSTANDING OF THESE CONCEPTS

bases for classifying structure
continuum of architectural style
substandard housing
arbitrary nature of definitions
regions

isopleth map
correlation coefficient
location
spatial distribution
choropleth map

SUGGESTED ACTIVITIES

1. Investigate the spatial distribution of some aspect of housing within a given state or for the United States, and try to account for it. A variety of data is given in the U.S. Census of Housing for characteristics such as median value; sound, deteriorating, and dilapidated; median number of rooms; population per dwelling unit; and vacant and for sale or rent. Select one of the categories for which data are given by counties if you have selected a single state, or by states for the entire United States.

   a) Show the spatial variation on a map. Rank the data and group the observations into five equal classes. Show the classes on a choropleth map* using either different patterns or shadings of one color, from light to dark, representing respectively smaller to larger amounts or proportions of the phenomenon. If you wish to use other ways of grouping the data you may for example determine the arithmetic means of the observations and have two groups above the mean and two below. An isopleth map may also be constructed, similar to the one in Hartmann and Hook's study. For other methods of grouping data and portraying them on maps, refer to a standard text on cartography.

b) By studying the spatial distribution portrayed on the map, identify phenomena which you believe to be spatially distributed in a similar manner. Using these phenomena as independent variables, formulate hypotheses to account for the observed spatial distribution.

2. a) Observe the houses in some area of your city and list the types found. Explain the classification scheme which you used in determining types of houses and your reasons for using this scheme. Plot the distribution of these classes on a map.

b) Attempt to explain the observed spatial variation of different house types by finding factors which are related to the one you have shown on the map.

3. For a community of your choice, obtain data related to one or more characteristics of housing from the local planning office or from census data. Show their spatial variation on a map of the city and attempt to account for it.

REFERENCES

Hance, William A. (1951), "Crofting settlements and housing in the Outer Hebrides," *Annals* of the Association of American Geographers **41**, 75–87.

Hartman, George W. and John C. Hook (1956), "Substandard urban housing in the United States: a quantitative analysis," *Economic Geography* **32**, 95–114.

Kniffen, Fred B. (1936), "Louisiana house types," *Annals* of the Association of American Geographers **26**, 179–193.

Pownall, L. L. (1960), "Low-value housing in two New Zealand cities," *Annals* of the Association of American Geographers **50**, 439–460.

Rose, A. J. (1955), "The border between Queensland and New South Wales," *The Australian Geographer* **6**, No. 4, 3–18.

Rose, A. J. (1962), "Some boundaries and building materials in southeastern Australia,"

---

*A choropleth map shows spatial variation in the quantity or quality of a phenomenon by areal units. Each areal unit is assigned to a particular class of the phenomenon.

Land and Livelihood: Geographical Essays in Honour of George Jobberns. Christchurch, N.Z.: New Zealand Geographical Society.

Scott, Peter (1959), "Building materials in greater Hobart," *The Australian Geographer* 7, 149–163.

Seth, Mary (1964), "Coventry Cathedral," *Presbyterian Life* 17, No. 7, 2–9, 35.

Skole, John (1962), "Adobe in Africa," *Landscape* 12, No. 2, 15–18.

Wagner, Philip L. (1960), *The Human Use of the Earth.* New York: The Free Press of Glencoe.

Zelinsky, Wilbur (1953), "The log house in Georgia," *The Geographical Review* 43, 173–193.

Additional Readings

Amato, Peter W. (1970), "Elitism and settlement patterns in the Latin-American city," *Journal of the American Institute of Planners* 36, 96–105.

Aronin, Jeffrey Ellis (1953), *Climate and Architecture.* New York: Reinhold.

Davis, J. Tait (1965), "Middle class housing in the central city," *Economic Geography* 41, 238–251.

Finley, Robert and E. M. Scott (1940), "A Great Lakes-to-Gulf profile of dispersed dwelling types," *The Geographical Review* 30, 412–419.

Fletcher, Sir Banister F. (1961), *A History of Architecture: On the Comparative Method,* 17th ed., revised by R. A. Cordingley. London: Athlone Press.

Fuchs, Roland J. (1960), "Intra-urban variation in residential quality," *Economic Geography* 36, 313–325.

Gowans, Alan (1958), *Looking at Architecture in Canada.* Toronto: Oxford University Press.

Gregor, Howard F. (1951), "A sample study of the California ranch," *Annals* of the Association of American Geographers 41, 285–306.

Hamlin, Talbot (1940), *Architecture Through the Ages.* New York: Putnam.

Johnston, R. J. (1969), "Processes of change in the high status residential areas of Christchurch, 1951–1964," *New Zealand Geographer* 25, 1–15.

Johnston, R. J. (1969), "Toward an analytical study of the townscape: the residential building fabric," *Geografiska Annaler* 51B, 20–32.

Kniffen, Fred B. (1965), "Folk housing: key to diffusion," *Annals* of the Association of American Geographers 55, 549–577.

Kniffen, Fred B. and Henry Glassie (1966), "Building in wood in the eastern United States," *The Geographical Review* 56, 40–66.

Krautheimer, Richard (1965), *Early Christian and Byzantine Architecture.* Baltimore: Penguin Books.

Lee, Douglas H. K. (1951), "Thoughts on housing for the humid tropics," *The Geographical Review* 41, 124–147.

Marsden, Brian S. (1966), "A century of building materials in Queensland and Brisbane, 1861–1961," *The Australian Geographer* **10**, 115–131.

Paulsson, Thomas (1959), *Scandinavian Architecture*. Newton, Mass.: Branford.

Reid, Margaret G. (1962), *Housing and Income*. Chicago: University of Chicago Press.

Rickert, John E. (1967), "House facades of the northeastern United States; a tool of geographic analysis," *Annals* of the Association of American Geographers **57**, 211–238.

Sanford, Trent E. (1950), *The Architecture of the Southwest: Indian, Spanish, American*. New York: Norton.

Spencer, Joseph E. (1945), "House types of southern Utah," *The Geographical Review* **35**, 444–457.

Spencer, Joseph E. (1947), "The house of the Chinese," *The Geographical Review* **37**, 254–273

Tewari, A. K. (1966), "A house type in Jaunsar-Himalaya," *The Australian Geographer* **10**, 35–46.

Vidal de la Blache, Paul (1926), "Building materials," Ch. 4 in *Principles of Human Geography*. London: Constable.

Whiffen, Marcus (1969), *American Architecture Since 1780: A Guide to the Styles*. Cambridge: The Massachusetts Institute of Technology Press.

World Architecture: An Illustrated History (1963). New York: McGraw-Hill.

Zelinsky, Wilbur (1968), "The New England connecting barn," *The Geographical Review* **48**, 540–553.

CHAPTER 3
RELIGION

3.1 INTRODUCTION

We shall begin our exploration of the spatial aspects of religion on a world scale, and then consider some of the studies which have been made within smaller areas. We hope, finally, to be able to make generalizations about some of the aspects of religion which we have studied, and to see whether these appear to be equally valid for different universes.

3.1.1 Definition of Religion

Religion is difficult to define but easy to classify. No two authorities agree on a definition; many refuse to attempt one. For our purposes, we shall use the term *religion* to refer to the accepted, institutionalized phenomenon.

   The religions of the world are so different that it is difficult to find any element which is common to them all. Some elements are, however, common to many and may be present in different religions to different degrees. These elements include: (1) a set of beliefs or doctrines, usually involving a deity or deities; (2) a code of ethics or ethical standards; (3) an organization; (4) certain practices or rituals; (5) the existence of a type of experience different from that of everyday life, referred to as religious experience or, in its more extreme form, as mysticism; and (6) a body of religious literature or scriptures.

3.1.2 Classification of Religions

Using the definition which we have accepted above, we can see that there is no problem of classification, since the major living religions of the world, which include a majority of the world's population as adherents, are generally known and recognized as religions. For convenience, they may be considered in two large geographic groupings. The Eastern religions include Hinduism; Buddhism; an amalgamation of Confucianism, Taoism, and Buddhism which is often referred to as Chinese religions; and Shinto. The Western religions—Judaism, Christianity, and Islam—stem from the ancient Hebrew tradition. There are also a number of minor religions such as Sikhism, Bahaism, and Jainism, which are confined to relatively few adherents in restricted areas, and a diverse assortment of beliefs and practices often grouped under the term of *animism* or *primitive* or *tribal religions*. The present distribution of religions is shown in Fig. 3.1.

3.2 EASTERN RELIGIONS

3.2.1 Hinduism

Hinduism is one of the oldest of the living religions of the world, having originated over 4,000 years ago in India. To an outsider it appears to be full of contradictions; for example, it has one god and over 300 million gods at the same time. The one basic doctrine on which most Hindus agree is the idea of *karma* or divine justice, which is closely bound up with the notion of transmigration of souls. The soul of an animal or person who dies is believed to be re-born into a new individual; whether it goes up or down in the hierarchical scale depends on what the individual has done in his former life. The goal of the individual Hindu is to achieve release from this endless cycle of transmigration through union with Brahman, the eternal spirit. This release is the highest and best that can happen. The doctrine of *karma* is closely tied up with the caste system. The existence of castes is part of the eternal plan; social arrangements and religion are inseparable. Caste in this life is determined by behavior in past life; caste in the next life is dependent upon behavior in the present life.

Hinduism has absorbed ideas from other religions introduced into India. Although Buddhism originated in India in the sixth century B.C. as an organized religion, it became virtually extinct there until a recent revival, mainly among the casteless. Many of its concepts were, however, incorporated into Hinduism. Christianity was brought to India at many times over the centuries; for the first time perhaps less than a hundred years after the death of Christ and subsequently in the succeeding Dutch, Portugese, and British occupations of the country. In spite of this continuing contact, only about two percent of the Indians are Christians. The influence of Christianity is felt primarily as it has been assimilated into Hindu beliefs; the message of the Sermon on the Mount, for example, is preached by Hindu holy men or gurus.

By the beginning of the Christian era Hinduism had spread eastward along established trade routes as far as what is now Indonesia. Later, however, with the Muslim conquest, the majority of the population in these areas became Muslims. Today Hinduism is found primarily in India, on the island of Bali, and among expatriate Indians in Asia, Africa, and throughout the rest of the world,

3.2.2 Buddhism

Buddhism also began in India, during the sixth century B.C. Gautama, called the Buddha, grew up in the Hindu tradition and was dissatisfied with many of its

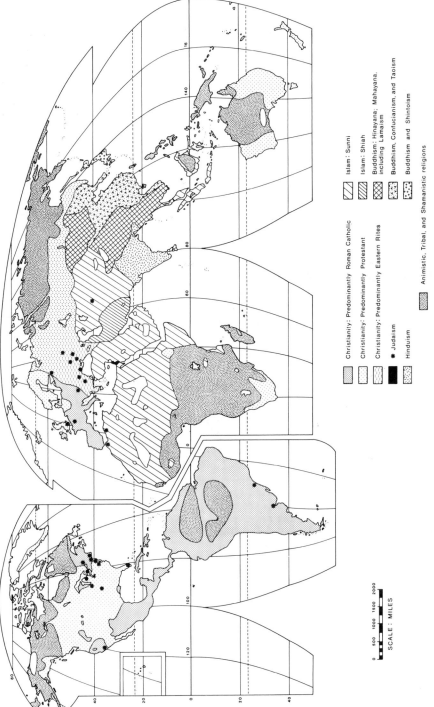

Fig. 3.1. Major religions of the world. Adapted from map of religions in *Man's Domain: A Thematic Atlas of the World*. ©Copyright, General Drafting Co., Inc. and Western Publishing Company, Inc. Goode's base map © copyright, University of Chicago. Used by permission of the University of Chicago Press.

Christianity: Predominantly Roman Catholic

Christianity: Predominantly Protestant

Christianity: Predominantly Eastern Rites

Judaism

Hinduism

Islam: Sunni

Islam: Shiah

Buddhism: Hinayana, Mahayana, including Lamaism

Buddhism, Confucianism, and Taoism

Buddhism and Shintoism

Animistic, Tribal, and Shamanistic religions

0   500 1000 1500 2000

SCALE : MILES

tenets. His doctrines were based on the traditions of *karma* and the concept of the world as an abode of ignorance and sorrow. He taught that escape from the evils of life is to be sought through meditation, the aim of which is to achieve a condition of mind termed Nirvana—that is, the extinction of all craving, resentment, and covetousness. This escape alone constitutes true happiness, and brings with it release from future reincarnations. The ethical precepts of Buddhism include tolerance, non-violence, respect for the individual, love of all nature, and belief in the fundamental spiritual equality of all human beings. Hinduism teaches that salvation is intimately related to caste, but in Buddhist doctrine, salvation is attainable by any man without regard for caste. For this reason many outcastes in India today are becoming Buddhists, often in mass ceremonies.

There are at present two major forms of Buddhism: Hinayana, the lesser vehicle, and Mahayana, the greater vehicle. According to the beliefs of the Hinayana Buddhists, man must and can attain his own salvation here and now, without the assistance of any gods, by following the teachings of Buddha. Mahayana Buddhism, on the other hand, offers salvation for the masses rather than for the select few who are able to win it through intense self-denial and meditation. Its essence is mutual helpfulness: stronger souls build up a treasury of merit upon which lesser persons can draw for their own salvation.

After a long period of decline, Buddhism is currently undergoing reformation and revival. Missionaries are moving into less strongly Buddhist areas and many Buddhists, especially in China and Japan, are repudiating the doctrine of *karma*, with its rejection of the world, in favor of taking an active part in the building of contemporary society.

In the first three centuries following the death of Buddha in 489 B.C., Buddhism spread throughout India and Ceylon; for part of the third century B.C. it had more adherents than Hinduism. As word of the new religion reached China by way of traders, Chinese philosophers came to India to learn about it. Missionaries traveled from India to China, and the works of Buddha were translated into Chinese during the sixth century. About the same time, the special form of Buddhism known as Lamaism developed in Tibet. It was compounded of early Buddhism plus Tibetan beliefs in magic and spirits and the later addition of a mixture of Mahayana Buddhism and certain magical and mystical doctrines derived from Hinduism. Buddhism was carried from China to Japan by the seventh century.

Buddhism today has an estimated 175 million adherents, not including those in China. As can be seen from the map (Fig. 3.2), it predominates over a much smaller area than at its height. It is relatively unimportant in India, where it began. Hinayana Buddhism has many adherents in Ceylon, Burma, Thailand, Laos, and Cambodia, and a smaller proportion in Vietnam. Mahayana Buddhism, in the form of Lamaism, is strongest in Tibet and parts of Nepal; in China it is mingled with other religions, all of which are being displaced by Communism; in Korea and Japan it is one of several religions.

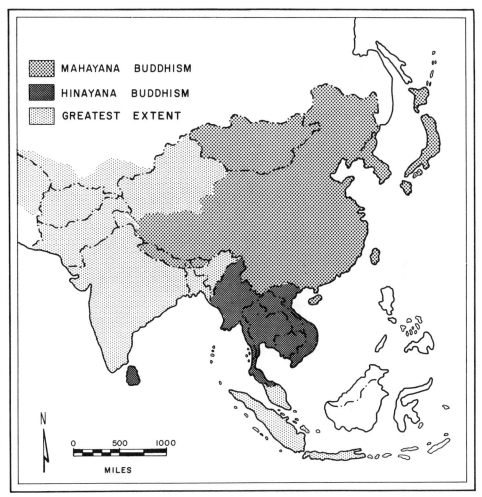

Fig. 3.2. Extent of Buddhism. Adapted from Editorial staff of *Life* (1963), *The World's Great Religions*: Vol. 1, *Religions of the East*. New York: Time Inc. Used by permission of the publisher and Antonio Petruccelli, artist.

3.2.3 Chinese Religions

Another group of religions and philosophies often referred to collectively as Chinese religions is composed of four major traditions: ancient Chinese traditions, Taoism, Confucianism, and Buddhism. From the ancient Chinese traditions came the belief in the unity of man and nature and the practice of making ritual sacrifices to ancestors to symbolize that each man is an indispensable link in the endless chain of humanity. Both Lao-Tzu and Confucius (Kung-Fu-Tzu) lived during the sixth century B.C., and each developed different aspects of the earlier traditions. Lao-Tzu emphasized man's dependence on nature; he preached the way of the Tao, suggesting that man should accept what life offers him. Confucius, by contrast, was primarily an ethical and moral philosopher who preached about ideal relationships among persons and emphasized filial piety. The teachings of both philosophers became distorted in later centuries. Lao-Tzu was worshipped as a god, and much emphasis was placed upon propitiating evil spirits and demons. Confucius was elevated to higher status, sacrifices offered to his spirit became more elaborate, and a state cult of Confucianism evolved.

Mahayana Buddhism was introduced into China in the first century A.D. All three traditions continued to exist side-by-side until the twentieth century. Since Taoism and Confucianism had become essentially state cults which emphasized worship of and obedience to the emperor, they were officially disbanded in 1911, when China became a republic. Since 1948 the Communists have actively repressed all religions and discouraged filial piety by encouraging children to denounce their parents' incorrect ideas and actions. Mao Tse-tung's *Red Book* has become the scripture of the Chinese people.

The two distinctively Chinese traditions, Taoism and Confucianism, have remained primarily within the boundaries of China, except as they are practiced by expatriate Chinese living in other areas. It seems likely that they may perish on their home grounds.

3.2.4 Shinto

Shinto, "the way of the gods," is the native religion of Japan which combines a love of the land, the nation, and the emperor. It is bound up with the Japanese reverence for nature and their acceptance of man as a part of all nature. There are several manifestations of Shinto: state Shinto, which until 1945 was the national faith and which is now called Shrine Shinto; domestic Shinto; and a variety of Shinto sects. State Shinto involved a government-fostered program of patriotic rites in shrines which were national property, aimed at systematic cultivation of patriotic fervor within the nation. Domestic Shinto centers around the god-shelf in the home, upon which families place objects of special respect and before which daily rites are performed. The practice of Shinto does not exclude other religions; for example, Buddhist priests are often called to the home to officiate at special occasions such as funerals. Before World War II, thirteen Shinto sects were recognized; now there are more than 800, representing a wide range of religious faith and practice aimed at attaining ultimate truth and personal spiritual security.

Shinto is confined to the Japanese people, and is found in Japan and in other areas to which Japanese have migrated.

3.3 WESTERN RELIGIONS

The Western religions—Judaism, Christianity, and Islam or Muhammadanism—all originated in the Near East and share a common history. They also share a belief in one God who created all nature, including man, and who stands apart from the world but is involved in man's day-to-day life. The relationship between man and God is conceived of as a person-to-person one in which both moral and spiritual elements are prominent.

3.3.1 Judaism

The origins of the Jewish tradition can be traced back to the time of Abraham, the patriarch, now dated at about the nineteenth century B.C. One of the major concepts is that of the oneness of God, constantly repeated by the Jews in the *Shema*: "Hear, O Israel, the Lord our God, the Lord is One." Not only is there one God, and only one, but He is a personal God, who speaks directly to mankind and intervenes in men's everyday affairs.

Since their beginning as a nomadic desert tribe, the Jews have suffered a series of conquests, persecutions, and exiles. Moses led them out of Egypt to Canaan, the promised land. They were not established there long before they were shaken by civil war and split into two kingdoms, Israel and Judah. After the kingdom of Israel was destroyed by the Assyrians, only the southern kingdom, Judah, remained. Its people were conquered and carried into captivity by the Babylonians; they returned to Jerusalem and rebuilt it and the temple, only to suffer under a succession of masters: the Greeks, the Egyptians, the Syrians, and finally, the Romans. Jerusalem was destroyed again in 70 A.D. and the Jews were driven out to communities scattered all over the Near East. There they survived, intermittently persecuted and tortured, but retaining their faith in God and awaiting the coming of the Messiah who would deliver them from their oppressors. Until the eighteenth century, most Jews were denied citizenship or participation in the life of the countries in which they lived. Then, gradually, they came out of the ghettos and began to take active parts in affairs of the world. Hitler tried to exterminate all Jews in Germany, Czechoslovakia, and Poland. After a long struggle and much fighting, the Jews won for themselves a homeland in Palestine, and created the new state of Israel which continues to be in conflict with its Arab neighbors.

Judaism reflects its contact with many different peoples over the centuries. The idea of ethical dualism, and of the existence of angels and devils, heaven and hell, was derived from the teachings of Zoroaster, a Persian, in the sixth century B.C. Many beliefs and rituals of other nations were rejected, often dramatically, as in Elijah's conflict with the Phoenician worship of Baal, which was being practiced by many Jews. The basic beliefs in the oneness and uniqueness of God, and in His directives to His chosen people as revealed in the Law and by the Prophets have remained over the centuries.

In the United States today, there are three major branches of the Jewish faith. Orthodoxy, the largest group, tries to maintain the traditional way of life and to follow the Law as closely as possible, keeping the Sabbath strictly and obeying dietary rules. The Conservative branch is less strict, trying to strike a middle road between orthodoxy and reform. The Reform branch has modified the traditional services, allowing women and men to sit together, using an organ and choir, and being less concerned with strict adherence to traditional rituals, but continuing to emphasize the personal relationship between God and man and the ethical teachings of Judaism. Similar trends exist in other parts of the world.

Ever since the Diaspora, or Dispersion, which began in 70 A.D. with the destruction of the temple in Jerusalem, Judaism has been a dispersed religion. Jews have lived in colonies, or, more recently, concentrated in cities but not in separate communities. Prior to World War II, there were large groups of Jews in most European countries, as well as in both North and South America and throughout the Near East. It is estimated that there are 14 million Jews; about 5.7 million live in the United States, 2.8 million in Israel, and 2.5 million in the U.S.S.R.

3.3.2 Christianity

At the time of Christ's birth, Jerusalem was seething under Roman rule. Throughout the Jewish world, the Messianic hope was high; the Jews were waiting for a Savior to deliver them from their oppressors and bring on a new order. When Jesus of Nazareth began preaching, some Jews were ready to accept Him as the Messiah, but most were looking for a more worldly deliverance. Even His apostles expected Him to be a temporal ruler. Although they were rudely disillusioned by the Crucifixion, after recovering from the shock they gained courage and began preaching in the streets, winning many converts.

Although the original apostles continued to adhere to the Jewish Law and considered themselves as Jews, Christianity developed as an independent religion only as Paul, a Hellenized Jew, began preaching to the Gentiles. Ritual and worship gradually became institutionalized, a church organization developed, and doctrine was formalized in the early writings of the New Testament. Although many Christians were put to death between 250 and 300 A.D. for refusing to make sacrifices to the emperor, by 380 Christianity was declared the official religion of the Roman Empire. The papacy was established, and the temporal power of the church began to grow. During the seventh century, Rome was invaded by barbarians from the north and Moslems from the south. With the subsequent weakening of the Pope's power, the Eastern churches gradually drifted away from Roman control, and by 1054 the break was complete.

During the Middle Ages the papacy reached its all-time height of spiritual and temporal power, and many abuses developed. Although these abuses were fought by many people within the church, no major reforms were made. During the fifteenth and sixteenth centuries, the Protestant Reformation occurred, not only as a protest against the papacy, but also as the result of political and economic changes in Europe. Sparked by Luther in Germany, and Zwingli and Calvin in Switzerland, it soon spread over much of Europe. War broke out between Protestants and Catholics in France and the Netherlands. Some of the Protestant areas were later re-converted to Catholicism by the Jesuits.

Although it is difficult to discern common elements among the many groups calling themselves Christians, Christianity has certain characteristics which distinguish it from other religions. Christians believe in the One God of the Jews and the Muslims, but they alone recognize Jesus Christ as a personal Saviour. They believe in the essential unity of soul and body and that, as Christ said, "He who loseth his life shall find it." Redemption comes not by escape from the problems of this world but by living in a right relationship with God here and now.

As with other religions, the number of Christians and their spatial distribution have fluctuated over time. Jesus himself preached to a relatively small number of Jews in a few towns in what is now Israel. After his death his apostles reached audiences in some areas beyond the borders of their home country. By 45 A.D. churches were established in Antioch and Tarsus in Asia Minor, and in Rome. In the fifteen years from 50 A.D. to 65 A.D., Paul and other apostles preached in many provinces of the Roman Empire. Paul's aim was to travel along trade routes, establishing churches in the major cities, whence he hoped their influence would spread to the surrounding territory. He preached to Gentiles as well as Jews; by the end of his ministry, Christian churches had been established in areas bordering the Mediterranean as far west as Greece and there were isolated groups of Christians in and near Rome and along the southern shore of the Black Sea, as well as on the islands of Crete and Cyprus. By 185 A.D., there had been some spread of Christians from these locations. In addition, new foci had been established in Spain, Gaul, the west coast of the Adriatic, and the south coast of the Mediterranean at Alexandria, Cyrene, and Carthage.

By the time of Constantine, 325 A.D., when Christianity became the official religion of the Roman Empire, there were Christians in almost all of the Empire, including southeastern Britain. There had also been some spread to the north and east, although its exact location and extent are unknown. Since the death of Jesus, the spread of Christianity as a minority religion had proceeded slowly but steadily by active missionary efforts, often in the face of persecution and torture.

Expansion of Christianity continued, primarily into the rest of Europe, until the seventh century A.D., when the Moslem conquests began. From Arabia, the Moslems moved outward in all directions and succeeded in replacing Christianity with Islam in most of Asia Minor and North Africa. Beginning in the tenth century, Christians first recaptured the southern half of Spain, then moved into Asia Minor through Hungary. They reached Constantinople in 1096 and conquered Jerusalem in 1099. Their victory was, however, short-lived, as much of the territory was subsequently regained by the Arabs.

The next spread of Christianity occurred with the colonization of the New World. In Central and South America the Spanish *Conquistadores* were accompanied by priests. The Indians were enslaved, their culture was obliterated, and Catholicism was imposed as a universal religion. European settlers who later immigrated to the South American countries came primarily from areas which were Catholic. As a combined result of the conversion of the native population and the immigration of Catholic settlers, South America today is almost entirely Catholic.

Much of North America, on the other hand, was originally settled mainly by Protestants, often those who were escaping religious persecution in Europe. But French explorers, accompanied by Jesuit priests, converted Indians as they opened up the northern and central portions of the continent to settlement. Catholic missions had already been established in Florida and California by the Spaniards at the time of the English settlement of the original thirteen colonies. When the United States was established as a new nation, the principle of separation of church and state was laid down in the Constitution, and has been adhered to ever since. Immigrants, from all parts of Europe, brought their religions with them. In the United States today, Catholicism is the largest single religious group; although there are more Protestants than Catholics, the Protestants are split up into a multitude of denominations and sects.

Christianity today is divided into three major branches: the Roman Catholic Church, the Orthodox churches, and the many Protestant denominations and sects. It is the dominant religion of the Americas and most of Europe. Protestantism is strongest in Anglo-America and much of northern Europe, while Roman Catholicism predominates in Latin America and southern Europe. The Orthodox churches are located mainly in the eastern European countries. The proportion of Christians throughout Africa and Asia is relatively small. In these areas, Christianity has become associated with colonialism in the minds of many people, and is therefore being rejected in the face of strong nationalistic sentiments.

3.3.3 Islam

Like Buddhism and Christianity, Islam was originated by one man. Its creed is summed up in the oft-repeated statement, "There is no God but Allah; Muhammed is the messenger of Allah."

At the time of Muhammed's birth, the Arabs were divided both politically and religiously, and tribes were constantly at war with each other. Although there were some converts to both Judaism and Christianity, the majority of people worshiped local gods and goddesses. Theirs was a religion which had developed from the same Semitic background as that described in the early parts of the Old Testament.

Muhammed was born into a well-to-do Bedouin family in the city of Mecca about 570 A.D. and grew up in its cosmopolitan atmosphere. He learned to respect the ideas of Jewish and Christian monotheism more than the polytheistic religion of his fellow Bedouins. According to legend, one day when he was wandering in the hills meditating, as was his habit, he suddenly heard a voice saying, "Recite!" Words began to come from his lips with no effort on his part. His recitations continued for a decade or more, until he had spoken all of what is now known as the Koran. Although some of it was written down as he spoke, much of it was preserved in oral tradition and written down later, when the entire Koran was compiled.

The Muslims believe that Allah reveals his will to mankind in three ways: through Muhammed, His prophet; through the Koran, His revelation; and through the angels. According to the Koran, Allah is the One, Supreme God. For all who submit unquestioningly to His will, there will be happiness, but for the idolater and unbeliever only eternal damnation awaits.

Every Muslim has the duty to observe the "Five Pillars of Islam:" (1) proclamation of the unity of God as expressed in the creed, "there is no God but Allah; Muhammed is the messenger of Allah;" (2) prayer, five times daily, facing Mecca, and in the mosque on Friday; (3) almsgiving, as an offering to Allah and an act of piety; (4) keeping the fast during the month of Ramadan; and (5) pilgrimage to Mecca at least once in his lifetime. In addition, he must live according to the rules laid down by Muhammed and his successors. These cover many aspects of life; for example eating pork, drinking wine or other alcoholic beverages, and smoking are forbidden. The Koran and the "Five Pillars" are unifying factors in the divided Moslem world of today. Despite them, Islam is not a monolithic faith, any more than the Arab countries are themselves united. Of the many branches and sects which have appeared and disappeared, the Sunnites and the Shiites are the best known today.

Even though Islam acts as a strong unifying force in the otherwise divided Arab World, changes are being forced upon it. The concept of blind submission to the will of Allah conflicts with contemporary belief in the need for knowledge to improve the lot of man in this world. Although culture and learning flourished in the Arab world during the ninth, tenth, and eleventh centuries—the "Dark Ages" of Europe—little change took place from then until the twentieth century, when first Turkey and then Egypt began the process of westernization and secularization, with emphasis on the use of human reason and concern with man's temporal welfare.

Under the theocracy established by Muhammed, Islam spread rapidly. Arab tribes drove out of the Arabian peninsula, toppling the Byzantine and Persian empires which had already been weakened by years of fighting with each other. Within twenty years after Muhammed's death, Syria, Iraq, Palestine, Egypt, and the Persian empire had been overcome. Recruiting subjects from the conquered countries into their armies, the Muslims spread across North Africa into Spain and France, where they were finally stopped at Tours in 732. At the same time their armies moved into India, Chinese Turkestan, and Mongolia.

Although it has receded some from the greatest extent of the Conquest, Islam remains strong today in the Arab world: throughout North Africa, the Arabian peninsula and the Middle East, with the exception of Lebanon, Cyprus, and Israel. Beyond that area, Indonesia is the largest of the 32 predominantly Muslim nations. Islam continues to grow largely through its association with African and Asian nationalism. It is a symbol of freedom from white domination not only to the Black Muslims of America but also to Blacks in many countries of Africa.

3.4 ANIMISM

The group of religions often called *primitive* or *tribal religions*, or *animism* comprise a miscellaneous or residual category. Because of the wide range of beliefs and practices represented, we cannot describe them in any detail here. In general these beliefs and practices represent some attempt of man to understand and, where possible, to control the world in which he lives. The term animism refers to the belief that spirits dwell within inanimate objects. In many of the animistic religions, the attempt is made to influence these spirits by means of rituals and magical practices; dances may be performed for rain, or for good crops, or for victory in warfare. As the term tribal religions implies, the specific beliefs are restricted to relatively small numbers of people.

Tribal religions are generally found in those areas which are relatively inaccessible, such as the interior of New Guinea or the Amazon jungles. They are declining at present, as they tend to be replaced by one of the major religions when continuing contact with persons holding these beliefs is established.

3.5 DISCUSSION AND EXPLANATION

In discussing each religion we have looked not only at the present-day spatial distribution of its adherents, but also at the way in which it spread from the point of origin. Using our observations, we can make certain broad generalizations about the spread and distribution of the religions we have studied. Using these generalizations, we can see that many aspects remain unexplained, and that we have raised many questions which remain to be answered.

We have noted that some religions dispersed rapidly, whereas others were confined to relatively small areas. Spread occurred by means of person-to-person contact which was at some times peaceful and at others forcible. We have noted, for example, that Buddhism and Christianity each began at a specific time and place. They were at first disseminated peacefully by missionaries through person-to-person contact. Buddhist monks followed the established trade routes between India and China, spreading their religious ideas to Tibet and other countries along the way. Similarly, Paul and the early Christian missionaries traveled about the Roman world preaching their new religion, as missionaries have done ever since. Islam, on the other hand, grew at first primarily by conquest. People were forced to become Muslims or to die unless they could pay exceedingly large sums as tribute to their conquerors. Forced conversion was also practiced at various times and places in the history of Christianity, such as during the Inquisition and the Spanish conquest of the New World. Catholics and Protestants fought in so-called holy wars, each trying to force their way of thinking upon the other.

Less militant religions such as Hinduism and the Chinese religions, in contrast, were passed on from generation to generation, spreading primarily as people migrated from one area to another. Migration also brought adherents of many different religious beliefs to North America, often seeking asylum from religious persecution in their own countries. Judaism has, in general, also been passed along as part of the cultural heritage of the Jewish people. From the earliest times, their history has been that of persecution, exile, and eventually, dispersion.

We have also noted that although a particular religion may have ceased to exist in its institutionalized form in a given area, many of its ideas and practices were adopted by persons of other religions. Christianity as it is practiced today bears little resemblance to the way of life preached by Jesus. The beliefs and rituals of the church have evolved from many sources besides the Hebrew and Greek origins of the New Testament. The magical beliefs and folk practices of many different groups may still be seen in many areas today as part of their Christian worship. The traditional Christmas celebration, for example, has its roots in Teutonic festivals marking the winter solstice. Similarly, Buddhism is now dominant over a much smaller area than it was at its height. In India and China many Buddhist beliefs and practices were assimilated into prevailing religions and Buddhism virtually ceased to exist as an organized religion.

Our brief survey of the distribution and spread of the major religions of the world raised many questions. To date, few, if any, studies have been made which would help to explain our observations systematically. We could ask, for example, why Christianity spread rapidly in certain areas at certain times and was decisively rejected in other areas at other times. Various people have hypothesized that Christianity was poorly accepted in Asia because of its association with colonialism, and is now being rejected by black Africans for the same reason. We might also like to specify the conditions under which religions which are forced upon a group of people, as Christianity was upon the Negro slaves who were transported to America, continue to be passed down to their children. Similarly, we would like to know when and why they reject them, as many black Christians are doing in the United States.

In summary, we find that religion tends to be perpetuated as one aspect of the total cultural heritage of a group of people. It may be spread peacefully by missionaries and by migration of its adherents, or forcefully by conquest and subjugation. Both physical barriers, such as mountains and deserts, and human barriers, such as language or opposition to new religious ideas, may interfere with the spread of religion. Conversely, a religion may decrease in extent through assimilation, persecution, or replacement by a different religion, either peacefully or forcibly. We shall examine these mechanisms again in the next section as we consider the distribution of different religious groups over the United States.

3.6 THE SPATIAL DISTRIBUTION OF CHURCH MEMBERSHIP IN THE UNITED STATES

In the section above, we were dealing with both a different aspect of religion and a different universe than those we shall be concerned with in this section. The dependent variable was the nominal religious preference of large numbers of people; we were not concerned with actual religious belief or affiliation. In this section, in contrast, we shall be dealing with actual church membership, as reported by various religious bodies such as denominations and sects. The study area, or universe, is a single country, the United States, rather than the entire world.

The distribution of church membership in the United States in 1952 was studied by Zelinsky (1961). He found that the most accurate data avalable were those in *Churches and Church Membership in the United States* (1953), compiled by the National Council of Churches of Christ in the U.S.A., from questionnaires returned by 112 of the 251 religious bodies to whom they were sent. The membership data reported were those given by each church organization and are not, therefore, comparable. Some churches, such as the Roman Catholic, reported all baptized members; others, including most of the Protestant denominations, reported only those confirmed into full membership, usually over thirteen years of age. The religious bodies which did not report included the majority of the predominantly Negro churches in the south, various Eastern Orthodox churches, and the Church of Christ, Scientist.

Regarding the analysis of these data, he says,

> Since it is obviously impractical to deal individually with each of 112 religious bodies for which data are furnished . . . it was decided to combine various bodies of common origin or close affinities into a relatively small number of denominational groups . . . Twenty-two groups, comprising 80 religious bodies, were selected for further analysis. (p. 144)*

He analyzes three aspects of the spatial distribution of church membership: (1) the variation among states and counties in the percentage of population reported as members of church bodies, (2) differences in the strength of membership in the various denominational groups as between rural and urban areas, and (3) the distributional patterns of membership in the different denominations.

3.6.1 Regional Variations in Reported Church Membership

The variation among states in the percentage of population reported as members of religious bodies is indicated in Table 3.1. Zelinsky's explanation of these variations is:

---

*This and the following excerpts from Zelinsky (1961) are reprinted by permission from the *Annals* of the Association of American Geographers, Volume 51 (1961).

Table 3.1   Reported church membership as percentage of total population

UNITED STATES	49.2	*South Atlantic*	(cont.)
New England	62.5	Virginia	38.5
Maine	41.2	West Virginia	32.8
New Hampshire	53.0	North Carolina	39.9
Vermount	52.7	South Carolina	40.0
Massachusetts	67.1	Georgia	38.3
Rhode Island	75.7	Florida	36.4
Connecticut	60.5	*East South Central*	38.6
Middle Atlantic	59.3	Kentucky	44.8
New York	60.1	Tennessee	40.2
New Jersey	57.6	Alabama	34.2
Pennsylvania	58.9	Mississippi	33.9
East North Central	49.2	*West South Central*	49.0
Ohio	46.4	Arkansas	31.3
Indiana	43.6	Louisiana	53.7
Illinois	53.6	Oklahoma	42.4
Michigan	42.3	Texas	53.6
Wisconsin	63.8	*Mountain*	50.4
West North Central	53.6	Montana	46.7
Minnesota	61.6	Idaho	44.1
Iowa	53.6	Wyoming	43.6
Missouri	48.9	Colorado	41.6
North Dakota	63.0	New Mexico	64.9
South Dakota	58.4	Arizona	44.9
Nebraska	53.4	Utah	73.3
Kansas	46.6	Nevada	37.6
South Atlantic	39.5	*Pacific*	37.7
Delaware	44.3	Washington	30.5
Maryland	47.7	Oregon	27.7
District of Columbia	46.6	California	40.7

Source: *Churches and Church Membership in the United States*, Series A, No. 3, Table 4. Reprinted by permission from the National Council of Churches of Christ in the U.S.A.

The incidence of church membership is highest in those areas, particularly in the Northeast, where settlement is old, dense, and stable and where strongly organized denominations, especially the Roman Catholic, are well represented. It is lowest in those places with heavy in-migration—and thus a temporary loosening of church associations—such as California, Washington, Oregon, Nevada or Florida—or those areas which are relatively inaccessible, thinly settled, or characterized by low incomes. (pp. 149–150)

3.6.2 Urban-Rural Differentials Among Different Denominations

For the United States as a whole, 60.8 percent of the reported members in 1952 lived in the 168 standard metropolitan areas (S.M.A.'s) in which 56.8 percent of

Table 3.2   Denominational groups by percentage of reported members in metropolitan and non-metropolitan areas, ca. 1952

Denominational group	Metropolitan counties	Non-metropolitan counties	
		Intermediate counties	Rural counties
Jewish Congregations	97.5	2.5	.0
Roman Catholic	74.5	23.0	2.4
Reported members of all Protestant Groups	45.6	45.3	9.0
Unitarian and Universalist Churches	74.4	25.6	
Protestant Episcopal	72.8	25.1	2.1
Moravian Bodies	70.3	29.7	
Congregational Christian Church	59.9	34.9	5.1
Evangelical and Reformed	59.5	37.0	3.5
Presbyterian Bodies	58.1	37.6	4.3
Reformed Bodies	54.9	45.1	
Assemblies of God	54.5	45.5	
Adventist Bodies	52.1	47.9	
Lutheran Bodies	51.1	40.5	8.4
Latter-day Saints	45.8	44.5	9.8
Friends	44.8	55.2	
Church of the Nazarene	43.8	56.2	
Evangelical United Brethren	42.0	50.6	7.4
Methodist Bodies	40.1	49.8	10.1
Mennonite Bodies	37.9	62.1	
Disciples of Christ	36.0	53.3	10.7
Brethren Churches	35.7	64.3	
Baptist Bodies	34.9	52.2	12.9
Churches of God	34.6	65.4	
Total Reported Church Members	60.8	33.5	5.8
United States population, 1950	56.8	36.4	6.8

Source: *Churches and Church Membership in the United States*, Series D, Nos. 3 to 6, Tables 136 to 139 and Series E, No. 1, Table 140. Reprinted by permission from the National Council of Churches of Christ in the U.S.A.

the population resided in 1950. The percentage of reported members living in these urban areas varied from 97.5 percent for Jewish congregations to 34.6 percent for Churches of God (Table 3.2).

3.6.3 Distributional Patterns of Membership in the Denominations

The United States is distinctive in the number and diversity of its religious denominations. In 1969 there were 238 religious bodies, with 126, 445, 110 members in

321, 079 local churches. In his study, Zelinsky commented on the distribution of members in 1952:

> One of the surprising facts about the American religious scene ... is the extent to which most of the major groups tend to be national in distribution. No two of the areal patterns closely resemble each other, and each of the denominational groups does have one or more regional concentrations. (pp. 151–152)

He made a number of observations about these areal patterns. The Roman Catholics, Presbyterians, and Episcopalians are relatively evenly distributed nationally in proportion to the total population. Methodism is the largest Protestant denomination; it is nationwide in extent, but relatively stronger in the southern and midwestern sections of the country.

Historically, the United States was settled by people with diverse ethnic backgrounds and religious faiths, with members of each ethnic group tending to concentrate in certain areas. In tracing the distribution of church membership today, therefore, we might look first to history to find where members of various groups originally settled. In addition, we should know about subsequent changes brought about through internal migration. Although Zelinsky discusses these two aspects in detail, we shall consider only a few highlights of his analysis and relate his findings to our observations of the worldwide distribution of religions.

As we observed, members of Jewish congregations throughout the world are heavily concentrated in metropolitan areas. This is also true in the United States, as we saw above. Zelinsky suggests that there is a positive correlation between size of metropolis and the percentage of Jews among its total church membership. He notes also a correspondence between the importance of a city as a wholesaling center and the size of its Jewish population.

Roman Catholics are a majority in fourteen of the sixteen largest metropolitan areas and most of the northeastern states. French Catholics predominate in southern Louisiana, while Mexicans in southern Texas form another nucleus. Catholicism is relatively unimportant in the Mormon region of Utah and surrounding states, most of the south, and in most rural areas throughout the nation.

The Methodists and Baptists are two largest Protestant denominations. Both are spatially distributed in about the same way as the total population, but with a heavier concentration in the South, among both Blacks and whites. Members of both denominations migrated to this country in small numbers, but their active evangelistic policies and the freer, less formal worship helped to spread them widely over the country. Although both Episcopalians and Congregationalists are nationwide in their distribution, their heaviest concentration is on the east coast, in the original areas of British colonial settlement, among persons of middle and upper class with urban residence. Presbyterians are distributed in about the same manner as the general population, in part because of active missionary effort as the frontier advanced. All of these denominations were brought to this country by British or Scottish immigrants and have spread so that there is no longer any ethnic significance to their distribution.

The religions of other immigrant groups, on the other hand, remain more strongly ethnically centered, and are to be found primarily in areas where persons of the relevant ethnic origin live. For example, the Lutherans comprise one of the major Protestant groups west of the Hudson and north of the 40th parallel. Various denominations of German origin—the Evangelical and Reformed, now merged with the Congregational Christian Church to form the United Church of Christ, the Evangelical United Brethren, and various Brethren and Mennonite groups— are found primarily in areas of German settlement from Pennsylvania west to Iowa. The Reformed Church is found mainly among a few concentrations of Dutch settlers, especially in New York, Michigan, Iowa, and northwest Washington.

There is a large number of native American denominations and sects. The Unitarian-Universalist churches are found primarily in cities among the educated and relatively well-to-do, and in many college communities. The Latter-Day Saints, or Mormons, originated in New York State and moved westward in the face of successive persecutions until they finally settled in Salt Lake City. Today, they have one of the most active missionary movements of any group, both at home and abroad. The denomination remains, nevertheless, heavily concentrated in the inter-mountain west, with some outposts, notably along the Pacific coast. Other groups, such as the Disciples of Christ, now the sixth largest Protestant denomination, the Church of the Nazarene, the Assembly of God, and the Church of God are widely distributed throughout the country.

3.6.4 Regionalization

Zelinsky also did a regionalization of the United States on the basis of religion (see map, Fig. 3.3). He delineated seven major religious regions and five subregions. Because there was no clear-cut basis for establishing the regions or for drawing the boundaries between them, he did so,

> ... only by a certain loose areal association among certain groupings of church members, i.e. some moderate degree of areal homogeneity apparent to the map analyst ... and the little we know of the configuration of the general culture areas of the United States. (p. 163)

The areas so delineated are:

1. *New England:* Roman Catholic is widely dominant. There is also a relatively larger proportion of Congregationalists, Unitarians, Universalists, and Episcopalians than in the country as a whole.

2. *Midland:* Although religious composition within this region varies from place to place, Methodism is the dominant Protestant denomination, with a wide variety of others represented. Roman Catholics are in the majority in

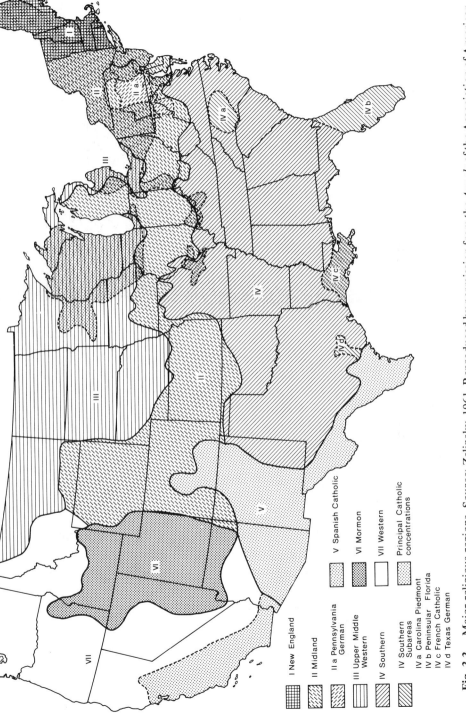

Fig. 3.3. Major religious regions. Source: Zelinsky, 1961. Reproduced by permission from the *Annals* of the Association of American Geographers, Volume 51 (1961).

Legend:

- I New England
- II Midland
- II a Pennsylvania German
- III Upper Middle Western
- IV Southern
- IV Southern Subareas
- IV a Carolina Piedmont
- IV b Peninsular Florida
- IV c French Catholic
- IV d Texas German
- V Spanish Catholic
- VI Mormon
- VII Western
- Principal Catholic concentrations

many cities and some rural areas. A sub-region can be delimited in southern Pennsylvania and portions of Maryland, West Virginia, and Virginia in which churches of German origin are of major importance.

3. *Upper Middle West:* Lutheranism is the dominant Protestant denomination, and in some areas even exceeds Roman Catholicism.

4. *South:* Baptists are strongly dominant and Methodists form large minorities. Although Roman Catholics are relatively unimportant, there are islands of Catholic strength in Texas, Louisiana, and Florida. Another sub-region in the Carolina Piedmont has a greater proportion of Presbyterians, Friends, Congregationalists, and members of various German groups.

5. *Spanish Catholic:* Members of various Protestant denominations, especially Baptists and Methodists, form sizeable minorities alongside the Catholic plurality.

6. *Mormon:* The Church of Latter-Day Saints is the largest single denomination in this region. There are also some Catholics, Jews, and members of other Protestant denominations.

7. *Western:* This region contains members of all religious groups, with no clear patterns of dominance.

3.6.5 Explanations of the Findings

Let us review briefly the approach used in this study and its findings. Among the stated purposes was "a first approximation of the nation's religious regions." Using the best data available, and recognizing their shortcomings, Zelinsky analyzed several aspects of the distribution of religious groups in the United States: (1) the variation among states and counties in the percentage of population reported as members of church bodies, (2) differences in the strength of membership in the various denominational groups as between rural and urban areas, and (3) the distributional patterns of membership in the different denominations. In the course of discussing each topic, he suggested several tentative hypotheses which might possibly account for the observed distribution of the phenomena.

1. With regard to church membership, he made the generalization that areas which were settled early and which have smaller amounts of in-migration have a larger percentage of the population as members of religious bodies than those areas which are more recently settled, or which have larger amounts of in-migration.

2. Differences between the relative proportions of rural and urban members in a religious body may be related to (a) the nature of its religious beliefs, and the adherents which it tends to attract; (b) the implied social status attached to a given denomination; or (c) the occupation of persons who profess that religion.

3. The nationwide distributional pattern of each religious body is influenced by one or more of the following factors: (a) areas of original settlement to which the religion was brought by in-migrants; (b) subsequent migration of its adherents within the country; (c) spread of the religion through missionary efforts, or, conversely, its decrease or failure to spread through lack of such efforts; and (d) the extent to which the denomination has remained ethnically centered and areally restricted rather than becoming "Americanized" and, in many instances, spreading over a wider area among people of various ethnic stocks.

Although none of these hypotheses was formally tested, all are well supported by the evidence given, and many of them could be tested if one desired to do so.

3.7 COMMENTS ON REGIONS AND REGIONALIZATION

Regions were delineated in three of the studies we have reviewed: Kniffen's investigation of Louisiana house types and Zelinsky's studies of log houses in Georgia and church membership in the United States. Since regionalization is an important facet of geographic study, some ideas relating to it will be discussed. Regionalization may be defined as a grouping or classification of phenomena on an areal basis; that is, it represents the spatial aspects of classification. A region, therefore, is an area which is homogeneous according to one or more arbitrarily selected criteria, the selection having been made from a number of phenomena related to the purposes for which the regionalization is being done. Examples of *single-criterion regions* would be those based on the dominant religion, language, or type of land use. *Multiple-criterion regions* can be based on a combination of cultural, economic, or physical features. Both single- and multiple-criterion regions are often referred to as *uniform* or *formal* regions. In Zelinsky's study of religions, for example, regionalization was based on the dominant religious denomination, considered in conjunction with the distribution of other groups. It is more difficult to delineate multiple- than single-criterion regions because the criteria used do not co-vary perfectly, and decisions on where to draw boundaries between regions must often be made more or less subjectively. It is also more difficult to show that such regions are homogeneous; that is, that there is less variation within than among them. Although regions are usually thought of as contiguous, they need not necessarily be so. All urban areas in the United States, for example, could be considered as constituting a single non-contiguous region.

Regions are often delineated according to one or more functions for which an area has been organized spatially, such as school or park and recreation districts. These areas are termed *functional regions*. The United States Forest Service, for example, has divided the United States into ten regions; each of these in turn contains a number of forests, and each forest is subdivided into ranger districts for administrative purposes. This regionalization is based solely on the administration of land under jurisdiction of the Forest Service. We may think of one of the larger units, such as a forest, as consisting of a number of nodes, the headquarters of the ranger districts. Each of these headquarters is a node, or center, about which the activities of that district are organized. Other nodes which serve as centers of *nodal regions* are individual churches within a diocese, schools within a school district, or parks within a park and recreation district. Sometimes a functional region consists of a single node, such as a hospital or university, which serves as a center of attraction for the population of the surrounding area. In this case, the region would be delimited according to the residence of the people coming to the node.

Regionalization is often helpful for organizing data, as it helps to simplify a quantity of data so that it can be more easily comprehended. It is also useful for selecting a study area with certain desired characteristics, as well as for distinguishing between areas. There are, however, certain problems associated with regionalization. The difficulty of establishing boundaries between regions has already been mentioned; because of it, the location of the boundary is often somewhat arbitrary and imprecise. Perhaps a more serious difficulty is that regions once defined tend to be thought of as things which actually exist, rather than simply as a convenient way of grouping areas, which may change over time or be changed by use of different criteria for regionalization. Regions are probably most useful when they are defined with a specific purpose in mind, using clearly-identified criteria.

3.8 A MICROSTUDY IN THE GEOGRAPHY OF RELIGION

Our last study concerns yet another aspect of the geography of religion—the location of churches—in a still smaller area—a single county. Stoddard (1960) studied the location of churches in Nemaha County, Nebraska, in selected years from 1894–1959 (Fig. 3.4). After mapping the distribution of all churches within the county (see Fig. 3.5), he found the town churches to be clustered and the open-country churches to be unevenly distributed throughout the remaining area. In attempting to explain this uneven distribution of churches—the dependent variable—he studied its relationship to many other independent variables, only a few of which are discussed below.

1. The only clearly discernible relationship with physical features was that most churches were constructed on ridges bordering streams.

2. Various cultural features were examined. The absence of towns in some parts of the county was found to be associated with the greatest number of open-country churches and the highest density of churches per area intervening between towns. There was also a relationship to transportation routes: those churches which persisted over the years were located on or near improved roads, often at crossroads. Several less accessible churches became defunct. While there was a fairly close relationship between the location of open-

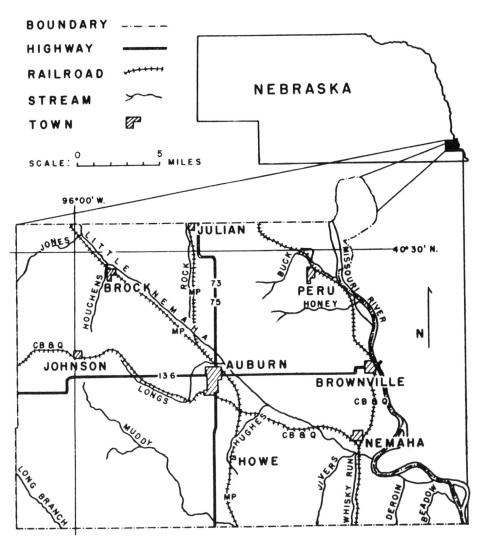

Fig. 3.4. Nemaha County, Nebraska. Source: Stoddard, 1960. Reprinted by permission.

country churches and the location of schools in 1894, this was no longer observable in 1959.

3. With regard to various characteristics of the population, it was found that more church buildings were located in areas where there was a greater density of people. There was also a relationship between the location of churches and nationality; 100 percent of the group of churches such as Lutheran and Catholic which served primarily persons of restricted ethnic origin, usually

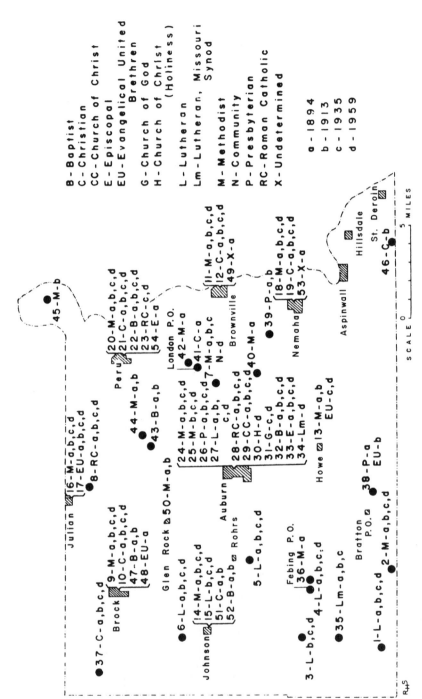

Fig. 3.5.   Location of churches in Nemaha County. Source: Stoddard, 1960. Reprinted by permission.

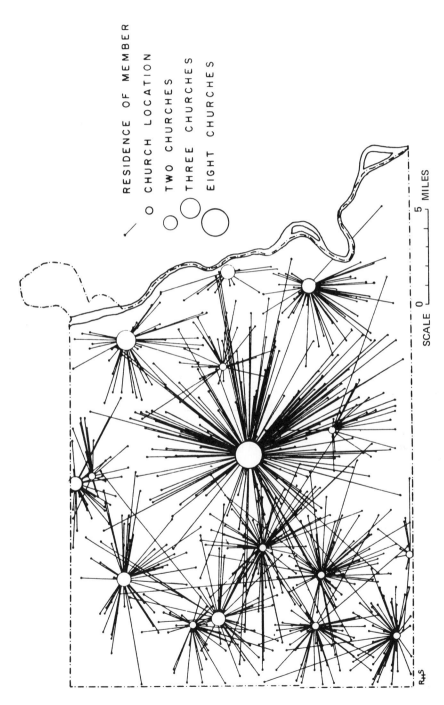

RESIDENCE OF MEMBER
O CHURCH LOCATION
TWO CHURCHES
THREE CHURCHES
EIGHT CHURCHES

SCALE 0   5 MILES

Fig. 3.6.   Service areas of churches in Nemaha County 1959. Source: Stoddard, 1960. Reprinted by permission.

first- or second-generation immigrants, had survived from 1894 to 1959. On the other hand, only 18 percent of the group of churches such as Presbyterian, Baptist, and Methodist, which served primarily persons of native-born American stock, which were active in 1894 were still in use in 1959.

4. The servicing areas of the various churches was also investigated. By referring to Fig. 3.6, it can be seen that the more churches there were in an area, the larger was the area from which the membership was drawn. Rural members of town churches tended to attend church in the town to which they went for other services, such as postal service, education, and shopping.

While these findings were restricted to Nemaha County, some of the generalizations developed could be used as the basis for deriving hypotheses for future studies. They might also contribute to the formulation of a theory of the location of churches and, if we consider the location of churches to be an indicator of the presence of persons with a given religious belief, a theory of the location of religion.

3.9 SUMMARY AND POSSIBILITIES FOR FUTURE EXPLORATIONS

In our exploration of religion we examined spatial aspects of three religious phenomena which we considered as dependent variables: religious affiliation, church membership, and the location of church buildings. The spatial characteristics of other phenomena, however, could also have been selected—for example, Buddhist shrines, Hindu holy sites, or Christian monasteries or missions.

We explored each of these phenomena for different universes, from the entire world to a single county of the United States. By studying different phenomena on a variety of scales, we might eventually determine whether some or all of the hypotheses suggested to account for the observed distributions were equally valid for other areas and for other time periods.

We also considered the spread of different religions over space and time, and tried to identify factors which were related to the spread of different religions. We observed that the most important means of transmission of religious beliefs is by person-to-person contact, and that religious phenomena are spread in this way by missionaries, migration of believers, forceful conversion, and conquest. Although we did not pursue the matter, it seems reasonable to believe that the means used to propagate a particular religion depend to some extent upon the nature of the religion and the beliefs of its followers. Some religions have spread very little spatially, whereas others have spread widely; some were disseminated peacefully, others more forcibly. The same religion has been spread differently at different times and places; Christianity, for example, was originally spread peacefully but later by conquest and subjugation.

Some religions are more closely related to the total culture of their believers than others. We have noted that the more intimately a particular set of religious beliefs and practices is bound up with the culture, the greater is the tendency for that religion to remain associated with a particular ethnic group and to remain areally restricted. This tendency has been illustrated by Hinduism, Shinto, and the religions of ethnic groups in the United States such as the Mennonite and Dutch Reformed denominations. Further study of the diffusion of religions might proceed along lines similar to those by which Johnson (1966) studied the spread of the Church of Jesus Christ of Latter-Day Saints, or Mormons. We shall consider this approach to the study of spatial diffusion in Chapter 12.

After many additional studies have been made, we will have a better understanding of some of the more abstract spatial aspects of a number of religious phenomena, and how these relate to spatial aspects of other cultural phenomena; in other words, a closer approach to a theory of the spatial organization of cultural phenomena, of which religion is but one.

REVIEW YOUR UNDERSTANDING OF THESE CONCEPTS

religion
geographic grouping
spread or dispersion of religious
study area or universe

regionalization
uniform, nodal, and functional regions
internal homogeneity

SUGGESTED ACTIVITIES

1. For a selected community, determine the generalized distribution of persons with a given religious preference (e.g. Catholic, Jewish, Lutheran). If data are not available for the above, identify and map the location of all churches of the selected group and attempt to account for the observed distribution. Individuals can do this investigation for different groups and then compare results.

2. For Canada or some other country where data on expressed religious affiliation or preference are available, obtain the data and construct a map showing the location and spatial distribution of religions. Describe and explain the observed spatial distribution of one of these.

3. For a specific church or congregation, determine the location of residences of the members and formulate hypotheses which may help to explain the observed spatial distribution. Next, note the spatial pattern formed by the distribution and attempt to describe and explain it.

4. Consider religion as an independent variable and list several phenomena, such as voting behavior, educational level, or sale of certain food items, whose spatial distribution may be accounted for in part by the consideration of religion.

REFERENCES

Churches and Church Membership in the United States (1953). New York: National Council of the Churches of Christ in the U.S.A.

Johnson, Paul T. (1966), "An analysis of the spread of the Church of Jesus Christ of Latter-Day Saints from Salt Lake City, Utah, utilizing a diffusion model," unpublished doctoral dissertation, Department of Geography, University of Iowa.

Stoddard, Robert H. (1960), "The geography of churches and their rural congregations in Nemaha County," unpublished M.A. thesis, University of Nebraska.

Zelinsky, Wilbur (1961), "An approach to the religious geography of the United States: patterns of church membership in 1952," *Annals* of the Association of American Geographers **51**, 139–193.

Additional Readings

Aharoni, Yohanan and Michael Avi-Yonah (1968), *The Macmillan Bible Atlas*. New York: Macmillan.

Braden, Charles S. (1939), *The World's Religions*. New York: Abingdon Press.

Brush, John E. (1949), "The distribution of religious communities in India," *Annals* of the Association of American Geographers **39**, 81–98.

Clark, A. H. (1960), "Old World origins and religious adherence in Nova Scotia," *Geographical Review* **50**, 317–344.

Cowgill, Donald O. (1960), "The ecology of religious preference in Wichita," *Sociological Quarterly* **1**, 87–96.

Dornbush, Sanford M. and Elijah L. White (1952), "Segregation of churches, Chicago 1950: the cost utility approach applied to the spatial patterns of social institutions," *Urban Analysis Report No. 7*, University of Chicago Population Research and Training Center.

Duke, Keith E. (1965), "Geographical factors in the location of church sites in urban Los Angeles," unpublished doctoral dissertation, University of California at Los Angeles.

Gaustad, Edwin S. (1962), *Historical Atlas of Religion in America*. New York: Harper and Row.

Government of the State of Israel (1969), *The Official National Atlas of Israel*. New York: Elsevier.

Hebert, Budd H. (1964), "An investigation of the church as a central place employing the central place theory," unpublished M.A. thesis, Department of Geography, Arizona State University.

Hotchkiss, Wesley A. (1959), *Areal Patterns of Religious Institutions in Cincinnati*, Department of Geography Research Paper No. 13, Chicago: University of Chicago Press.

Isaac, Erich (1959), "The citron in the Mediterranean: a study in religious influences." *Economic Geography* **35**, 71–78.

Johnson, Hildegard Binder (1967), "The location of Christian missions in Africa," *Geographical Review* **57**, 168–202.

Kohn, Clyde F. (1970), "Regions and regionalizing," *Journal of Geography* **69**, 134–140.

Kostabade, J. Trenton (1968), "The regional concept and geographic education," *Journal of Geography* **67**, 6–12.

Martin, R. R. (1941), "The church and changing ecological dominance," *Sociology and Social Research* **25**, 246–257.

McDonald, James R. (1966), "The region: its conception, design, and limitations," *Annals* of the Association of American Geographers **56**, 516–528.

Meer, Frederick van der (1966), *Atlas of the Early Christian World*, 3rd ed. London: Nelson.

Meinig, Donald W. (1965), "The Mormon culture region: strategies and patterns in the geography of the American West, 1847–1964," *Annals* of the Association of American Geographers **55**, 191–220.

Minshull, Roger (1967), *Regional Geography: Theory and Practice*. London: Hutchinson.

Myers, George C. (1962), "Patterns of church distribution and movement," *Social Forces* **40**, 354–363.

Noss, John B. (1963), *Man's Religions*. New York: Macmillan.

Ross, Floyd H. and Tynette Hills (1965), *The Great Religions by Which Men Live*. Greenwich, Conn.: Fawcett.

Schlunk, D. Martin and Horst Quiring (1966), *Map of the World's Religions and Missions*. Berne: Kümmerly and Frey.

Sopher, David E. (1967), *Geography of Religions*. Englewood Cliffs: Prentice-Hall.

Stein, Martin M., John Yasnowsky, Jr., Floyd I. Thiel, and Michael R. Horwitz (1968), "Highway interchange locations for Churches: a pilot study in Washington, D.C.," *Public Roads* **35**, 9–17.

Tawney, R. H. (1926), *Religion and the Rise of Capitalism*. New York: Harcourt, Brace.

Warkentin, John (1959), "Mennonite agricultural settlements of southern Manitoba," *Geographical Review* **49**, 342–368.

CHAPTER 4
METHODOLOGY

4.1 INTRODUCTION

In the preceding two chapters we explored some spatial aspects of shelter and religion and tried to explain our observations, but did not concentrate on the way in which we studied these phenomena. In this chapter we shall emphasize the conceptual framework within which our explorations are carried out, and introduce some aspects of methodology. In succeeding chapters we shall discuss content and methodology concurrently, in the hope that the reader will learn not only geographic facts but also different ways of analyzing and studying geographic or spatial aspects of phenomena.

4.2 DEVELOPMENT OF THE SCIENTIFIC APPROACH TO GEOGRAPHIC STUDY

The scientific approach is relatively new to the solution of geographic problems. Hartshorne (1939) suggests that although the precursors of modern discipline of geography may be found in the Greek and Renaissance periods, it was not until about 1750 that it began to develop as a scholarly discipline. Even then, primary emphasis were placed upon the utilitarian nature of geography; that is, upon the assistance which the study of geography lent to the understanding of other disciplines such as politics and history. As geography developed, however, certain concepts were abstracted from the mass of facts which had accumulated. Geographers began to apply the scientific method to the study of geography in the attempt to discern laws which governed the distribution of various phenomena over the face of the earth.

By 1820, Humboldt and Ritter were leaders in geography. According to Schaefer (1953, pp. 227–228)

> . . . both of these men recognized as the major concern of geography the manner in which the natural phenomena, including man, were distributed in space [that is, over the face of the earth].

They accepted the proposition that all natural relations and, therefore, all spatial relations, were governed by laws. . . . Hence, geography had to be conceived as the science concerned with the formulation of laws governing the spatial distribution of certain features on the surface of the earth.*

They believed that while it was essential for geographers to begin their study with observations and empirical findings about the location of things, it was also necessary for them to seek to determine laws about the spatial distribution of the phenomena. Description alone was not enough; it was justified as a basis for the formulation of scientific laws.

More recently, de Geer (1923), a Swedish geographer, defined geography as "the science of the present-day distribution phenomena on the surface of the earth." He emphasized that this definition does not regard the actual crust of the earth and the material things to be found thereon as in themselves the objects of geography. Instead, the emphasis common to all branches of geography is on the phenomena associated with the distribution: the location of objects, their size, form, or distribution in general; that is, certain abstract spatial properties of the objects.

This concern with the study of the location and distribution of things in space distinguishes geography as a scholarly discipline. As de Geer pointed out, geographers may study physical features of the earth, cultural features such as the language, housing, or artifacts of a group of people, economic systems, or political systems. They seek to abstract the distributions of the phenomena from the matrix in which they occur and to study these distributions rather than the phenomena as such. It is important to note that they are concerned with the distributions of the phenomena and with their covariation or areal association; that is, with the way in which any two or more phenomena are associated together in different areas. Geographers are interested in such ideas as the development of cultures or languages, or the processes by which the artifacts are produced only as they are relevant to explanation of the distributions and other spatial aspects.

4.3 KINDS OF EXPLANATIONS

If we are trying to find explanations for observations, we need to consider what an explanation is; that is, what statement or series of statements we will accept as an explanation of a particular observation or set of observations. Philosophers of science recognize different kinds of explanations: genetic, or historical; functional, or teleological; and scientific, or deductive. Since we are primarily interested in scientific explanations, we shall discuss them in greater detail than the other two types.

---

*Reprinted by permission from the *Annals* of the Association of American Geographers, Volume 43 (1953).

4.3.1 Genetic Explanations

When we ask why something exists in the form or location in which it is found at a given time, we may be told the history of the area or the particular set of circumstances preceding a given event. This series of statements constitutes a genetic explanation, which accounts for the occurrence of a single event or a complex series of events in terms of the sequence of events leading up to it. In general, genetic explanations are concerned with unique events or sets of events and little attempt is made to generalize from these events to other similar ones. We have used a genetic explanation in our exploration of the spread of certain religions in that we have described some of the events which occurred as Christianity, Islam, and other religions spread and diminished.

4.3.2 Functional Explanations

Functional explanations tell us what purposes are served by a given phenomenon at a particular time and place and, by extension, that the phenomenon exists where and as it does because it serves these functions. Functional explanations account for the existence of phenomena in terms of their value for or contribution toward the systems of which they are parts. To cite a familiar biological example, we may say that the heart exists because it pumps blood throughout the body. A similar geographic example would be the statement that a city exists in order to supply farmers in the surrounding countryside with the goods and services they require.

4.3.3 Scientific Explanations

The purpose of a scientific or hypothetico-deductive explanation is to show the way in which a particular event or set of events is an example of a more general law. Nagel (1961) states,

> The sciences seek to discover and to formulate in general terms the conditions under which events of various sorts recur, the statements of such determining conditions being the explanations of corresponding happenings. (p. 4)

Stated differently, in the deductive scientific explanation a single observation is shown, by the deductive processes of formal logic, to be one instance of a more general case embodied in the relevant law or laws which are considered to be explanations for these observations. A scientist asks questions about something which he has observed. He wishes to find out how that thing behaves and why, in the sense of discovering relationships between his observations and other phenomena. In thinking about possible explanations he attempts to discern patterns of regularity among his observations. He draws upon both previous knowledge and explanations proposed by himself or others to formulate a series of educated guesses which, when formulated as proposed statements of regularity, are termed *hypotheses.* He constantly works back and forth between hypotheses and observations, testing his guesses, reformulating them, and retesting them in the light of new observations. When necessary, he revises his hypotheses to fit new observations.

Hypotheses which have been confirmed by observations are termed *laws.* More precisely defined, a law is a statement of regularity about the properties or behavior of a set of phenomena under specified conditions. Laws may be either invariate or probabilistic. The laws of classical physics are mainly invariate, whereas many laws of modern physics are probabilistic; in the social sciences most laws can be stated only in probabilistic terms. They are not as well verified as laws in the physical sciences.

Laws may be expressed in various ways and with different degrees of precision. Because verbal expressions tend to be lengthier and less precise than mathematical ones, they are often used in early, tentative formulations of relationships between variables. That is, we might first hypothesize simply that two variables are related and only later, when we had studied the matter more fully, would we be able to express the relationship mathematically. In our explorations, we shall be using both verbal and mathematical statements, and translating from one to the other.

Figure 4.1 illustrates the way in which scientists go about finding and testing new knowledge and integrating it into existing laws and theories.

4.3.4 An Example of the Use of the Scientific Approach in Solving a Problem

A simple example may help to illustrate the way in which the scientist goes about answering a question he has formulated. First, however, let us review the elements involved.

The scientist seeks to answer the questions "how?" and "why?" In order to do so, he formulates a hypothesis, or a series of hypotheses, based upon present knowledge. He then makes his observations to confirm or fail to confirm the various alternatives. He often makes them experimentally, so that the conditions may be carefully controlled. After organizing his observations, often submitting them to a series of mathematical calculations and statistical tests, he is able to state that certain hypotheses have been confirmed, while others have failed to be confirmed. If he can eliminate all hypotheses but one, as if he is sure that his hypotheses have taken into account all the possibilities, he may accept tentatively the remaining hypothesis as the correct explanation. Should future observations disclose information which casts doubt upon this hypothesis, however, he would have to formulate a new set of hypotheses and submit these to the testing process. This verification of a law by successive rejection of untenable hypotheses is known as indirect proof.

Our example is drawn from the work of the detective, which is familiar to most of us, if only through reading or from watching television. Faced with a

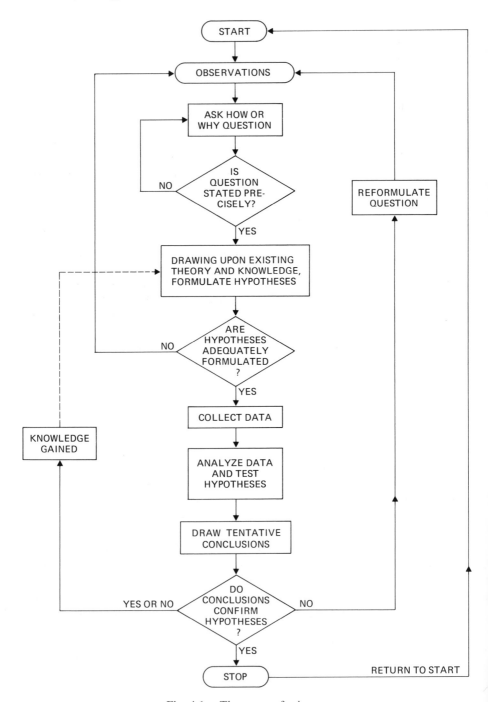

Fig. 4.1. The game of science.

murder, our detective considers all the possibilities as to "whodunnit." Was it the butler, the nephew, or the maid? Assisted by devices which extend and improve upon his own direct observations, he checks fingerprints, bullets, tire treads, and other clues. These observations help him to rule out the maid and the butler, and cast increasing suspicion upon the nephew. Since, however, the deceased and the culprit were the only witnesses to the crime, our detective can never be positive that it was not the butler, or that it was the nephew. Later evidence may disclose that an unknown party entered the house by a back window at the time the crime was committed. This would of necessity lead to a reformulation of hypotheses, and a new search for the unknown culprit.

Although this example is somewhat frivolous, it points out the main elements of the scientific approach. In this instance, the question was, "Whodunnit?" To answer this question, a set of alternative hypotheses was formulated and observations were made which would either support or fail to support these alternatives. All alternatives but one were discarded on the basis of these observations. But that one alternative could be accepted only on a tentative basis, not as having been conclusively proved. In the example, an alternative arose which had not been previously considered. It, too, would have had to be submitted to the testing process until a new tentative conclusion could be reached.

4.3.5 The Heuristic Nature of Scientific Inquiry

As has been suggested, scientific inquiry is heuristic; that is, it results in the accumulation and integration of knowledge. It builds upon what has preceded, adds something new, and raises questions for further speculation and investigation. Whereas observations are related to each other by means of laws, laws are interrelated by theory. A *theory* is a statement proposed to explain a number of related scientific laws and/or observations. Unlike a law, a theory cannot be tested directly, its validity is determined by the testing of hypotheses derived from it, and by its adequacy as an explanation of observations related to it.

Building theory involves two types of reasoning, induction and deduction. Deduction is the process of reasoning from a generalization to a specific example; that is, from the abstract to the concrete. For example, hypotheses may be deduced from theories. Induction is the process of reasoning from specific observations to a generalization, or from the concrete to the abstract. Hypotheses can be induced from observations as well as deduced from theories. Theories can be arrived at only by induction, as they represent the most abstract level of scientific study.

A second diagram (Fig. 4.2) may help to illustrate the relationships between observations, hypotheses, and theory, and to show the way in which the scientist may move from observation to hypothesis to theory by induction, or from theory to hypothesis to observation by deduction. A number of observations may be

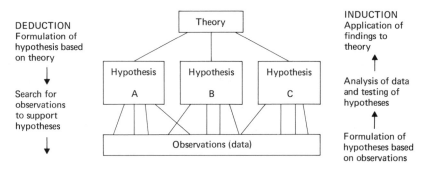

Fig. 4.2.   Relationships between observation, hypotheses, and theory.

used to test a number of different hypotheses which, in turn, may help to confirm a theory. Hypotheses may be derived either inductively, by consideration of a serious of observations, or deductively, on the basis of what one would expect to find if the proposed theory were in fact correct.

4.4 EXPLANATIONS OF GEOGRAPHIC PHENOMENA: AN EXAMPLE

If we were attempting to explain a geographic phenomenon such as the location of the city of Chicago, we could use any one of the three types of explanation. According to an historical explanation, Chicago is in its present location because early traders found it a convenient place for meeting the Indians. As settlers moved westward it became a supply point. Access to transportation, an adequate water supply, availability of wood for building material, and good farming land all encouraged its continuing growth. With the coming of the railroad, it also became a shipping point for many agricultural products, and an industrial center. We can thus explain its location in terms of this very oversimplified series of events leading up to the present.

A functional explanation, in contrast, would emphasize that Chicago is located where it is because it serves many important functions both for the surrounding area and for the entire nation. It is, for example, a transportation center for the entire midwest, with access by water from the St. Lawrence Seaway, by rail from all parts of the country, and by air from all parts of the world. It is a major industrial center for the production of iron and steel, a trading center for agricultural products throughout the midwest, and the financial center of a large area. We would thus have explained its location in terms of the functions which it serves for the system or systems of which it is a part—that is, for the area in which it is located.

Whereas genetic explanations concentrate upon a particular phenomenon or set of phenomena, or the unique features of a given time or place, scientific explanations are more concerned with general principles. If we were to study the locations of many cities in the United States and Canada, for example, we would find many common factors. Most would have good access by rail, road, air, and often water. They would also be important industrial and commercial centers. By knowing these common factors, we could examine a number of specific instances—in this case, the location of many different cities—to determine the extent to which the factors which we had identified applied in each instance. In this framework, the location of Chicago is but one instance of the generalizations. Any deviations which this and other cities exhibited from them might, in turn, suggest additional generalizations to be tested.

4.5 FRAMEWORK OF THE EXPLORATIONS

As stated in Section 1.5, we are concentrating on the definition, location, and explanation of the observed distribution of each phenomenon we have chosen to study; we want to know *what* phenomenon or aspect of it we are studying, *where* it is located, and *why* it is located there. We are more likely to achieve this goal if we proceed in an orderly and systematic fashion in well-defined phases or steps. It is helpful to distinguish these phases conceptually, even though in actuality we may work back and forth from one to another during our exploration.

4.5.1 What: Identification and Definition of the Dependent Variable

Careful identification and definition of what we are studying is an important prerequisite to answering the other two questions, because we need to know as unambiguously and precisely as possible what we are investigating. The topic, or the particular aspect of it being studied, is termed the *dependent variable*. It is called a variable because it varies in quality or quantity; it is a dependent variable because we are interested in knowing how its quality or quantity varies with changes in the quality or quantity of other phenomena which we think are related to it. These other phenomena are called *independent variables*. A particular phenomenon may be used as a dependent variable in one study and an independent variable in others; as our explorations progress, we shall be using as independent variables some phenomena which we have studied as dependent variables. In later chapters we shall examine the interrelationships among a number of variables which constitute a system without designating any of them as dependent or independent.

    The precision with which a variable is defined depends on many things, including the nature of the phenomenon being studied, the particular way in which it is conceptualized, and data availability. Ideally, we would like to define every variable precisely and operationally; that is, to state the definition in such a way that the data are completely replicable by any person. As we saw in Section 2.4.5, for example, Hartman and Hook used a census definition of dilapidated housing. Anyone wishing to replicate the study could obtain exactly the same data by referring to the U.S. Census of Population. Our definition of religion in Section 3.1.1 as "the accepted, institutionalized phenomenon" is less clear and open to various ways of interpretation, but it appears to be satisfactory for the purpose.

In the process of defining or analyzing the spatial aspects of the dependent variable, it may be desirable to organize the data in some manner. Quantitative data may be ordered readily; they may be ranked by size and then grouped so as to yield a smaller number of classes than the original number of observations. Sometimes one approach is used for mapping and another for data analysis. Qualitative data, such as we used in our explorations of religion and shelter on a world scale, may be classified. We were able to use generally accepted classes of religions such as Buddhist, Muslim, and Christian. Since, however, no generally accepted classification scheme existed and it was more difficult to identify house types over the entire world, we proposed a classification scheme for this variable. We also examined other schemes used in studies of smaller areas and considered some of the merits and deficiencies. In subsequent chapters we shall look further at some problems associated with classification and consider some of the characteristics of a satisfactory classification scheme.

4.5.2 Where: the Spatial Distribution of the Dependent Variable

Having defined the dependent variable, we shall examine its spatial variations; that is, how it varies with respect to either quality or quantity over the particular area designated as the study area, also referred to as the universe or sample space. Our individual observations will be based on selected areal units for which data are available, such as individual residences or centers of activity, census tracts, cities, counties, states, or countries. The smaller the areal unit the greater the locational specificity. Using these unit areas, we obtain data for the dependent variable. These data may be depicted by using devices such as maps, tables, charts, or graphs. Often these devices are used to supplement each other; for example, precise values for each observation may be given in a table, whereas values shown on the accompanying map are grouped.

4.5.3 Why: Explanation of the Observed Spatial Distribution

By examining the spatial distribution of the dependent variable as portrayed on a map or table, we can get clues as to why it is distributed in that way. We shall concentrate upon obtaining a scientific explanation as outlined earlier in this chapter, and attempt to determine the relationships among the variables, or the conditions under which the observations occur. Having defined the conditions of the system, we should then be able to say that when certain phenomena within this system vary, we can expect to find corresponding variations in the other variables.

4.6 OBJECTIVES OF THE EXPLORATIONS

We shall use parts of each of these types of explanations to help us in our overall goal of accounting for spatial aspects of the phenomena we are exploring. We have already looked at the sequences of events by which different religions spread over the earth, and how one religion gained adherents as others lost them. Using some of our common findings from these genetic explanations, we then looked for general principles which applied to the distribution and spread of several religions.

We hope to discover other such interrelationships among variables as we explore additional topics. We may find that some variables are related to almost all the others, or that different phenomena spread in much the same manner. If this is the case, we will be able to suggest more abstract and more powerful laws which apply to a number of phenomena. We can also attempt to conceptualize the interrelationships which we have found to exist among a number of variables; that is, to consider these variables as being part of a system, and how changes in one or more variables relate to changes in other variables.

Our overall goal, then, is to find laws explaining certain spatial aspects of the phenomena we are studying. Some of these laws may be quite restricted in their scope, others more general. In the long run we would like to develop general laws and even more general theories to explain these laws. We can achieve this goal only by synthesizing and building upon what is already known, and by considering each phenomenon as it relates to others rather than in isolation. We recognize, however, that we are far from answering the ultimate *why* question, since with each explanation found, many new questions can be raised. In short, the more we know, the more we realize that there is to know.

We have used the word explorations in the title of the text because we recognize that geographers are still exploring the relatively new domain of spatial analysis. As yet, they have found few laws, and these laws have not been interrelated to form the basis for more inclusive theories such as exist in the more advanced disciplines like biology and physics. We are, therefore, assessing some of what is already know about the topics we are studying, finding out how this information became known, and suggesting areas for further study which might lead to greater knowledge in the future.

REVIEW YOUR UNDERSTANDING OF THESE CONCEPTS

abstract properties of distributions	hypothesis
geography as distinct from other disciplines	law
covariation or areal association	theory
kinds of explanation: genetic, functional,	deduction
and scientific	induction

dependent variable
independent variable
operational definition

quantitative data
qualitative data

SUGGESTED ACTIVITIES

1. From geographic journals, select two or three articles reporting substantive research. Analyze each article, following the "Guide for Analyzing Articles," Appendix A.
2. Similarly, select one article focusing on some aspect of methodology and determine the contribution which it makes to present knowledge.

REFERENCES

De Geer, Sten (1923), "On the definition, method and classification of geography," *Geografiska Annaler* **5**, 1–37.

Hartshorne, Richard (1939), "The nature of geography according to its historical development," Ch. 2 in *The Nature of Geography*. Lancaster, Pa.: Association of American Geographers.

Nagel, Ernest (1961), *The Structure of Science*. New York: Harcourt, Brace and World.

Schaefer, Fred K. (1953), "Exceptionalism in geography: a methodological examination," *Annals* of the Association of American Geographers **43**, 226–249.

Additional Readings

Agnew, Neil McK. and Sandra W. Pyke (1969), *The Science Game: An Introduction to Research in the Behavioral Sciences*. Englewood Cliffs: Prentice-Hall.

Angel, R. B. (1967), "Explanation and prediction: a plea for reason," *Philosophy of Science* **34**, 276–282.

Bunge, William (1966), *Theoretical Geography*, 2nd rev. ed., Lund Studies in Geography, Series C, No. 1. Lund: C. W. K. Gleerup.

Burton, Ian (1963), "The quantitative revolution and theoretical geography," *The Canadian Geographer* **7**, 151–162.

Chamberlin, T. C. (1897), "The method of multiple working hypotheses," *Journal of Geology* **5**, 837–848.

Chorley, Richard J. (1964), "Geography and analogue theory," *Annals* of the Association of American Geographers **54**, 127–137.

Golledge, Reginald and Douglas Amedeo (1968), "On laws in geography," *Annals* of the Association of American Geographers **58**, 760–774.

Haggett, Peter (1966), *Locational Analysis in Human Geography*. New York: St. Martin's Press.

Hartshorne, Richard (1959), *Perspective on the Nature of Geography.* Chicago: Rand McNally.

Harvey, David (1969), *Explanation in Geography.* London: Edward Arnold.

Jones, Emrys (1956), "Cause and effect in human geography," *Annals* of the Association of American Geographers **46**, 369–377.

Kemeny, John G. (1959), *A Philosopher Looks at Science.* Princeton: D. Van Nostrand.

King, Leslie J. (1966), "Approaches to location analysis: an overview," *The East Lakes Geographer* **2**, 1–16.

Lowry, Ira S. (1965), "A short course in model design," *Journal of the American Institute of Planners* **31**, 158–165.

Lukermann, Fred (1961), "The role of theory in geographical inquiry," *The Professional Geographer* **13**, 1–6.

Madden, Edward H., ed. (1960), *The Structure of Scientific Thought: An Introduction to Philosophy of Science.* Boston: Houghton Mifflin.

McCain, Garvin and Erwin M. Segal (1969), *The Game of Science.* Belmont, Calif.: Wadsworth.

Morgenbesser, S. (1963). "The explanatory-predictive approach to science," in Bernard Baumrin, ed., *Philosophy of Science, The Delaware Seminar.* Vol. I. New York: Interscience.

Nystuen, John D. (1963), "Identification of some fundamental spatial concepts," *Papers of the Michigan Academy of Science, Arts, and Letters* **48**, 373–384.

Rescher, Nicholas (1963), "Fundamental problems in the thoery of scientific explanation," in Bernard Baumrin, ed., *Philosophy of Science, The Delaware Seminar,* Vol II. New York: Interscience.

Scrivens, Michael (1962), "Explanations, predictions, and laws," in Herbert Feigle and Grover Maxwell, eds., *Minnesota Studies in the Philosophy of Science,* Vol. III. Minneapolis: University of Minnesota Press.

Watson, J. W. (1955), "Geography—a discipline in distance," *Scottish Geographical Magazine* **71**, 1–13.

CHAPTER 5
FOOD*

5.1 INTRODUCTION

Food is something with which we are familiar; we deal with it several times daily, if we are so fortunate as to live in areas where it is plentiful. At the same time, we recognize that the supply of food is unevenly distributed among the nations of the world and within each country. Scrimshaw (1963) has vividly described the problem existing in many areas of the world.

> Nearly half the world's population is underfed or otherwise malnourished. The lives of the people in the underdeveloped areas are dominated by the scramble for food to stay alive. Such people are perpetually tired, weak and vulnerable to disease— prisoners of a vicious circle that keeps their productivity far below par and so defeats their efforts to feed their families adequately. Because their undernourishment begins soon after birth, it produces permanently depressing and irremediable effects on the population as a whole. Malnutrition and disease kill a high proportion of the children by the age of four; the death rates for these young children are 20 to 60 times higher than in the U.S. and western Europe. Among those who survive, few escape physical or mental retardation or both. (p. 73)†

Scrimshaw is obviously interested in the immediate practical problems associated with the uneven distribution of food over the surface of the earth. In our exploration, however, we are more concerned with theoretical or basic aspects of this distribution. We are interested in observing, describing, and explaining spatial aspects of the phenomena we have chosen to study. In our exploration of food, we would like to get some idea of the dietary patterns of people living in different areas of the world: what foods are eaten and how nutritionally adequate the diet of the average person is. We shall then look for factors to explain the distribution we have observed. These factors might then, in turn, prove helpful in analyzing some of the practical problems associated with the uneven distribution of food.

---

*Much of the material in this chapter has previously appeared in Kariel, 1966.
†From Scrimshaw, Nevin S., "Food" from *Scientific American*, No. 3, Sept. 1963. Copyright © 1963 by Scientific American, Inc. All rights reserved.

5.2 DEFINITION OF THE PROBLEM

Let us consider how we might study the geography of food, since we realize that
the general subject is too big to consider all at once. If we first identify some aspects or elements of it which we might study, we can then assess how studying
each of these might contribute to our overall goal of learning about dietary patterns of people throughout the world. We could investigate what foods are eaten
and in what proportions. Knowing the amounts of different foods eaten, we could
assess the nutritive value of the diet of an average or typical individual. Alternatively, we might consider the presence or absence of certain foods or the way food
is prepared. When we had assembled data related to these topics and others and
achieved some explanation of the spatial aspects which we set out to study, we
might be able to apply some of the resulting knowledge to solution of some of the
social problems stemming from the uneven distribution of food over the world.
Our knowledge of nutritional adequacy of the diet would be helpful in determining
those areas in which people are receiving diets which are inadequate in one or
more respects. Our information about staple items of diet and preparation of foods
would suggest what foods might be acceptable to persons living in different areas,
and how unfamiliar foods might be prepared. For example, at a time when the
Japanese were short of rice, wheat was shipped to them. It was found that they
were not accustomed to using it as bread but would use it if the flour was made into
noodles. Similarly, throughout many areas of the world there is a severe shortage
of protein foods. Although low-cost supplements have been developed, these must
be produced in a form which is acceptable to persons in each area, and which will
be readily incorporated into their customary diets.

5.3 CHOICE OF SCALE

The degree of detail with which we can make statements about our observations
within the study area is related to the scale at which a study is conducted. In our
explorations of shelter and religion, for example, we first got an overview of the
spatial distribution of the phenomenon by studying it on a world scale, and then
studied various spatial aspects over smaller areas. We found that our observations could be more detailed when we were studying smaller areas. For example,
when reviewing Zelinsky's (1961) study of the distribution of religious affiliation
over the United States, we learned that he studied the membership of different denominations by states. When Stoddard (1960) studied churches within a single
county of the state of Nebraska, however, he located each church, and found out
when it had been built and when it was abandoned, if it was no longer in use. He
also studied the residence of each church member and the distance it was located
from the church which he attended.

Arbitrarily, we have decided to study food only on a world scale; in later
chapters we shall explore other phenomena on different scales, and compare the

results obtained. Since we are exploring the field of human geography, we would like not only to get some idea of what foods are eaten by people living in different areas of the world, but also to organize our observations in a manner which will assist us to explain spatial aspects such as the uneven distribution of food. Since our aim is to get a general overview, we shall consider only the average diet of the majority of people living in each area. Such a survey is, of necessity, macroscopic; that is, it is concerned with large areal units and ignores variations within them related to individual or group food preferences, natural or man-made catastrophes, or seasonal fluctuations in diet.

5.4 DEVISING A SCHEME FOR CLASSIFYING DIETARY PATTERNS

5.4.1 General Considerations

In order to analyze and explain spatial aspects of a phenomenon it is helpful to organize the data representing the observations. There are so many individual observations, or bits of data, that without organization it is impossible for us to visualize and derive relationships among them. Quantitative or metric data are ordered numerically; non-quantitative data may be classified or grouped so as to sort like kinds from unlike. What classification scheme is selected depends upon a number of factors, including the purpose of the study, the existence of accepted classification schemes, the aspect of the phenomenon which is being investigated and the availability of data for the desired areal units within the study area.

We have already encountered some of the problems of classifying data in our study of shelter, although we did not consider them explicitly at that time. We found that since no generally accepted classifications of shelter existed, as one did for religion, researchers devised their own schemes. Each scheme was set up according to the overall purpose of the study and the particular aspect of the phenomenon being investigated. Researchers, such as Zelinsky (1953), who collected their own data were less restricted by data availability than were Hartmann and Hook (1956), who used census data.

5.4.2 Possible Schemes

In our present problem of classifying dietary patterns, we need to consider which of the aspects of the phenomenon of food would be most useful as criteria on which to base our classification scheme. Since there are many elements which could be studied, we need first to decide which likenesses to concentrate on.

Among the first things that may occur to us when we think of food in different parts of the world are a number of national dishes or regional specialities: sauerbraten brings to mind Germany, pizza is associated with Italy, egg foo yung with China, curries with India, and tamales with Mexico. Although such an approach may be satisfactory for the author of a gourmet "round-the-world" cookbook, it is not as suitable for our purposes, as it fails to describe the diet as a whole in any area.

We might, alternatively, study the distribution of a single food such as potatoes, oranges, or horsemeat. To do so, we could either conduct a study of the presence or absence of this food in the diet, or carry out a more complex study of the amount consumed in different areas. Although this study would be interesting and hypotheses could be formulated to explain the presence or absence of particular items, we can easily see that this approach also would not serve our purpose of describing food patterns or dietary habits as a whole.

Another possibility would be to study the consumption of foods in various groups such as meats, cereal grains, dairy products, fats, fruits, and vegetables. Study of the average consumption per capita of foods within each food group is often used by nutritionists to give an overall picture of the nutritional adequacy of the diet of an individual or group. Unfortunately, however, the necessary data for such a study are not available by country for the entire world. In addition, by restricting ourselves to studying food groups, we would be less successful in describing variations in diet from area to area, as we would not know what kinds of meat or cereal grain, for example, were predominant in different areas.

In seeking a more inclusive approach, we might consider the particular combination of foods which is characteristic of the diet in a given area. For example, people living near the Mediterranean eat mainly wheat, barley, olives, grapes, and mutton or goat. Similarly, the diet often termed North American is composed of a variety of meats, vegetables, fruits, and many cereal grains, of which wheat is most important. Such an approach gives us a good picture of what foods people in different areas eat, and it also gives us some notion of the variety and nutritional adequacy of their diets. On the other hand, it is cumbersome because many foods must be listed for each group. Perhaps a more serious disadvantage is that this scheme is based on area rather than on components of the diet.

If we are interested primarily in nutritional adequacy, we might look for one or two components of the diet which would help us to characterize it in this respect. We know that calories and proteins are two nutritional components which, when considered together, provide a reasonable approximation of the nutritional adequacy of a diet. A *calorie* is a measure of energy; a person who consumes a diet deficient in calories over a period of time is unable to perform his daily work adequately, particularly if it involves heavy physical labor, and loses weight. *Protein* is necessary for growth and repair of body tissue. Although the amount of essential vitamins and minerals is disregarded when we consider only the number of calories and the amount of protein consumed per capita per day, a diet which has enough calories and protein is often adequate in other respects as well. The use of these two components has the disadvantage of lacking a description of the actual foods eaten. It has the advantage, however, that data are available for both variables. In addition, because the data are quantitative, they are amenable to statistical analysis.

These suggestions indicate but a few of the many ways in which we might approach our world-wide study of dietary patterns; hopefully, they are enough to indicate that there is a wide range of possibilities. We have also suggested enough topics that we can choose one or more of them, or a combination of several, as criteria upon which to base the following classification scheme.

5.4.3 The Proposed Classification Scheme

In this scheme we shall list the major foods eaten, as was suggested in the regional diet approach, but consider them in two categories: major sources of calories and important sources of protein. A scheme using these criteria is suitable for our overall purpose of describing the average diet of typical individuals within a class, under usual circumstances. A distinction between the proposed scheme and the regional diet approach is that the delineation of classes is based on characteristics of the dependent variable, foods eaten, and not upon area.

5.4.4 Sources of Data

Some data are available in publications of governmental and international agencies such as the United States Department of Agriculture (USDA) and the Food and Agricultural Organization of the United Nations (FAO). The Office of Foreign Agricultural Research of the USDA has developed a method of estimating consumption from production and trade figures.* In this method, food production of a country is estimated; the amount of each commodity exported is then subtracted, and the amount of each commodity imported is added in order to calculate the total food supply for the country of all commodities included in the estimate.† These estimates were used for all countries for which they were available. For other countries, the *Production Yearbook* and the *Trade Yearbook* of the the FAO (1947-various years to date) as well as maps in various atlases and books, provide data about staple crops. These data are also of value in delineating boundaries between classes.

Additional sources of data include studies of food consumption on a world scale or of a portion of the world (Bennett, 1941; Brown, 1961; Githens and Wood, 1943; Jones, 1959). Data have also been drawn from a variety of sources which range in accuracy and completeness from casual comments about food made by travelers to detailed case studies of food consumption of many individuals living in a particular area. Some case studies contain references to food which are in-

---

*A distinction is made between food *consumption* and *ingestion.* Consumption refers to the bringing of food into the home; ingestion to the actual eating. There is a certain amount of wastage between purchase and ingestion. In the data, for example, the average calorie consumption per capita per day in the United States is given as 3,100 calories. Few people actually eat this much, so that ingestion is considerably lower. In our report, however, no distinction is made between consumption and ingestion.

†The procedure by which food balances are computed is described in *Agricultural Production and Food Consumption in Western Europe*, (USDA, 1951).

cidental to the main purpose of the study; food has been the major topic of investigation of still other studies. Many case studies of areas or groups of people have been made by nutritionists, whose main concern was the nutritional adequacy of the diet. Similar surveys, covering larger areas, have been sponsored by governmental agencies and nonofficial research institutions.

5.4.5   Determination of Classes

The next problems we need to consider are how many classes to use and what areas should be placed in each class. Our objective is to make each class relatively homogeneous; a classification scheme is obviously meaningless unless there is greater variation between classes than within them. The problem of drawing boundaries enclosing areas which are relatively homogeneous as to diet, using the criteria we have selected, is complicated by the fact that data are given only by country. Since there may be more than one class of diet within a country, additional sources of data, such as case studies and maps of climate and agricultural production, have to be used. In our explorations, decisions as to what areas to include in each class and where to draw boundaries between classes were made subjectively, using approximate guidelines as to what constituted a major source of protein or an important source of calories. If more accurate and complete data had been available, it would have been better to use an objective criterion such as a specified percentage of the total protein or calories consumed.

5.4.6   Evaluation of the Proposed Classification Scheme

We have devised a scheme which appears to be suitable for our purpose of describing world dietary patterns, is related to the aspect of the problem upon which we wish to focus, and is possible to work with because data are available. We should next evaluate whether it will, in fact, be as acceptable. According to philosophers of science, classes within a scheme must be both mutually exclusive and exhaustive. This means that any given observation can fall in one and only one class, and that every observation must fall in some class. The scheme we are using here is suitable for describing the average diet of people over the world, and the classes are both mutually exclusive and exhaustive because we can arbitrarily place every observation in some class. It has the shortcoming of being based on two criteria rather than a single one, with neither criterion being precisely and operationally defined. Despite this disadvantage, it is suitable enough for our purpose to outweigh the disadvantage. None of the classes delineated here is completely homogeneous, since there are variations within each class based on factors such as personal taste, income, ethnic origin, and the local availability of of foods. Fish, for example, is often important for people living near the ocean, lakes, or inland waterways, even though it may be relatively insignificant for a class as a whole. Such microvariations cannot be taken into account in a world-wide classification scheme. Overall, however, there is greater variation among classes than within any particular class.

5.5 THE CLASSES AND THEIR SPATIAL DISTRIBUTION

The resulting classification of foods, on a world-wide scale, is shown in the combined table and map legend (Fig. 5.1); their spatial distribution is depicted on the map. The following discussion is an expanded description of the diet in each class. As may be seen from the map, most of the classes are located in a single area; Class 1 is a notable exception.

Classes are arranged in the table according to major food grains. Within each class, the major sources of calories are listed in the approximate order of their importance in the diet. In Classes 1–6, wheat is the major food grain. It is dominant in Class 1, and about equal to other grains in Class 6. In the next five classes, Classes 7–11, rice is the major food grain; in Classes 12–14, maize; and in Classes 15–17, millet and sorghum. Each of the remaining three classes is different from all others. Barley is dominant in 18, while tropical fruits and tubers substitute for grain in 19, and meat in 20.

5.5.1 Location and Description of the Diet of Each Class

Class 1.   *Location: Anglo-America, Argentina, Chile,*
Uruguay, most of Europe, U.S.S.R., Australia,
New Zealand, South Africa.

We find a highly varied diet in the areas included in this group. Although meat, potatoes, wheat, and dairy products are the staples, many other items are available to most people. Wheat is the major food grain, but others are also found. Rye is consumed more heavily in eastern and northern Europe, whereas oats are important in the British Isles, especially in Scotland and Ireland. Potatoes are consumed most heavily in Ireland; sugar consumption is high throughout the region.

This is the only class including large numbers of people in which animal products are major sources of calories as well as important sources of protein. Beef and pork are the most important meats. More pork than beef is consumed in most of the European countries, whereas beef is more important in the other areas. Total meat consumption is highest in Argentina and Uruguay, where large amounts of beef are eaten. The greatest amount of fish is eaten in Norway. Dairy products are used both as fresh milk and as cheese. Chicken and eggs are of secondary importance; even though the total consumption is high in many areas, they are not major sources of either calories or protein according to the criteria used.

Class 2.   *Location: Northern India and West Pakistan*

In Northern India and West Pakistan, wheat is the dominant food grain, but millet and sorghum and barley are also eaten. Rice is also found in some areas. Various pulses provide most of the protein; fish is important mainly along the Indus River and other waterways.

*Class 3.   Location: European and Middle East Mediterranean.
          North Africa, Arabian Peninsula, Soviet Central Asia.*

Wheat is by far the predominant food grain, and fats and oils are the other major sources of calories. Maize, barley, and rice are eaten as supplementary food grains; more maize is consumed in Egypt and Portugal, but barley is more important in northwest Africa. In some areas dates and figs are major sources of calories. Dates are especially important in the oases of Libya and Tunisia; figs are staple items of diet in parts of Algeria, Morocco, and Tunisia. Meat is less important than in Class 1, and the amount of meat eaten decreases from north to south. Beef and veal are found throughout the region, but pork is unimportant in Israel and the Moslem areas, where it is forbidden by religious tenets. Dry broad beans are the most important of the many pulses which provide a large amount of the protein. Fish is important primarily in Portugal, but is also eaten wherever it is available in coastal areas and along rivers.

The diet of the pastoral nomads living in the mountains of Morocco, Algeria, the Sahara, and on the Arabian Peninsula is distinctive in that they are almost entirely dependent upon their herds for food. Meat and milk are important dietary items, and the other foods mentioned above are of relatively less importance.

Class 4.   Location: Highlands of Ecuador, Peru and Bolivia.

In many ways, this diet is similar to the preceding one. Wheat is the major food grain, but maize is a close second. Barley and potatoes are also important sources of calories; small amounts of fats and oils are eaten. Dry beans are the major and almost the only source of protein.

Class 5.   Location: Brazil, other than the Amazon Basin.

In this region, wheat, maize, and rice are approximately equal in importance. Sugar is another major source of calories. In addition to the dry beans which provide most of the protein in Class 4, some beef is also found.

Class 6.   Location: Paraguay, lowlands of Bolivia.

The dietary pattern of people in this area is distinguished from that of Class 5 mainly by the dominance of cassava and the lesser importance of sugar. Wheat and maize are the major food grains, while dry beans and beef are the major sources of protein.

Class 7.   Location: Northeastern India, Bangladesh.

In this and the next four classes, rice is the major food grain. Dry beans and peas are the major sources of protein. Fish is important locally, along waterways, but not in the region as a whole.

Class 8.   Location: Coastal Southeast Asia, Japan, South Korea, Taiwan.

Rice is dominant and wheat is of lesser importance. Fish and soybeans are the

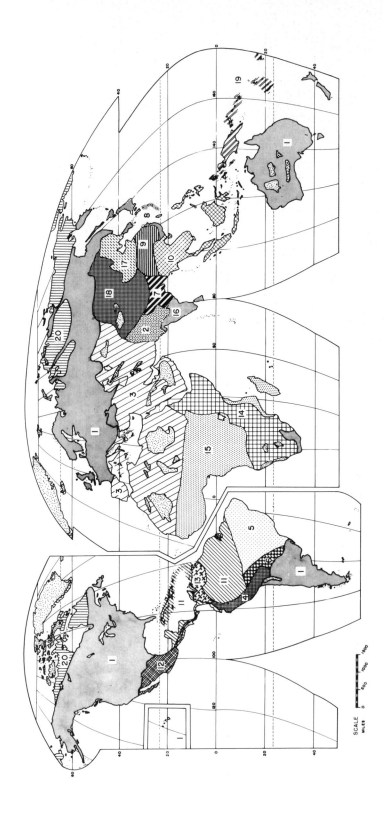

DIETARY PATTERNS

		MAJOR SOURCE(S) OF CALORIES [1]	IMPORTANT SOURCE(S) OF PROTEIN [2]
	1	Wheat, potato, sugar, meat, fats and oils	Beef, pork, mutton, dairy products
	2	Wheat, millet and sorghum, barley, rice	Dry beans, dry peas, chickpeas, lentils
	3	Wheat, maize, barley, rice, fats and oils	Beef, pork, mutton, dry beans, dry broad beans, chickpeas
	4	Wheat, maize, barley, potato	Dry beans
	5	Wheat, maize, rice, sugar	Beef, dry beans
	6	Wheat, maize, cassava	Beef, dry beans
	7	Rice	Dry beans, dry peas
	8	Rice, wheat	Fish, soybeans
	9	Rice, maize, sweet potato	Pork, fish, soybeans, peanuts
	10	Rice, maize, sweet potato, coconuts, cassava	Fish, soybeans, peanuts, dry beans
	11	Rice, maize, bananas, yams, cassava, sugar	Dry beans, dry peas
	12	Maize	Dry beans
	13	Maize, wheat, potato	Beef, dry beans
	14	Maize, millet and sorghum	Dry beans, dry peas, dry broad beans, chickpeas, lentils
	15	Millet and sorghum, maize, rice, yams, cocoyams, sweet potato, cassava, bananas	Dry beans, dry peas, peanuts
	16	Millet and sorghum, rice, cassava, coconuts	Fish, dry beans, lentils, peanuts
	17	Millet and sorghum, wheat, maize, potato	Pork, mutton, soybeans, peanuts
	18	Barley	Dairy products, mutton, goat
	19	Cassava, yams, taro, bananas, coconuts	Fish, pork
	20	Animal fats, wheat	Fish, local game animals
		Uninhabited Areas	

1. *Major sources derived from starchy staples and other sources where applicable.*
2. *In addition to that protein which is derived from grains.*

Fig. 5.1. Dietary patterns. Source: Kariel, 1966. Reproduced by permission from the *Annals* of the Association of American Geographers, Volume 56 (1966). Goode's base map © copyright, University of Chicago. Used by permission of the University of Chicago Press.

major sources of protein. Consumption of wheat and milk is increasing, especially in Japan. Meat, primarily pork, is of greatest importance in Taiwan.

Class 9. Location: Eastern China (Yangtze River Valley).

Although rice is the dominant food grain, maize is also eaten. Sweet potatoes are also a major source of calories. As in Class 8, fish and soybeans are important sources of protein; these are supplemented by peanuts and pork.

*Class 10. Location: Southern China, Southeast Asia,
Indonesia, Malaysia, Philippines.*

Coconuts and cassava are major sources of calories in addition to the rice, maize, and sweet potatoes of Class 9. Cassava is most important in Indonesia. Fish, soybeans, peanuts, and dry beans are the major sources of protein. Meat is important mainly in Singapore, where some pork is eaten. Fish is eaten locally, and is of greatest importance in Thailand.

*Class 11. Location: Lowlands of Central America, Ecuador and Peru,
Amazon River Basin, Caribbean Islands.*

Rice and maize are the most important grains in this class. Some millet is found in Haiti. Total cereals consumed are greatest in Cuba and Panama; the consumption of cassava is high in Cuba, the Dominican Republic, and Haiti. Bananas provide a large number of calories in the Dominican Republic. Consumption of sugar is generally high throughout the area. Prior to the food shortages of the Castro regime, the largest amounts of meat, fats and oils were consumed in Cuba. Pulses, especially dry peas and beans, are the major sources of protein.

Class 12. Location: Mexico, uplands of Central America.

The diet in this region is distinctive in its heavy dependence upon maize and dry beans. When meat is eaten, it is usually beef or veal. This diet has little variety, and unless it is supplemented with dairy products, fruits, and vegetables, is nutritionally inadequate.

Class 13. Location: Uplands of Columbia and Venezuela.

The diet in this area is somewhat more varied, since wheat and potatoes, as well as corn, are staple items of diet. More beef is found than in Class 12.

*Class 14. Location: Highlands of East Africa, southern Africa
except portions of South Africa.*

This is a transitional class in that, although the total amount of cereals is relatively constant, the proportions of millet and sorghum, maize, and rice vary from place to place. In Ethiopia, teff is the most important grain; although favored in that country it is little known elsewhere. Millet and sorghum are the major cereals eaten in the Sudan. While they are found to some extent in Kenya, Rhodesia, Zambia and Malawi, maize is the major cereal. In Tanzania, the proportion in reversed, millet and sorghum being more important than maize. The dietary pattern in South Africa is difficult to describe. In general, the Europeans and the wealthier urbanized Africans conform to Class 1. Other Africans eat corn as the major food grain, although other grains are also found. Pulses provide most of the protein; a variety of these is found, including dry beans, peas, broad beans, chickpeas and lentils. Little meat is eaten except in South Africa where beef and mutton are the primary meats.

Class 15.   Location: Africa south of the Sahara including the Congo and the coastal lowlands of East Africa.

Total grain consumption is lower than in the preceding class. It is divided among millet and sorghum, maize, and rice. Yams, coco-yams, sweet potatoes, cassava, and bananas provide a large proportion of the calories. Rice consumption is highest in Malagasay, Liberia, and Guinea, where the climate is more favorable to its growth. In Rwanda, Urundi, and the Congo total grain consumption is very low, and the consumption of cassava is correspondingly high. Protein is derived mainly from dry beans, dry peas, and peanuts. Almost no meat or milk are found.

Class 16.   Location: Southern India and Ceylon.

Rice is the major cereal grain eaten in the coastal areas, while millet and sorghum are more important in the interior. Cassava and coconut are also important sources of calories. Dry beans, lentils, and peanuts are important sources of protein throughout, but fish is eaten primarily along the coast.

Class 17.   Location: North and northeastern China.

Millet, sorghum, and wheat are the major food grains. Maize is also found, and the potato is becoming increasingly important as a starchy staple. Soybeans and peanuts provide most of the protein, but pork and mutton are consumed in large enough quantities to be of dietary significance.

Class 18.   Location: Highlands of Central Asia.

The diet of people in this area, like that of other nomadic herdsmen, is distinctive because of its dependence upon animals. Locally grown barely is almost the only cereal eaten, although some wheat and millet are imported. Cheese and butter, mutton, goat and, in some areas, yak provide the balance of calories and much of the protein. In general, meat is not consumed in large enough quantities to be considered a major source of protein.

Class 19.   Location: Tropical Pacific Islands.

In these areas, as in most others, the native diet has been greatly modified by increasing contact with other peoples. Among those living in more remote villages, however, cassava, yams, taro, bananas, and coconuts are still staple items of diet. Breadfruit is locally important. Fish and pork are the primary sources of protein.

Class 20.   Location: Remote parts of the Arctic.

As in the preceding class, the original native diet scarcely exists today. Traditionally, the Eskimos derived all their food from fish and local game animals such as whales, seals, and polar bears. By consuming almost all parts of the animal, they obtained the essential nutrients. Large quantities of fat, especially whale and seal blubber, were eaten. Increasingly, however, wheat flour and sugar are coming to be considered as essentials, and canned goods are in demand as luxury items.

5.6 SUGGESTED EXPLANATIONS

In trying to explain the distribution of dietary patterns over the entire world, we should like to formulate generalizations which applied to a large number of classes.

5.6.1   Food Production and Technology as Independent Variables

We can draw not only upon our general knowledge but also upon some of the conclusions from our explorations of shelter and religion. In our study of shelter we found that people tended to use building materials which were available in the natural environment. As the amount of technology in an area increased, however, building materials could be transported over greater distances, and more use tended to be made of materials brought in from outside the immediate area.

We can make a similar generalization about the distribution of food, and formulate an hypothesis at a low level of abstraction which explains some of the spatial variation. Without considering technology, we can state that people tend to eat foods which are naturally available or can be grown in the area in which they live. A rough evaluation of this hypothesis can be made with the aid of the data as arrayed in Fig. 5.1; persons living in remote parts of the Arctic rely heavily on game animals such as whale, seal, and caribou or reindeer (Class 20), whereas people living in tropical areas eat such foods as cassava, yams, taro, bananas, and coconuts (Classes 10, 11, 15, 16). Between these two extremes, however, we find that a wide variety of food grains and pulses, supplemented by starchy vegetables and animal products, form the basis of the diet of much of the world's populations. Figures 5.2 through 5.9 show major production areas of important food items. Study of maps showing the production of various food grains (Figs. 5.2–5.4) suggests that in any area, those grains which are consumed in the greatest quantity tend to be those which can be raised most efficiently in that area. We find maize as the predominant food grain in hot, relatively dry areas, and rice as the predominant one in hot, more humid areas. Wheat is most common in cooler, relatively dry areas. We can conclude, therefore, that factors such as types of soils, the amount and timing of rainfall, amount of sunshine, and winter and summer temperatures are related to what crops grow in an area and, in turn, what foods tend to be consumed there.

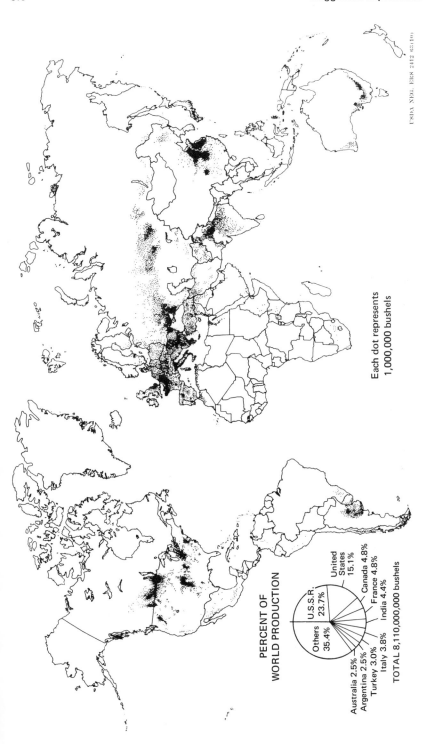

PERCENT OF
WORLD PRODUCTION

United
States
15.1%

Canada 4.8%

France 4.8%

India 4.4%

U.S.S.R.
23.7%

Others
35.4%

Australia 2.5%
Argentina 2.5%
Turkey 3.0%
Italy 3.8%

TOTAL 8,110,000,000 bushels

Each dot represents
1,000,000 bushels

Fig. 5.2. Areas of wheat production. Source: U.S. Department of Agriculture, 1964.

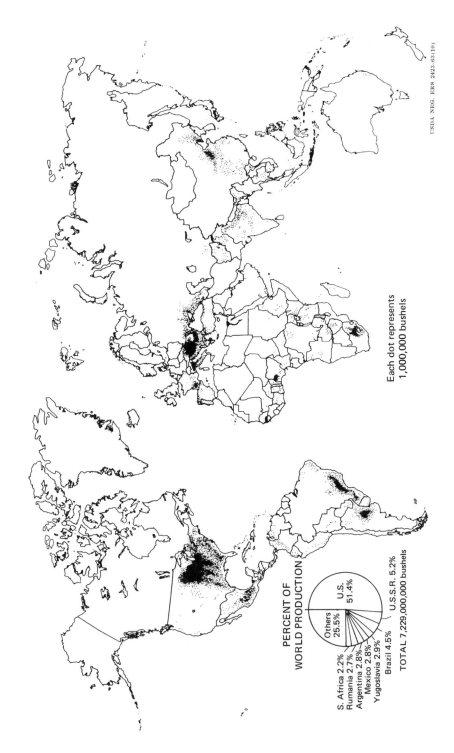

Each dot represents
1,000,000 bushels

PERCENT OF
WORLD PRODUCTION

Others
25.5%

U.S.
51.4%

S. Africa 2.2%
Rumania 2.7%
Argentina 2.8%
Mexico 2.8%
Yugoslavia 2.9%
Brazil 4.5%
U.S.S.R. 5.2%
TOTAL 7,229,000,000 bushels

Fig. 5.3. Areas of corn production. Source: U.S. Department of Agriculture, 1964.

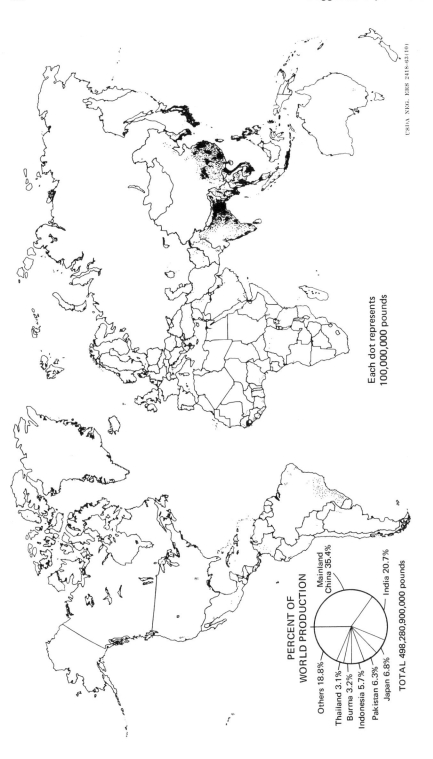

USDA NEG. ERS 2418-63(10)

Each dot represents
100,000,000 pounds

PERCENT OF
WORLD PRODUCTION

Mainland China 35.4%

India 20.7%

Others 18.8%

Thailand 3.1%

Burma 3.2%

Indonesia 5.7%

Pakistan 6.3%

Japan 6.8%

TOTAL 498,280,900,000 pounds

Fig. 5.4. Areas of rice production. Source: U.S. Department of Agriculture, 1964.

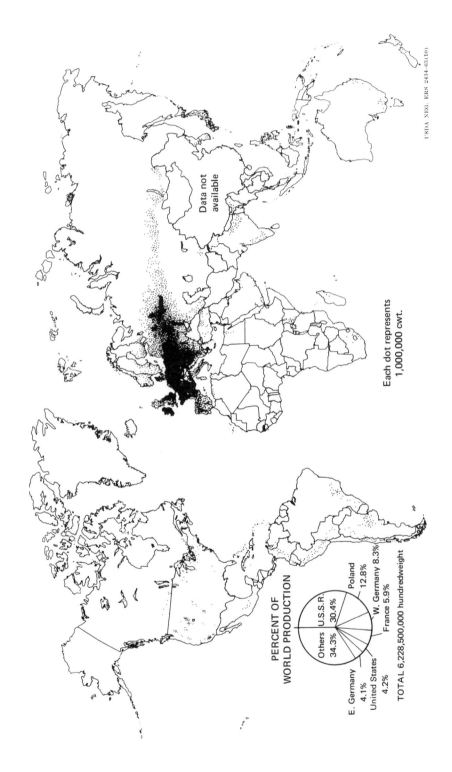

Data not
available

Each dot represents
1,000,000 cwt.

PERCENT OF
WORLD PRODUCTION

Others
34.3%

U.S.S.R.
30.4%

Poland
12.8%

W. Germany 8.3%

France 5.9%

E. Germany
4.1%

United States
4.2%

TOTAL 6,228,500,000 hundredweight

Fig. 5.5.   Areas of potato production. Source: U.S. Department of Agriculture, 1964.

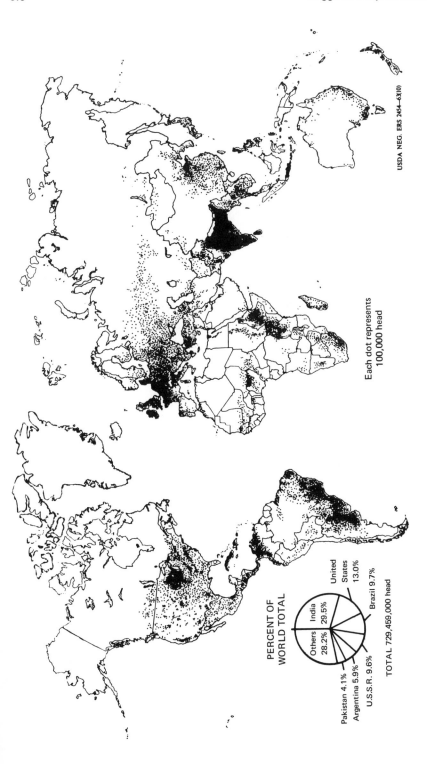

Fig. 5.6.   Areas of cattle production. Source: U.S. Department of Agriculture, 1964.

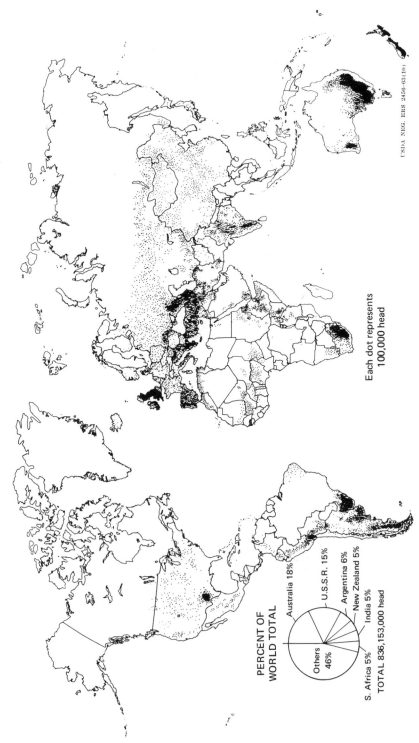

Each dot represents
100,000 head

PERCENT OF
WORLD TOTAL

Australia 18%

U.S.S.R. 15%

Argentina 6%

New Zealand 5%

India 5%

Others
46%

S. Africa 5%

TOTAL 836,153,000 head

Fig. 5.7. Areas of sheep production. Source: U.S. Department of Agriculture, 1964.

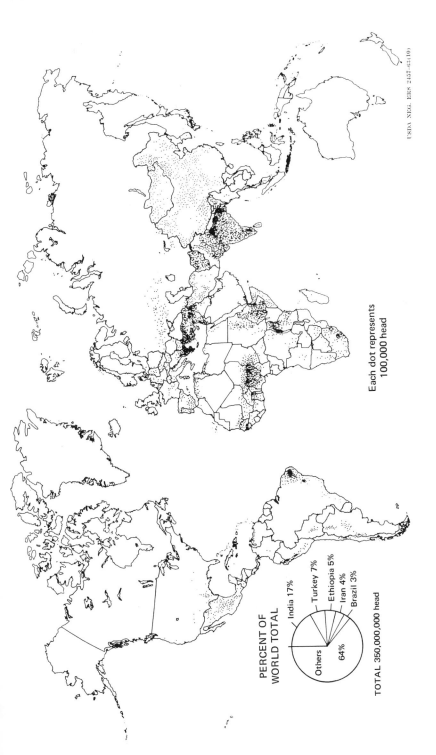

Fig. 5.8.   Areas of goat production. Source: U.S. Department of Agriculture, 1964.

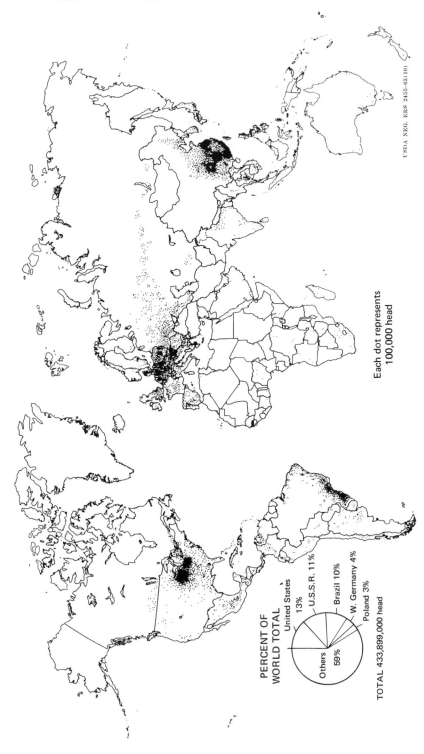

Each dot represents
100,000 head

PERCENT OF
WORLD TOTAL

United States
13%

U.S.S.R. 11%

Brazil 10%

W. Germany 4%

Poland 3%

Others
59%

TOTAL 433,899,000 head

USDA NEG. ERS 2455-63(10)

Fig. 5.9. Areas of hog production. Source: U.S. Department of Agriculture, 1964.

Looking at the distribution of Class 1, however, we find that this hypothesis does not offer an explanation of the observations. This is one of the few classes distributed widely over the earth's surface in many non-contiguous areas. Although wheat is the major food grain, the growing of wheat is concentrated in relatively few places: parts of Australia, Argentina, Russia, and the western plains of the United States and Canada. Production of potatoes, sugar, beef and pork is similarly specialized areally. We might formulate an additional hypothesis: The amount of technology in an area is related to diet. The greater the amount of technology, the less reliance there is on foods which are raised locally and the greater the distance over which foods are transported both into and out of the area. In areas with more technology, more transportation is available and it is more rapid. There are means of keeping perishable items refrigerated while they are being transported, so that milk, meat, and produce can be transported long distances from producer to consumer. It is obvious that without refrigerated trucks, planes, and railroad cars, it would be impossible to transport fresh fruits and vegetables from areas such as Florida, Texas, Arizona, and California to other parts of the United States and Canada.

5.6.2 Other Independent Variables

Although these two hypotheses together appear to explain much of the spatial variation in the distribution of diet, other factors must also be considered if we are to achieve a more complete explanation. People become accustomed to eating certain foods, and may reject unfamiliar ones even when they are hungry. Although persons living in the United States eat some rice, most of them would find it monotonous if eaten three times a day in place of cereal, bread, potatoes, and most of their usual meat. When people travel or migrate, therefore, they take their food habits along, and continue to eat at least some of the foods to which they are accustomed. Persons of Chinese or Indian origin, for example, usually continue to eat their customary diets wherever they live; Americans have the reputation of wanting steaks or hamburgers wherever they travel.

5.7 TESTING THE HYPOTHESES

We have suggested four factors related to dietary patterns of people throughout the world, as we have classified them. (1) The availability of a particular food in an area, in either the natural or cultivated state, is in turn related to (2) physical factors such as rainfall, sunshine, temperature, and soils. The dependence upon food locally is related to (3) the amount of technology in the area and (4) food habits which are related to customs, religion, or other cultural factors. We have tested these hypotheses simply by comparing the data and map giving the distribution of our dependent variables with maps of the distributions of some of the independent variables and our knowledge about others.

In order to test hypotheses more rigorously, we have to define the variables more precisely and state the nature of the relationship which exists between them. When we attempt to do so, we find that although the twenty classes we have identified are useful for descriptive purposes, they are not adequate as operational definitions for testing hypotheses. We shall, therefore, select one particular characteristic of diet as a dependent variable to test.

5.7.1 A Quantitative Test of the Relationship between Technology and One Element of Diet

We have suggested that the kind of food eaten in an area is related to the amount of technology in that area. We can also hypothesize that one element of the nutritional adequacy of the diet in an area, calories consumed per capita per day, is related to the amount of technology in that area. Although there is no generally accepted measure of technology comparable to that of food energy, we can use a measure which has been found to reflect the amount of technology: energy consumption per capita. This variable represents the total amount of all types of energy consumed in an area: human, animal, electrical, coal, gas, and others. Data for this variable are available for many countries, although their accuracy varies from country to country, with some figures being rough estimates and others reasonably accurate. A more detailed explanation of and justification for the use of total energy consumption per capita as a measure of technology is found in Chapter 10.

With both variables in operational form, we can state the relationship which we expect to find between them: The more technology there is in an area, the more calories are consumed per capita per day. We can test this hypothesis in a number of ways. One of the simplest, which requires no mathematics, is to use a scatter diagram. The dependent variable, average number of calories consumed per capita per day, is plotted on the Y-axis, and the independent variable, total energy consumption per capita, on the X-axis. Data are plotted by countries, for those countries for which data are available.

In order to evaluate the closeness of the relationship between the variables, we need to know that, if the relationship between them were perfect, the dots would lie on a straight line; if no relationship existed, the dots would be randomly distributed. When the distribution of dots is somewhere between these extremes and is generally elliptical, the variables are related to some extent, and the hypothesis is supported. Examination of the scatter diagram (Fig. 5.10) reveals that the dots are in a generally elliptical pattern, and so we may conclude that the variables are related, and accept the hypothesis tentatively. The closeness of the relationship could be determined by computing a coefficient of correlation, done in Section 10.4.2, and employing tests of statistical significance.

We can, nevertheless, tell by observation that the relationship between the variables, although close, is not perfect. Although part of the unexplained variation may be due to the inaccuracy of the data, it is likely that we would have to use other measures to achieve a higher level of explanation. We know, for

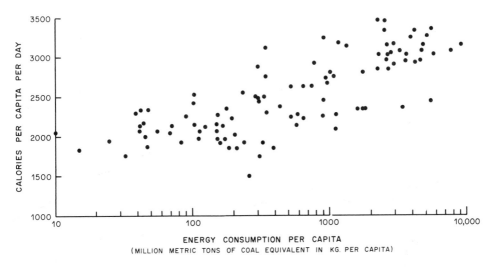

Fig. 5.10. Relationship between energy consumption per capita and calorie consumption per capita, around 1965.

example, that caloric requirements vary with size and activity of individuals, as well as the amount of energy required to maintain body temperature. We could, therefore, if data were available, change the operational definition of the dependent variable, and use percent of caloric requirement actually consumed. In areas with more technology, most people perform less physical labor and therefore tend to have lower caloric requirements. Additional dependent variables could also be selected which would measure different aspects of the dietary pattern. In addition, we might identify other independent variables which would contribute to a more complete explanation of the variation in the various dependent variables. When we had formulated and tested hypotheses using these variables, we would have a more comprehensive idea of the factors related to dietary patterns throughout the world. From these ideas, it might be possible to formulate more general and inclusive laws which would explain a number of the relationships we had discovered, and help us to relate our knowledge about this phenomenon to that of other phenomena.

5.8 CONCLUSION

In attempting to explain spatial variations in dietary patterns, we found that it was necessary to define precisely the phenomenon we wished to study and determine the scale at which we would examine it. It was also helpful to organize the data by means of a classification scheme. We learned that the classification scheme which we devised was adequate for describing dietary patterns throughout the world, but less satisfactory as a basis for explaining them. Further progress in explanation would require new approaches.

In addition to the suggestions for further study which we have already made, there are other possibilities for investigation which might lead to a more complete understanding. We might study the diffusion of various items of diet or combinations of food through time and space. People have a definite order of preference for different food grains: wheat and rice are considered most desirable and tend to replace the less-wanted grains such as barley, millet, and sorghum wherever and whenever circumstances permit. Study of changes in dietary habits such as these might lead to new insights.

Another possibility would be to study dietary patterns on various scales and for a number of different universes, in order to see how well the factors we have found on a world scale explain spatial variations on a smaller scale. We might expect to find variations related to ethnic origin and income, as well as physical features, as we have already done. We might also look for differences between urban and rural dwellers, or among persons with different occupations or religions.

Combining the findings on a world scale with those of smaller scales would then help to give us a better understanding of the distribution of dietary patterns. This broader empirical study could then be tied in with existing knowledge by relating all the information to a broader theoretical framework. We have made a start at doing this by drawing upon studies of shelter and religion in formulating some of the hypotheses to explain the distribution of diet. Further work along these lines would be likely to result in achieving a more general explanation at a higher level of abstraction; that is, contribute to the building of geographic theory.

REVIEW YOUR UNDERSTANDING OF THESE CONCEPTS

dietary patterns
nutritional adequacy
staple items of diet
macroscopic view
microvariations
criteria used for classification
classification by area or phenomenon

between- and within-class variation
level of abstraction
completeness of an explanation
relationship between technology and
    calorie consumption
scatter diagram

SUGGESTED ACTIVITIES

1. Make a list of specialty food items, such as cheeses, wines, delicatessen, or lutefisk. Determine the location of stores where these items are sold. Attempt to explain why these items are sold at these locations.

2. a) Analyze what is meant by adequate food supply in terms of minerals, proteins, calories, animal proteins, etc. Formulate an operational definition for adequate food supply.

   b) For some area such as a city, county or state, determine which people have an inadequate food supply, their location, why they have an inadequate supply and why these people are located where they are. Attempt to answer the question, "Why are these the areas in which hunger in some form exists?"

3. Determine the spatial changes occurring over a period of time in the quantity of consumption of a particular food or food group such as tomato, meat, or frozen orange juice. Plot the data on a map and attempt to account for the observed spatial variation of change in food consumption.

4. For one selected country, such as Japan or the United States, determine and attempt to explain changes in food consumption.

REFERENCES

Bennett, M. K. (1941), "International contrasts in food consumption," *Geographical Review* **31**, 365–376.

Brown, Lester. R. (1961), *An Economic Analysis of Far Eastern Agriculture*, Foreign Economic Report No. 2, Washington, D.C.: U.S. Department of Agriculture.

Food and Agricultural Organization of the United Nations (1947)—various years to date, *Yearbook of Food and Agricultural Statistics*, *Production Yearbook*, *Trade Yearbook*. Rome: United Nations.

Githens, T. S. and C. E. Wood, Jr. (1943), *The Food Resources of Africa*. Philadelphia: University of Pennsylvania Press.

Hartman, George W. and John C. Hook (1956). "Substandard urban housing in the United States: a quantitative analysis," *Economic Geography* **32**, 95–114.

Jones, W. O. (1959), *Manioc in Africa*. Stanford: Stanford University Press.

Kariel, Herbert G. (1966), "A proposed classification of diet," *Annals of the Association of American Geographers* **56**, 68–79.

Scrimshaw, Nevin S. (1963), "Food," *Scientific American* **209**, No. 3, 72–80.

Stoddard, Robert H. (1960), "The geography of churches and their rural congregations in Nemaha County," unpublished M.A. thesis, University of Nebraska.

U.S. Department of Agriculture (1951), *Agricultural Production and Food Consumption in Western Europe*, Agricultural Monograph No. 10, Washington, D.C.: U.S. Department of Agriculture, p. 4.

U.S. Department of Agriculture (1964), *A Graphic Summary of World Agriculture*, Economic Research Service, Miscellaneous Publication No. 705. Washington, D.C.: U.S. Government Printing Office.

Zelinsky, Wilbur (1953), "The log house in Georgia," *Geographical Review* **43**, 173–193.

Zelinsky, Wilbur (1961), "An approach to the religious geography of the United States: patterns of church membership in 1952," *Annals* of the Association of American Geographers **51**; 139–193.

Additional Readings

Addison, H. (1961), *Land, Water and Food*. London: Chapman and Hall.

Bennett, M. K. (1954), *The World's Food*. New York: Harper and Brothers.

Berry, Brian J. L. (1958), "A note concerning methods of classification," *Annals* of the Association of American Geographers **48**, 300–303.

Block, M. R. (1963), "The social influence of salt," *Scientific American* **209**, No. 1, 88–98.

Bourne, Geoffrey, H., ed. (1959 to date), *World Review of Nutrition and Dietetics*. Basil: S. Karger A.G.

Brown, Lester R. (1963), *Man, Land and Food: Looking Ahead at World Food Needs*, Foreign Agricultural Economic Report No. 11, Washington, D.C.: Regional Analysis Division, Economic Research Service, U.S. Department of Agriculture.

Burk, Marguerite C. (1961), *Influences of Economic and Social Factors on U.S. Food Consumption*. Minneapolis: Burgess.

Burk, Marguerite C. and Mordecai Ezekiel (1967), "Food and nutrition in developing economies," in Herman M. Southworth and Bruce F. Johnston, eds. *Agricultural Development and Economic Growth*. Ithaca, New York: Cornell University Press.

Castro, Josué de (1952), *The Geography of Hunger*. Boston: Little Brown.

Culter, Hugh (1954), "Food sources in the new world," *Agricultural History* **28**, 39–41, in Philip L. Wagner and Marvin W. Mikesell, 1962, *Readings in Cultural Geography*. Chicago: University of Chicago Press, pp. 282–289.

Farber, Symour M. and Nancy L. Wilson, eds. (1966), *Food and Civilization*. Springfield, Ill.: Charles C. Thomas.

Fonaroff, L. Schuyler (1965), "Was Huntington right about human nutrition?" *Annals* of the Association of American Geographers **55**, 365–376.

Gould, Peter R. and Jack P. Sparks (1969), "The geographical context of human diet in southern Guatemala," *Geographical Review* **59**, 58–82.

Guthe, Carl E. and Margaret Mead (1943), *The Problem of Changing Food Habits*, Publication of the National Research Council No. 108, Washington, D.C.: National Academy of Sciences.

Johnston, Bruce F. (1953), *The Staple Food Economies of Western Tropical Africa*. Stanford: Stanford University Press.

Johnston, R. J. (1968), "Choice in classification: the subjectivity of objective methods," *Annals* of the Association of American Geographers **58**, 575–589.

Lamartine-Yates, P. (1960), *Food, Land and Manpower in Western Europe*. New York: St. Martin's Press.

Lloyd, E. M. H. (1956), *Food and Inflation in the Middle East 1940–45*. Stanford: Stanford University Press.

Mackay, J. Ross (1959), "Regional geography: a quantitative approach," *Cahiers de Geographie de Quebec* **6**, 57–63.

May, Jacques M. (1961 and 1964), *Studies in Medical Geography: The Ecology of Malnutrition*. New York: Hafner.

May, Jacques M. (1967), *The Ecology of Malnutrition in Northern Africa*. New York: Hafner.

McMaster, David N. (1962), *A Subsistence Crop Geography of Uganda*, The World Land Use Survey, Occasional Papers No. 2. Bude, Cornwall, England: Geographical Publications.

President's Science Advisory Committee Panel on the World Food Supply (1967), *The World Food Problem*, Vols. I and II. Washington, D.C.: The White House.

Simoons, Frederick J. (1961), *Eat Not This Flesh*. Madison: University of Wisconsin Press.

Sorre, Max. (1952), "The geography of diet," from "La geographie de l'alimentation," *Annales* de Geographie **61**, 184–199, in Philip L. Wagner and Marvin W. Mikesell (1962), *Readings in Cultural Geography*. Chicago: University of Chicago Press, pp. 445–456.

Symposium on Food And Population Growth, London (1962), *Food Supplies and Population Growth*. Edinburgh: published for the Royal Statistical Society, Oliver and Boyd, 1963.

Vidal de la Blache, Paul (1926), "Means of sustenance," *Principles of Human Geography*. London: Constable.

Weldon, E. D. (1953), "Sources of selected foods," Plate 8 and "Diets and deficiency diseases," Plate 9, Study in human starvation 2, in *Atlas of Diseases*. New York: The American Geographical Society.

CHAPTER 6
LANGUAGE

6.1 INTRODUCTION

The cultural phenomena which we have already studied have involved basic human needs and activities: food, shelter, and religion. Like them, language is an essential element of human culture. By means of it, men can communicate a wide range of ideas to each other. Without it, abstract thought would be almost impossible; it is difficult for us to imagine, for example, how young children and animals solve problems or manipulate ideas without using words. Although relatively simple ideas can be communicated without the use of language, humans depend on it for manipulating and communicating more complex thoughts.

As with other cultural phenomena, we are interested in knowing enough about language to describe and explain its spatial distribution at a given time. In the long run, we would like to learn about the process by which languages change and how the distribution of speakers of a language changes over time. One step toward this goal is the identification of factors associated with the distribution of speakers of various languages at a given time, as has been done in earlier chapters with the study of the spatial distributions of other cultural phenomena. We may then extend such a study to consideration of change over a period of time, with the aim of discovering the process by which change has occurred.

In this chapter, the nature of language is surveyed briefly to provide background knowledge of selected aspatial aspects believed relevant for explaining the spatial distribution. Study of the spatial aspects begins with the distribution of some of the many language families, language groups, and individual languages of the world. Some possible explanatory factors are then proposed. The process of change is next examined, and hypotheses proposed to explain it. Two studies of word geography in smaller areas are then reviewed, and the proposed hypotheses applied to the findings.

6.2 ASPATIAL ASPECTS

6.2.1 Definition of Language

The word *language* is used in many different ways. Although we speak of animal language or sign language as forms of communication which do not use words, we are concerned here with a definition of language which involves the communication of ideas between human beings by words. We shall therefore adopt Gray's (1939) definition of language:

> In its specific and usual sense, language is such expression and communication to or from human beings by means of speech and hearing, the sounds uttered or heard being so combined in systems evolved, conventionalised, and recognized by common usage at any given period in the history of the human race within a given community or within given communities that they are mutually intelligible to all approximately normal members thereof. (p. 13)

Many important ideas are included in this definition. (1) It emphasizes the nature of language as oral communication of ideas between human beings. We shall be primarily concerned with the oral form of language rather than with the symbols used in writing or printing it. (2) Every language employs conventionalized symbols agreed upon by its speakers. Sounds are combined in some way which is accepted by speakers of the language as conveying a specific meaning. When A speaks to B, he thinks of an idea, or concept, which he wishes to convey. He converts this idea into words in his own mind, then utters a series of sounds which, when heard by B, are converted into the concept intended by A. The intended meaning is not always clearly transmitted; the frequency of misunderstandings and failures of communication between individuals is evidence of the complex nature of this process. (3) Language is not static, but changes continually. (4) In order for mutual intelligibility to exist, it is necessary that there be general agreement among speakers at any given time and place as to the meaning of each group of sounds, and that these groups of sounds be combined in a specified fashion.

6.2.2 Components of Language

Analyzing a language into its components, we can see that in each language there are a number of distinct sounds which are combined to form phrases and sentences. Each sound is called a *phoneme*. The English language is composed of over 30 phonemes: twelve to fourteen pure vowel sounds, a number of diphthongs, or combinations of vowels, and 22 consonant sounds. These phonemes are represented by the 26 written letters of our alphabet. Each vowel represents several different sounds; some consonants also represent more than a single sound, although others represent just one.

These sounds are combined to form words, each of which has one or more symbolic meanings. A word is composed of a base, or root, sometimes called a *semanteme*, which has a symbolic meaning, and may also have one or more *morphemes*, which indicate the relationship of the word to the rest of the sentence. We have, for example, a base semanteme such as *work* or *play*. We may then add a morpheme, *ing* or *ed*, to the base to indicate when the action took place. Study of the forms of a language is termed *morphology*; study of the meanings, *semantics*.

Words are combined to form sentences, or groups of words, in accordance with specified rules. Students studying a foreign language often contend with the difficulty of learning new ways of arranging words in a sentence. For example, in German verbs usually come at the end of sentences, whereas in English they are in the middle; in French, adjectives usually follow nouns rather than preceding them, as in English. This aspect of language is called *syntax*.

To review briefly: Language is a form of mutually intelligible symbolic communication between humans. It is made up of individual sounds, phonemes, arranged into words composed of semantemes and morphemes. Words are arranged into sentences according to conventions defined in the syntax of the language.

6.2.3 Variations within Languages

One problem which is met in the classification of languages is deciding what constitutes a language. According to our definition, mutual intelligibility is a major criterion. We know, however, that there may be so much variation in the way a language is spoken by different groups of people that some of the dialects are almost unintelligible to other speakers of the language.

In English, for example, there are wide variations in the spoken language. We speak of people having a Southern, British, or American accent. Some professional groups use terminology unintelligible to persons outside their group. By the criterion of mutual intelligibility, however, these people nevertheless speak the same language. They are generally able to understand each other, no matter how the words are pronounced and in spite of variations in the meanings attached to some words by different speakers. There is a standard language which more educated speakers tend to use, while less educated ones have their own variations. The literary standard language is, in turn, distinguished from the spoken; if people talked as they wrote, they would sound stilted and unnatural. Within the spoken language, sub-standard variations occur, such as the forms *he seen* or *he done*, which are not acceptable in standard usage. *Professional language*, *slang*, and *argot* are variations of a standard language involving primarily the use of special terms or phrases. Slang usually refers to a class of recently coined terms, which tend either to pass out of usage or to become acceptable as standard language. Argot may involve both the use of special terms and the application of familiar words in an unfamiliar way; for example, some of the language associated with the use of narcotics, such as *pusher* and *fix*.

Such variations in a language may be considered social, in contrast to regional ones. Dialects are regional variations in language marked by deviations from the standard in vocabulary, pronunciation, and usage. We tend to speak of accents rather than dialects in the United States, although the variations are similar to those of dialects. A person with a Southern accent, for example, not only pronounces words differently from a midwesterner, but also uses certain phrases and words in ways which are unfamiliar to the midwesterner. There are no clear distinctions between *dialect* and *patois*, although the latter conveys the impression of being more provincial and perhaps more difficult for speakers of the standard language to understand.

6.2.4 Classification of Languages

Linguists have studied and classified a large number of the estimated 2500 to 3500 languages of the world. The classification scheme used today is primarily a *genetic* one, based on the presumed developmental relationships between languages, rather than a *generic* one, based on some element or elements such as morphology. The development of a genetic classification requires intensive study, which has not been done for all areas of the world. In some areas, therefore, a geographic classification is used which groups together all languages in the area without regard for their possible relationship to each other.

In classifying languages genetically, linguists consider many elements, including phonemes or language sounds, semantics, morphology, and syntax. They draw upon knowledge of the history of the speakers of different present day languages, including their contacts with speakers of other languages through trade, migration, or conquest. From all available clues, they deduce that certain languages probably were derived from other earlier languages, either known or unknown. By such study they are often able to discern relationships among words in different languages which appear to the uninitiated to be completely different, and so to establish some connection between the languages. For example, the Romance languages, French, Italian, and Spanish, are derived from Latin. They exhibit many similarities in all the elements pointed out above: phonemes, semantemes, morphemes, and syntax. This, however, is one of the few language groups for which written records exist over several centuries; others must be traced by inferential methods, perhaps to unknown but presumed pre-existing languages such as Proto-Indo-European posited as a precursor of the present-day Indo-European languages. Like experts in many other areas of study, linguists do not always agree on the origins of a given language or the relationship between various languages. As new information is discovered, classifications may be modified in the light of it.

The classification scheme presented here represents a compromise among the formulations of several linguists. Although no one authority would be likely to agree with every aspect of it, the general outline would be accepted by most. The smallest units with which we are concerned are individual languages, not dialects or other regional variations. The arrangement of languages into families and groups is given. Wherever a genetic classification is generally accepted, it will be used; where none is known, a geographical one will be substituted.

6.3 SPATIAL ASPECTS OF LANGUAGE

As we have learned from consideration of the aspatial aspects of language, many possible dependent variables dealing with language could be selected: the distribution of the number of speakers of each language, the different languages spoken in an area, or the official languages of different areas are but a few which come to mind. We shall concentrate upon the distribution of the speakers of some of the many languages throughout the world, emphasizing those areas in which each language is spoken either as a vernacular or as an official language, or both, as is often the case.

In discussing the spatial distribution of speakers in the different language families, language groups, and languages, it is essential to be selective. It is estimated that between 3,000 and 4,000 languages are spoken in the world today. Not all of the languages of the world are known to linguists; because of the limitations of space, we can study only a fraction of those which are known. Because of the large number of languages, we shall deal mainly with language families and groups rather than individual languages, and cite certain languages as examples. The selection of examples is based primarily on data availability, and to a lesser extent on the number of speakers of a language and its interest and familiarity to the student. The Indo-European languages are therefore discussed in more detail than others.

The universe to be studied is the entire inhabited world; the time period is the present, and the scale of areal analysis is, in most cases, the area occupied by speakers of each language group or language discussed, which may or may not coincide with existing political boundaries. Although it is sometimes relatively simple to demarcate a clear boundary between two language areas, more often it is not. Especially in areas where approximately equal proportions of speakers of two or more languages live, such as Brazil and Uruguay, it is impossible to draw precise boundaries between areas, and the line shown on the map is an approximation. Such a demarcation is also difficult because of the scale at which data are available. In any given area many different languages may be spoken; one or two are recognized as official, and several additional ones may be spoken as vernaculars by a majority or sizeable minority of the population. Drawing boundaries between language areas therefore involves making many arbitrary decisions. Their locations are therefore subject to different interpretations by different authorities.

6.3.1 Location and Distribution of Speakers of Different Language Families, Language Groups, and Languages Throughout the World

The study of the distribution of speakers of different language families, language groups, and languages will be facilitated by frequent reference to the map (Fig. 6.1). Language families are indicated by capital letters, as ALTAIC. The first time a language group is mentioned, it appears in boldface type, as **Turkic**; and an individual language appears in italic type, as *Turkish*.

ALTAIC

The Altaic family is commonly divided into three groups: **Turkic**, **Mongolian**, and **Manchurian**, even though there is some question as to whether these three are, in fact, related genetically. Languages in this family are spoken in Turkey, in European Russia from the Volga eastward, and throughout Asiatic Russia, Chinese Turkestan, Mongolia, and Manchuria, as well as in parts of northwestern Iran and northern Afghanistan. The Turkic group includes *Turkish*, or *Osmanli*, which is spoken in Turkey and by some people in Yugoslavia, Bulgaria, Greece, and Cyprus; *Azerbaijani*, spoken in northwest Iran and the Caucasus; *Uzbek*, found in the Uzbek SSR; and a number of other languages of Central Asia. The Mongolian group includes several languages often classed together as Mongolian. Speakers of languages in this group are found in eastern Sinkiang, the Mongolian SSR, parts of Chinese Inner Mongolia, and in areas of the USSR where the Buryats live. The main language is *Khalka*, or *Mongol* proper. The Manchurian group includes two languages: *Manchu*, spoken in scattered regions in northern Manchuria, and *Tungus*, whose speakers live in sparsely settled regions of eastern Siberia.

JAPANESE

Although some authorities include Japanese, Korean, and Aleut in the Altaic family, they are usually considered as separate language families. Two languages, *Japanese* and *Ryukyu*, are spoken in Japan and on the Ryukyu Islands and Taiwan respectively.

KOREAN

Korean, the only language in this family, is spoken primarily on the Korean peninsula.

ESKIMO-ALEUT

Some scholars connect Eskimo-Aleut with Altaic, others associate it with Paleo-Siberian or Sino-Tibetan. Until further study is done, it is best to consider it as a separate family. Speakers of languages in this family live in an area extending from eastern Siberia to Greenland, including the entire Arctic coast of North America and along the coast of Alaska.

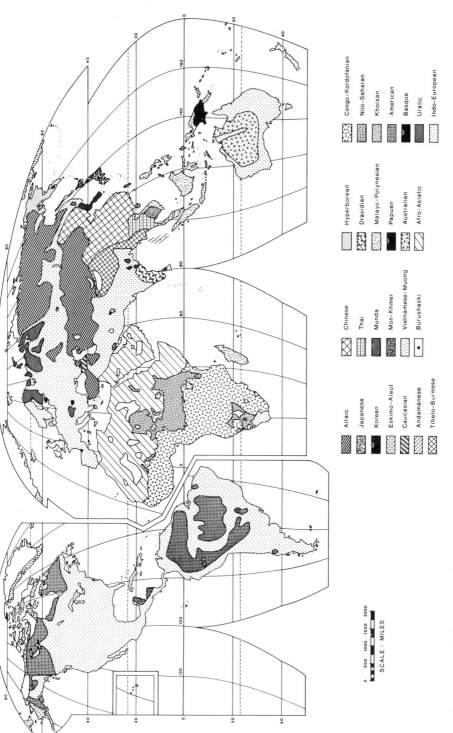

Fig. 6.1. Major languages of the world. Adapted from map of languages in *Man's Domain: A Thematic Atlas of the World.* © Copyright, General Drafting Co., Inc. and Western Publishing Company, Inc. Goode's base map © Copyright, University of Chicago. Used by permission of the University of Chicago Press.

Legend:

Altaic
Japanese
Korean
Eskimo-Aleut
Caucasian
Andamanese
Tibeto-Burmese

Chinese
Thai
Munda
Mon-Khmer
Vietnamese-Muong
Burushaski

Hyperborean
Dravidian
Malayo-Polynesian
Papuan
Australian
Afro-Asiatic

Congo-Kordofanian
Nilo-Saharan
Khoisan
American
Basque
Uralic
Indo-European

0 500 1000 1500 2000
SCALE : MILES

CAUCASIAN

Those languages spoken on the northern and southern slopes of the Caucasus Mountains which are neither Indo-European nor Turkic are placed in this family. It is not clear whether the two groups in this family, North and South Caucasian, are in fact related. There are about twenty languages in the northern group, the best known of which include *Abkhasian*, *Avar*, *Chechen*, and *Kabardian*; and four in the southern group, including *Georgian* and *Mingrelian*. A large number of different languages belonging to this family are spoken in remote mountain valleys of the Caucasus.

ANDAMANESE

Several variants of *Andamanese* are spoken by the indigenous inhabitants of the Andaman Islands in the Bay of Bengal. No kinship with any other language family has been shown, although a suggestion has been made that it may be related to languages of aboriginal Australians and Papuans.

> Note: Until recently, most of the many languages spoken in southeast Asia have been classified geographically rather than genetically, but genetic classifications of some have now been made. The former Sino-Tibetan family has been divided into four families, and the Southeast Asiatic family into three, although some authorities still believe that they are related.

CHINESE

The Chinese family contains a number of mutually unintelligible languages, each of which has a wide variety of dialects. The major languages are *Mandarin* and *Cantonese*. Mandarin is spoken by the largest number of people; it has been the official language of China since 1949, and is the standard language of many of the people of northern China in an area which covers nine-tenths of the area of mainland China, where three-fourths of the people live. Cantonese is standard in the extreme southern provinces and Hong Kong, and is also spoken in parts of Thailand, Vietnam, Burma, and Cambodia. Nearly all Chinese living in the United States speak Cantonese. Many other languages are used locally, among them *Wu* in the Shanghai area and Chekiang province, and *Fukienese* in Fukien and in Taiwan, Indonesia, Malaysia, and the Philippines by its speakers who have migrated to these areas. In Kwangtung, a land-locked enclave between the areas of Mandarin, Fukienese, and Cantonese speech, *Hakka*, a mixture of the three, is spoken.

TIBETO-BURMESE

The Tibeto-Burmese family has eight divisions. Most of the languages are spoken by various tribes in the area south and east of southern Tibet and Nepal, including parts of Assam, Burma, northern India, Pakistan, and southeastern China. *Tibetan* is native to Tibet, Bhutan, and Nepal; since the occupation of Tibet by the Chinese in 1950, however, its use has been actively discouraged in favor of Mandarin. The **Burmese-Lolo** group includes *Burmese*, the official language of Burma, a number of Kachin languages of northern Burma, and the Lolo subgroup, spoken in southwestern China, northern and eastern Burma, Vietnam, Thailand, and Laos. The **Karen** language of southern Burma constitutes another group.

MIAO-YAO

Both *Miao* and *Yao* are spoken in parts of southern China, northern Vietnam, and the hills of Laos and northern Thailand.

THAI

Although formerly thought to be related to Chinese, Thai is now classified as a separate family. It includes *Thai* and *Siamese*, the official language of Thailand.

MUNDA

The Munda family is made up of five languages, the speakers of which live in isolated portions of the state of Orissa in central India.

MON-KHMER

Speakers of languages in the Mon-Khmer family live primarily in Cambodia and in Burma east of Rangoon. Groupings within this family are still largely on a geographic basis. *Khmer* is the official language of Cambodia.

VIETNAMESE-MUONG

The majority of speakers of *Vietnamese* live in North Vietnam, with the rest in South Vietnam, Cambodia, Laos, and Thailand. There are two main dialects: Hanoi in the north and Saigon in the south. *Muong* is spoken in the highlands of northern Vietnam.

BURUSHASKI

No relationship has been established between Burushaski and any other language. It is spoken by the Hunzas, who live in the Karakoram Mountains in the western part of Kashmir. Its territory is completely surrounded by other languages of the Turkic, Tibeto-Burman, and Indo-Iranian groups.

HYPERBOREAN OR PALEO-ASIATIC

This family is composed of six languages spoken in the northeastern corner of Siberia, on the Kamchatka Peninsula and the Kurile and Sakhalin Islands. It represents remnants of a family whose speakers earlier extended over much more of Asia; one enclave remains as far west as the Yenisey River. The number of speakers of *Ainu*, the language of the Ainu, the aboriginal inhabitants of Japan, is decreasing. The few remaining Ainu live on the coast of Hokkaido and in southern Sakhalin.

DRAVIDIAN

The Dravidian languages are now spoken primarily in southern India, the Laccadive Islands, and on the northern and eastern coasts of Ceylon. They are believed to have developed from an unknown uniform language spoken throughout the Indian peninsula before the coming of the Indo-Europeans in the second millenium, B.C. *Gond*, a tribal language, is spoken in areas of central India; *Telugu* is spoken in Andra Pradesh; *Tamil* in Madras, Ceylon, and by people who have migrated from these areas to the southern portion of the Malay peninsula, Singapore, and South Africa; *Malayalam* in Kerala and on the Laccadive Islands, *Kannada* in the central portion of Mysore; and *Brahui* in Baluchistan, Pakistan, and Iran, an area which is isolated and distant from the territory of the other Dravidian languages.

MALAYO-POLYNESIAN, OR AUSTRONESIAN

Speakers of the languages in this family are distributed over an extensive area of the earth's surface. Many of them live on islands separated by vast stretches of water. The area extends from Malagasay on the west to Easter Island on the east, and from Hawaii on the north to New Zealand on the south. Languages of the Australian aborigines and the tribes in the interior of New Guinea are not included in the family. The common origin of the speakers of these languages has been traced to a homeland presumed to be near Malaya, from which ancestors of the present speakers spread by successive migrations to the outlying areas.

Probably at least five hundred languages are in the family. They are named primarily by the area in which they are spoken. Languages in the **Indonesian** group are spoken on the Malay Peninsula and in Taiwan, the Philippines, Borneo, and Indonesia. It is estimated that about two hundred languages and dialects are spoken in Indonesia alone. The *Malay* language of Southeast Asia has long been used in a pidginized form known as *Bazaar Malay* as the *lingua franca** in coastal regions from Sumatra to the Philippines. In 1945, after twenty years of development, a version of Malay based on Bazaar Malay became the national and official language of Indonesia. Called *Indonesian*, it was eagerly accepted by patriotic youth of the nation as a nationalistic symbol. *Tagalog*, originally the

---

*A *lingua franca* is a common language usually used for purposes of trade or commerce by persons speaking different languages. It is often composed of elements of several different languages, with simplified vocabulary and grammar.

language of central Luzon, has been declared the official language of the Philippines. It supersedes Spanish and English, which were associated with colonialism in the minds of many Filipinos.

Polynesian languages include *Samoan*, *Tahitian*, *Maori*, and *Hawaiian*. Hawaiian is seldom used today as a vernacular; words from it have become pidginized or entered the English spoken by inhabitants of Hawaii. Languages in the *Micronesian* and *Melanesian* groups are spoken in much of the South Pacific.

PAPUAN

This family includes an estimated 150 languages, some spoken by less than fifty people. Its speakers are found primarily in New Guinea and neighboring islands. Because these languages have been little studied, the classification is areal rather than genetic. *Bentoeni*, spoken in the western part of New Guinea may have the largest number of speakers.

AUSTRALIAN

It is believed that there are about 100 aboriginal languages of Australia. No genetic classification of these is available. Their use is rapidly decreasing in favor of English.

> Note: Languages spoken on the African continent are divided by Greenberg (1963) into four major families: Afro-Asiatic, Niger-Kordofanian, Nilo-Saharan, and Khoisan. Because he worked to identify relationships among languages formerly classified only on a geographic basis, his genetic classification differs from earlier ones in many respects. In general, we have followed Greenberg, although other sources have been used to fill in details for those groups which he studied less intensively, especially the Bantu.

AFRO-ASIATIC

The former name of the Afro-Asiatic language family was Hamito-Semitic, derived from the names of two of Noah's sons, Ham and Shem. Languages in it were spoken by the people described in the Bible, and are still used in the same areas today. By the fifth century B.C. languages in this family were spoken throughout Africa north of the Sahara, in all of Arabia, and in Asia from the Mediterranean to western Asia, generally called the Middle East.

There are five coordinate groups: **Semitic, Egyptian, Berber, Cushitic**, and **Chad**. Within the Semitic group, *Arabic* in its many variants is most widely spoken. A standard Arabic, Fusha, is coming into common usage, and has been adopted by the mass communications media. Arabic is used by the majority of people in northern Africa, the Arabian Peninsula, and most countries of the Middle East, with the exception of Israel. *Hebrew*, now the official language of Israel, was not spoken as a vernacular after the fourth century B.C., but was used only in Jewish religious services. With the founding of the modern state of Israel in 1948, Hebrew was revived and modernized, making the grammar and vocabulary relevant to contemporary usage. *Amharic*, which belongs to the Ethiopic sub-group, is the official language of Ethiopia. *Aramaic-Syriac* is a remnant of the vernacular spoken in Palestine at the time of Christ, and is found only in a few isolated communities in eastern Turkey and adjacent countries.

Coptic, the major language within the Egyptian group, is no longer spoken as a vernacular, but is still used in services of the Coptic churches of Egypt and Ethiopia. Languages in the Berber group are spoken mainly in Morocco, Algeria, and a few other parts of North Africa, primarily by nomadic herdsman. Since Arabic is the predominant language in most of this area, the men, who deal with outsiders, are usually bilingual, whereas the women, who live in seclusion, speak only Berber. Languages in the Cushitic group are spoken in East Africa, including all or part of Ethiopia, Sudan, Somalia, Kenya, and Tanzania. *Somali*, the most wisely used, is spoken in Somalia and southern Ethiopia. *Hausa*, the major language of the Chad group, is spoken in the Northern Territory of Nigeria, Niger, Cameroun, Togo, and Dahomey. It is also used as a *lingua franca* in neighboring countries, where it was originally introduced by Arab slave traders.

CONGO-KORDOFANIAN

Because of the genetic resemblance of the Kordofanian subfamily to the Niger-Congo subfamily, Greenberg has placed them both in one family, which he calls the Congo-Kordofanian. Languages in the Niger-Congo subfamily are spoken both within the Niger River basin, in a narrow belt between the Sahara and the Gulf of Guinea, extending from the Atlantic on the west as far east as Cameroun, and in most of central and southern Africa, including the Congo basin. There are six groups within this subfamily.

Speakers of *Fula* or *Fulani*, a major language of the **West Atlantic** group, are concentrated in Nigeria and Guinea, although others are scattered north and west as far as Dakar. Speakers of languages in the **Mande** group live primarily in Guinea, Sierra Leone, Mali, northern Liberia, and northwestern Ivory Coast. Persons speaking languages in the **GUR** group are found in southern Mali, Upper Volta, northeastern Ivory Coast, Northern Ghana, Togo, and Dahomey. The **Kwa** group is just south, along the coast of the Gulf of Guinea from Liberia to Nigeria. *Yoruba* and *Ibo* are the two major languages of Nigeria. *Ewe*, the vernacular of the coastal areas of Togo and Dahomey, is also used as a *lingua franca* in a wider region.

Although the Bantu languages are often classified as a separate group, Greenberg includes them within the **Benue-Congo** group. Speakers of languages in this group are spread over most of southern and central Africa; there are about 250 languages in the Bantu subgroup alone. Because of this distribution, it is believed that the Bantu peoples spread southeastward from the region where other languages in the Niger-Congo subfamily are concentrated. *Swahili*, which began as a *lingua franca* developed by Arab slave traders, is composed of both Bantu and Arabic words, with Bantu grammar. It is now spoken primarily in East Africa: in Tanzania and neighboring islands, Kenya, the Congo, Burundi, and Uganda. It is also used as a *lingua franca* in Kenya, the Congo, and Tanzania by speakers of other languages. Additional languages in the Bantu group with over a million speakers each include *Kikuyu* in central Kenya, *Ganda* in Uganda, *Ruanda* in Rwanda and the Congo, and *Rundi* in the Congo and Burundi. Speakers of nine major Bantu languages live in South Africa. *Sotho* and *Zulu* have the largest numbers, followed closely by *Xhosa* and *Tswana*. The last is also found in Botswana and Rhodesia.

Languages in the **Adamawa-Eastern** group are spoken primarily in eastern Nigeria and an adjoining section of Cameroon.

Languages in the Kordofanian subfamily are spoken by only a small number of persons living in central Sudan, in the Nuba hills of Kordofan.

NILO-SAHARAN

The Nilo-Saharan family, as classified by Greenberg, includes the Eastern Sudanic languages formerly included in the Nilotic and Nilo-Hamitic groups but placed by him in the larger Chari-Nile subfamily. Of the six subfamilies identified, only Chari-Nile and Saharan are widely distributed. The Chari-Nile languages are spoken primarily in northern Cameroun and across southern Chad into the northern Central African Republic and southwestern Sudan, with small pockets on both sides of the border between Sudan and Ethiopia, and in parts of Kenya and Tanzania. Languages in the Saharan subfamily are spoken in northern Chad, a small area of eastern Niger, and northeastern Nigeria. One of these, *Kanuri*, is spoken in northeastern Nigeria, in the proximity of Lake Chad.

KHOISAN

The Khoisan family includes the languages of the Hottentots and Bushmen, for whom it was named by Greenberg. Khoi is the self-appelation of the Hottentots, and San that of the Bushman. Members of these two groups now live in remoter areas of Botswana and Southwest Africa. *Sandawa* and *Hatsa* are two other languages in this family. The total number of speakers for the entire family is less than one million.

AMERICAN

The native languages of North and South America are usually classified geographically. Although some work has been done on genetic classification, especially in Latin America by McQuown (1955), it is too detailed and complex to summarize here. We shall therefore rely on the geographic classification, according to which there are two major areal divisions: **North American** and **Mexican, Central, and South American**. It is estimated that at the time of European discovery there may have been as many as 1800 separate languages; many of these have been replaced by the languages of the European colonists. Probably about 200 languages in the northern division and 500 in the southern are still being spoken.

Languages in the North American division have been separated into five major groups: **Athabascan, Algonquian, Penutian, Hoka-Siouan,** and **Uto-Aztecan**. Although Eskimo-Aleut is sometimes placed in this family, some authorities place it in the Paleo-Asiatic family; we have already discussed it under that classification. The Athabascan languages are spoken mainly in the interior of Alaska and northwest Canada, but a southern enclave is found in eastern Arizona, New Mexico, and southwest Texas. This is thought to be the result of a migration about 1000 B.C. of tribes whose present-day descendants include the Navajo. Speakers of languages in the Algonquian group are spread over the largest territory, from Vancouver Island east through Canada to Newfoundland, and south along the Atlantic coast to North Carolina. Languages in the Hoka-Siouan group are spoken on the central Great Plains; the Penutian group in Oregon, southern Washington and northern California; and the Uto-Aztecan group from Nevada and Utah south into Mexico.

Much less is known about languages in the Mexican, Central, and South American division. In most of the countries European languages, especially Spanish and Portuguese, are spoken by the majority of people; in Guatemala Indian speakers are in the majority, and they are thought to constitute about 50 percent of the population in Peru, Bolivia, and Paraguay. Not enough is yet known to make a complete genetic classification of the individual languages in this division, although a start has been made. *Quecha*, which was the administrative language of the Inca Empire, is still spoken in Peru, Bolivia, Ecuador, Brazil, and Argentina. *Maya*, derived from the language of the Mayan civilization, is spoken in Yucatan, Guatemala, Honduras, and British Honduras. *Arawak* is spoken in Venezuela, the Guianas, and the Greater Antilles and *Carib* in the Lesser Antilles and the territory between the Orinoco and the Amazon rivers. *Guarani* is spoken in Paraguay and parts of Brazil.

BASQUE

Speakers of *Basque* today live primarily in a small area in the western Pyrenees, in southwestern France and northeastern Spain. This is the only language in Europe that has no known relation to any other language. Most of its speakers are bilingual, also speaking Spanish or French.

URALIC

The Uralic language family is sometimes combined with the Altaic family, and the combination referred to as URALIC-ALTAIC. Speakers of languages in this family extend from eastern Europe through Russia and Siberia to the Pacific Ocean, although the areas in which they live are not all contiguous. There are three main divisions: **Finnic**, **Ugric**, and **Samoyedic**. Languages of the Finnic group include *Finnish, Estonian, Mordovian*, the language of the Mordovian ASSR, located east of Moscow, and *Lapp*, spoken by nomads living north of the Arctic Circle. The Ugric division includes *Hungarian*, which is spoken in Hungary and by Hungarians living in Transylvania, an autonomous region of Romania, as well as in other countries such as the United States, Yugoslavia, Czechoslovakia, the USSR, and the Balkans. The Samoyedic languages are spoken in northwestern Siberia near the mouths of the Ob and Yenisey rivers.

INDO-EUROPEAN

Languages in the Indo-European family are spoken by almost half the world's population. Because they have been studied more than those in any other family, their classification is more definite and accurate. From comparison of the many languages in this family, the previous existence of a hypothetical language, Proto-Indo-European, has been posited; it is thought that all present-day languages in the family have developed from it. In order to determine the area in which this hypothetical language originated, words from different languages in the family were compared. It was found that words for winter, cold, and snow were often similar, whereas words for tropical plants or animals were not. From these and other clues, linguists guessed that the area of origin was in a cold rather than a hot climate, now thought to be somewhere in central Europe, between the Elbe and Vistula rivers. From there, the people spread south and southeast.

We shall discuss the languages in this family in greater detail than we have any of the others, first, because more is known about them, and second, because many of them are familiar at least by name. At least nine groups are commonly recognized: **Indo-Iranian**, **Armenian**, **Greek**, **Albanian**, **Romance**, **Celtic**, **Teutonic**, **Baltic**, and **Slavic**.

Indo-Iranian. Languages in the Indo-Iranian, or Indic, group are thought to be derived from an early Indo-European language spoken by people who migrated into India sometime in the second millenium B.C. Although languages of the aboriginal group, the Dravidians, are still spoken in southern India, almost all of the remainder of the languages spoken in India and Pakistan are Indo-European. This group contains more individual languages than any other in the family. It is divided into the eastern, or Indic, and the western, or Iranian, subgroups.

Languages in the Indic subgroup are spoken by almost all the inhabitants of Pakistan, Bangladesh, and Nepal, four-fifths of the inhabitants of India, and the majority of Ceylonese. In Pakistan, *Urdu*, a variant of *Hindi*, is the principal verna-cular as well as the official language; in Bangladesh and the adjacent Indian state of West Bengal, *Bengali* is the official language. Hindi was declared one of the co-official languages of India in its Constitution. The largest settlements of Hindi-speaking peoples outside of India are found on Mauritius and the Fiji Islands. Other languages spoken as vernaculars by significant minorities include: *Punjabi*, *Rajasthani*, *Marathi*, *Gujarati*, *Oriya*, and *Assamese*. Hindi was to have replaced English entirely by 1965. When this date arrived and it was declared the official language of India, rioting began in southern India in protest, since the languages of the people there are unrelated to Hindi, which few people speak even as a second language. It appears likely that English will continue as a co-official lan-guage for some time, even though only about 3 percent of the population speak or understand it.

   Romany, the language of the gypsies, is spoken primarily outside India. It is thought that the ancestors of the present gypsies migrated into Europe from India between the ninth and the fifteenth centuries. Gypsies now live mainly in Spain and some of the Eastern European countries.

   Languages in the Iranian subgroup include *Persian*, spoken in Iran and Afghanistan; *Pashto*, *Baluchi*, *Tadzhik*, and *Kurdish*, all spoken in parts of the area between Pakistan, Iran, Turkey, and the USSR.

Armenian, Greek, and Albanian. Each of these languages comprises a group. *Armenian* is spoken in the Armenian SSR, *Greek* in Greece and on Cyprus, and *Albanian* in Albania. When Greece was at the height of its power, the Greek language was spoken throughout the world then known to the Greeks. It con-tinued as the literary language long after Rome had surpassed Greece politically; the New Testament was originally written in Greek.

Romance. The common precursor of languages in the Romance group is *Latin*. This group is commonly divided into eastern and western subgroups. In the eastern subgroup *Italian* is spoken not only on the Italian peninsula but also by Italians living in France, Argentina, Brazil, Yugoslavia, Switzerland, and the United States. There are many dialects, with variations among them so great that speakers of one dialect are often unable to understand speakers of another, but communicate in standard Italian. *Sardinian* and *Corsican* are so different as to be considered separate languages. *Rhaeto-Romanic* is thought to be more directly related to the Vulgar Latin of the Roman Empire than to Italian. With many variations, it is spoken in parts of Switzerland and in the area near the borders of Austria, Italy, and Yugoslavia. Speakers of *Romanian* are spatially separated from those of other Romance languages; they live primarily in Romania and the neighboring Moldavian SSR.

   There are more languages in the western subgroup than the eastern. *Spanish* is spoken in Spain as well as in eighteen Latin American republics from Mexico south through South America; in Cuba, Puerto Rico, and the Dominican Republic in the Caribbean; and in the Philippines, Spanish Morocco, and the remaining Spanish possessions in Africa. There are a number of dialects, with *Castilian* being considered the standard language. It differs from Latin American Spanish in both pronunciation and vocabulary. A creolized version, *Papiamento*, is spoken in the Caribbean Islands of Curacao and Aruba.

Portuguese is spoken in Portugal, as well as in Brazil and in Portuguese colonies in Africa and Asia such as Angola, Mozambique, Timor, and Macao. *Catalan* is spoken in Catalonia, on the Balearic Islands, and in a small region in southern France. *Ladino* is spoken by Sephardic Jews who migrated from Spain to areas of the eastern Mediterranean. It is the counterpart of Yiddish, and developed from a mixture of fifteenth-century Spanish, Hebrew, Greek, and Turkish.

French is the vernacular of people in France, southern Belgium, five western cantons of Switzerland, the British Channel Island of Jersey, Monaco, and Luxembourg. There are also many French-speaking people in Africa, Algeria, and former French and Belgian possessions. The largest number of French speakers in the western hemisphere lives in Canada, primarily in Quebec but also in Nova Scotia and Manitoba, as well as other provinces. Many French Canadians have migrated to New York and the New England states, where they continue to speak their own language. French is also spoken by some people of Louisiana and parts of the Caribbean. It is the official language of twenty-one independent countries and eighteen African nations that were formerly French or Belgian colonies, and is co-official in seven more. It is second to English as a foreign language studied in schools throughout the world, and is one of the five official languages of the United Nations. In Haiti, *French Creole* is spoken by the majority of people; it consists of a mixture of French and various African languages. Efforts are now being made to develop a standardized version of this language and to teach it in the schools.

Celtic. There are only a few remnants of languages in the Celtic group, which were once spoken in most of central and southern Europe as far east as Asia Minor. *Gaelic* is spoken in the western and northern counties of Eire and by some people in Northern Ireland. It is an official language of the Irish people and is co-official with English in Eire. Scottish Gaelic is spoken in the northwestern Scottish Highlands and Islands, as well as on and around Prince Edward and Cape Breton Islands in Canada. *Welsh* is growing in popularity in Wales, but most speakers are bilingual. *Breton* is used in Brittany.

Teutonic. The Teutonic group is divided into four subgroups: English, Dutch, German, and Scandinavian. *English* is spoken in areas throughout the entire world and is more widely distributed spatially than any other language. In the western hemisphere it is the official language of the United States and many of the Caribbean islands and is co-official with French in Canada. In Africa it is spoken in many countries, including South Africa, Kenya, Tanzania, Nigeria, and Ghana. In Asia, it is an associate official language of India, and is used by many people in Malaysia and the Philippines. In Oceania, it is spoken in Australia, New Zealand, and other islands of the Pacific. It is the official language of shipping, aviation and sports, and one of the official and working languages of the United Nations. An increasing number of sicientific and technical periodicals are published in English.

The greatest distinction in the spoken language exists between British and American English, which differ in pronunciation, usage, vocabulary, and the spelling of certain words. The standard language in Britain was formerly spoken primarily by members of the upper classes; today it is used by the British Broadcasting Corporation and is being taught increasingly in the schools. There are over twenty dialects in Britain. Speech is more uniform in the United States, where only three major variants are recognized: standard American, native to the Middle and Far West; Southern; and New England. A trading language, *Pidgin English*, of which there are many variants, is used throughout the Pacific. *Frisian*, which is genetically related to Old English, with later borrowings from Dutch, is spoken primarily in the northernmost provinces of the Netherlands and along the North Sea coast of Germany.

German is spoken in the Federal Republic of Germany (West Germany) and the German Democratic Republic (East Germany), Austria, Liechtenstein, and part of Switzerland. Its use also extends into border areas of Denmark and France. *Yiddish* developed from Medieval German in the ghettos of Central and Eastern Europe. After the liquidation of most of the Jews in Germany, Poland, and other countries dominated by the Nazis, few Yiddish-speaking people remained in Europe. Some still live in Russia, and at least half of them live around and in New York City. In spite of efforts to preserve the language, it appears to be used less and less as younger American-born Jews become assimilated.

Dutch is spoken in the Netherlands, while *Flemish*, a variant of it which is mutually intelligible, is spoken in the neighboring portion of Belgium. *Afrikaans* developed from the original language of the Dutch settlers of South Africa, with the incorporation of many Bantu words. It is now spoken in South Africa, Botswana, Basutoland, and Lesotho.

The four major Scandinavian languages, *Icelandic*, *Swedish*, *Norwegian*, and *Danish*, developed from a common precursor, *Old Norse*. Icelandic, which because of its isolation has been relatively little influenced by other languages, remains most like this original language. The other three have influenced each other and have been influenced by other European languages. Norwegian has two official forms, book language and rural language, which are mutually intelligible. Each Scandinavian language is spoken in the corresponding country and adjacent areas. Many Scandinavians have migrated to the United States where they live in isolated communities and continue to use their own language, but most of the younger generation is now becoming assimilated.

Baltic. The only two languages in the Baltic group are *Latvian* and *Lithuanian*, each spoken in the corresponding SSR.

Slavic. Speakers of languages in the Slavic group extend eastward from Central Europe through Russia to the Pacific Ocean. These languages are very similar, so that speakers of one can usually understand most others within the group. *Russian*, originally the dialect of the Moscow region, is now used throughout the USSR and is one of the five official languages of the United Nations. It is spoken as the vernacular by the majority of people in the Russian SFSR and many people in the other fourteen republics of the USSR, and taught as a foreign language in the Communist countries of Europe. *Ukrainian* and *Byelorussian* are spoken within the corresponding SSR's. *Polish* is the official language of Poland, while both *Czech* and *Slovak*, which are closely related, are the languages of Czechoslovakia. *Lusatian* is found in a small area in East Germany. Yugoslavia is a federation of six republics with three official languages: *Serbo-Croatian*, *Slovenian*, and *Macedonian*. Serbo-Croatian is a single language, written in the Cyrillic alphabet by Serbs and in the Latin alphabet by Croatians. It is spoken in five of the republics. Slovenian is spoken mainly in the Slovenian republic and adjacent territory; Macedonian is found in Macedonia, western Bulgaria, and northern Greece. *Bulgarian* is spoken in Bulgaria and in adjoining areas of the USSR and Hungary.

6.4 PROCESSES OF CHANGE IN THE SPATIAL DISTRIBUTION OF LANGUAGES

6.4.1 Processes of Linguistic Change

Linguists recognize that languages change over time, in part as speakers of different languages come into contact with each other. For example, the Latin of the Roman empire gradually evolved into French, Spanish, Italian, and other Romance languages which are obviously related to each other although each is a distinct language. At the same time, elements of Latin were incorporated into Teutonic languages spoken in northern and western Europe, so that present-day German, Dutch, and English show strong influences of both roots. Usage is constantly being modified, as we can see from the difference between the English used by Chaucer, Shakespeare, and contemporary American writers. When speakers of a language migrate and become isolated from the mainstream of speakers of their own language, within a generation or two separate dialects begin to develop, so that when descendants of the original migrants return to their parents' or grandparents' homeland, they find difficulty in communicating with others. In addition, technological change brings about the constant introduction of new words. Not only would the language used a century ago sound stilted and awkward to us if it were spoken today, we would also soon find it inadequate for communicating about phenomena such as missiles and space exploration.

Some of the changes in individual languages are the results of what might be considered as random variations, whereas others come about as speakers of different languages interact. Since non-verbal communication can convey meaning in relatively few situations, when speakers of different languages interact they usually develop some way of communicating with each other. We have already observed some of these adaptations: (1) almost complete isolation of the speakers of one language from those of the other, (2) incorporation of words and phrases of one language into the other, (3) creolization, (4) pidginization, often with the development of a *lingua franca*, and (5) bilingualism. Since these developments are not mutually exclusive, several may occur simultaneously.

1. Isolation occurs when there is a lack of social interaction which requires communication. Since language is an essential means of communication between human beings, it is difficult for speakers of two language groups to remain in the same area without at least some members of a group learning the other's language. In Quebec, for example, many persons living in cities are bilingual, whereas many rural dwellers speak only French. In the cities French speakers come into contact with persons who speak English, and obtaining employment often depends on having a knowledge of both languages.

2. Borrowing, the incorporation of words or phrases from the other languages, occurs continuously. Words such as *jazz* and *sex appeal* have come into use in several different languages.

3. Creolization occurs when two or more languages, instead of retaining their identities, tend to merge into a distinctive language which is understood with difficulty, if at all, by speakers of any of the original languages. We have observed the presence of French Creole in Haiti and Louisiana; Papiamento, a Spanish Creole in the Caribbean; and Portuguese creole in parts of Spain.

4. Pidginization involves a similar process, except that the resulting amalgamation of languages is an extremely simplified tongue, with a limited vocabulary, in which only the most basic ideas can be expressed. It is useful for trade or simple communication, but not for literature or the expression of complex abstract ideas. We have observed several such languages, including Bazaar Malay and Swahili. In some cases these languages develop further, often by deliberate effort on the part of a government, to become complete languages; Indonesian, for example, was derived from Bazaar Malay.

5. Bilingualism is found in many areas. In some countries or regions governmental business is transacted in two or more official languages. These countries include Switzerland, Canada, Belgium, India, and many African states which were formerly European colonies. In some countries speakers of one language are relatively concentrated in a few areas; in others they are more evenly distributed throughout the country. Bilingualism is also often found among members of a minority group, and may be restricted to those members who have frequent contact with the majority. When the children of immigrants attend school in the new country, they quickly learn the language or speak one language at home, the other at school.

6.4.2 Toward an Explanation of Spatial Change

We can use this information about the process of linguistic change to help us formulate hypotheses accounting for changes in the spatial distribution of languages and in the relative proportions of speakers of different languages in a given area. We have noted, in our explorations of other human phenomena, that food, shelter, and religion are all intimately related to economic, political, and social factors; we may expect, therefore, to find the same to be true of language. Languages are not simply means of communication, but have emotional as well as utilitarian implications. For utilitarian purposes, such as economic gain or political power, it is often necessary for speakers of a minority language to learn the language of the majority in order to receive an education, obtain employment in certain fields, or vote and exert political influence. In some areas the language used in higher education is neither a vernacular nor the majority language. Knowledge of English, for example, is essential for this purpose in India, Pakistan, Bangladesh, and other former British colonies, even though it is spoken by a small minority of the population.

Besides these utilitarian implications, language also has strong emotional connotations for people. Many immigrants retain their love of the mother tongue even after they have been speaking the language of their new country for many years. Language is often associated with nationalistic movements. In the years since World War II, as many nations have become independent, some have sought to reject the European language introduced by their former rulers which has become a second language of the educated people. Such a language is often the only one mutually intelligible to many persons over the entire country, who speak many different vernaculars. When India gained its independence, for example, English was adopted as the language for higher education, government, business, and many newspapers. It was to be co-official with Hindi during the early period of independence, after which Hindi would become the only official language. At the date when this was to occur some speakers of Dravidian languages, who lived in South India, rioted to express their dissatisfaction. Not only did the possibility of having to learn a new language threaten their chances at many jobs in business and government, but their desire to retain their own vernacular was also an attempt to assert and maintain their ethnic identity. Similarly, the development of Indonesian in Indonesia and the revival of Hebrew in Israel have been encouraged by the respective governments as means of arousing national identity and fervor.

6.5 DEVELOPMENT OF GENERALIZATIONS AND THEIR APPLICATIONS

We are now ready to formalize the ideas in the above discussion, and state them as hypotheses:

1. When speakers of two or more languages interact, some means of verbal

communication usually develops. Accomodations include: (a) almost complete isolation of speakers of one language from those of the other, (b) incorporation of words and phrases of one language into the other, (c) creolization, (d) pidginization, often with the development of a *lingua franca*, and (e) bilingualism.

2. Over time, the number of speakers of the dominant language, whose speakers derive greater economic benefits, social prestige, and political power, will tend to increase; at the same time, the number of speakers of other languages will tend to decrease.

3. The greater the interaction between the speakers of different languages in an area, the fewer languages or dialects will be spoken in that area.

It should be remembered that since these hypotheses describe general tendencies, they will apply to many, but not all, situations. They can be used to predict what one might expect to find in an area where certain conditions prevailed, as we shall see in the following examples:

Situation 1. Let us begin by considering a hypothetical area populated by groups of people speaking different languages, each living relatively independent of the other, and isolated by physical features such as mountain ranges, rivers, or dense vegetation. A low amount of technology prevails in the area.

Tentative prediction: In areas such as these, we would expect that the amount of interaction between speakers of different languages would be low, because of physical barriers and the relatively low amount of technology prevailing. We might therefore expect to find a relatively large number of mutually unintelligible languages being spoken within a relatively small area, or a large number of languages per unit area.

Examples: Situations such as this exist in New Guinea, the Caucasus, and remote parts of South America and India.

Situation 2. Let us modify some conditions of the original system, so that neighboring groups trade with others on each side of them, but do not travel farther.

Tentative prediction: With some increase in circulation and interaction among speakers of different languages, we might expect to find some similarity of language or provision for communication between neighboring groups.

Examples: In Africa, the languages of neighboring tribes are often mutually intelligible, but when an individual travels farther from his home, he is no longer able to understand the language spoken.

Situation 3. Let us now assume that the distance traveled and the amount of interaction between speakers of different languages increase to the point that speakers of each language trade with those of all other languages.

Tentative prediction: Some additional means of mutual intelligibility will probably develop.

Examples: Hausa developed in Africa as a *lingua franca*; similarly, Bazaar Malay was found in Indonesia, and Chinook in the northwest United States and adjoining parts of Canada.

Situation 4. Let us now modify the amount of technology in the area we are considering, so that there is a society with a large amount of technology, and the concomitant high interaction of persons over a large area.

Tentative prediction: We would expect to find a single language predominating over the area, although there might also be bilingualism in some or all of it.

Examples: A single language, English, is spoken as both official language and vernacular by the majority of the people in the United States and as a second language by many others. Although Canada is officially bilingual, most speakers of French live in Quebec, small areas of the Maritime Provinces, and other small enclaves. In western Europe, on the other hand, many different languages are found in a smaller area. Some are closely enough related to approach mutual intelligibility; for example, Spanish, French, and Italian; Dutch and German; and the Scandinavian languages. At least one language, and often two or more, are studied in school.

Thus we find that many of the explanatory hypotheses which applied to other cultural phenomena are also relevant to the spatial distribution of languages. Contact among peoples modifies their customs, habits, and beliefs, and tends to accelerate the pace of change. Greater circulation tends toward increased provision for communication, through either decrease in the number of languages used or learning of additional languages.

6.6 DIALECT GEOGRAPHY: THE STUDY OF MICRO-VARIATIONS IN LANGUAGES

6.6.1 Some Implications of Changes in Scale

In studying other phenomena not only over the entire world but also over smaller areas, such as a single city or county, it has become clear that the scale of areal analysis selected often influences the manner in which a study is carried out as well as the resulting findings. Variations in the quality or quantity of the phenomenon may be less over a smaller area than over a large one. Thus, in a small-scale study the phenomenon not only may be defined differently, but also may be studied in more detail. We have found that in spite of these differences many of the same explanatory factors are relevant for both large- and small-scale studies.

6.6.2 Methods Used in Dialect Geography

The study of languages over a more limited area, in which variations are less marked, is often called dialect geography. In studying micro-variations, linguistic geographers investigate such phenomena as the pronunciation of certain sounds, different words used for a given item or event, and different meanings of the same word. Data are usually gathered by interviewing at least two individuals in each of the sample locations throughout the area being studied. The oldest living individuals who have resided in the area continuously since birth are preferred as informants. Data are collected on a standardized schedule which provides for quick, convenient notation of responses. The responses of each individual are plotted on a dot-type map, using different symbols for each possible response (see Fig. 6.10). From such a map, an isogloss map (Fig. 6.11) is constructed, in which boundary lines are drawn to separate the various usages as accurately as possible.

Just as isotherms and isobars may be drawn on a weather map joining points having the same temperature or barometric pressure, so linguists draw isoglosses to indicate and enclose regions with the same linguistic features. These may be isophonic, indicating use of the same sounds; isotonic, the same tones; isomorphic, the same forms, isosyntagnic, same syntax; or isolexic, same vocabulary. Unfortunately these lines do not coincide; instead they intertwine in a complex fashion. Drawing a boundary therefore involves making arbitrary decisions, and as such is subject to different interpretations by different authorities. Wherever a number of isoglosses coincide sufficiently to justify the establishment of a distinctive speech area, dialect regions may be delineated.

6.6.3 Dialects in the Northeastern United States

Zelinsky (1955) studied the geography of place names in the northeastern United States. Using data obtained from topographic maps, he investigated the distribution of generic terms appended to place names for such topographic features as stream, lake and hill, as well as for vegetational features, agglomerated settlements and highways. We shall review here only the words used to denote a small or medium-sized stream; other terms were similarly analyzed. *Creek* is the most common over the entire region except for New England, where it is used only occasionally. *Brook* is the common term in New England, eastern New York, and New Jersey. *Run* is concentrated in West Virginia, western Pennsylvania, Ohio, and northern Virginia. *Branch* is found primarily in eastern Kentucky and the bordering area of West Virginia, but also occurs in Virginia, Delaware, Maryland, and southern New Jersey, as well as scattered throughout the remaining states except Massachusetts and Rhode Island. *Fork* and *lick* are concentrated in West Virginia, northern Kentucky, and southern Ohio; *Stream* in Maine; and *kill* in extreme southeastern New York. A dot map was constructed for each name (Figs. 6.2–6.9).

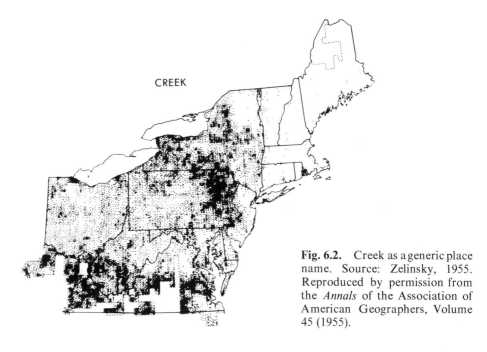

CREEK

Fig. 6.2. Creek as a generic place name. Source: Zelinsky, 1955. Reproduced by permission from the *Annals* of the Association of American Geographers, Volume 45 (1955).

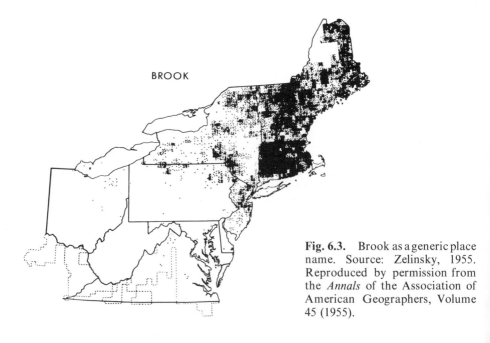

BROOK

Fig. 6.3. Brook as a generic place name. Source: Zelinsky, 1955. Reproduced by permission from the *Annals* of the Association of American Geographers, Volume 45 (1955).

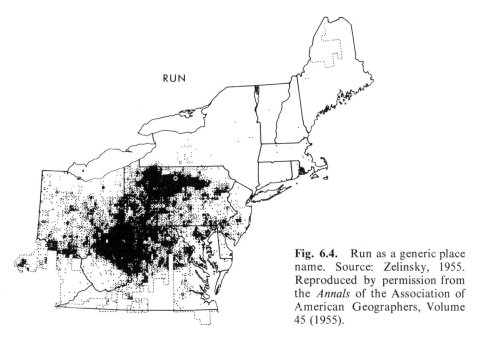

Fig. 6.4. Run as a generic place name. Source: Zelinsky, 1955. Reproduced by permission from the *Annals* of the Association of American Geographers, Volume 45 (1955).

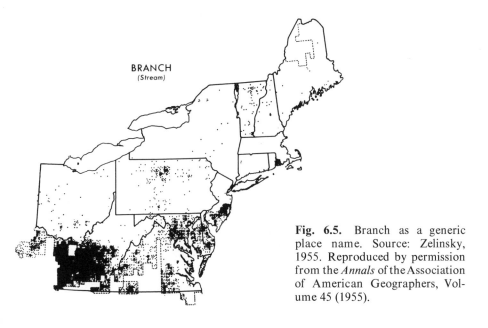

Fig. 6.5. Branch as a generic place name. Source: Zelinsky, 1955. Reproduced by permission from the *Annals* of the Association of American Geographers, Volume 45 (1955).

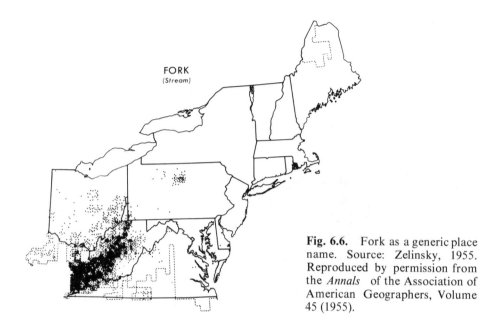

FORK
(Stream)

Fig. 6.6. Fork as a generic place name. Source: Zelinsky, 1955. Reproduced by permission from the *Annals* of the Association of American Geographers, Volume 45 (1955).

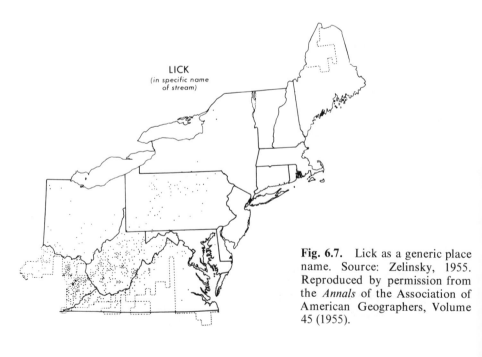

LICK
(in specific name
of stream)

Fig. 6.7. Lick as a generic place name. Source: Zelinsky, 1955. Reproduced by permission from the *Annals* of the Association of American Geographers, Volume 45 (1955).

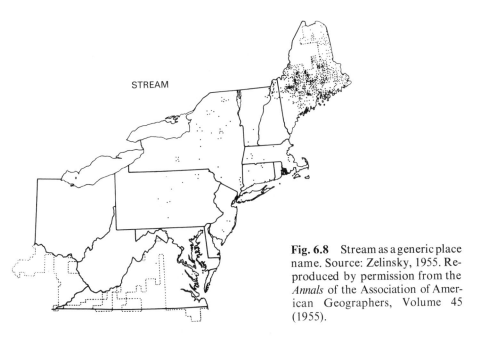

STREAM

Fig. 6.8   Stream as a generic place name. Source: Zelinsky, 1955. Reproduced by permission from the *Annals* of the Association of American Geographers, Volume 45 (1955).

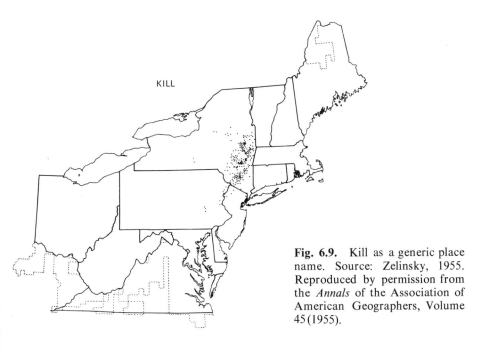

KILL

Fig. 6.9. Kill as a generic place name. Source: Zelinsky, 1955. Reproduced by permission from the *Annals* of the Association of American Geographers, Volume 45 (1955).

After studying many such terms, Zelinsky found that usages for no two of the terms he studied were similarly distributed. He therefore did not attempt to draw regional boundaries, but instead designated the following general areas: Old Colonial (entire sea-board), New England, Midland, South, Northern Frontier, and Southern Frontier. He found that the majority of terms used were of either American or British origin. Dutch names were found only in a small area of early

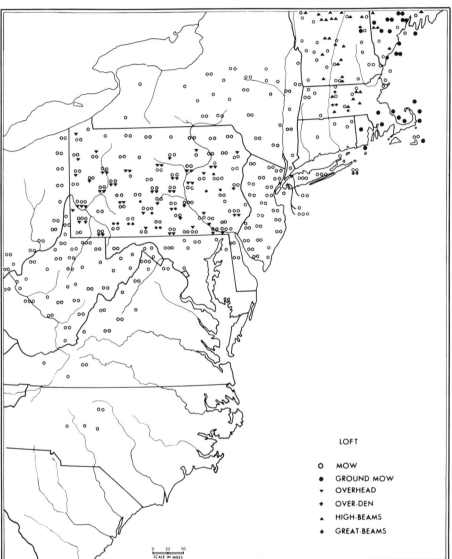

Fig. 6.10. Distribution of six terms used to denote the loft of a barn. Source: Kurath, 1949. Reprinted by permission from the University of Michigan Press.

Dutch settlement in New York, and names from other countries represented by early settlers seldom occurred.

6.6.4   Kurath's Studies of Dialect Geography

Kurath carried out a similar geographic investigation of dialects in the eastern United States. Beginning in 1931, data were collected by interviewing over 1,200

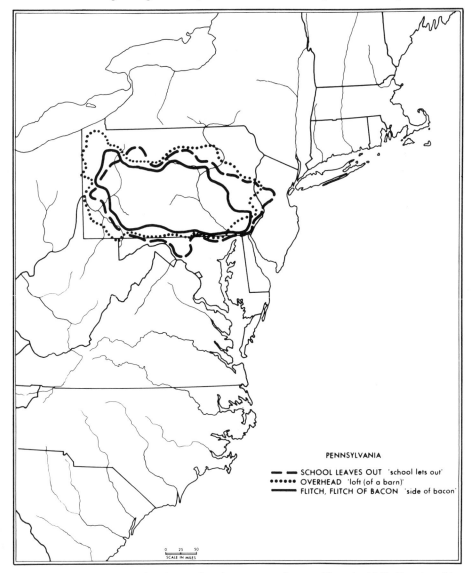

PENNSYLVANIA

— — SCHOOL LEAVES OUT 'school lets out'
•••••• OVERHEAD 'loft (of a barn)'
———— FLITCH, FLITCH OF BACON 'side of bacon'

0   25   50
SCALE IN MILES

Fig. 6.11.   Pennsylvania isoglosses for three terms. Source: Kurath, 1949. Reprinted by permission from the University of Michigan Press.

persons throughout the eastern states. His studies of the pronunciation of different sounds were published in *The Pronunciation of English in the Atlantic States* (Kurath and McDavid, 1961); studies of the different terms used to denote the same phenomenon are found in *A Word Geography of the Eastern United States* (Kurath 1949). In the latter book, Kurath reports on an investigation of over 400 terms, a few of which we have selected to discuss in order to illustrate his proce-

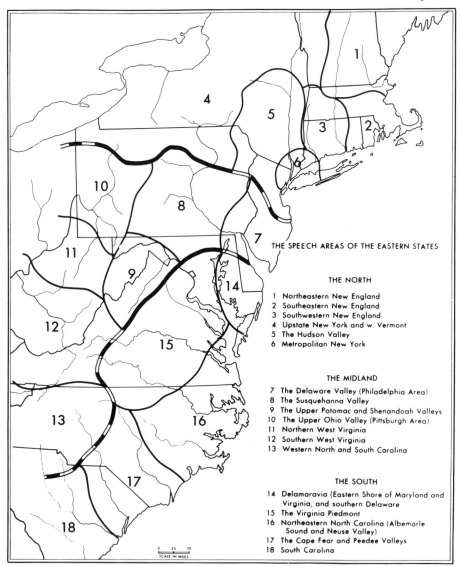

THE SPEECH AREAS OF THE EASTERN STATES

THE NORTH

1   Northeastern New England
2   Southeastern New England
3   Southwestern New England
4   Upstate New York and w. Vermont
5   The Hudson Valley
6   Metropolitan New York

THE MIDLAND

7   The Delaware Valley (Philadelphia Area)
8   The Susquehanna Valley
9   The Upper Potomac and Shenandoah Valleys
10 The Upper Ohio Valley (Pittsburgh Area)
11 Northern West Virginia
12 Southern West Virginia
13 Western North and South Carolina

THE SOUTH

14 Delamarvia (Eastern Shore of Maryland and Virginia, and southern Delaware
15 The Virginia Piedmont
16 Northeastern North Carolina (Albemarle Sound and Neuse Valley)
17 The Cape Fear and Peedee Valleys
18 South Carolina

Fig. 6.12.   Speech areas and sub-areas of the Eastern States. Source: Kurath, 1949. Reprinted by permission from the University of Michigan Press.

dure. He followed the steps outlined above: collection of data, mapping of individual observations, determination of isoglosses and regionalization.

The distribution of six terms used to denote the loft of a barn is shown in Fig. 6.10. *Mow* is used over the entire area, and is the only term found south and east of Pennsylvania. *Overhead* occurs throughout Pennsylvania, and *overden* in scattered parts of that state. *Ground mow, high beams,* and *great beams* are re-

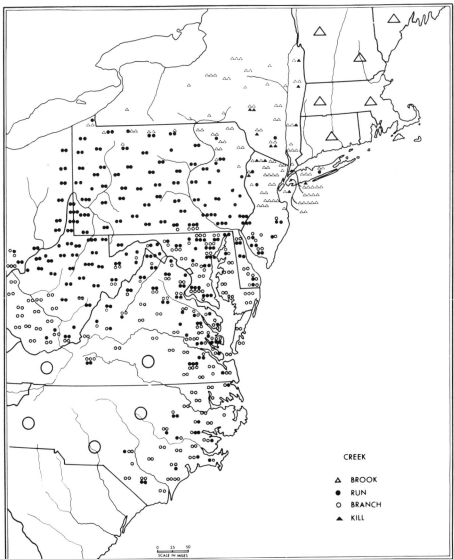

CREEK

△ BROOK
● RUN
○ BRANCH
▲ KILL

0   25   50
SCALE IN MILES

Fig. 6.13. Distribution of four terms used to denote creek. Source: Kurath, 1949. Reprinted by permission from the University of Michigan Press.

stricted to New England, excluding Connecticut. The isoglosses for Pennsylvania which have been derived from these usages are depicted in Fig. 6.11, along with those for two other terms. As can be seen from this map, there is some correspondence among them. The final delineation of speech areas and subareas, derived from consideration of many such isoglosses, is shown in Fig. 6.12. As a result of this study, Kurath concluded that in the eastern United States there is no clear distinction between northern and southern speech areas at the Mason-Dixon line. Rather, a distinct Midlands speech area extends west and south from New Jersey, which is separated from the south by the Blue Ridge Mountains. Northern New Jersey and Pennsylvania are included in the north rather than the midlands.

Kurath investigated one of the terms which was also studied by Zelinsky (1955) and found that four different words for *creek* were used (Fig. 6.13). *Brook* is common throughout New England, New York, northeastern Pennsylvania, and New Jersey. In the remainder of Pennsylvania and the bordering areas of Ohio, West Virginia, Delaware, and Maryland, and in southern New Jersey and parts of Virginia and North and South Carolina, *run* is the common term. *Branch* is most common in the entire area of south of Pennsylvania, whereas *kill* is used only in a few parts of northern New Jersey and New York.

He proposes two explanations of the origin and spread of word usage. First, many terms brought to the United States by the original settlers can be traced to British, German, or Dutch origins. Second, usage tended to become more uniform throughout an area over time as transportation routes were developed and trade and communication between urban centers and their hinterlands increased.

6.6.5 Explanations Suggested by Kurath and Zelinsky

These two studies have been reviewed here not only to illustrate studies of microvariations in language, but also to show that different authorities can reach different conclusions in studying similar phenomena. Kurath delineated regions partly by using isoglosses, whereas Zelinsky did not feel justified in doing so. Kurath proposed two explanations for the origin of names of physical features: (1) Certain words, or usages, were brought to this country by migrants. Words from a given country are found primarily in areas settled by persons from that country; (2) Uniformity of usage increases with increasing circulation of people within an area. In his study, which was more limited both areally and topically, Zelinsky did not find support for either of these hypotheses. Both of them, however, agree with the ones formulated in Section 6.4.

6.7 LANGUAGE AS AN INDEPENDENT VARIABLE

Language can also be studied as an independent variable. Selection of one phenomenon as independent and another as dependent is often purely arbitrary; one could equally well study the influence of migration upon the spread of language or that of language upon migration. It has been found, for example, that people tend to migrate to areas where other speakers of their native language have already gone. As archeologists seek to determine the origin of peoples who have lived in an area, they investigate clues such as what languages were spoken, what artifacts were used, and what foods were eaten. Relationships found between languages previously not thought to be related have often helped to open up new areas of investigation, and to suggest migrations, trade or other contact between peoples formerly thought to have been isolated from each other.

6.8 SUGGESTIONS FOR FURTHER RESEARCH

In this chapter, it has been possible to suggest only a few of the lines of inquiry along which geographers interested in the study of language might proceed. Although emphasis has been placed upon the distribution of the speakers of different languages, a number of other dependent variables have also been suggested, some of which merit further investigation. For example, many additional hypotheses could be proposed to explain the number of languages in an area of a given size; our suggestions of the amount of contact and communication among the speakers of different languages, the relative social and economic status of the languages, and political considerations are but a few. A systematic investigation of the phenomenon in different parts of the world might both disclose other relevant explanatory variables and point out some of the conditions under which each of the independent variables would be related to it. The findings of such investigations would result in a more complete explanation.

Study of the way in which languages change spatially over time would be in part an extension of the proceding topic. If we knew the distribution of speakers of different languages at any given time, the number of languages per unit area, and other variables, then we could study any given phenomenon in the same areas at different times. Certain explanatory variables come to mind: Migration of the speakers of a language has long been recognized as one way in which its distribution is influenced, and conquest has played a part. But the use of these factors still leaves much of the change unexplained; more investigation must be done to determine why one language is no longer used while another one persists. A more adequate understanding of the ways in which these factors have operated in the past should, in turn, enable us to predict future changes; given a specified set of conditions, in what direction might it be anticipated that changes would occur?

Other aspects of spoken languages could be investigated over smaller areas. Pronunciation of words, as we know, varies from place to place. What factors account for such variation, and for the persistence of greater variations within the United States in New England and the South than in most of the remainder of the country? Variations exist in meaning, too, as between American and British English. Different terms may be used for the same idea or the same term may be used to denote different ideas. How do such variations arise? Under what conditions do they persist, and for how long? Why do they disappear? These are questions to which there are as yet no clear answers.

Differences between written and spoken languages are often greater than those with which we are familiar. Hebrew and Latin persisted as written languages long after they dropped out of use as vernaculars. In many countries today, such as Iran, the written language would be almost incomprehensible to persons familiar only with the spoken vernacular. The same aspects of written languages that we have suggested for spoken ones could be investigated: for example, distribution of their use, the number of languages in an area, and change over time.

We might also investigate the alphabets by which words are committed to paper or other record. Some alphabets, like ours, are phonetic; others, like the Chinese and Japanese, are ideographic, with each character standing for an idea rather than a sound. What are the distributions of different alphabets? How did they develop and change over time? What is the result of forced or planned change, as was carried out in China, where the classical Chinese characters were reduced in number and simplified, so that written Chinese is now easier to learn than it was previously?

Nor have we touched on constructed languages, which have been proposed as supplements to existing ones which have evolved naturally. These include not only Esperanto and Interlingua, which are used for communication between human beings, but also FORTRAN and ALGOL, which are used for communication between men and computers. Mathematical and musical notation symbols have become almost universal, so that they may be read by educated individuals regardless of what language they speak. Will a similar universal computer language also develop, or will machine translation become practicable, so that works written in one language may be translated into any other language? Why has the use of constructed languages not spread, in spite of the many apparent advantages to be gained from their use? The number of questions which could be asked regarding these artificial languages is large, and answers to them would help to shed light upon other aspects of language as well.

REVIEW YOUR UNDERSTANDING OF THESE CONCEPTS

definition of language
phoneme
semanteme
morpheme
morphology
semantics
syntax
mutual intelligibility
variations from a standard language
distinction between genetic and generic classification
language families and groups

vernacular
process of linguistic change
isolation
incorporation
creolization
pidginization
bilingualism
dialect geography
isogloss
language as an independent variable

SUGGESTED ACTIVITIES

1. Select one topographic map from each of three widely separated sections of a single country. List the names given streams, water courses and other bodies of water on each map. Account for the observed variations of the names of these physical features.

2. Interview about fifty fellow students. From each, find out what languages he speaks and/or reads, what languages his grandparents speak and/or read, and his home address. From these data attempt to determine whether there is any locational pattern and attempt to account for it.

3. Watch newspapers and periodicals for items related to the distribution of languages, the locational change in language and the influence upon the language of one group of speakers by speakers of another language. Relate these specific instances to the general hypotheses proposed above.

REFERENCES

Gray, Louis H. (1939), *Foundations of Language*. New York: Macmillan.

Greenberg, J. H. (1963), *The Languages of Africa*. Bloomington: Indiana University Press.

Kurath, Hans (1949), *A Word Geography of the Eastern United States*. Ann Arbor: University of Michigan Press.

Kurath, Hans and Raven I. McDavid (1961), *The Pronunciation of English in the Atlantic States*. Ann Arbor: University of Michigan Press.

McQuown, Norman A. (1955), "The indigenous languages of Latin America," *American Anthropologist* **57**, 501–570.

Zelinsky, Wilbur (1955), "Some problems in the distribution of generic terms in the place-names of the northeastern United States," *Annals* of the Association of American Geographers **45**, 319–349.

Additional Readings

Allen, Harold B., ed. (1964), *Readings in Applied English Linguistics*. New York: Appleton-Century-Crofts.

Bloomfield, Leonard (1958), *Language*. New York: Holt.

Bottiglioni, Gino (1954), "Linguistic geography: its achievements, methods and orientations," *Word* **10**, 375–387.

Bruck, Solomon I. and V. S. Apenchenko, eds. (1964) and Telberg, V. G. (1965), *Atlas Narodov Mira* (Atlas of the People of the World). Moscow: Telberg.

Burling, Robbins (1965), "The languages of Southeast Asia," appendix in *Hill Farms and Padi Fields: Life in Mainland Southeast Asia*. Englewood Cliffs: Prentice-Hall.

Chao, Yuen Ren (1968), *Language and Symbolic Systems*. Cambridge: Cambridge University Press.

Delgado de Charvalho, C. M. (1943), "The geography of languages," in Philip L. Wagner and Marvin W. Mikesell, 1962, *Readings in Cultural Geography*. Chicago: University of Chicago Press, pp. 75–93 (Translated from *Boletim Geografico* **1**, 45–62).

Deutsch, Karl (1953), *Nationalism and Social Communication*. Cambridge: The Massachusetts Institute of Technology Press.

Dominian, Leon (1917), *The Frontiers of Language and Nationality in Europe*, American Geographical Society Special Publication No. 3. New York: Holt.

Dyen, Isidore (1956), "Language distribution and migration theory," *Language* 32, 611–624.

Eyre, Edward, ed. (1934), *European Civilization: Its Origin and Development*. Oxford University Press.

Fishman, Joshua, Charles A. Ferguson, and Jyotirindra Das Gupta, eds. (1968), *Language Problems of Developing Nations*. New York: Wiley.

Greenberg, Joseph H. (1957), *Essays in Linguistics*, Viking Fund Publications in Anthropology No. 24. Chicago: University of Chicago Press.

Hockett, Charles F. (1958), *A Course in Modern Linguistics*. New York: Macmillan.

Hymes, Dell, ed. (1964), *Language in Culture and Society*. New York: Harper and Row.

Jones, Emrys and Ievan L. Griffith (1963), "A linguistic map of Wales 1961," *Geographical Journal* 129, 192–196.

Kurath, Hans and Bernard Bloch, eds. (1939–1943), *Linguistic Atlas of New England*. Providence: Brown University Press.

Lieberson, Stanley (1965), "Bilingualism in Montreal: a demographic analysis," *The American Journal of Sociology* 71, 10–25.

Loukotka, Cestmir (1967), "Ethno-linguistic distribution of South American Indians," *Annals* of the Association of American Geographers 57, 437–438 and map.

McCormack, William C. (1967), "Language identity: an introduction to India's language problems," in Joseph W. Elder, ed., *Chapters in Indian Civilization, Vol. II, British and Modern India*. Madison: Department of Indian Studies, The University of Wisconsin.

Meillet, Antoine and Marcel Cohen, eds. (1952), *Les Langues Du Monde*. Paris: H. Champion.

Muller, Siefgried H. (1964), *The World's Living Languages*. New York: Ungar.

Pei, Mario A. (1957), *Language for Everybody*. New York: Devin-Adair.

Potter, Simon (1960), *Modern Linguistics*. London: A. Deutsch.

Reinicke, John E. (1938), "Trade jargons and Creole dialects as marginal languages," *Social Forces* 17, 107–118.

Thieme, Paul (1958), "The Indo-European language," *Scientific American* 199, No. 4, 63–74.

Voegelin, Charles F. and F. M. Voegelin (1965–1966), "Fascicles on the languages of the world," *Anthropological Linguistics* 7, 8, passim.

Wagner, Philip L. (1958), "Remarks on the geography of language," *Geographical Review* 48, 86–97.

Whatmough, Joshua (1956), *Language: A Modern Synthesis*. New York: St. Martin's Press.

Whorf, Benjamin L. (1956), *Language, Thought and Reality: Selected Writings*. Cambridge Technology Press of M.I.T. and Wiley.

CHAPTER 7
EDUCATION AND LITERACY

7.1 INTRODUCTION

7.1.1 Reasons for Studying Education and Literacy

Education is recognized as essential in contemporary society and its social importance in reducing poverty at home and overseas is widely known. Although education and literacy may, at first glance, seem to be less essential to human existence than some of the phenomena discussed in preceding chapters, education is becoming increasingly vital for obtaining the necessities of life, such as food and housing. In order to hold a job and so to procure even these essentials, people must not only possess an elementary knowledge of reading and writing, but also progress to higher levels of educational attainment. Until recently, only a small proportion of the world's population could read or write. Some people lived in cultures without written languages; others simply had never learned to read or write and had had no need to do so. In many countries only a small percentage of children ever attend primary school, and a small fraction of them continue through secondary and higher education. Literacy rates and educational levels are continually rising in many countries. In the United States and Canada a high school diploma is virtually essential for any young person, and soon two years of post-high school education will be the acceptable minimum. Similar trends toward higher educational levels are present in other areas. Even with all the communications media which exist, the printed word remains an important one for the transmission of knowledge.

Emphasis on education as a social issue should not obscure other benefits for the individual. People desire education not only because they gain knowledge and skills which provide access to better jobs, but also because they are curious about the world in which they live. Knowledge of the past, scientific advances, music and art are gained by reading. This fact has been dramatized during newspaper strikes in various large cities; although people had access to radio and television news, very few of them believed that these were adequate substitutes for newspapers.

135

7.1.2 Overview of the Chapter

Following the pattern of previous chapters, we shall select three areas of different sizes for study: the world, the United States, and the state of Rhode Island. A choice will be made of one topic in each area from among many possible topics which could be investigated. The dependent variable will first be operationally defined and some aspatial aspects considered. Observations will then be made about its spatial distribution, and relevant factors selected as independent variables which might help to explain it. Finally, the resulting hypotheses will be examined and tested, and tentative conclusions about their relationships to the dependent variable will be suggested. The hypotheses examined in this chapter are presented less as answers than as suggestions of the ways in which answers to questions like the ones posed here might be obtained. Although the analysis is largely static or cross-sectional, it provides a basis for subsequent dynamic or longitudinal studies aimed at understanding the process and the changes which take place over time—that is, the workings of the system.

7.2 THE DEPENDENT VARIABLE

7.2.1 Possible Topics for Study

Many topics within the broad area of education and literacy can be identified. An impression of the vastness of the field may be gained from a partial listing of them:

Literacy: stated and functional

Educational level: median school years completed, percentage of persons completing primary, secondary, and higher education; level of achievement with respect to norms

Teachers: salary, teaching loads, teacher-pupil ratios, conditions of work, qualifications, percent of teachers in the population

Libraries: number of volumes, expenditures per pupil

School Enrollment: primary, secondary, higher education

Curricula

Special educational programs: adult education and mass literacy

Types of educational institutions: primary, secondary, colleges and universities, liberal arts colleges, technical and vocational schools, agricultural colleges

In studying these topics, individuals comprising the population could also be classified according to characteristics such as age, sex, ethnic origin, or religion, and each of the subsets analyzed.

7.2.2 Selection and Definition of the Dependent Variable

Before deciding which topics to study, we would look for one which can be expected to contribute as much as possible to the building of a general explanation. Final selection is, however, contingent upon data availability; unless we are prepared to conduct a personal survey of the world, we must use data which have been collected. We shall therefore select as the dependent variables to be studied, literacy rates on a world scale, and median school years completed for the United States and for Rhode Island.

For many reasons it is difficult to select a single measure of educational level. Comparable data are often not available for different areas, and the data which exist are difficult to interpret. Even within the United States, completion of a given school year does not ensure that a given individual has attained that level of educational achievement. On a world scale, difficulties are increased because of the even greater variations among school systems, not only in formal organization but also in the quality of education offered.

For the present exploration, we shall adopt the definition of literacy used by the United Nations Educational, Scientific, and Cultural Organization, UNESCO, (1957). Whether or not a person is deemed to be literate rests on his answer to the question, "Are you able to read and write a simple message in any one language?" The respondent is taken at his word, and no test of achievement is given. Perhaps a more informative definition might involve functional literacy, which is generally assumed to have been reached after completion of four years of schooling. Since, however, data are available regarding self-statements of literacy but not of functional literacy, we shall study the former.

One man's perception of his ability does not always coincide with another's. A story is told by an American reporter of his conversation with a citizen of one of the new nations of Africa. The reporter was asked, "Why do you Americans always write that large numbers of the citizens of this country are illiterate?" The journalist's reply was "Can you and your friends all read and write?" To which the African replied, "We certainly can, we just have never learned how." To him, the implication was that being illiterate was somehow shameful and reflected upon his inherent abilities rather than upon the opportunities he had had for formal schooling.

7.3 WORLD LITERACY

7.3.1 Aspatial Aspects

Rapid changes in literacy rates are occurring all over the world. In nations with high literacy rates, the number of years of school completed is continually rising. In countries with very low literacy rates, increasing emphasis on compulsory

LITERACY TRENDS IN THE WESTERN HEMISPHERE

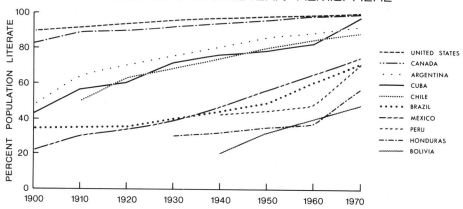

------	UNITED STATES
-·-·-	CANADA
· · ·	ARGENTINA
———	CUBA
········	CHILE
••••	BRAZIL
- - -	MEXICO
- - -	PERU
-·-·-	HONDURAS
~~	BOLIVIA

LITERACY TRENDS IN ASIA

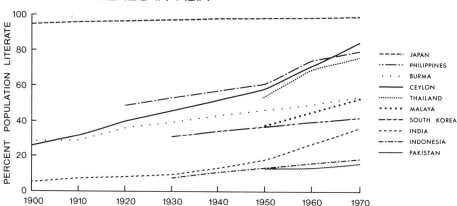

------	JAPAN
-·-·-	PHILIPPINES
· · ·	BURMA
———	CEYLON
········	THAILAND
••••	MALAYA
- - -	SOUTH KOREA
- - -	INDIA
-·-·-	INDONESIA
~~	PAKISTAN

LITERACY TRENDS IN WESTERN EUROPE

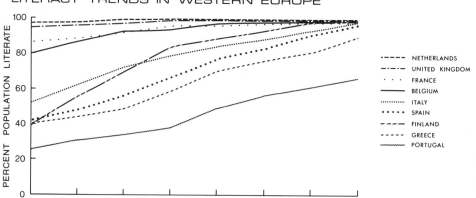

------	NETHERLANDS
-·-·-	UNITED KINGDOM
· · ·	FRANCE
———	BELGIUM
········	ITALY
••••	SPAIN
- - -	FINLAND
- - -	GREECE
~~	PORTUGAL

primary education for children and basic literacy education for adults are raising educational levels and making more people literate. These trends in many countries from 1900 to 1970 may be seen in Fig. 7.1.

Because of the continuing increase in the number of children being educated and the length of time they are remaining in school, literacy rates are higher for persons in younger age groups than for those in older age groups. Other long-standing differences in educational level exist between males and females and between urban and rural dwellers. Women have traditionally received less formal schooling than men, and this is still the case in many countries. In the United States, however, until recently the median school years completed was higher for females than for males, but this differential has now disappeared. The gap in educational achievement between urban and rural dwellers is also narrowing in many countries.

7.3.2 Spatial Aspects: The Distribution of Literacy

The extent and distribution of illiteracy throughout the world, as well as some factors related to its distribution, were investigated in a study sponsored by UNESCO (1957), *World Illiteracy at Mid-century*. It was the first such worldwide study conducted and is still the authoritative work on the topic. We shall therefore cite it extensively, even though the data are from about 1950, and supplement the findings with those based on more recent data. Since we are interested in literacy rather than illiteracy, we shall express the data in these terms; that is, the percentage of the population which is literate equals 100 minus the percentage of the population illiterate.

Data from this source for world literacy rates, by country, are presented in Table 7.1. They represent the percentage of persons 15 years of age and over who claim to be able to read and write a simple message in at least one language. Since about 1 to 2 percent of all persons are mentally incapable of learning to read or write, a literacy rate of 98 or 99 percent indicates that virtually all educable persons are literate.

The organization of data in tabular form helps us to make certain observations about the distribution of literacy. First, we can see that there are many countries with literacy rates of 90 percent and over, and many with rates of 10 percent and under. When this frequency distribution is plotted on a graph as

---

Fig. 7.1. Literacy trends for selected areas, 1900–1970. Trends plotted for all years data available and estimated for 1970. Sources: U.S. Department of Agriculture, 1965. Foreign Agricultural Economic Report No. 25, *Increasing World Food Output* by Lester R. Brown; Inter-American Development Bank, 1970, *Socio-Economic Progress in Latin America*, Social Progress Trust Fund Ninth Annual Report, 1969; and authors' estimates.

Table 7.1   Literacy rates for selected countries about 1950–1965

Country	Year	Percent literate	Country	Year	Percent literate
Portuguese Guinea	1950	0.3	Gabon	1960/61	12.4
Niger	1960	0.9	Morocco	1960	13.8
Mozambique	1950	1.5	Iraq	1957	14.5
Mali	1960/61	2.2	Congo Republic	1955/57	15.4
Guinea	1950	2.5	Tunisia	1956	15.7
Ivory Coast	1950	2.5	Sikkim	1961	15.9
Mauritania	1950	2.5	Laos	1950	17.5
Saudi Arabia	1950	2.5	Vietnam	1950	17.5
Togo	1950	2.5	Pakistan	1961	18.8
Upper Volta	1950	2.5	Algeria	1959	19.0
Afghanistan	1950	3.0	United Arab Republic	1960	19.5
Angola	1950	3.0	Botswana	1946	20.5
Central African Republic	1950	3.0	Libya	1964	21.7
Chad	1950	3.0	Malaysia	1960	22.3
Dahomey	1950	3.0	Ghana	1950	22.5
Ethiopia	1950	3.0	Kenya	1950	22.5
Somali Republic	1950	3.0	Southern Rhodesia	1950	22.5
Yemen	1950	3.0	Iran	1966	23.0
Senegal	1961	5.6	Swaziland	1956	22.8
Malawi	1945	6.5	Uganda	1959	25.1
Sierra Leone	1963	6.7	Bahrain	1959	25.3
Burundi	1950	7.5	Cape Verde Islands	1960	27.2
Cameroun	1950	7.5	India	1961	27.8
Gambia	1950	7.5	Syria	1960	29.5
Tanzania	1950	7.5	South Africa	1960	31.5
Nepal	1961	8.8	Bolivia	1950	32.1
Liberia	1962	8.9	Jordan	1961	32.4
Haiti	1950	10.5	Malagasy Republic	1953	33.5
Nigeria	1952/53	11.5	Ifni	1960	35.3
Sudan	1956	12.0	Korea	1950	37.5

Sources: UNESCO *Statistical Yearbook* 1965 and 1967 and *World Illiteracy at Mid-Century: A Statistical Study.* Used with the permission of UNESCO.

Data on which this table and Fig. 7.3 are based were compiled from the most recent and accurate data available at the time. The midpoint of a range of values is used for the 1950 data. Several of the values are estimates, and the fact that some data are given to the nearest tenth of a percent may give the impression of greater accuracy than is warranted. The data give a general indication of the ranking of countries with respect to literacy; although the absolute values should not be taken too seriously, the general pattern among countries is valid. Comparability is also limited by the fact that in some countries certain segments of the population are excluded—for example the indigenous population, Bedouins, Muslims, Europeans, or persons who are semi-literate. Although for most countries data include persons 15 years of age and over, persons as young as 10 are counted in some.

Data for countries in Africa were adjusted to conform to boundaries and nations as of 1970.

Country	Year	Percent literate	Country	Year	Percent literate
Rwanda	1950	37.5	Panama	1960	73.3
Guatemala	1964	37.9	Trinidad and Tobago	1946	73.8
Turkey	1960	38.1	Paraguay	1962	74.3
South West Africa	1960	38.4	Ryukyu Islands	1950	74.6
Cambodia	1962	41.0	Ceylon	1963	75.1
Brunei	1960	42.6	Cyprus	1960	75.9
Indonesia	1961	42.9	Guyana	1946	75.9
Honduras	1961	45.0	Yugoslavia	1961	76.5
Kuwait	1961	46.8	Cuba	1953	77.9
China	1950	47.5	Greece	1961	80.4
Lebanon	1950	47.5	Puerto Rico	1960	80.6
Singapore	1957	47.5	Jamaica	1960	81.9
El Salvador	1961	49.0	Chile	1960	83.6
Nicaragua	1963	49.6	New Caledonia	1963	83.8
Lesotho	1950	52.5	Israel	1961	84.2
Zambia	1963	53.2	Costa Rica	1963	84.3
China (Taiwan)	1956	53.9	Bahamas	1953	85.1
Malta	1948	57.6	Bulgaria	1956	85.3
Burma	1954	57.7	Western Samoa	1951	85.6
Peru	1961	60.6	British Honduras	1960	86.6
Brazil	1960	60.7	Spain	1960	86.7
Mauritius	1962	61.6	Guam	1950	87.5
Portugal	1960	61.9	Romania	1956	88.6
Fiji	1946	64.4	Uruguay	1963	90.3
Dominican Republic	1960	64.5	Barbados	1946	91.1
North Vietnam	1960	64.5	Argentina	1960	91.4
Mexico	1960	65.4	Italy	1961	91.6
Gibraltar	1951	65.5	Cook Island	1951	91.8
Venezuela	1961	65.8	French Polynesia	1962	94.5
Ecuador	1962	67.3	Poland	1960	95.3
Thailand	1960	67.7	Mongolia	1956	95.4
Macao	1960	70.4	France	1946	96.4
Republic of Korea	1960	70.6	American Samoa	1950	96.5
Hong Kong	1961	71.4	Luxembourg	1950	96.5
Albania	1955	71.5	Belgium	1947	96.7
Philippines	1960	71.9	Hungary	1963	97.4
French Guiana	1961	72.2	Czechoslovakia	1950	97.5
Netherlands Antilles	1950	72.5	Japan	1960	97.8
Surinam	1950	72.5	United States	1959	97.8
Colombia	1964	72.9	Bermuda	1960	98.0

(cont.)

Table 7.1 (cont.)

Country	Year	Percent literate	Country	Year	Percent literate
Australia	1950	98.5	New Zealand	1950	98.5
Austria	1950	98.5	Norway	1950	98.5
Canada	1950	98.5	Sweden	1950	98.5
Denmark	1950	98.5	Switzerland	1950	98.5
Finland	1950	98.5	United Kingdom	1950	98.5
Germany, East	1950	98.5	U.S.S.R.	1959	98.5
Germany, West	1950	98.5			
Iceland	1950	98.5			
Ireland	1950	98.5			
Netherlands	1950	98.5			

a histogram, it appears generally U-shaped, as in Fig. 7.2. The world mean is 56 percent. Of the 136 countries included in the table, 40 percent, representing 40 percent of the world population, have literacy rates above this mean. Also, 43 percent of the countries, accounting for 31 percent of the world population, have literacy rates of 25 percent or below.

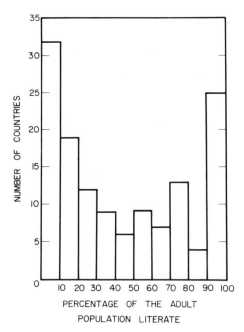

Fig. 7.2.   Frequency distribution of literacy rates by countries, as of 1965 or closest date for which data were available.

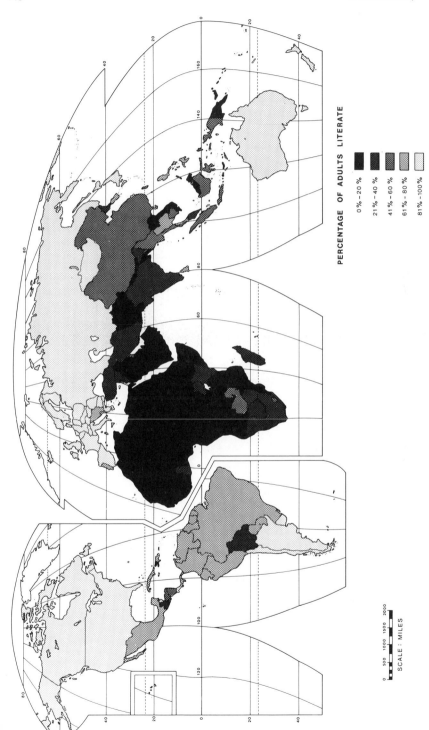

Fig. 7.3. Percentage of adults literate, as of 1965 or closest date for which data were available. Goode's base map © copyright, University of Chicago. Used by permission of the University of Chicago Press.

7.3.3 Proposed Explanations of the Spatial Distribution

Study of Table 7.1 and the World Map of Literacy, Fig. 7.3, based on more recent data for most countries, leads us to ask what conditions are present in countries with high literacy rates and absent from those with low ones. Although we recognize that we are dealing with a complex network of interrelated variables, we shall suggest only a few of them, indicate how they might be related to literacy, and test these hypothesized relationships. In the process, we may find that they are neither as simple nor as self-evident as they appear to be.

In the UNESCO study three independent variables were used and we shall suggest a few more. Some are directly related to education, whereas others relate less directly. Of the variables related directly to education, one, primary school enrollment ratios, is considered in the UNESCO study. This was selected because most of the adults literate at any given time were children who attended primary school several years earlier. In order to take this time lag into account, literacy rates about 1950 are compared with primary school enrollment ratios about 1930, twenty years earlier. Primary school enrollment ratio is the number of children enrolled in primary school per 100 children between the ages of 5 and 14 in the population. Data for 29 countries are shown in the contingency table, Table 7.2a; the number of countries in each cell is summarized in Table 7.2b. Each

Table 7.2a   Adult* literacy rate (1950) and primary school enrollment per 100 children ages 5–14 (1930 and 1935) in selected countries

Literacy rate	Primary school enrollment ratio		
	Low: 39 or less	Medium: 40–59	High: 60 or more
Low: 49% or more	Algeria, Bolivia, Dominican Republic, Egypt, El Salvador, Guatemala, Haiti, Honduras, India, Madagascar, Mozambique, Nicaragua, Turkey, Portuguese Guinea	(0)	(0)
Medium: 50–79%	Ceylon, Ecuador, Panama, Philippines, Thailand	Chile, Costa Rica, Paraguay, Puerto Rico, Yugoslavia	Greece
High: 80% or more	(0)	Argentina, Spain	Belgium, France Japan, U.S.

Adapted from: *World Illiteracy at Mid-Century: A Statistical Study.* Used with the permission of UNESCO.
*Adult refers to the population aged 15 years old and older.

Table 7.2b Summary of Table 7.2a Number of countries by primary school enrollment ratio and literacy rate

Literacy rate	Primary school enrollment ratio		
	Low: 39 or less	Medium: 40–59	High: 60 or more
Low: 49% or less	14	0	0
Medium: 50–79%	5	5	1
High: 80% or more	0	2	4

variable is arbitrarily grouped into three classes, high, medium and low. We can see that, for countries in this sample, those with low primary school enrollment ratios tend to have low literacy rates, whereas those with high primary school enrollment ratios tend to have high literacy rates; that is, there is a positive relationship between the two spatial distributions. Since this is a sample based on data availability, rather than a systematic sampling procedure, caution should be used in generalizing from it to all countries of the world. An analysis of more recent data for 148 countries, however, confirms this finding (Section 10.4.2).

Additional variables which might be considered include: school enrollment ratios at the secondary and post-secondary levels, number of schools, number or percent of teachers in the population, median school years completed, and governmental expenditures on education. We shall test only two of these hypothesized relationships.

The relationship between percent of teachers in the population and adult literacy is shown in Table 7.3. As in Table 7.2b, only the number of countries in each category is shown. We can note that the majority of countries which are high in literacy also have a high percentage of teachers in the population. This concentration is most striking in the group with less than 0.5 percent of the population teachers and literacy rates of 49 percent and below.

Operational definition of governmental expenditures on education is not as simple as it might seem. Although we could use per capita expenditures on educa-

Table 7.3 Adult literacy rate and percent of the population which are teachers

Literacy rate	Percent of the population which are teachers		Total
	Less than 0.5	0.5 or more	
Low: 49% or less	29	4	33
Medium: 50–79%	9	7	16
High: 80% or more	6	16	22
Total	44	27	71

Sources: *World Illiteracy at Mid-Century: A Statistical Study.* Used with the permission of UNESCO. "Teachers in the Countries," International Yearbook of Education. Vol. 24 (1962).

Table 7.4   Adult literacy rate and governmental expenditure on education as percentage of national income (around 1950) in selected countries

Literacy rate	Governmental expenditure on education as percentage of national income	
	Less than 2 percent	2 percent or more
Low: 49% or less	Bolivia, Brazil, Dominican Rep., El Salvador, Guatemala, Honduras, India, Malaya, Turkey	Egypt
Medium: 50–79%	Ecuador, Paraguay, Portugal, Thailand, Venezuela	British Guiana, Ceylon, Chile, Cyprus, Panama, Philippines, Puerto Rico, Yugoslavia
High: 80% or more	Argentina, France, Spain	Australia, Belgium, Canada, Denmark, Finland, Japan, Norway, Sweden, United Kingdom, United States

Adapted from: *World Illiteracy at Mid-Century: A Statistical Study.* Used with the permission of UNESCO.

tion, the difficulty is that the purchasing value of a given amount of money in any country cannot precisely be equated to dollar value. In countries where the cost of living is lower than in the United States, a smaller amount of money will purchase a year's education for a child. A variable which minimizes this problem is governmental expenditures on education as a percentage of national income. As Table 7.4 shows, a relationship between this variable and literacy rates is evident.

Since we have seen in our earlier explorations that other phenomena are related to the amount of technology in an area, it seems worthwhile to investigate the relationship between education and technology, or variables related to it. Here we are using variables associated with technology as independent variables; in Chapter 10 we shall first consider technology as a dependent variable, and then look at how the variables may be considered as parts of an interrelated system. At present, we shall leave technology as undefined, using the term as it is generally understood. We can note that countries which are considered to have more technology have higher productivity, usually measured by gross national product (GNP) or national income per capita. They are more highly urbanized and industrialized, and smaller percentages of the workers are engaged in agriculture. There is more movement of people and ideas both within the country and between that country and others. To see how all these factors relate to education, we can recognize that as the productivity of a country increases, there is an increased demand for workers with basic education and a variety of technical skills. More persons will therefore wish to attend school to attain the necessary qualifications. At the same time, education acquires a certain status value in and of itself and is perceived as being increasingly desirable. But the amount of education which can be made available will depend upon such things as the wealth of the country and the amount of money the people are willing to spend on education. Increase in the number of schools is limited also by the availability of teachers and physical facilities.

Considering first the relationship between literacy and national income, we can see from Table 7.5 that all but two of the countries with low and medium literacy rates also have less than $300 per capita national income; and all but one of the countries with high literacy rates have more than $300 per capita.*

Similarly, we can see from Table 7.6 that those countries with more than 50 percent of the economically active male population engaged in agriculture tend to have lower literacy rates than countries with less than 50 percent of the economically active male population engaged in agriculture. This variable is negatively related to industrialization: the higher the percentage of the population employed in agriculture, the less industrialized the country.

The closeness of the relationship may be visualized by constructing a scatter diagram, plotting the data for the dependent variable, literacy rate, on the

Table 7.5 Adult literacy and per capita national income, around 1950, in selected countries

Literacy Rate	Per capita national income	
	Less than $300 (U.S.)	$300 (U.S.) or more
Low: 49% or less	Bolivia, Brazil, Dominican Rep., Egypt, El Salvador, Guatemala, Haiti, Honduras, India, Malaya, Nicaragua, Turkey	
Medium: 50–79%	Ceylon, Chile, Costa Rica, Ecuador, Greece, Panama, Paraguay, Philippines, Portugal, Thailand, Yugoslavia	Puerto Rico, Venezuela
High: 80% or more	Japan	Argentina, Australia, Belgium, Canada, Denmark, Finland, France, Netherlands, New Zealand, Norway, Spain, Sweden, Switzerland, United Kingdom, United States

Adapted from: *World Illiteracy at Mid-Century: A Statistical Study.* Used with the permission of UNESCO.

---

*We have used national income instead of GNP because this is the variable used in the UNESCO study. Although there are minor technical differences between the two, for our purposes they may be used interchangeably.

Table 7.6 Relationship between adult literacy rates and percentage of active male population in agriculture, in 35 selected countries

Adult literacy around 1950	Percentage of active male population in agriculture	
	50 percent or more	less than 50 percent
Low literacy (50 percent or less)	Algeria, Bolivia, Brazil, Dominican Rep., Egypt, El Salvador, Guatemala, Haiti, India, Malaya, Nicaragua, Portuguese, Guinea, Turkey	
Medium literacy (51–80 percent)	Ceylon, Costa Rica, Ecuador, Greece, Panama, Paraguay, Philippines, Portugal, Thailand, Venezuela, Yugoslavia	British Guiana, Chile, Mauritius, Puerto Rico, Trinidad, Venezuela
High literacy (more than 80 percent)	Spain	Argentina, Belgium, France, Japan, United States

Adapted from: *World Illiteracy at Mid-Century: A Statistical Study.* Used with the permission of UNESCO..

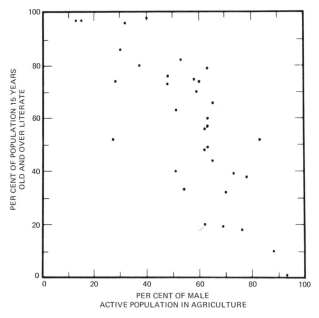

Fig. 7.4. Relationship between percent of male active population in agriculture and percent of population 15 years old and over literate. Adapted from *World Illiteracy at Mid-Century: A Statistical Study.* Used with permission of UNESCO.

Y-axis and for the independent variable, percent of the active male population employed in agriculture, on the X-axis, as an ordered pair of values for each country. If the relationship were perfect, all the points would lie on a straight line. If there were no relationship, the dots would appear to be scattered randomly. If the relationship lay somewhere between these two extremes, we would expect to find a generally elliptical pattern of dots. When the slope is positive, the relationship between the variables is direct; when it is negative, the relationship is inverse. In Fig. 7.4, we can observe such an elliptical pattern with a negative slope. We can therefore conclude that countries which have higher literacy rates tend to be those with smaller percentages of the active male population engaged in agriculture.

In earlier explorations we have also seen that circulation of people and ideas, both internal and external, tends to be greater in countries with more technology. It is reasonable to assume that newspaper circulation will also be more directly related to technology, since people who cannot read are unlikely to subscribe to newspapers. This hypothesis, too, is supported by the data portrayed in the scatter diagram, Fig. 7.5, although the relationship is far from perfect.

In summary, we have seen from this analysis that literacy is related to the six independent variables we have examined: primary school enrollment ratios, percent of population teachers, government expenditures on education as a percentage of national income, per capita national income or GNP, percent of economically active male population engaged in agriculture, and newspaper circulation. The tests have involved both visual evaluation of contigency tables and examination of scatter diagrams. We were able to determine that in each instance there was a relationship between literacy and the independent variable. In Chapter 10 we shall go on to examine the closeness of this relationship as well as of the interrelationships among all the variables, to analyze the way in which a number of variables taken together are related to technology, and to consider all the variables as comprising a system.

7.4 EDUCATIONAL LEVEL WITHIN THE UNITED STATES

7.4.1 Selection and Definition of the Dependent variable

Although it is recognized that spatial variations in educational attainment, as measured by literacy rates, exist within each of the countries used as areal units on a world scale, it is usually not practicable to be concerned with these micro-variations when studying such a large area. Within a single country, however, smaller areal units such as states, counties, cities, or census tracts may be used and greater detail revealed. Instead of taking an average value for each variable for the entire country, we can use an average value for each of the smaller

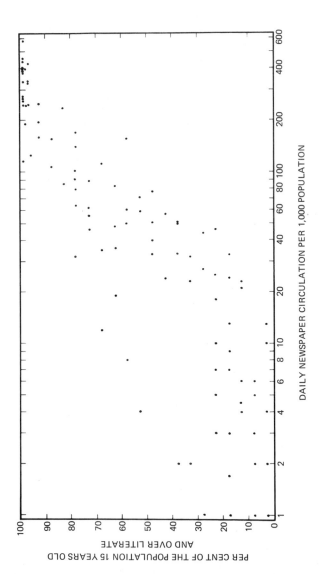

Fig. 7.5. Relationship between daily newspaper circulation per 1000 population and percent of the population 15 years old and over who are literate.

areal units selected. At the same time, we recognize that there are further variations with it.

When the scale of areal generalization is changed, it is often desirable to select a different operational definition of the dependent variable by which finer discrimination between values of this variable among the unit areas can be achieved. Over the entire world, we found that literacy rates ranged from near 0 to about 98 percent, which meant that areal variations could be measured by use of this operational difinition of educational achievement. Literacy is generally so high throughout the United States, however, that a different variable has to be selected in order to reveal area variations. Median school years completed is chosen because it meets this criterion, is suitable for the purpose of the study, and data for it are available in the *Census of Population.*

For census purposes, years of school completed is based on the last school grade completed. The median number of school years completed is defined in the census as "the value which divides the population into two equal parts—one-half having completed more schooling and one-half having completed less schooling than the median." Final tabulations are based on adults 25 years old and over, most of whom are assumed to have completed their formal education. It should be noted, however, that this assumption is becoming less accurate with the passage of time. As increasing numbers of college students continue into graduate school and as more adults return to school to earn graduate degrees or to update their skills, formal education comes to be thought of as a process continuing throughout life rather than terminating sometime during the early twenties or before.

7.4.2 Aspatial Aspects

Perhaps the most noticeable trend is that more students are remaining in school longer, as shown by the fact that, for the United States as a whole, median school years completed was 8.6 in 1940, 9.3 in 1950, 10.6 in 1960, and 12.2 in 1970. This rise is reflected by the differential in median school years completed for various age groups in the population. In 1970, median school years completed by persons aged 25 to 29 was 12.6. It remained about the same up to age 54. For the group aged 55 and over, however, the figure was 9.3. With an increase in the number of people now attending college, we might anticipate a rise in median school years completed by the group now under 25 years of age.

While some long-standing differentials in educational level are disappearing, others remain. For the population as a whole, the educational levels of men and women were almost the same in 1970: 12.2 for males and 12.1 for females. Marked differences existed, however, among the Negro population: 9.6 for males and 10.1 for females. The gap in educational achievement between urban and rural dwellers is also narrowing. The median school year completed by residents of metropolitan areas was 12.3, but higher outside central cities than within them. Values

Table 7.7 Median school years completed and selected variables, their ranks, the difference in rank between each selected variable and median school years completed by states: 1960

State	Median school years completed by the population age 25 years old and over		Per capita revenue of state and local governments		
	Years	Rank	Dollars	Rank	Difference in Rank
Utah	12.2	1	307.03	19	−18
Alaska	12.1	4.5	384.21	3	1.5
California	12.1	4.5	373.67	4	0.5
Colorado	12.1	4.5	346.64	9	− 4.5
Nevada	12.1	4.5	418.75	2	2.5
Washington	12.1	4.5	334.09	12	− 7.5
Wyoming	12.1	4.5	470.48	1	3.5
Idaho	11.8	8.5	288.52	25	−16.5
Oregon	11.8	8.5	342.36	10	− 1.5
District of Columbia	11.7	10.5	336.35	11	− 0.5
Kansas	11.7	10.5	303.17	20	− 9.5
Massachusetts	11.6	13	295.49	21	− 8
Montana	11.6	13	351.03	6	7
Nebraska	11.6	13	254.24	38	−25
Hawaii	11.3	16	350.31	8	8
Iowa	11.3	16	290.40	23	− 7
Arizona	11.3	16	308.12	18	− 2
New Mexico	11.2	18	342.43	13	5
Delaware	11.1	19	285.30	26	− 7
Connecticut	11.0	20.5	278.02	29	− 8.5
Maine	11.0	20.5	262.83	32	−11.5
Florida	10.9	23.5	269.28	31	− 7.5
New Hampshire	10.9	23.5	259.28	36	−12.5
Ohio	10.9	23.5	261.27	35	−11.5
Vermont	10.9	23.5	317.65	14	9.5
Indiana	10.8	27	248.26	39	−12
Michigan	10.8	27	288.74	24	3
Minnesota	10.8	27	312.32	15.5	11.5
New York	10.7	29	365.75	5	24
New Jersey	10.6	30	262.75	33	− 3
Illinois	10.5	31	272.83	30	1
Maryland	10.4	34	261.59	34	0

Percent of the population Negro			Percent of the population urban			Median family income in 1959 of families, 1960		
Percent	Rank	Difference in Rank	Percent	Rank	Difference in Rank	Dollars	Rank	Difference in Rank
.5	8	− 7	74.9	11	−10	5.899	17	−16
3.0	21	−16.5	37.9	49	−44.5	7.305	1	3.5
5.6	27	−22.5	86.4	4	0.5	6.726	5	− 0.5
2.3	20	−15.5	73.7	14	− 9.5	5.780	21	−16.5
4.7	25	−20.5	70.4	19	−14.5	6.736	4	0.5
1.7	14	− 9.5	68.1	20	−15.5	6.225	12	− 7.5
0.7	9.5	− 5	56.8	32	−27.5	5.877	19	−14.5
0.2	4	4.5	47.5	41	−32.5	5,259	30	−21.5
1.0	13	− 4.5	62.2	28	−19.5	5,892	18	− 9.5
53.9	51	−40.5	100.0	1	9.5	5,993	15	− 4.5
4.2	23.5	−13	61.0	30	−19.5	5,295	29	−18.5
2.2	18	− 5	83.6	6	7	6,272	10	3
0.2	4	9	50.2	40	−27	5,403	27	−14
2.1	17	− 4	54.3	36	−23	4,862	37	−24
0.8	11	5	76.5	9	7	6,366	8	8
0.9	12	4	53.0	37	−21	5,069	32	−16
3.3	22	− 6	74.5	12	4	5,568	26	−10
1.8	15	3	65.9	22	− 4	5,371	28	−10
13.6	39	−20	65.6	23	− 4	6,197	13	6
4.2	23.5	− 3	78.3	8	12.5	6,887	2	18.5
0.3	6.5	14	51.3	39	−18.5	4,873	36	−15.5
17.8	42	−18.5	73.9	13	10.5	4,722	38	−14.5
0.3	6.5	17	58.3	31	− 7.5	5,636	23	0.5
8.1	32	− 8.5	73.4	15	8.5	6,171	14	9.5
0.1	1.5	22	38.5	47	−23.5	4,890	34	−10.5
5.8	28	− 1	62.4	27	0	5,798	20	7
9.2	36	− 9	73.4	16	11	6,256	11	16
0.7	9.5	17.5	62.2	29	− 2	5,573	25	2
8.5	33.5	− 4.5	85.4	5	24	6,371	7	22
8.5	33.5	− 3.5	88.6	2	28	6,786	3	27
10.3	37	− 6	80.7	7	24	6,566	6	25
16.7	41	− 7	72.7	17	17	6,309	9	25

(cont.)

Table 7.7   (cont.)

State	Median school years completed by the population age 25 years old and over		Per capita revenue of state and local governments		
	Years	Rank	Dollars	Rank	Difference in Rank
Oklahoma	10.4	34	279.90	28	6
South Dakota	10.4	34	312.32	15.5	18.5
Texas	10.4	34	246.95	40	− 6
Wisconsin	10.4	34	282.74	27	7
Pennsylvania	10.2	37	231.46	41	− 4
Rhode Island	10.0	38	256.59	37	1
Virginia	9.9	39	204.80	46	− 7
Missouri	9.6	40	225.86	42	− 2
North Dakota	9.3	41	350.32	7	34
Alabama	9.1	42	200.00	49	− 7
Georgia	9.0	43	221.85	43	0
Arkansas	8.9	45	204.36	47	− 2
Mississippi	8.9	45	208.17	45	0
North Carolina	8.9	45	201.45	48	− 3
Louisiana	8.8	48	308.72	17	− 31
Tennessee	8.8	48	204.93	22	26
West Virginia	8.8	48	217.72	44	− 4
Kentucky	8.7	50.5	192.39	51	− 0.5
South Carolina	8.7	50.5	198.75	50	0.5

Sources: U.S. Bureau of the Census, *County and City Data Book, 1962.*
U.S. Bureau of the Census, *Statistical Abstract of the United States: 1962.*

for rural non-farm and rural farm residents were 11.8 and 10.0 years, respectively. Median school years completed by whites remains higher than that for non-whites; 12.2 years for whites and 9.6 years for non-whites. It is also lower for persons with lower incomes and for those in certain occupational groups, such as laborers.

These six variables are interrelated. For example, Blacks* tend to have lower incomes, higher unemployment rates and, when employed, to work at less skilled jobs than whites. Migration is also an important factor in changing educational levels of areas, since migrants tend to be younger and have more education than the general population. In order to discover the workings of the system, inter-

---

*Whenever a census definition is used or referred to, we adhere to the official term *Negro*; in other contexts, however, we use *Black*.

Percent of the population Negro			Percent of the population urban			Median family income in 1959 of families, 1960		
Percent	Rank	Difference in Rank	Percent	Rank	Difference in Rank	Dollars	Rank	Difference in Rank
6.6	29	5	62.9	26	8	4,620	39	− 5
0.2	4	30	39.3	46	−12	4,251	43	− 9
12.4	38	− 4	75.0	10	24	4,884	35	− 1
1.9	16	18	63.8	24	10	5,926	16	18
7.5	30	7	71.6	18	19	5,719	22	15
2.1	19	19	86.4	3	35	5,589	24	14
20.6	43	− 4	55.6	33	6	4,964	33	5
9.0	35	5	66.6	21	19	5,127	31	9
0.1	1.5	39.5	35.2	51	−10	4,530	41	0
30.0	47	− 5	54.8	35	7	3,937	48	− 6
28.5	46	− 3	55.3	34	9	4,208	44	− 1
21.8	44	1	42.8	43	2	3,184	50	− 5
42.0	50	− 5	37.7	50	− 5	2,884	51	− 6
24.5	45	0	39.5	45	0	3,956	46	− 1
32.0	48	0	63.3	25	23	4,272	42	6
16.5	40	8	52.3	38	10	3,949	47	1
4.8	26	22	38.2	48	0	4,572	40	8
7.1	31	19.5	44.5	42	8.5	4,051	45	5.5
34.8	49	1.5	41.2	44	6.5	3,821	49	1.5

relationships among these variables would have to be studied and additional variables identified before a reasonably adequate explanation of the spatial variation of educational achievements could be said to have been reached.

7.4.3 Spatial Aspects

Median school years completed, by states, for the entire United States as of 1960, is shown in Table 7.7. From examination of the histogram depicting the frequency distribution of these data, Fig. 7.6, it can be seen that it differs from that of world literacy, Fig. 7.2. The latter is definitely U-shaped, with concentrations at both ends; the former cannot be said to show any clear-cut, easily describable pattern.

    Study of the map (Fig. 7.7) of the spatial distribution reveals some regional patterns. Educational levels are lowest in the southern states, plus Kentucky and West Virginia; they are highest in the western states, including Alaska. No spatial pattern can be discerned for the remainder of the country.

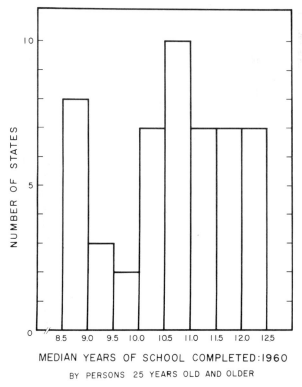

MEDIAN YEARS OF SCHOOL COMPLETED:1960

BY PERSONS 25 YEARS OLD AND OLDER

Fig. 7.6. Frequency distribution of median school years completed for the United States by states, 1960.

7.5 PROPOSED EXPLANATIONS

7.5.1 Selection of Independent Variables and Testing of Hypotheses

Some of the independent variables thought to be related to educational level were initially derived from knowledge of variables found to be related for the entire population. We have seen that for the United States as a whole, educational levels are lowest among Blacks, older persons, persons with low incomes, unskilled laborers, and persons living on farms. On a world scale, we found a relationship between the educational level of persons in an area and expenditures spent on education for which various measures are available. Since a large proportion of state and local tax revenues is used for this purpose, we shall use it.

The next step is to test these hypothesized relationships for the selected areal units—in this case, individual states—to determine whether they are valid for this level of areal generalization as well as for the entire country. If not, reasons should be sought for the lack of relationships. This analysis may then lead to new insights which will contribute to revision of the hypotheses and formulation of new ones.

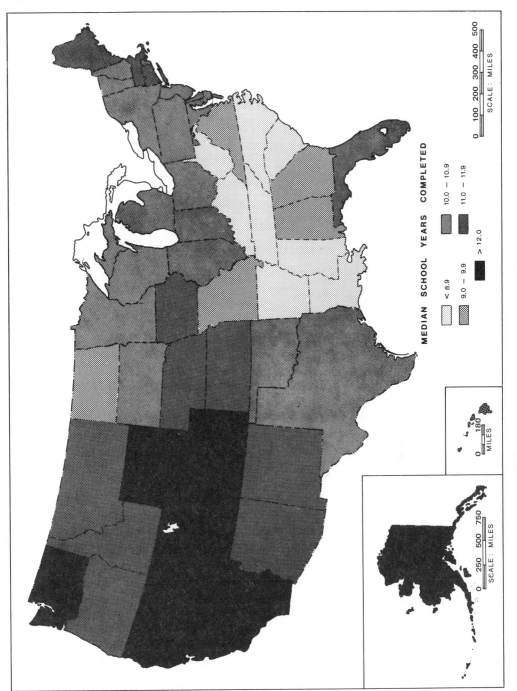

Fig. 7.7   Median school years completed, 1960.

Values for median school years completed and each of the selected independent variables are shown in Table 7.7. States are listed by the rank order of the dependent variable; value and rank are also shown for each independent variable.

Figure 7.8 illustrates graphically the relationship between the values of each independent variable and those of the dependent variable. By studying the table and the scatter diagrams together, it can be seen that the variable which appears to be most closely related to median school years completed is per capita state and local tax revenue. The relationship to median family income is also close, indicating that educational level is higher in those areas with higher median family incomes. This relationship might be different if smaller areal units such as a single metropolitan area were used, since the educational level of people in the inner city tends to be lower than that of people in the surrounding suburbs.

As can be observed from Fig. 7.8, the percent of population Negro is inversely related to median school years completed. Twenty percent or more of the population is Negro in seven of the ten states in which educational level is lowest. Although West Virginia and Kentucky are also in this lowest group, less than 10 percent of their populations are Negro. In contrast, Washington, D.C., which has the highest percentage of the population Negro in the entire country also has one of the highest literacy rates. In the seventeen other areas with educational levels of 11.2 and above, less than 6 percent of the population is Negro.

There appears to be relatively little relationship between educational level and percent of the population classified as urban.

Relationships between the variables may also be determined more objectively as well as quantitatively by using descriptive statistics. In Table 7.7 we have shown the rank of each observation for each variable, together with the differences in rank between that of each independent variable and the dependent variable. This difference indicates how closely the two distributions correspond. If the areal association were perfect, which would not be expected, the rank would be the same for all variables for every observation. A small difference in rank indicates close correspondence, a large difference little correspondence. A coefficient of rank correlation can be computed for each pair of variables, using these differences, to show how close this correspondence is. As shown in the figure, the coefficient of rank correlation (r_s) between median school years completed and total state and local tax revenue is highest: 0.70. For median family income it is 0.64; for percent of the population Negro, -0.54; and for percent of the population living in urban areas, 0.34. These figures confirm the conclusions drawn from inspection of the table and scatter diagrams.

We could use other statistical measures, such as the Pearson product-moment coefficient of correlation, r. In addition, we might want to know how much of the variation in the dependent variable all the independent variables together explain; this would require a multivariate technique such as multiple correlation analysis. These techniques will be explained in Chapter 8.

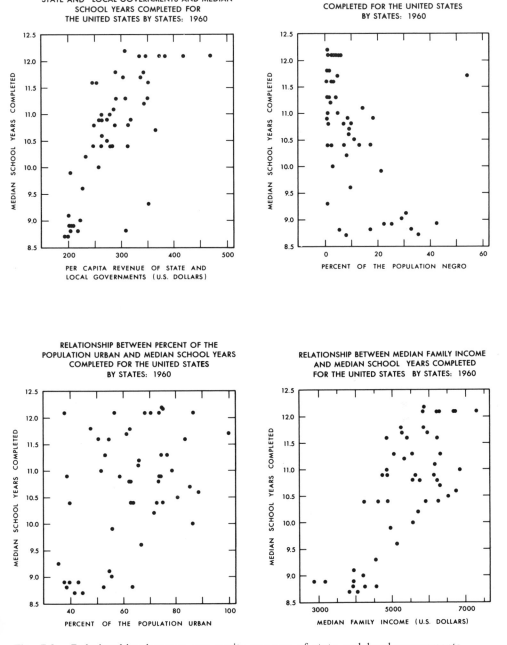

Fig. 7.8. Relationships between per capita revenue of state and local governments, percent of the population Negro, percent of the population urban, and median family income and median school years completed for the United States by states, 1960.

7.5.2 Possible Relevance of the Observed Relationships to Theory

Having partially explained the spatial distribution of educational level by finding factors which are areally associated with it, we would like to know how and why these factors are related. When an anticipated relationship is not found, some possibilities are: (1) The operational definition used may not be an adequate measure of the concept; (2) data for one or more variables may be inaccurate, so that even though relationships exist between them, they are not revealed; (3) the measure does not discriminate sufficiently for the range of values represented in the study area; (4) an unsuitable areal unit may have been used; and (5) there may in fact be no relationship. Each hypothesis tested above is evaluated in this manner, and suggestions made as to why it was or was not supported by the data. This analysis leads to the suggestion of new or revised hypothesis for further study; that is, asking the next question.

We found that the two variables which appeared to be most closely related to median school year completed were per capita state and local tax revenues and median family income. The interrelationship between these two might be expected to be high, since people with higher incomes pay more taxes in all forms: property, sales, income, and others. Either or both of these variables might be considered to be an index of general wealth of the people in an area, which we found to be related to literacy on a world scale, as measured by gross national product per capita.

The relationship between percentage of Negroes in the population and median school years completed may be ascribed to several factors. Negroes have traditionally been barred from more skilled, higher-paid jobs requiring a high level of educational attainment. In the South, as well as in some areas in the North, educational systems tend to discriminate against Negro students, so that they drop out of school earlier. Other social factors also operate to augment this dropout rate. Economically, since the majority of Negroes have lower incomes, we might expect the percent of Negroes in the population to be related to median family income.

The lack of relationship between percent of population urban and educational level is more difficult to account for. It might be ascribed to use of an inadequate measure of urbanization. The census definition of urban may no longer be adequate for today's patterns of living in the United States. Many people within standard metropolitan statistical areas live in unincorporated areas around cities, but work within them. Perhaps the percent of the employed labor force in agriculture would be a more adequate measure of urban versus rural orientation of people in an area. It is probable that, in addition to the foregoing possibilities, the educational distinction between rural and urban dwellers is rapidly disappearing. With the almost universal advent of consolidated high schools and school bus transportation, a large percentage of farm youths attend and complete high school. As agriculture becomes increasingly mechanized and industrialized, the demand for unskilled agricultural labor also decreases. We might find that the differential between the educational levels of rural and urban dwellers tends to decrease as the level of technology rises, since a distinction was found on a world scale but not for the United States.

Since we would like to develop laws about the relationships between phenomena which hold for different levels of areal analysis and so provide the basis for the development of theories, it is desirable to compare the findings of this brief study at the two levels. We found that, both on a world scale and within the United States, educational level tends to be related to the general wealth of people in an area. The rural-urban differential seems to be relevant on a world scale but not within the United States. Other factors are less closely related.

7.6 THE USE OF SCALE

Although the word *scale* is used in many different ways, its meaning generally involves ordering observations in some way. One familiar use is the scale of a map, for which there is a precise mathematical interpretation. For example, 1 inch on the map may represent some larger distance on the earth's surface, such as 1 mile, or the scale may be expressed in a ratio such as 1:63,360, where one unit on the map represents 63,360 of the same units on the earth's surface. On a map scale the size of this ratio defines the size of scale; that is, on a small-scale map a large area is represented, since the ratio is a small fraction; on a large-scale map a smaller area is shown, since the ratio is a larger fraction.

We are using the term scale throughout these explorations, however, in a broader and less specific sense. As in section 6.6.1, scale is usually expressed relatively rather than absolutely. We can say, therefore, that one scale is finer than another; scales can be ranked, although precise values can not be assigned. Used in this way, the concept of scale has two components: the size of the universe or area studied and the relative size of the areal units used to study it. The areal units are, of course, subdivisions of the universe and therefore always smaller than it is.

It is helpful to distinguish between observational units and areal units. *Observational units* are those on which data collection is based. Many different ones may be used: Individuals, families or households, dwelling units, parks, schools, or parcels of land are but a few. *Areal units* may include, for example, city blocks, acres, square miles or kilometers, census tracts, cities, counties, states or provinces, countries, and continents. Sometimes observational units and areal units coincide, although often they do not. We might, for example, study the number of cities having a city manager form of government, or states with unicameral legislatures. In these examples the areal unit is the smallest for which the phenomenon can be observed. Table 7.8 gives examples of scales.

When areal units and observational units do not coincide, data obtained for all observational units are generalized for each areal unit. Three ways of doing this are: (1) Some average quantitative value of the phenomenon for all observa-

Table 7.8 Examples of scales in rank order

Universe	Areal units	Fineness of the category
World	Continents	Grosser
	Countries	
Continent	Countries	
	States, departments, or provinces	↑
Country	States, departments, or provinces	
	Counties, prefectures, cantons, or municipios	
State, province, or department	Counties, prefectures, cantons, or municipios	
County, prefecture, canton, or municipio	Townships, sq mi, sq km, hectares, or acres	↓
Metropolitan area or city	Census tracts, precincts, wards, city blocks, or households	Finer

tional units may be used as the value for the entire area; for example, energy consumption per capita, or median school years completed. (2) The predominant class of a given phenomenon (food eaten or religious denomination, for example) may be taken as representative of the entire areal unit. (3) When measures of distance between the areal units are used, some point within the area is usually used as a single reference point for the entire area, from which distances to other localities are measured.

We study a phenomenon at a particular point in time or over a specified time period. In some circumstances there is temporal as well as areal generalization, with the value at a given time used for the entire time period. When phenomena are mapped, both temporal and areal generalizations may be employed. It is obvious that the greatest possible variability is shown when each observational unit is mapped, and the larger the area over which observations are averaged, the less the variations within it are taken into account. Similarly, there are less detail and locational specificity on a map of a large area, such as the world, than of a relatively small one, such as a city block.

For some of the phenomena we have already explored—literacy, for example —countries have been the areal units over which observations were averaged; for others—languages, food, religion—areal units have been delineated with respect to the dominant element or elements in a given area, without regard for political boundaries. In mapping these two types of distributions, a choropleth map was used for the first type (Fig. 7.3) and isopleth maps for the second (Figs. 3.1, 5.1 and 6.1).

Three implications related to the use of different scales are of particular interest in these explorations. (1) As we have found, different operational definitions of dependent variables are often needed for studying the same general phenomenon at different scales. A variable reflecting gross differences is often adequate for consideration of the entire world, where the range of variation is large, but inadequate within smaller areas, where there is less variation. For example, we used literacy as an operational definition of educational level over the entire world. Shifting scale, we found that for the United States median school years completed had greater variability, and was therefore more useful. (2) Because of the generally greater homogeneity as well as the smaller number of observational units within a smaller area as opposed to larger ones, smaller variations in quality or quantity can be investigated when using smaller scales. For example, in studying the distribution of religions over the entire world the major religious groupings such as Christianity or Buddhism were used; within the United States, however, we used subdivisions of these major groupings; and within a single county, the location of individual church buildings. (3) Finally, as is noted in many of the explorations, generalizations found to apply at one scale do not necessarily apply at others. Hopefully, if phenomena are studied over a number of areas and at several different scales, some findings may emerge which appear to be more widely applicable.

7.7 EDUCATIONAL LEVEL OF SMALLER STUDY AREAS

In studying the same phenomenon over different-sized areas, using different areal units, we can attempt to determine the extent to which hypotheses which are supported at one level of areal generalization also apply at other levels. In this chapter we have seen that some generalizations on the world scale also seem to be applicable for the United States, even when different operational definitions of the phenomena under study are used. For example, on a world level literacy rates were closely related to national wealth as measured by gross national product per capita; in the United States median school years completed was closely related to wealth in an area as measured by both median family income and total state and local tax revenues.

7.7.1 Rhode Island

We shall use the state of Rhode Island as a sample study area in which to test some of the hypotheses which have already been examined, using smaller areal units—in this case cities and New England towns, as identified by Goldstein and Mayer (1963). Median school years completed will be used as the operational definition of educational level, as was done for the United States. We can use two of the independent variables used in our investigations of both the world and the United States: general wealth, as measured by median family income, and degree of industrialization, as measured by percent of the population classified as rural farm. The percent Negro, used in our study of the United States, is too small and shows

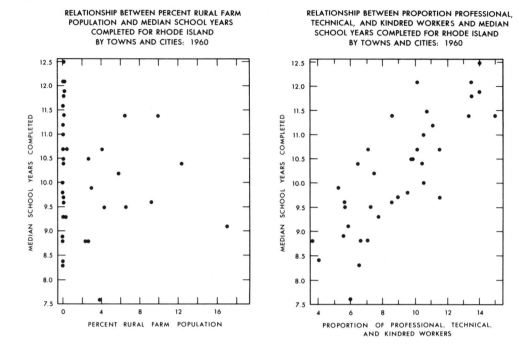

RELATIONSHIP BETWEEN PERCENT RURAL FARM
POPULATION AND MEDIAN SCHOOL YEARS
COMPLETED FOR RHODE ISLAND
BY TOWNS AND CITIES: 1960

RELATIONSHIP BETWEEN PROPORTION PROFESSIONAL,
TECHNICAL, AND KINDRED WORKERS AND MEDIAN
SCHOOL YEARS COMPLETED FOR RHODE ISLAND
BY TOWNS AND CITIES: 1960

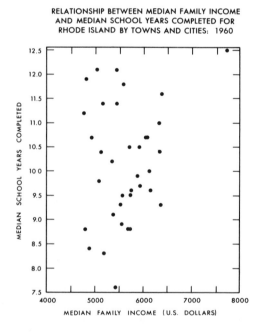

RELATIONSHIP BETWEEN MEDIAN FAMILY INCOME
AND MEDIAN SCHOOL YEARS COMPLETED FOR
RHODE ISLAND BY TOWNS AND CITIES: 1960

Fig. 7.9. Relationships between percent rural farm population; proportion professional, technical, and kindred workers; and median family income and median school years completed for Rhode Island by towns and cities, 1960.

too little variation to be useful here. We shall also try an additional variable, the percent of employed males in the census classification of professional, technical, and kindred workers. Since these occupations usually require a relatively high level of educational attainment, we would expect to find some relationship to median school years completed.

The relationship of each of these variables to the dependent variable is shown in the scatter diagrams, Fig. 7.9. There is almost no relationship between educational level and either median family income ($r_s = 0.102$) or percent of the population classified as rural farm ($r_s = 0.042$). Only for the percent of employed males classified as professional, technical, and kindred workers do we find a close relationship ($r_s = 0.800$).

This brief investigation can merely serve to indicate that hypotheses supported at one level of areal generalization or scale are not necessarily valid at other levels. It is, therefore, important to be cautious in generalizing from findings at one scale to others, that is, in applying what we have found to be valid on a world level to a single country, or state, or city. Our findings illustrate the need for testing hypotheses even though they appear to be trivial or self-evident, using a variety of areas and areal units. Hypotheses often fail to be confirmed by the empirical evidence, however plausible they may at first appear.

7.7.2 The Netherlands

An informal test of one of the above hypotheses for another small area, the Netherlands, gives conflicting results and emphasizes the needs for further study. A report based on the 13th General Census of Population of the Netherlands, 1960, suggests the existence of a close relationship between urbanization and educational level. The dependent variable used is "the percentage of the total economically active population having completed, in the field of general education, more than primary school." The areal unit is the economic-geographic region identified in the Census, of which there are 129 in the country.

Conclusions reported were based on visual comparison of the map of the dependent variable (Fig. 7.10) with knowledge of the degree of urbanization of the country. It is noted that percentages of 15 or more occur mainly in regions with high degrees of urbanization or in industrial areas, and percentages lower than 10 are found primarily in rural areas. Since visual comparison has been shown to be unreliable, we would be more confident if the findings were based on some objective test.

We find, then, the hypothesis of a relationship between urbanization and educational level holds for the world and for the Netherlands, but not for the United States as a whole or for the State of Rhode Island. A next step in understanding why this is so might be to identify other factors within the areas studied which might help to account for the discrepancy. It would also be necessary to study more areas before final conclusions could be drawn.

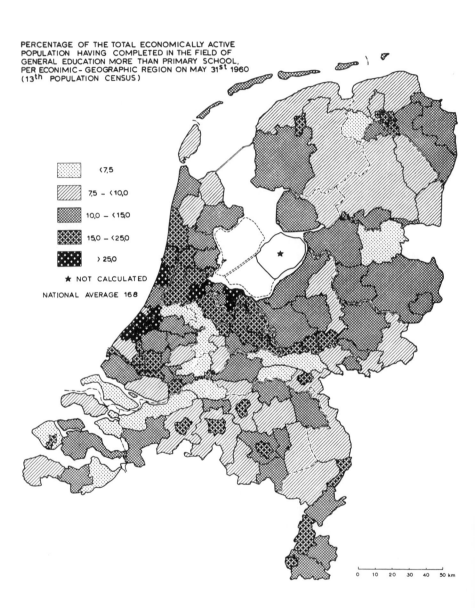

PERCENTAGE OF THE TOTAL ECONOMICALLY ACTIVE
POPULATION HAVING COMPLETED IN THE FIELD OF
GENERAL EDUCATION MORE THAN PRIMARY SCHOOL,
PER ECONIMIC - GEOGRAPHIC REGION ON MAY 31st 1960
(13th POPULATION CENSUS)

〈7,5

7,5 - 〈10,0

10,0 - 〈15,0

15,0 - 〈25,0

〉 25,0

★ NOT CALCULATED

NATIONAL AVERAGE 16.8

0   10   20   30   40   50 km

Fig. 7.10.   Percentage of the total economically active population of the Netherlands having completed in the field of general education more than primary school, per economic-geographic region on May 31st 1960 (13th population census). Source: Netherlands Central Bureau of Statistics and Government Physical Planning Service, 1964. Reprinted by permission.

7.8 SUMMARY AND CONCLUSION

In the study of education and literacy we have followed the pattern of earlier chapters in describing and analyzing the spatial variations in a few of the many variables related to education and literacy. We have examined these variations over different study areas, using different areal units. Since few, if any, studies of these topics have been made within the framework established here, our aim was primarily to suggest ways in which such studies might be carried out, and to explore a few of the possible explanatory variables which may be relevant.

These exploratory investigations have pointed out that relationships found on one level of areal generalization or scale and for one universe or study area, such individual countries of the world, are not necessarily valid at another level of areal generalization for another universe, such as individual states within the United States. We might look next, therefore, for conditions which differ between the two study areas, and attempt to specify conditions under which each set of findings might be expected to hold. The next step of an investigation would involve testing the revised hypotheses for selected areas which would fulfill the conditions established for those hypotheses.

Such studies are cross-sectional, in that they test hypotheses about relationships among the variables at given points in time. Ultimately, we would like to discover the processes by which spatial changes in the variables and their interrelationships take place; that is, to develop process laws. Carrying out a series of studies of the same variables at different time periods, which is called comparative statics, would be one step in their development. These laws could also be stated more precisely if we could discover how closely certain variables are related and how much change in one or more independent variable is associated with change in a particular dependent variable.

When we can explain a variable, we can also predict the amount and direction of change in it as the independent variables change. Although we have achieved only a limited and fragmentary explanation of the variables studied here, even this limited knowledge helps us to make rough predictions about these dependent variables. If we know, for example, the amount of technology in a given area, we can predict the approximate literacy rate with a fair degree of accuracy.

In this exploration we have concentrated upon the attempt to explain the dependent variables selected for study. We have been concerned very little with illiteracy as a social problem; for example, with the importance of and need for raising literacy rates in developing areas throughout the world and with means for accomplishing this goal. If, however, studies such as those outlined here were continued in the directions suggested above, it is probable that some of the findings would prove helpful in attacking illiteracy as a social issue. Conversely, in the process of raising literacy rates, new ideas might well arise which would be applicable to further basic research. This mutual relationship between basic and applied research has often been helpful in other disciplines, to the advantage of each.

REVIEW YOUR UNDERSTANDING OF THESE CONCEPTS

literacy   interrelationships among variables
educational level   coefficient of rank correlation
school enrollment   scale of areal generalization
functional literacy   observational unit
histogram   areal unit
contingency table

SUGGESTED ACTIVITIES

1. Select one dependent variable from the list of educational variables given in Section 7.2.1. Determine its spatial variation for any one area of your choice: a given city, county, state, or nation. Construct a map of the distribution of this variable and attempt to account for the observed spatial variation.

2. Select one of the independent variables shown in this chapter to be related to the educational level of the population. Collect and analyze data to ascertain the validity of the relationships for one of the following: (1) a different level of areal generalization, or scale; (2) a different area, or universe, or (3) a different time period.

3. It has been claimed that a relationship exists among education, unemployment, and income. Attempt to verify this relationship for any of the cities for which data are given by (a) mapping the data for all three variables, and comparing their spatial distributions and/or (b) plotting the data on scatter diagrams. Data may be obtained from U.S. Department of Labor publications. One which identifies neighborhoods in 36 of the larger cities in the nation where there are concentrations of disadvantaged youth is *Income, Education, and Unemployment in Neighborhoods* listed in the bibliography.

4. In the chapter, four independent variables were discussed as being related to median school years completed in the United States, by states. Although it was suggested that these variables might be interrelated, this possibility was not investigated. Using the data presented in Table 7.7, construct a scatter diagram, plotting per capita state and local tax revenue against median family income. Evaluate this diagram in terms of the closeness of the relationship between these variables, and explain your findings.

5. If one knows the relationships between variables existing at a given time, and the trend in one or more of them, it is often possible to project estimates for the other variable in the future. Assuming that the general conditions of the system remain the same, determine what changes in the spatial distribution of any of the educational variables used here as dependent variables will occur during the next ten years.

6. Refer to the original data and the corresponding scatter diagrams which indicate the relationship between median school years completed and any one of the independent variables within the United States. Determine which observations are deviant cases, i.e., do not fit the general pattern. Consider why this might be so, and formulate one or more revised hypotheses which might provide a more inclusive and adequate generalization.

7. Suggest some areas for further research which might be carried out and which would explain more fully the spatial variations in educational level at a particular scale.

REFERENCES

Goldstein, Sidney and Kurt B. Mayer (1963), *The People of Rhode Island: 1960*, State Planning Section Publication No. 8. Providence: Planning Division, Rhode Island Development Council.

Netherlands Central Bureau of Statistics and Government Physical Planning Service (1964), "Percentage of the total economically active population having completed in the field of general education more than primary school, per economic-geographic region on May 31st, 1960 (13th Population Census)," part of "The Netherlands in maps," *Tijdschrift voor Economische en Sociale Geografie* **55**, 256–257.

UNESCO (1957), *World Illiteracy at Mid-Century: A Statistical Study*, Monograph on Fundamental Education No. 11. Paris: UNESCO.

U.S. Bureau of the Census (1964), *U.S. Census of Population: 1960*, Vol. 1, Characteristics of the Population, Part 1, U.S. Summary. Washington, D.C.: U.S. Government Printing Office.

Additional Readings

Anderson, C. Arnold and Mary Jean Bowman, eds. (1965), *Education and Economic Development*. Chicago: Aldine.

Bogue, Donald J. (1959), *The Population of the United States*. Chicago: The Free Press.

Carey, George W., Lenore Macomber, and Michael Greenberg (1968), "Educational and demographic factors in the urban geography of Washington, D.C.," *The Geographical Review* **58**, 515–537.

Cipolla, Carlo M. (1969), *Literacy and Development in the West*. Baltimore, Penguin Books.

Coleman, James S. (1966), *Equality of Educational Opportunity*. Washington, D.C.: U.S. Department of Health, Education and Welfare, Office of Education.

Correa, H. (1962), *The Economics of Human Resources*. The Hague: Pasmans.

Dominion Bureau of Statistics (1968), *Educational Attainment in Canada: Some Regional and Social Aspects*, by M. D. Lagace, Special Labour Force Studies No. 7. Ottawa: Dominion Bureau of Statistics.

Jeffries, Sir Charles (1967), *Illiteracy: A World Problem.* New York: Frederic A. Praëger.

Robinson, Edward A. G. and John E. Vaizey, eds. (1966), *The Economics of Education.* New York: St. Martin's Press.

UNESCO (1953), *Progress of Literacy in Various Countries*, Monograph on Fundamental Education No. 7. Paris: UNESCO.

UNESCO (1955), *World Survey of Education*, triennial. Paris: UNESCO.

UNESCO (1963), *Higher Education in the United States*, by Harold A. Haswell, Educational Studies and Documents, No. 47. Paris: UNESCO.

UNESCO (1963), *Statistical Yearbook.* Paris: UNESCO.

UNESCO (1964), *Economic and Social Aspects of Educational Planning.* Paris: UNESCO.

United Nations Department of Economic and Social Affairs (1963), "Education," Ch. VI in *1963 Report on the World Social Situation.* New York: United Nations, pp. 62–73.

United Nations Department of Economic and Social Affairs (1963), "Housing, building and urban and regional planning," Ch. V in *1963 Report on the World Social Situation.* New York: United Nations, pp. 51–61.

United Nations Secretariat, Bureau of Social Affairs, in co-operation with International Labor Office, Food and Agriculture Organization, UNESCO, and World Health Organization (1957), "Education," Ch. V in *Report on the World Social Situation Including Studies of Urbanization in Underdeveloped Areas.* New York: United Nations, pp. 64–90.

U.S. Bureau of the Census (1967), *Education of the American Population*, by John K. Folger and Charles B. Nam, A 1960 Census Monograph. Washington, D.C.: U.S. Government Printing Office.

U.S. Department of Health, Education, and Welfare (1968), *State Data and State Rankings in Health, Education and Welfare*, Part 2 of Health, Education, and Welfare Trends. Washington, D.C.: U.S. Government Printing Office.

U.S. Department of Labor, Bureau of Labor Statistics (1963), *Income, Education, and Unemployment in Neighborhoods.* Washington, D.C.: U.S. Department of Labor.

Vaizey, John (1967), *Education in the Modern World.* New York: McGraw-Hill.

CHAPTER 8
LAND USE

8.1 INTRODUCTION

Land use is a topic which includes many basic elements in human geography. A thorough study of the pattern of land use in an area reveals much about the way in which the inhabitants live: their ways of earning a living, the prevailing level of technology, their dietary habits, and, to some extent, their values. In studying the pattern of agricultural land use, for example, we might be concerned first with finding out what crops are grown, so as to have some idea of what the people eat. We might then ask about the size of the fields, which provides a clue as to the level of technology, since large fields are needed for efficient use of machinery. Next, we would want to know what portion of the land is used for transportation and what kinds of transportation are available, since limited transportation is associated with low levels of technology.

As we examined cities and the pattern of urban land use, we could discover what the major industries were and where they were located. We would want to know where the people live, work, and shop, and how they move from one activity to another. We could find out how much space is provided for recreation, and whether schools were accessible to all children in the city. By the time we had answered these and other questions about land use patterns, we could begin to discern certain recurring patterns from place to place and make generalizations about them.

Land use has been studied by economists, planners, agricultural experts, geographers, and others in different ways. Some researchers have been concerned primarily with case studies of particular areas, describing their unique features. Others have concentrated upon applied or practical studies of land use. Agricultural geographers, for example, have analyzed existing patterns of land use in order to determine how the existing land could be used more efficiently. In developing countries, plans have been devised for improving crop yield by reform of the traditional patterns of land ownership and control, which is an essential prerequisite to other improvements.

In cities, urban geographers and planners have examined the ways in which land use is determined by economic competition. They have then attempted to devise an overall pattern or plan for orderly development which takes into account not only the greatest profit to be made by individual landowners and speculators, but also the general welfare, so that all inhabitants might live and work in decent surroundings.

In our exploration of land use, we shall begin by examining the distribution of various land uses over the entire world. In doing so, we shall deal with problems of defining and classifying the phenomenon and difficulties arising from the lack of comparable data on a world scale. Changing scales, we shall next examine briefly land use surveys in a few countries and, in more detail, the actual pattern of land use in the United States and Canada. These data will assist us in our search for possible explanations of why different land uses are located where they are.

Changing scale again, we shall examine patterns of urban land use. Rather than concentrating on one or two cities, however, we shall try to determine what is known about patterns of urban land use, and analyze some of the studies which have been made and theories which have been developed to explain these observations.

Because land use has also been studied by many geographers concerned with explaining their observations and using them to predict patterns of land use, we shall examine some of the models of land use which they have devised. Consideration of these models will provide a basis for our methodological study of models in general: what they are, why geographers are interested in them, and how they may be used.

8.1.1 Definition of Land Use

Although the term *land use* may appear to require little definition, it has been used in so many different ways that specification of the meaning to be used is desirable. Many different types of information have been included in different land use studies. Clawson (1965) lists nine concepts about land which are often of interest:

1. location,
2. activity on the land,
3. natural qualities of the land, including its surface and subsurface characteristics and its vegetative cover,
4. improvements to and on land,
5. intensity of land use, or amount of activity per unit area,
6. land tenure,
7. land prices,
8. interrelations in use between different tracts of land, or accessibility, and
9. interrelations between activities on the land and other economic and social activities.

Although activity on the land is the major criterion for classifying land use, many classification schemes include characteristics from one or more of the other concepts. For example, a parcel of land may be classed as "high-density residential," or "low-value residential," thus including concepts of intensity of use, land prices, and improvements. Ideally, a single-criterion classification scheme would not run this risk of confusion. We shall attempt here, therefore, to concentrate upon activity of the land, the criterion suggested by Clawson, as our definition of the dependent variable, and to avoid mixing in other factors, using them instead as independent variables which help to explain the distribution of activity on the land.

8.2 WORLD LAND USE

Since land use is a qualitative rather than a quantitative variable, we are faced with problems of classification encountered previously. Although the topic of land use has been studied by geographers and others for many years, as yet no generally accepted classification scheme exists. Criteria on which classification is based are seldom explicit, and often do not meet the requirements of being mutually exclusive and exhaustive. Classification schemes have been established for different purposes, such as prediction of world food supplies, regional planning of water supplies and overall land use, and zoning within cities. As we have already learned, it would be difficult to set up a single scheme which would adequately serve such diverse purposes.

8.2.1 Whittlesey's Study of Agricultural Land Use

A well-known classification and mapping of agricultural land use over the entire world was made by Whittlesey (1936) (Fig. 8.1). He showed only predominant land use over large areas, not microvariations within areas. In setting up the scheme, he considered both physical and cultural conditions of the environment. He recognized three elements of the physical environment which set the limits within which given crops can be grown and help to determine areas of optimal production: climate, soil, and slope. Cultural elements which influence what crops actually will be grown, and in what proportions, are: density of population, amount of technology, and tradition. Taking all these into account, he established five criteria as bases for classification, which he called "functioning forms which appear to dominate every type of agriculture." They are: (1) the crop and livestock association; (2) the methods used to grow the crops and produce the stock; (3) the intensity of application to the land of labor, capital, and organization, and the outturn of product which results; (4) the disposal of products for consumption, that is, whether used for subsistence on the farm or sold off for cash or other goods; and (5) the ensemble of structures used to house and facilitate the farming operations.

Although we shall use his map to look at agricultural land use on a world scale, we shall modify his classification scheme. In order to simplify and reorganize it, we shall use two criteria, which are included in, but not the same as, Whittlesey's

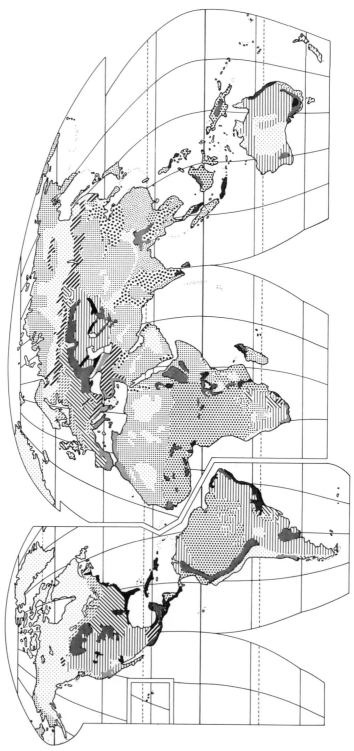

SUBSISTENCE METHODS – LOW TECHNOLOGY

A. EXTENSIVE LAND USE

Nomadic Herding

Shifting Cultivation

Rudimental Sedentary Agriculture

B. INTENSIVE LAND USE

Intensive Subsistence Tillage
Rice Dominant

Intensive Subsistence Tillage
Rice Not Dominant

NON-AGRICULTURE AREAS

CASH CROPPING – HIGH TECHNOLOGY

A. EXTENSIVE LAND USE

Livestock Ranching

Commercial Grain Farming

B. INTENSIVE LAND USE

Plantation Agriculture

Subsistence Crop and Livestock

Commercial Livestock and Crop

Commercial Dairy Farming

Specialized Horticulture

Mediterranean Agriculture

Fig. 8.1. Major agricultural regions of the World. Adapted from Whittlesey, 1939. Reproduced by permission from the *Annals* of the Association of American Geographers, Volume 56 (1966). Goode's base map © copyright, University of Chicago. Used by permission of the University of Chicago Press.

second, third, and fourth. These are: (1) approximate amount of technology used in farming, and (2) intensity of land use.

These two criteria are independent. The first includes Whittlesey's fourth, the disposal of products. When less technology is used to obtain food, more man-hours of labor are required to feed one individual. Consequently, such methods are usually associated with subsistence farming, in which each family is able to raise enough food only to feed itself, rather than with the growing of cash crops. Conversely, farming methods which use more technology make possible higher yields, so that a greater proportion of the crop can be sold for cash.

For simplicity the classes of agricultural land use identified by Whittlesey can be divided into two groups: low and high technology. Extensive and intensive land uses are found in both. The spatial distributions of most of the classes are shown in Fig. 8.1, adapted from Whittlesey's (1936) map of world agricultural regions, with a few changes. Hunting and gathering is not shown on the map and Mediterranean agriculture is not found in the classes below, since it is based on area rather than type of land use.

As modified, the classes of world agricultural land uses include:

I.   Subsistence Methods—Low Technology

A. Extensive land use

1. Hunting and gathering

This method of obtaining food is not discussed by Whittlesey, as it is not properly a type of agriculture. Since it is, however, a way in which land is used by man to procure food, it is included here. As the name suggests, persons dependent upon this means of obtaining food hunt animals and gather plants and animals which are readily available in the natural environment.

Location: This type of land use is found today in scattered, remote areas of the earth's surface: in Southeast Asia, the interiors of Malaya, Borneo, Papua, the aboriginal reserves in central and northern Australia, on the fringes of the Arctic Ocean, in North America and in remote portions of South America and Africa. Even where it predominates, it is not usually the only land use in an area.

2. Nomadic herding

This is referred to by Whittlesey as "the aboriginal form of the livestock business." Nomadic herdsmen are dependent upon the natural environment for forage and water. Sheep, cattle, goats, camels, and reindeer are among the animals which support their owners, providing meat, blood, milk, skin, bones, and horns to fulfill the basic needs of food, shelter, and clothing.

Location: Found primarily in areas that are too dry or too cold to produce crops. Scattered areas of this land use extend from northwestern Africa eastward through Arabia, Turkey, and southeastern European Russia, all the way to the Gobi country of Mongolia and western China. There are also some areas in the high latitudes of Russia, the Scandinavian countries, and North America, as well as southwestern Africa and Malagasay.

3. Low-intensity subsistence—shifting cultivation

This type of land use is named from the fact that plots are tilled for brief periods of time, usually one to three years, until fertility is depleted. A new area is then cleared for cultivation. Fire is usually used to clear the ground, and only simple tools such as digging sticks are used. Few crops are grown, and the yield is low. Animal protein is obtained by hunting and fishing.

Location: Widespread in tropical rain forests and on their borders, but also found in other areas.

4. Rudimental sedentary agriculture

This type may be thought of as a transition between shifting cultivation and cash cropping. It requires a high labor input because of crude tools and the lack of fertilizer to replenish soil fertility. Cash crops grown include tree crops such as cacao, rubber, oil and coconut palms, and annuals, especially peanuts and cotton. The farmer also grows crops to feed himself and his family, since return from the cash crops is insufficient to buy food for their needs.

Location: Areas of rudimental sedentary agriculture are usually found within regions of shifting cultivation where, for one reason or another, inhabitants remain permanently; for example, in mountain valleys with more favorable soil and climate than the surrounding areas. Some of these areas are located in portions of Malagasy, Borneo, the Philippines, and the interiors of New Guinea, New Hebrides, and tropical Pacific islands. They are also found in Burma and Laos, some valleys of the Andes, the coast of Mexico, Haiti, and scattered portions of tropical Africa.

B. Intensive land use

5. Intensive subsistence tillage

Intensive subsistence tillage supports the densest rural population found over large areas. Two crops a year may be grown in hot climates if the water supply is adequate. In much of this area, paddy rice is the predominant crop. In drier parts of it, however, other grains such as wheat, millet, or barley are grown. Oil seeds and cotton are grown on non-irrigated fields; trees such as mulberry, tea, and pepper on the hillsides. Tools used include plows, either steel or wooden, pulled by animals such as water buffaloes (carabaos). Primitive irrigation pumps, worked by man or animal power, are used. Because the labor input is high, per capita production is low even though output per acre is high.

Location: Intensive subsistence tillage is found primarily in the humid regions of south and east Asia and adjacent islands including parts of southern China, eastern India and Pakistan and southwest coastal India and in the valleys of the Tigris, Euphrates, and Nile Rivers.

II. Cash Cropping—High Technology

A. Extensive land use

6. Livestock ranching

Livestock ranching is a large-scale business operation. Usually sheep or cattle are the major livestock raised. Several acres are required to feed one animal; labor input is relatively low, and cash return per animal is high. The small, scattered human population associated with a single operation lives in or near the main ranch house, where facilities for care of the animals are also concentrated.

Location: Primarily in drier areas of North and South America, Australia, New Zealand, and South Africa, where there is enough water for grass but not enough to grow crops. Major areas are found in western Canada and the United States, into central Mexico; from Tierra del Fuego through Argentina and Brazil to the Atlantic, and the interior lowland of Venezuela; Africa south of central Angola and Rhodesia and northeast of the Caspian Sea in Asia. Transition from nomadic herding to ranching is occurring in Russian Turkestan, the Atlas Mountains, and the eastern and southern African highlands such as in Rhodesia.

7. Commercial grain farming

About half the total acreage of commercial grain farming is in wheat. Because farmers depend on natural rainfall, there are yearly variations in crop yields. The input of machinery is high, but labor input is low. Although the return per acre is low, return to the individual farmer is usually high, except in years of drought.

Location: The dry-land borders of crop farming regions which are too cold or too dry to support more intensive crop farming. Primarily in eastern Europe as far as western Siberia; the Prairie Provinces of Canada; Kansas, Montana, and the Dakotas in the United States; Argentina; and southwestern Australia.

B. Intensive land use

8. Plantation agriculture

One major cash crop, such as bananas, coffee, sisal, rubber, tea, or sugar cane, is usually grown. Machinery and capital come from European or American sources, and field labor may be either local or imported. Since many plantations were formerly owned by colonial settlers, they are on the decrease in many parts of the world where former colonies have become independent nations. The land is being broken up into smaller holdings, which are either sold to farmers or rented on a share-crop basis.

Location: The total amount of land in plantations represents only a small proportion of the world's land area. Plantation agriculture is widely dispersed in enclaves in mid-latitude regions of Africa, southeast Asia, and South and Central America.

9. Subsistence crop and livestock farming

   Grains grown may include rye, oats, barley, and maize, but usually not wheat. Although the land used may be suitable for cash farming, various factors, such as the existence of serfdom and the division of plots into small fields, prevent more profitable use. Many of these areas are in the process of transition to cash farming. In Poland and Russia this change is due primarily to collectivization, which makes possible larger fields and increased use of machinery.

   Location: Parts of northern and eastern Europe and the Mexican highlands.

10. Commercial livestock and crop—mixed farming

    Crops are grown both for sale and as feed for animals. Wheat, maize, and oats are the principal grains, but rye and barley are also grown. Root crops include potatoes, turnips, and sugar beets. Hogs, cattle, and poultry are raised. This type of land use involves a high input of labor, machinery and fertilizer. The return per acre is high, especially in parts of Europe where hand labor is less expensive than in the United States.

    Location: Humid middle latitudes of all continents.

11. Commercial dairy farming

    Forage crops grown include grasses and legumes, especially clover. Root crops, oats, and barley are also grown for feed. Increasingly, food is brought to cattle instead of their being allowed to graze in fenced-in pastures. Dairy farming involves high inputs of capital in the form of buildings, stock, and machinery for milking, and for holding and transporting milk. There is a high ratio of stock to land. The return per animal and per capita are high. With increasing automation, capital costs are rising relative to labor costs.

    Location: In areas where summers are too cool and moist for either maize or wheat and hay is the best crop, as well as in the vicinity of large cities which provide markets for fluid milk. This market orientation is decreasing, particularly in the United States. Concentrations of dairy farms are found throughout western Europe, the United States, Canada, in southeastern Australia, and on the North Island of New Zealand.

12. Specialized horticulture

This involves intensive use of land especially suited to particular crops or stock, such as fruits, vegetables, sugar beets, tobacco, cotton, and specialized poultry and egg production. Return per acre is high, although labor and capital inputs are also relatively high.

Location: In small areas scattered throughout the middle latitudes. Market gardens or truck farms are found near large cities, along the Channel Coast and Brittany and in the Rhone Valley of France, in the Netherlands, along the Algerian and Tunisian coasts of northern Africa, the plains of Morocco, and in the oases of the Sahara. In North America, along the Atlantic coastal plain, Mississippi Valley and Gulf Coast, the Rio Grande Valley, the lower Colorado basin, and interior and coastal valleys of California.

8.2.2 Other Studies of Agricultural Land Use

Reports of the Food and Agricultural Organization of the United Nations (FAO, 1958 to date) on world land use are concerned with present and potential food production, taking into account the total amount of land in each category, by country. Land use is not mapped. It was estimated that in 1969 the world's land surface was used as shown in Table 8.1.

Although this classification scheme is suitable for the purpose of estimating the world's land resources and their potential for food production, the categories

Table 8.1   Percent of world land in different uses

1. Agricultural area		33%
a. arable land and land under permanent crops	11%	
b. permanent meadow and pasture	22%	
2. Forested land		30%
3. Other		37%
a. unused, but potentially productive under present technology	1–33%	
b. built-up areas, wasteland, and other	4–36%	
		100%

Source: FAO 1970. From the *Production Yearbook*. Reproduced by permission from the Food and Agriculture Organization of the United Nations.

are not fine enough for many other purposes. Over one-third of the total land surface ends up in the miscellaneous category of *build-up areas*, *wasteland*, and *other*, which contains much of the land involved in regional and urban planning, and which is used for such diverse purposes as industries, housing, transportation, and recreation.

An earlier attempt at surveying the entire world was initiated in 1949 by the International Geographical Union and UNESCO. The aim was to provide a skeleton classification scheme which could be used by governmental bodies and other organizations in surveys and mapping. Nine major land use categories were distinguished: (1) settlements and associated non-agricultural lands, (2) horticulture, (3) trees and other perennial crops, including plantations and orchards, (4) cropland, (5) improved permanent pasture, managed or enclosed, (6) unimproved grazing land, (7) woodlands, (8) swamps and marshes, and (9) unproductive land. Although the emphasis is on agricultural uses, this scheme is more generally useful than that of the FAO, since settlements are separated from agriculturally unproductive land.

In this World Land Use Survey all maps were to be drawn on a scale of 1:1,000,000, the same as that of the international map of the world. To date, however, mapping has been completed only in widely scattered areas such as Cyprus, Hong Kong, Uboma, and Zanzibar (now part of Tanzania). Since the survey was started, techniques of obtaining data have changed from on-the-ground surveys, supplemented by aerial photographs, to collection of data, including photographs and other information, by satellite. Photographs taken from satellites show large portions of the earth's surface in minute detail, so that increased accuracy results, together with savings of time and money.

8.2.3 Non-agricultural Land Uses

Forested lands, which formerly occupied much more of the world's surface than they do now, are today found primarily in areas where, for reasons of climate, accessibility, or soil fertility, they still constitute the use of the land which yields the highest monetary return. Needle-leaf evergreen forests remain in the high latitudes of North and South America and Europe, as well as in the mountains of many countries where the terrain is too steep for cultivation. Although some deciduous and mixed forests remain in middle latitudes, they represent only a small portion of the original forested area. The other large area of forest is in the humid tropics which have not, as yet, been found profitable to farm commercially, except for scattered areas of plantation agriculture.

Although settlements and urbanized areas occupy a relatively small percentage of the world's land area, this small portion is where a large percentage of the population lives and earns its livelihood. Within the overall classification of urban land use are to be found a multiplicity of uses: residential, industrial, commercial, educational, governmental, and recreational—to mention but a few. On a world scale it is impossible to show these classifications within urbanized areas. We shall group all these together under urban land use, which will be studied in detail in Section 8.5 of this chapter.

Although many urbanized areas are too small to show up on a world map, four major areas of the world are highly urbanized. In some, one city merges into the next, resulting in what has come to be termed a megalopolis. In eastern North America, large urbanized areas extend from Lake Michigan to the Atlantic coast, and from just north of the Great Lakes in Canada to the Ohio River. There are also several more isolated urbanized areas, including Los Angeles-San Diego, Fort Worth-Dallas, Mexico City, and Vancouver, British Columbia. In South America, large cities are fewer and more scattered. Another concentration of urbanized areas occurs in Europe, from England east into the western part of Poland, north as far as southern Sweden, and south as far as northern Switzerland and Vienna. Again, a few large cities are located outside this concentration. Within the U.S.S.R., Leningrad and Moscow are the largest cities, but urbanized areas are found associated with manufacturing as far east as the Urals and in the Donetz Basin. Japan, one of the most heavily populated areas of the world, has many large urban areas, as do eastern China and Hong Kong. Although there are large cities throughout the rest of Asia, they are not concentrated.

8.3 LAND USES WITHIN COUNTRIES

8.3.1 The British Land Use Survey

One of the few detailed land use surveys of an entire country was carried out in Britain between 1931 and 1939. Land use was surveyed by 22,000 student volunteers, who entered their observations on maps at a scale of six inches to the mile. Each volunteer mapped six square miles of his home territory, a rectangle 2×3 miles. After these maps were assembled and checked for accuracy, they were reduced to a scale of one inch per mile and combined. The final publication of the maps of England and Wales required 140 sheets.

Each individual parcel of land was shown. Eight categories of land use were distinguished: (1) arable, (2) permanent grass and meadow land, (3) rough grazings, commons heath and moor, (4) forest and woods, (5) orchards, (6) nurseries, (7) houses with gardens, and (8) land agriculturally unproductive. Following the completion of this survey it was possible for the first time to obtain an estimate of the amount of urban or built-up land area by adding together the amounts of land in the last two categories; houses with gardens and land agriculturally unproductive. The total amount of agricultural land was determined by adding together the five agricultural uses—that is, all except the last two and forest and woods.

As can easily be seen, carrying out an on-the-spot land use survey such as this for an even larger area would be extremely expensive in terms of manpower, time, and actual cost, even if volunteers were again available. Enumerator errors can also result in inaccuracy. Moreover, newer techniques of mapping, using aerial and satellite photography, are useful aids. Land use studies must still rely on supplementary field observation, since it is not always possible to tell from photographs the use to which a given plot of land is being put.

8.3.2 Land Use in the United States and Canada

As in other countries, information about land use in the United States has come largely from studies by various governmental agencies. The Department of Agriculture, the Bureau of Land Management, and the Bureau of the Census have over a period of years collected data regarding the amount of land devoted to different agricultural uses. Most detailed land use surveys have been made of smaller areas, with some particular purpose in mind. Such diverse governmental and quasi-governmental units as national forests, soil conservation districts, counties, cities, and metropolitan areas have studied land uses within their boundaries in order to assess present use and plan for the future. It is not possible, however to combine the results of these surveys into a country-wide land use map. Among other things, only a small part of the total area has been mapped, and no consistent classification scheme has been used.

The best land use map available for the United States as a whole is based on studies by the U.S. Department of Agriculture (USDA), and published in *Land Use and Its Patterns in the United States* (Marschner, 1959). This map was compiled from data obtained by aerial photography, supplemented by information from a variety of sources including topographic and geologic surveys, census reports, type-of-farming studies, state publications, and county agents. Because it covers a large area on a single sheet, at a scale of 1:5,000,000 (approximately 80 miles to one inch), land use is of necessity generalized, with the major land use for each area being shown. It is not, therefore, comparable with the British survey, which showed the use of individual land parcels with no generalization.

Twelve classes were identified: (1) cropland and pasture land, (2) cropland, woodland, and grazing land, (3) irrigated land, (4) forest and woodland grazed, (5) forest and woodland mostly ungrazed, (6) subhumid grassland and semiarid grazing land, (7) open woodland grazed, (8) desert shrubland grazed, (9) desert mostly ungrazed, (10) alpine meadows and mountain peaks above timber line, (11) swamp, and (12) marshland. The location of metropolitan cities, a term which is undefined, is also shown.

The amount and proportion of land in broader classes as reported by the USDA are given in Table 8.2. Looking at the map of land use in the United States and Canada (Fig. 8.2), we can generalize about the location of some of these broader classes of land use. For purposes of this discussion, we shall be concerned with cropland, grazing land, forest and woodland, and urban and industrial areas.

Table 8.2   Major uses of land in the United States, 1964.

Land use	Million acres		Percent	
Cropland:				
Cropland used for crops	335		14.8	
Soil-improvement crops and idle	52		2.3	
Cropland used only for pasture	57		2.5	
Total cropland*		444		19.6
Grassland pasture and range†		640		28.2
Farmsteads, farm roads		9		.4
Forest land:				
Used for pasture and range	225		9.9	
Not grazed‡	507		22.4	
		732		32.3
Urban and other built-up areas§		55		2.4
Primarily for recreation parks and wildlife¶		76		3.4
Public installations and facilities‖		33		1.5
Miscellaneous other land**		277		12.2
Total land area		2,266		100.0

*Cropland harvested, crop failure, and cultivated summer fallow.
†Excludes cropland used only for pasture.
‡Excludes 28 million acres of reserved forest land and 2 million acres of unreserved forest land duplicated mainly in parks and other special use areas. It was not feasible to eliminate some overlap that exists because of multiple use.
§Urban and town areas; highway, road, and railroad rights-of-way; and airports.
¶National and state parks and related recreational areas, National and State wildlife refuges, and National Forest wilderness and primitive areas.
‖National defense (including military reservations and other land administered by Department of Defense), Federal flood control, Federal industrial (AEC land, etc.), and State institutional areas.
**Marshes, open swamps, bare rock areas, deserts, tundra, and other land generally having low value for agricultural purposes.

Source: Frey, Krause, and Dickason, 1968. United States Department of Agriculture.

Most of the cropland in the United States lies in the eastern two-thirds of the country. It is scattered throughout the eastern states, more concentrated in formerly wooded areas of western Ohio, Indiana, Wisconsin, and Kentucky, and most concentrated on the plains of the Central States. West of the Rockies, cropland devoted to dry grain farming is located mainly on the Columbia River plateau; most of the remaining cropland is in scattered irrigating valleys and basins. In Canada cropland devoted to general farming is located primarily in Prince Edward Island, southern Quebec and Ontario, and some valleys of British Columbia. Grain farming is found in southern Manitoba, Saskatchewan, and Alberta.

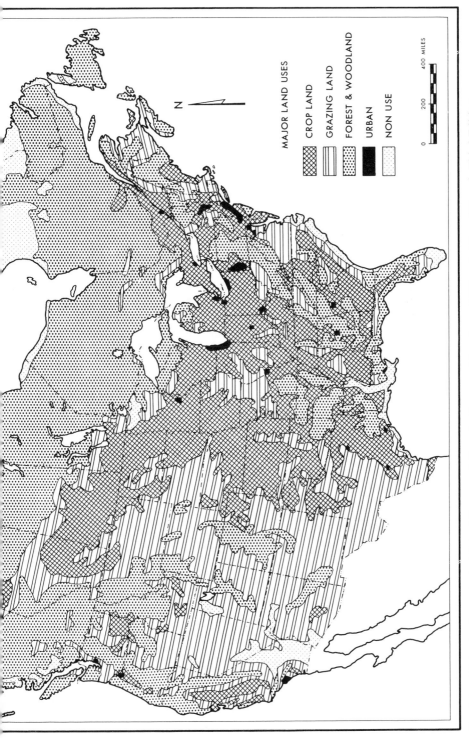

Fig. 8.2. Major land uses in the United States and Canada. Sources: Marschner, 1959 and *Atlas of Canada* Third Edition. Reprinted by permission.

MAJOR LAND USES

CROP LAND

GRAZING LAND

FOREST & WOODLAND

URBAN

NON USE

N

0   200   400 MILES

185

Most of the grazing land in the United States is located in the drier western portion of the country. Pastures are generally differentiated from grazing land by the carrying capacity of the land, which is related primarily to the amount of water available. Whereas less than an acre of humid or irrigated pasture is required to support a cow for a month, in arid areas where desert shrub is the prevailing vegetation type as much as 18 acres may be needed. In Canada, pastures and grazing land are found in New Brunswick, Nova Scotia, southern Quebec, Alberta, and the Cariboo region of British Columbia.

Forests and woodland are located throughout much of the United States, usually on land too rocky or hilly, or with too poor soil to be arable: in the Appalachian Highlands, extending northward into Maine, scattered throughout the South, in northern Wisconsin, Michigan, Minnesota, and in mountainous areas of the West, and along the Pacific Coast, as far south as San Francisco. Much of this land is in national forests, especially in the West. A large part of Canada is covered by forest: from the boundary of the farming and grazing areas on the south to the tundra on the north, and in mountainous areas of the West.

Urban industrial areas are concentrated along the east coast from Boston to Washington, D.C., and less concentrated around the Great Lakes. Other more isolated areas are found throughout the country, especially in the South and Gulf States, and along the Pacific Coast, especially from Los Angeles to San Diego. Urban areas in Canada are concentrated in south-eastern Ontario and the Montreal region.

8.3.3 Toward a Uniform System of Land Use Classification

Several different land use classifications have been presented and discussed. Looking only at the last two, those used in the surveys in Great Britain and the United States, it can be seen that reconciling them would be difficult, if not impossible. That is, if one were given the two maps, it would be difficult to develop a single classification scheme which could be used in drawing both maps. Part of the problem arises from the existence in the United States of certain types of land not present in Britain, especially alpine meadows and mountain peaks, the various types of subhumid and arid grazing land, and desert. This would not create as much difficulty, however, as reconciling the two British classifications *arable* and *permanent grass and meadow* with the two American ones, *cropland and pasture land* and *cropland, woodland and grazing land*. Orchards and nurseries are not shown at all on the United States map, in part because of the difference in scale.

The same sorts of discrepancies exist in land use data within the United States. In order to bring some uniformity into land use surveys, two United States governmental agencies have cooperated in developing a uniform classification system. The Urban Renewal Administration and the Bureau of Public Roads, in cooperation with other federal agencies, have published a *Standard Land Use Coding Manual* (URA-BPR, 1965). Its authors believe that the classification scheme suggested in the *Manual* is inclusive enough to be used for almost any type of land use survey, rural or urban, and flexible enough to adjust to the amount of detail required in the particular project. In developing the *Manual*, the attempt was made to devise a scheme based on a single criterion: human activities taking place on the land. It was hoped that such a classification would prove more accurate and easier to handle than some of the other schemes in use, which include within some of the classes factors other than activity on the land. Land values, intensity of use, and natural vegetation are among the many factors which have been included in classification schemes.

In practice, it is recommended that enumerators, the individuals doing the original data collection, whether by on-the-spot surveys or from other sources such as aerial photographs, report according to the smallest identifiable unit of land—preferably a single home or parcel of land within a farm devoted to a particular use. They simply list the location and use of the parcel, according to instructions in the *Manual*. These data are later coded and transferred to data processing cards.

As in the Standard Industrial Classification (SIC), which has been used since 1957, four digits are used in coding data. The first digit identifies the major type of activity. The nine one-digit activities identified are: (1) residential, (2) and (3) manufacturing, (4) transportation, (5) trade, (6) services, (7) cultural, entertainment, and recreational, (8) resource production and extraction, and (9) undeveloped land and water areas. Each succeeding digit provides greater detail, so that the entire four-digit number is highly specific. For example, a cattle ranch would be 8161, which is broken down as follows: One digit, 8: resource production and extraction. Two digits, 81: agriculture. Three digits, 816: farms and ranches (livestock other than dairy). Four digits, 8161: farms and ranches (predominantly cattle).

Supplementary codes are provided for auxiliary activities such as a supermarket parking lot. It is anticipated that some unforeseen problems may arise as this classification scheme is put into actual use. It is, nevertheless, a helpful and important first step in the standardization of land use data within the country.

8.4 PROPOSED EXPLANATIONS OF THE LOCATION OF NON-URBAN LAND USES

Looking at a land use map of the world or of a country, we ask why the different land uses are located where they are. Why, for example, are some areas used primarily for nomadic herding or forestry rather than cropland or wasteland? How can we explain the location of urban-industrial areas? Although we are far from knowing the answers to these questions, we can identify some of the factors which determine land use. We shall be concerned here mainly with non-urban land uses, and consider urban land uses in the following section.

As with other phenomena we have studied, the first generalization to be made is that no simple or complete explanation is presently available. We must, therefore, attempt to identify some of the variables which have been found to be related to land use, and which can be used in formulating hypotheses. We shall consider first agricultural land uses and then non-agricultural ones. A little thought reveals that many kinds of factors must be taken into account: physical, economic, political, and social. These categories are not clearly defined; we use them for convenience only, recognizing that they overlap, and that factors in all categories may be interrelated.

8.4.1 Physical Factors

A number of physical factors influence both the natural vegetation of an area and the particular crops which can be grown there. Climatic factors such as the amount of available soil mosture, range of temperatures over the year, amount of sunshine during the growing season, types of soils, and nature of the terrain are influential. Natural hazards caused by extreme variations in these phenomena, such as floods, storms, unseasonal frosts, or droughts, also affect crop yields. Some of these phenomena can be modified by man, whereas others have not yet come under his control. Soil moisture depends upon natural precipitation and the moisture-retention ability of the soil, subsoil, and substrate, but can be modified by irrigation, drainage, contour plowing, and treatment of the soil to retard run-off. Modifications of temperature and sunshine are usually profitable only for very high-value crops, such as flowers and some vegetables which may be grown out of season in greenhouses. Land with steep terrain may be terraced to yield small plots such as the ricefields of Japan or the vineyards along the Rhine in Germany. The range of a crop may be extended by the development of new hybrids which will grow under different conditions than will existing varieties.

These factors, however, are physical limits to the potentialities of a given area; they do not in themselves determine how the land will be used. Human beings make these decisions, either explicitly or implicitly.

8.4.2 Economic Factors

Economic factors help to explain much of the variation in land use, especially in a society with more technology and with a money exchange economy. They can be thought of as determining the economic limits within which a given land use will be profitable. Within the United States, for example, we would hypothesize that a farmer would grow whatever crops would bring him the greatest total profit from all his land. In their analyses, economists and economic geographers simplify the real-life conditions by making certain assumptions which either ignore or hold constant a number of factors so that they can consider only the effects of the economic ones. They assume a state of pure competition in the market for the produce, perfect knowledge on the part of the farmer as to his costs and anticipated selling price of the goods produced, and rational behavior in an economic sense—that is, that the individual farmer will make all decisions in such a way as to maximize his profit in the long run. It is obvious that many of these assumptions are only partially valid.

In making decisions as to what to plant on his land, our hypothetical economic man-farmer would first determine the anticipated gross return from the sale of any of the possible crops he could plant in terms of dollars per unit of land. This determination assumes, of course, that there is a market for his goods and that transportation from farm to market is available. From the anticipated gross return he would have to subtract all his expenses: rent of the land (or its equivalent if he owns it), labor, seeds, fertilizer, pest control, machinery, transportation to market, and all other costs involved in growing the crop and delivering it to the point of sale. If all the costs were known precisely, he would then have a relatively simple arithmetic problem to solve in deciding the anticipated profit from each crop per unit of land. This problem could be set up in the form of an equation, with all variables expressed in terms of dollars per unit of land:

Profit = Selling price − Inputs (land, labor, seeds, fertilizer,
pest control, machinery, transportation . . .)

In practice, of course, the determination is not so simple. He does not know what price his crop will bring at the end of the season, but must rely on estimates. He does not know the actual size of his crop, which may be influenced during the growing season by lack of rainfall, a severe hailstorm, or an unexpected frost before harvesting. He may need to rotate crops. He may already have certain parcels of land committed to particular uses, such as orchards or vineyards, which cannot be changed yearly, but only as revenues increase or decrease over several years. He makes decisions not for his land as a single unit, but as individual parcels, so that he may have to decide how much land to devote to wheat, potatoes, or pasture.

Combining the physical and economic analyses, we can consider land use competition. That is, when two or more different crops can be grown in an area, as is often the case, what factors determine which of these crops will be raised, and in what relative quantities? We have suggested that there are certain physical limits for any crop; there are also areas which are optimal for the raising of that crop, in which maximum yields will be produced. It is known, for example, that wheat can be grown with a higher yield per acre on land now devoted to corn than on land where wheat is being grown. On the other hand, growing corn and raising livestock yields a higher return on land located in the so-called Corn Belt. Wheat tends, therefore, to be grown in areas where it yields a relatively high return on land unsuitable for the higher-profit corn. Although the attempt is made to grow each crop in areas which will produce the optimum yield, or economic rent, when two crops are competing for the same land, the one with the highest monetary yield will usually be grown in the optimum area, and the other one pushed toward its limits.

Although we have been talking about agricultural land uses, these concepts may be extended to explain competition between any land uses, such as the displacement of orchards by housing, or of residential land use by commercial uses.

8.4.3 Political Factors

We have been assuming a condition in which the individual farmer makes his own decisions in a capitalistic system with pure competition. In reality, however, this situation does not exist; decisions are made by a central planning agency which may weigh other factors, such as the need for certain products, more heavily than profit. Crop support programs, usually based on crop quotas, may also limit the amount of land which a farmer devotes to any given use. In extreme cases, wars and political unrest may so imperil the prospects of growing and harvesting a crop that the farmer may prefer or be forced not to plant at all. We cannot, therefore, fail to take into account political factors which affect, among other things, who makes decisions about land use and what criteria are used.

8.4.4 Social Factors

Many of the remaining factors can be grouped under the general heading of social variables. The most important of these in relation to land use are social organization, land tenure, and custom, all of which are poorly defined.

Social organization and land tenure systems are closely related. In a tribal society the tribe itself often retains ownership and control of the land. The right to use it may be determined in many different ways such as by yearly decision of the chief or by inheritance.

In a communistic or communally organized society, land often technically belongs to the group as a whole. Although less common today, this type of land ownership and allotment was found among certain religious groups as the Amana colonies of Iowa, and still exists in the *Kibbutzim* of Israel and among the Hutterites. Homes are designated for families to use, and the land is farmed by members of the group who are assigned to the task. In Communist countries, especially the USSR and China, farms of large landowners were seized by the government and collectivized, and small farm owners were "encouraged" to join the collectives. These were run on the scale of a large business, with major decisions being made by the country's control planning agency. It was the responsibility of the farm manager to fulfill the quota set for him. When it was found that production was less than hoped, individual families were allowed to retain the use of small plots of land for growing their own vegetables and livestock, and were allowed to sell the surplus in the markets of nearby towns and cities. This incentive boosted the total amount of food available for consumption.

The system of land tenure in effect is often closely related to the size of land farmed. In France, for example, many farmers own or work a number of small, scattered parcels. Their total holdings are small, and the problem of optimal use of the land is complicated even more by their dispersion. The use of machinery is less economical, and a high labor input is required. In countries such as India, the land is divided into such small parcels that the amount of land farmed by one family is scarcely enought to support it, even at a bare subsistence level. In another country with different methods of farming, the same amount of land might produce not only enough food for the family, but some surplus for sale.

The relationship between land use and land tenure is complicated by a further factor of the relationship between owner and farmer. If the owner does not farm the land, how is its use and control allotted, and what is the relationship between owner and tenant? In the United States, land is usually leased on a cash basis, determined either by a flat amount or by a certain percentage of the yield from the land. In other countries, however, a sharecropping system may be in effect which gives the farmer no assurance that he will be permitted to stay on the land and binds him to the owner economically. The sharecropping system has almost disappeared in the southern United States, primarily because of the rapid growth in the use of machinery in farming. At its height, however, the tenant was often forced to buy at the company store run by the owner, and was continually in debt to him for food, seeds, and other goods. At the same time, because he had no assurance that he would be permitted to remain on the land, he had little incentive to work to improve it so that he might reap the rewards in later years. The same situation exists throughout much of Latin America today, and is a barrier to increasing the output from the land, as well as to diversifying the crops grown and introducing better farming practices.

Custom is often an important variable. Agricultural development workers in widely dispersed areas such as Latin America, India, and Southeast Asia have repeatedly learned that customs are difficult to change. Even people living at a bare subsistence level tend to reject new ideas which would increase the yield of their crops. Some Indians living in the Andes, for example, keep the poorest and smallest potatoes for seed rather than attempting to improve the quantity and quality of yield by improving the strain used for planting; it is difficult to persuade them to change this pattern. In addition, many religious beliefs and practices, such as the worship and protection of cows in India, interfere with the acceptance of what might appear to outsiders to be more economically rational practices, but which conflict with prevailing value systems. Desire for conformity and fear of being seen by friends and neighbors as different are also powerful deterrents to the acceptance of innovations.

The operation of these social factors is not restricted to areas of low technology. Studies of the adoption of innovations such as hybrid seed corn in Iowa and other parts of the United States have revealed the same reluctance to accept new products or practices in spite of the economic advantages. More generally, there is a gap between what could be done and what is actually being done at any given time.

From the foregoing discussion, it can easily be seen that physical and economic variables are easier to identify and work with than political and social ones. Many of the former have been operationally defined and quantified, whereas social variables such as land tenure remain ill-defined and qualitative. In analyses of land use we tend, therefore, to hold many of these political and social variables constant—that is, to assume them to be part of the given conditions in the system we are studying without explicitly stating what they are. We might, for example, consider a universe such as the United States and Canada, the countries of the West with high technology, or cities of Southeast Asia. By specifying the universe, we would imply the conditions of the system even if they were not explicitly stated. At this point, we are not in a position to formulate hypotheses about the relationships of these political and social variables to land use in any systematic fashion except to caution, "Watch out for them. They are important, and limit the extent to which it is possible to generalize from one area to another." People involved with development and planners who undertake a project assuming that the economic laws which apply in the United States will also be pertinent in countries of Latin America or other so-called developing areas have found that *other things being equal* does not apply, since the assumption is invalid. They must instead seek to determine the values of the people with whom they are working, and to present innovations in such a way that they are acceptable.

8.4.5 Effects of Technology on Factors Affecting Land Use

Obviously, in any area none of the factors mentioned above are fixed in either quantity or quality. Changes occur over time; since the factors are interrelated, change in one often is related to changes in others. Technology is related to almost all of the variables, so that the entire set of variables, including technology, may be seen as constituting a system such that changes in one or more of the variables will be associated with changes in others.

Changes in technology, for example, help to alter the optima and limits within which crops can be grown profitably. Development of new hybrids, techniques to increase soil moisture, and new machinery all help to extend the area within which a given crop can be grown. Improvements in transportation make it economically feasible to transport a given product a longer distance, thus opening up new areas for its production.

To cite another example of the effects of technology, transportation has been shown consistently to be related to the location of all land uses, urban and non-urban. From the earliest times of which we have records, either archeological or historical, cities have been located on major transportation routes, often at the junction of two routes. The particular form of transportation varies with the time and place. In Biblical times, ships and camel caravans provided long-distance transportation. In some European cities during the Middle Ages and later, rivers and canals were important for intra-city as well as inter-city transport. Later, the building of railroads influenced settlement patterns in the United States and Canada. Currently, the location of freeways and superhighways is helping to establish patterns of land use.

The interrelationships among these variables are just beginning to be studied, and quantitative relationships between them investigated. Some of the models in Section 8.7 are attempts at studying these interrelationships and analyzing the workings of the system.

8.4.6 The Use and Misuse of Land

Since a given piece of land can generally be used for only one purpose at a time, it is obvious that an increase in any one type of land use will result in a decrease in another. Over the years that man has inhabited the earth, he has taken over increasingly greater portions of its surface for his own use. From a long-term point of view, therefore, there has been a decrease in the amount of land which exists in its natural state. In North America, for example, much of what is now the Middle West of the United States was originally covered by mixed hardwood forest. The pioneers cleared land for cultivation, using what trees they needed for building and burning the rest. Similarly, in Europe and the Near East trees were cut down either for man's use or simply to clear the land. Gradually more and more land came under cultivation or was used as pasture.

The most noteworthy change in land use in this century has been associated with an increase in the rate of urbanization throughout the world. In the United States and Canada the resulting suburban sprawl has covered areas of fertile farmland with housing tracts. In Europe and Asia much of the housing has consisted of large multi-story apartment buildings, which house more people per unit of land than do single-family dwellings. Within cities, residential areas near the central business district tend to be engulfed by commercial and other related land uses, until finally little or no residential land remains.

No matter what amount of technology a civilization has, it is necessary that people be fed and clothed if that civilization is to survive. In a hunting and gathering economy a large land area is usually needed to provide people with the essentials of life. The Great Plains were capable of supporting far fewer Indians, who were dependent on buffalo for these necessities, than it now does when the land is occupied by agriculture (or, more accurately, agribusiness) and cities which employ many people in manufacturing and service occupations.

Changes in land use pose problems for planners. For example, a large area of fertile agricultural land in the vicinity of California cities, which was until recently used for market gardens, orchards, and other intensive horticulture, is being taken over by housing tracts. If the same number of people were housed in large apartment buildings they would require a much smaller land area. But a variety of political, economic, and social factors help to determine both what has happened in the past and what the trend is likely to be in the future.

8.5 PATTERNS OF URBAN LAND USE

Having looked briefly at land use on a world scale and in a few countries, we now change scale and turn to consideration of urban land uses. We are concerned here not with the location of cities, but rather with land use within cities or urbanized areas. We are not concerned here with defining the terms *urban* and *urbanized area*, as this will be done in Section 9.2. We shall simply use them in their commonly accepted usage. We shall continue to focus on the same dependent variable: land use, defined as the activity which takes place on the land. To do so is difficult, because many studies of urban land use have been concerned primarily with social problems related to housing conditions of the lower socio-economic classes or of certain ethnic groups. In considering these studies, therefore, we should bear in mind what we are trying to explain, and abstract from the findings factors which are related to land use as we have defined it. These factors can then be organized in the same manner as those related to non-urban land uses. (Section 8.4).

If a person acquainted with several cities in the United States and Canada were to visit one unfamiliar to him, he would still have some idea of where to look for certain facilities. Presumably he would find tourist facilities such as motels, restaurants, and service stations on or near highways. Near the edge of town, he would expect to see newer housing tracts, with single-family homes predominating. In or near these tracts, a variety of stores and services would be concentrated in shopping centers with large parking lots. As he approached the city center, he would expect to see different land uses. He might travel through industrial or commercial areas, and residential areas in which homes were older, smaller and possibly less well kept. He would be likely to find a central business district with department stores, specialty shops, banks, offices, new high-rise apartments, and large hotels. Somewhere nearby he would probably find a skid row, featuring burlesque shows, taverns, pawn shops, cheap hotels, rooming houses, and storefront churches. In large cities, he would also find an automobile row of new- and used-car dealers.

These generalizations would appear to be almost self-evident to a reasonably observant person, even if he had no formal knowledge of urban land use patterns. His expectations would, however, be less well fulfilled if he were traveling on a different continent. For example, in European cities he would find that large automobile-oriented shopping centers were replaced by small shops which were scattered throughout residential neighborhoods and accessible to housewives doing their daily shopping on foot.

8.5.1 Generalized Descriptions of Urban Land Use and Growth

Scholars interested in cities have sought to describe the regularities which they observed. As with any phenomenon, they recognized that, although each city was unique and had certain special features, there was at the same time some overall pattern of urban spatial structure.

Burgess (1925, 1929) was concerned primarily with the growth of cities. As a sociologist, his major interests were housing conditions and the movement of immigrants within the city. He formalized his observations of Chicago into what is now known as the concentric zone theory of city growth. He identified five concentric zones (Fig. 8.3), each of which contained certain types of land use.

A. The inner zone is the central business district (CBD) containing the down-town retail district, offices, banks, hotels, and civic and cultural buildings. This district is surrounded by the wholesale business district, recognized but not defined as a distinct zone by Burgess.

B. The zone in transition is an older residential area which is being invaded by business and light manufacturing. Many homes in this area have been divided up into small apartments or are used as rooming houses. This area, often referred to as the slums, provides housing for recent immigrants to the city.

C. The zone of independent workingmen's homes is primarily a residential area, often inhabited by second-generation immigrants, which provides housing relatively close to the place of work.

D. The zone of better residences is composed of one- and two-family dwellings and better apartment buildings.

E. The commuters' zone is located beyond the city limits, in satellite cities or urban fringe areas, along routes of travel to the city.

It was recognized that this formulation provided only a rough approximation to the actual situation in most cities. In an attempt to bring it closer to reality, Hoyt (1939) proposed that cities were organized not simply by concentric zones, but also radially by sectors; that is, that a given land use tended to spread outward from the center of the city along axes of transportation (Fig. 8.3). Like Burgess, he was especially concerned with the location of residential areas. He noted that a particular ethnic group or social class tended to continue to migrate away from the city in the same direction in which it began, following existing transportation arteries. He hypothesized that features which attracted high socio-economic class residential use included high ground, open country, homes of community leaders, the availability of fast transportation to the city, and trading centers or other existing nuclei.

Harris and Ullman (1945) developed further some of the ideas suggested by Hoyt. They recognized that, as a city grew, it was no longer organized around a single nucleus, the CBD, but that different land uses tended to be found together,

CONCENTRIC

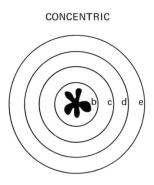

SECTOR

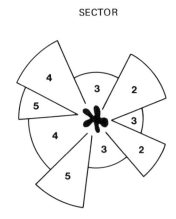

b. OLDER RESIDENTIAL INVADED BY
    BUSINESS
c. WORKING CLASS RESIDENTIAL
d. BETTER RESIDENCES
e. COMMUTER ZONE

MULTIPLE NUCLEI

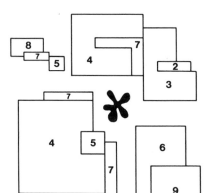

COMPOSITE

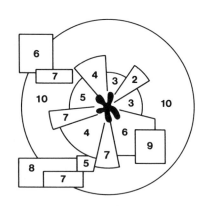

 CENTRAL BUSINESS DISTRICT
2. WHOLESALE AND LIGHT MANUFACTURING
3. LOW CLASS RESIDENTIAL
4. MEDIUM CLASS RESIDENTIAL
5. HIGH CLASS RESIDENTIAL

6. HEAVY MANUFACTURING
7. OUTLYING BUSINESS DISTRICT
8. RESIDENTIAL SUBURB
9. INDUSTRIAL SUBURB
10. COMMUTER ZONE

Fig. 8.3. Spatial structure of urban land use. Adapted from Harris and Ullman, 1945. Reproduced by permission from the authors and *The Annals* of The American Academy of Political and Social Science, Volume 242 (1945). *Composite* by author.

or organized around a number of nuclei (Fig. 8.3). They hypothesized that the rise of separate nuclei reflected the operation of four factors:

1. Certain activities require specialized facilities such as access to intra-city or extra-city transportation or large amounts of land.

2. Certain like activities tend to group together: retail stores, offices, and wholesale business.

3. Certain activities, such as industrial and residential land use, are usually not associated spatially.

4. Certain activities require land with lower cost than that available near the center of the city.

Using these four principles, they identified several major types of specialized districts, each developed around different kinds of nuclei.

1. The CBD, containing the retail shopping center, is the area most accessible from all points of the city by public transportation. Office and government buildings are located nearby, as is the financial district.

2. The wholesale and light manufacturing district is in the central city in a location accessible to extra-city transportation facilities, both rail and road.

3. The heavy industrial district is often located near the periphery of the city, where large expanses of land are available. As the city increases in size, industrial areas may become surrounded by areas of other types, and new industry locates near the new periphery.

4. Residential districts may be subdivided by social class. Usually low socio-economic class districts are located nearer the city center and in areas considered less desirable because of noise, dirt, or odors from nearby factories and railroads. The higher-class residential areas tend to be away from the city center, in more desirable areas.

5. Minor nuclei include cultural centers, parks, outlying business districts, small industrial centers, and universities.

6. As the city expands, existing suburban and satellite communities act as nuclei for the development of new higher-class residential areas.

All three theories are valid to some degree. The actual pattern in many cities is a composite of those described by Burgess, Hoyt, and Harris and Ullman (Fig. 8.3). The major pattern of concentric zones around the CBD is not a completely circular one, but may be distorted by transportation axes or the existence of other nuclei. Around the edges of the city may be found residential or industrial complexes, along with other compatible uses.

Firey (1947) was concerned that these theories did not emphasize sufficiently the importance of social values in the determination of urban land use. He formulated two general hypotheses emphasizing the importance of these values:

1. Socially rooted values influence urban land use patterns.
2. Rationally functioning (i.e. economically based) forces are part of large cultural systems, and cannot be viewed as ends in themselves.

He contended that social values, such as the desirability of a given location because of its historical or status value, were often more important than economic values alone. For example, he found that residence in Boston's North End was considered desirable by many Italians in spite of the deteriorated and undesirable housing conditions because by living there they could identify with the prevailing Italian culture. Similarly, Beacon Hill is an upper-class residential area which is near the city center.

8.5.2 Current Trends in Urban Land Use

At the time Burgess, Hoyt, and Ullman wrote, they recognized that their theories merely provided approximations to the actual patterns of cities. Because of changes in urban land use since that time, these generalized descriptions conform even less closely to the actual situation than they did previously. Anglo-American cities of the 1960's have been modified by increasing use of the automobile and the building of freeways and expressways. Because of changes in time-distance relationships made possible by these transportation developments, there has been a trend toward dispersion of many activities away from the CBD as a nucleus. Residential land, in particular, is found farther from the CBD. Although the commuting range has not changed appreciably, more people are living farther away from the city center. New retail and wholesale businesses tend to be located away from the city center, as do new industries, for which the presence of open land is a strong attractive force.

Countering this trend for certain activities to be located away from the city center is a movement of others toward the city center. As land in and around the CBD is vacated, and as buildings which have deteriorated are torn down, new office buildings, hotels and motels, and luxury apartments are being constructed on land formerly occupied by retail businesses, wholesaling, light industry, rooming houses, and other dilapidated housing.

It is obvious, therefore, that in explaining or predicting the location of land uses in a given city, it is necessary to take into account the rate at which the entire urban area is expanding. Newer cities, or older ones which have been expanding rapidly in the past two decades, might be expected to follow the newer patterns. Although the same trends could be noted in cities with relatively stable populations, change would be slower, and the differences would not be as marked.

Some attempts are now being made to check this trend toward dispersion and decentralization. City planners are recognizing that urban and suburban sprawl are undesirable. Open land, especially in and around large metropolitan areas, is becoming an increasingly scarce commodity. Planners believe that it should be used for the benefit of large numbers of people rather than restriced to those who can benefit economically from its development and exploitation. Zoning and planning are tools for imposing some sort of predetermined order on the otherwise individually determined processes of change and development.

A possible solution for the future is the development of New Towns. The original intention of planners was to develop relatively self-sufficient satellite towns away from the congested city center, and to check the trend toward dispersion of residential areas away from the center without corresponding dispersion of other activities, especially those providing employment. People could live nearer their work, in relatively self-contained communities which to some extent counteracted the growing impersonality of contemporary urban life. In practice, however, things have not worked out as planned. Often the new communities have simply become additional dormitory suburbs, most of whose residents commute into the central city for work.

New Towns can be found in scattered places of the Western World. Radburn, New Jersey was among the early ones. Reston, Virginia, near Washington D.C., has become a pleasant dormitory suburb for government workers. Irvine, California was planned with a university campus as its nucleus. Other towns built by industries or government such as Kitimat, British Columbia or Los Alamos, New Mexico to provide services and amenities in previously unsettled areas. Other such cities may be found in England, France, Czechoslovakia, the U.S.S.R. Israel, and Finland, to mention but a few.

8.5.3 Proportions of Land in Different Uses

In spite of the large number of studies which have been made of individual cities, many of the data about many aspects of urban land use have not been compiled. In order to carry out their research, Niedercorn and Hearle (1964) made such a compilation of selected aspects of urban land use, including the percentage of land area devoted to different uses. Questionnaires were sent to 63 large American cities in 1962. Forty-eight of the returns contained usable data on the proportions of land devoted to various uses. Averages for these cities are shown in Table 8.3 With few exceptions, these proportions tend to be relatively constant from city to city.

Wingo (1963) points out that as cities grow, the proportion of land devoted to each use remains relatively constant, not only for urbanized areas as a whole, but also for both central cities and surrounding suburbs. His findings agree with those of Niedercorn and Hearle. Transportation is taking up more space as 80-foot highway rights-of-way are replaced by 300-foot freeway rights-of-way. Residential density, or intensity of residential land use, decreases with distance from the city center; the same is true of the intensity of other land uses. As residential land expands on the periphery of an urbanized area, it is accompanied by

Table 8.3   Mean proportions of land devoted to various uses in 48 large American cities

Type of use	Proportion of total land	Proportion of developed land
Total Developed	.770	1.000
Residential	.296	.390
Industrial	.086	.109
Commercial	.037	.048
Road and highway	.199	.257
Other public	.153	.197
Total Undeveloped	.230	
Vacant	.207	
Underwater	.023	

Source: Niedercorn and Hearle, 1964. Reprinted by permission from *Land Economics*, Volume 40 (1964).

a spread of commercial land, also at a lower intensity than that in the CBD. Industries too, are moving away from the center of the city; and new industries are often one-story and more spread out than the older industrial buildings nearer the city center. In summary, the change appears to be in the intensity of land use rather than in the proportion of land devoted to each use.

8.5.4 Urban Land Use in Areas other than the United States and Canada

We have been referring primarily to cities in the United States and Canada, trying to discern and describe certain regularities in the distribution of various land uses. Although it would be interesting to extend this study to other areas, the findings of existing studies are often not comparable, and it is difficult to generalize from them. It may be interesting, nevertheless, to consider a few examples of land use in cities in different areas, simply to see some of the other possible patterns which exist.

Schnore (1965) cites seven studies of Latin American cities. All at one time exhibited the traditional Latin American pattern: a plaza in the center of town, surrounded by upper-class Spanish homes. The poor, primarily Indians, lived in *barrios* on the edge of the city. Now, however, the Anglo-American pattern is beginning to appear. The center is becoming a business district, the wealthier people are moving to new homes on the periphery, and those of lower socio-economic classes are filling in the vacated area near the city center.

In the older cities of Europe the pattern of land use also differs from that of Anglo-America. There is much less separation of residential and commercial land use. Small shops are found throughout residential areas, usually on the ground floor of buildings, the upper floors of which contain apartments. There are more multiple-family residences and fewer one- or two-family ones. Streets are seldom arranged in a rectangular grid pattern, especially in older areas, and they are often narrow and winding. The transition between city and surrounding countryside is more abrupt, with large new apartment houses being located at the edge of the city, immediately adjoining open country. Urban fringe areas of suburban sprawl found in Anglo-American cities are rare. As has been pointed out above, attempts are being made by planners to decentralize industrial location, so that people may live closer to their work in more nearly self-contained communities which have a mixture of land uses.

It is more difficult to generalize about land use in non-Western areas, since few of the studies which have been made are suitable for this purpose. Ginsburg (1965) has, however, noted certain general characteristics of cities in non-Western areas. Indian cities tend to be multi-nucleated, with no clearly defined CBD. Residential and commercial land uses are intermingled in almost all areas. The impact of colonialism is shown by the existence of special districts formerly occupied exclusively by foreign residents, usually European. Many Indian residential districts are segregated according to ethnic origin, language, caste, or religion, with little spatial interaction among them. The absence of adequate transportation tends to minimize movement between areas.

A study of Tokyo showed a high concentration of commercial uses at the center of the metropolis and along major rail lines. Areas of residential and industrial land are clumped in areas widely scattered over the metropolitan region. Suburbanization has taken place rapidly since World War II; suburban residential areas tend to be occupied by members of the poorer classes. Industries are also tending to locate toward the periphery.

8.5.5 The Distribution of Individual Land Uses

In the studies which we have examined, all land uses in an area were considered simultaneously. It is often simpler to examine and attempt to explain one type of land use at a time, in the hope that such an analysis may eventually provide the basis for a synthesis, in which several land uses are again considered.

We can think of the location of land uses as being arrayed in a matrix, with the types of land use in the rows and their locations in the columns, as shown in Fig. 8.4. It would be possible to look at a certain row and find the locations for any given land use; conversely, we could look at a given column and find the types of land use in a particular area. This matrix would then portray the land use pattern for the entire city.

In effect, this is what we plan to do here: Having considered the types of land use in different areas, such as the CBD or wholesale district, we shall now look at each type of land use individually and attempt to make generalizations about its location. By organizing our material in this manner, we hope to lay the groundwork for an analytical approach to the study of land use, employing land use models which have been developed.

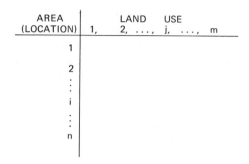

Fig. 8.4.   Two-dimensional matrix for the location land use by area.

Although any attempt to describe or generalize the distribution of land uses in a typical city is difficult, because cities differ in many respects and each is in some respects unique, it is possible to distinguish certain patterns which are relatively constant from place to place. In the foregoing generalized descriptions, usually referred to as theories, although no explicit classification schemes were presented, many of the same types of land use were recognized and discussed: retailing, wholesaling, manufacturing, residential, and others. The scheme used by Bartholomew (1955) gives classes representative of those used by planners and others studying urban land use. In outline, the major classes are as follows:

A. *Developed*

    1. Private

        a) Single-family dwellings
        b) Two-family dwellings
        c) Multiple-family dwellings
        d) Commercial
        e) Light industry
        f) Heavy industry

    2. Public and Semi-Public

        a) Streets and roads
        b) Railroad property
        c) Parks and playgrounds
        d) Other: includes hospitals, cemeteries, schools, churches, airports.

B. *Unimproved vacant land*

C. *Water areas not included in parks*

The Standard Land Use Classification (SLUC) offers a number of advantages for urban land use study. Perhaps most important, data collected by use of this scheme will be comparable from study to study, and compatible with the existing Standard Industrial Classification (SIC). Detailed instructions for coding are given in the *Manual*, so that classification of a given piece of property by any person trained to use the scheme should be the same. Since it is based on a single criterion, activity taking place on the land, it is difficult for a researcher using the SLUC to become sidetracked into discussing quality of housing, intensity of land use, population density, or land values. If on the other hand, he is interested in these or other factors, he may use or devise supplementary codes for each factor which he wishes to study.

Our discussion of the SLUC is intended to illustrate its structure as well as to summarize the location of different land uses. The first one-digit category, residential, is therefore given in full, including all four-digit classes. The discussion of succeeding one-digit classes has been shortened by combining the two- and three-digit classes wherever it seemed feasible. It must be recognized that generalizations about the locations of activities would be more precise if the categories were more specific, but in this instance brevity was considered more desirable than complete locational precision.

1. Residential land use

In discussing residential land use (Table 8.4), we shall present the entire classification to show the function of each successive digit. The first digit, *1*, identifies the major class: residential. The second digit gives the first breakdown: *11* household units, *12* group quarters, and so on. The third digit gives a further breakdown by Bartholomew's residential classes. Classes *114*, *115*, and *119* are not strictly comparable, as they tell us something about the structure itself: for example, *114*, converted structures, would apply to older single-family homes which had been converted to duplexes or apartments. The fourth digit adds detail about the structure: detached, semi-attached or apartments. The last class, *119*, takes into account such situations as families living in storefronts or old warehouses which serve as housing although they have never actually been converted for residential use.

Location: Residential areas are scattered throughout the city, with a preponderance of multiple-family dwellings nearer the city center, and of single-family dwellings nearer the periphery and in suburban and satellite cities. As the city increases in size, residential land use gives way to other land uses with higher returns per unit of land; single-family to multiple-family residential and commercial.

2. and 3. Manufacturing

Fifteen two-digit classes are identified; these classes are further subdivided into three four-digit classes, in a manner comparable to that used in the SIC, with which the SLUC is compatible.

Location: Land used for manufacturing tends to be located with respect to the availability of extra-city transportation, in sites where vacant land was available at the time of building. Non-noxious industry may be intermingled with wholesaling on the fringes of the CBD, whereas noxious industry tends to be near the periphery of the city at the time the plant was built.

Table 8.4 A standard system for identifying and coding land use activities—two-, three-, and four-digit levels for residential land use

Code	Category	Code	Category	Code	Category
11	Household units	111	Single family structures	1111	Single units—detached
				1112	Single units—semiattached
				1113	Single units—attached row
		112	Two family structures	1121	Two units—side-by-side
				1122	Two units—one above the other
		113	Multifamily structures	1131	Apartments—walk up
				1132	Apartments—elevator
		114	Converted structures	1141	Converted from—detached
				1142	Converted from—semidetached
				1143	Converted from—attached row
		115	Mobile homes	1151	Mobile homes—on permanent foundation
				1152	Mobile homes—not on permanent foundation
		119	Nonresidential structures	1190	Nonresidential structures
12	Group quarters	121	Rooming and boarding houses	1210	Rooming and boarding houses
		122	Membership lodgings	1221	Fraternity and sorority houses
				1229	Other membership lodgings, NEC

Table 8.4 (cont.)

Code	Category	Code	Category	Code	Category
		123	Residence halls or dormitories	1231	Nurses' homes
				1232	College dormitories
				1239	Other residence halls or dormitories, NEC
		124	Retirement homes and orphanages	1241	Retirement homes
				1242	Orphanages
		125	Religious quarters	1251	Convents
				1252	Monasteries
				1253	Rectories
				1259	Other religious quarters, NEC
		129	Other group quarters, NEC	1290	Other group quarters, NEC
13	Residential hotels	130	Residential hotels	1300	Residential hotels
14	Mobile home parks or courts	140	Mobile home parks or courts	1400	Mobile home parks or courts
15	Transient lodgings	151	Hotels, tourist courts, and motels	1510	Hotels, tourist courts, and motels
		159	Other transient lodgings, NEC	1590	Other transient lodgings, NEC
19	Other residential, NEC	190	Other residential, NEC	1900	Other residential, NEC

Source: U.S. Housing and Home Finance Agency and Department of Commerce, 1965.

Planners usually recognize two classes of industry: light and heavy. For their purposes, light industry is defined as that which is not noxious to users of land surrounding it; that is, it does not produce objectionable noise, smoke or odors. From the more detailed breakdown given in the SLUC, it would be possible to determine such information; in addition, the SLUC gives more information, especially at the four-digit level.

4. *Transportation, communication and utilities*

41   Railroad, rapid rail transit and street railway transportation
42   Motor vehicle transportation
   421   Bus transportation
   422   Motor freight transportation
   429   Other motor vehicle transportation, NEC
43   Aircraft transportation
44   Marine craft transportation
45   Highway and street right-of-way

The transportation network provides access from points outside the city to the CBD, as well as from point-to-point within the city. Railroad and bus terminals tend to be located in or near the CBD, with subsidiary stations between the CBD and periphery in larger cities. Railway and motor freight terminals are located on the periphery of the CBD, often in the wholesaling district, at points where freight is transferred from one form of transportation to another. Airports are located on vacant land, often at a distance from the city center. Marine terminals are found along the waterfront, usually near the original location of the CBD. A system of streets and roads, ranging from freeways and expressways to arterial streets, local access streets and alleys provides access to all parts of the city. The convenience and speed of access varies from city to city, with the amount of traffic and the adequacy of the road network.

46   Automobile parking

Location: Lots and garages are located in or near areas of trip origin and destination such as homes, apartments, offices, shopping centers, and industrial plants.

47   Communications

Location: Offices and radio and television studios are usually located near the CBD, or in outlying areas with ease of access and parking. Transmitting facilities are on higher ground or at tops of tall buildings.

48   Utilities

Location: Lines for utilities usually parallel the street network. Telephone and electric wires may be either above ground or, increasingly, underground. Business offices are usually located near the CBD, and production and distribution facilities in outlying areas.

5. *Trade*

51   Wholesale trade

Location: Wholesaling tends to be concentrated around the edge of the CBD, in areas accessible from outside the city by rail and truck and convenient to the CBD, where total distance traveled for deliveries tends to be at a minimum.

52–59   Retail trade

Location: Retail businesses are clustered in the CBD, and tend to spread away from that district radially along main transportation arteries. Smaller retail areas are scattered throughout the city; in older areas strung out along main streets, and in newer ones clustered in shopping centers, which are often located at or near the intersection of arterials convenient to residential areas and away from the city center.

6. *Services*

Location: Services are usually located close to the CBD or other retail trade centers. Certain services requiring large amounts of land, such as hospitals, cemeteries, and universities, may be located in outlying areas. Hospitals often serve as nuclei for associated professional services such as doctors' and dentists' offices and optical, dental, and medical laboratories. Governmental services to residential areas, such as fire and police stations, and schools, are located in or near those areas.

7. *Cultural, entertainment, and recreational*

Location: Smaller parks, swimming pools, and other recreational activities and amusements are dispersed throughout the city, convenient to residential areas. Larger parks, museums and other types of recreation are located near scenic areas and where vacant land was available at the time of their establishment, and where parking space can be provided.

8. *Resource production and extraction*

This category includes primarily non-urban land uses except for a few activities such as market gardens and other specialized horticulture on the periphery of the city, some agricultural processing, oil wells, and lumber processing in specialized areas.

9. *Undeveloped and water areas*

91   Undeveloped and unused land area (excluding noncommercial forest development).

Location: Usually on periphery of the urbanized area, especially where the city boundary has extended far beyond the developed area.

92   Noncommercial forest development
93   Water areas
94   Vacant floor area
95   Under construction
99   Other undeveloped land and water areas, Not Elsewhere Coded.

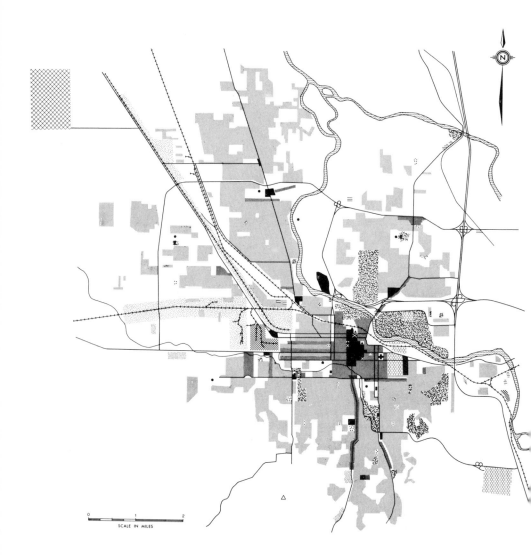

Fig. 8.5.   Various land uses in Eugene, Oregon.

Figure 8.5 illustrates land uses in a city of about 80,000 people in the United States. The SLUC one-digit categories are used, with some breakdown into subcategories, as appeared appropriate for the area and the degree of detail in a map of this size. Study of it will reveal many similarities to the location of individual land uses discussed in this section.

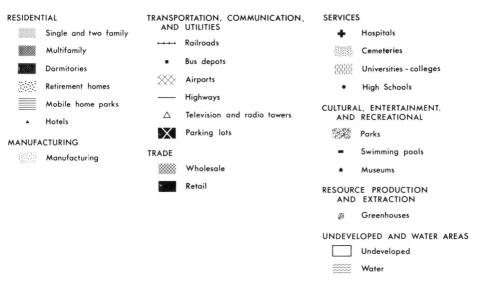

RESIDENTIAL

Single and two family

Multifamily

Dormitories

Retirement homes

Mobile home parks

▲ Hotels

MANUFACTURING

Manufacturing

TRANSPORTATION, COMMUNICATION, AND UTILITIES

⊢—⊣ Railroads

■ Bus depots

Airports

—— Highways

△ Television and radio towers

Parking lots

TRADE

Wholesale

Retail

SERVICES

✚ Hospitals

Cemeteries

Universities – colleges

• High Schools

CULTURAL, ENTERTAINMENT, AND RECREATIONAL

Parks

▬ Swimming pools

▲ Museums

RESOURCE PRODUCTION AND EXTRACTION

⌀ Greenhouses

UNDEVELOPED AND WATER AREAS

Undeveloped

Water

8.6 EXPLANATIONS OF THE LOCATION OF URBAN LAND USES

In identifying some of the factors related to urban land uses, we shall follow the same plan used in the explanation of non-urban land uses. We shall identify and discuss some of the physical, economic, political, and social or cultural factors which have been cited as being related to urban land use. We must repeat the caution that this division is purely arbitrary and for convenience only; in reality, each factor cannot be designated as purely physical or economic or political or social. All are interrelated, and each affects others. Economic values, for example, may be considered to be concrete manifestations of social values; zoning regulations are explicit statements of many implicit values and beliefs about land use. Technology is related to almost all factors, and changes in it bring about corresponding changes in land use.

8.6.1 Physical Factors

In considering the location of different land uses within a given city or urbanized area, some of the physical factors which were found to be related to non-urban land uses over larger areas, such as climate, might be considered to be relatively homogeneous. In any area, however, there are microvariations in sunshine, precipitation, wind, and temperature which make some sites more desirable than others for various activities. More important, perhaps, are characteristics of the site itself: topography, soil, drainage, and the substrate which supports buildings. All of these factors influence the use to which the site may be put. A person wishing to locate a steel mill would look for a large plot of level land, with substrate capable of supporting a large building and heavy machinery. For residential purposes, however, a hillside site with a view might be preferable, provided that the soil and subsoil were relatively stable and would not slide down the hill, taking the house along. Another factor to be considered is the presence or absence of natural vegetation. A wooded lot is considered desirable for a single-family residence, whereas the presence of weeds and brush simply adds to the cost of clearing a site for building.

8.6.2 Economic Factors

In speaking of economic factors, we are referring to those factors which can be measured in dollar costs, and not to social costs, which are more difficult to measure. These factors include: (1) the location of a site with respect to other parcels of land in the city and to transportation—that is, accessibility, (2) land values, (3) tax structure, and (4) the availability of credit.

In considering these economic factors, we can make use of the general equation:

Profit = Gross return − costs.

When the assumption is made that the maximization of profit is the sole determinant of location, this equation tells us that the individual seeking to locate a given activity will place it so as to have a maximum return or minimum costs.

1. Location with respect to other land uses is a major factor. Returns will be maximized if the total travel time to the site is minimized. In selecting a site for a retail enterprise, for example, this will be accomplished if a location is convenient for prospective customers, on a well-traveled route, and with adequate parking available close to the store to minimize the total time spent in shopping. If in addition, the site is located in a shopping center or complex of stores close to other businesses and services, the customer finds it even more attractive because the total shopping time is minimized

   Transportation costs are also important considerations for other activities. In selecting a residential site, the prospective buyer is concerned about the time consumed in journeys to many different activities: work, school, recreational activities, and the homes of friends. For any industrial or commercial activity, cost of transporting goods to and from the site must be considered; location near a railroad, water transportation, or major highways is an asset.

2. Land values are also an important element of the total cost. In general, high-value land tends to be used for high-yield activities, whereas lower-value land is used for activities with lower yields per unit area.

3. A factor which is often crucial in determining land use is the tax structure. When land is assessed according to the highest-yield use in the area, uses with lower yields tend to be pushed out, because tax costs become too high. For example, when agricultural land which is being encroached upon by housing is taxed at the same rate as the residential land next to it, farming becomes more costly, and the land is soon converted to residential use. Similarly, in a neighborhood of single-family dwellings which is changing to multiple-family dwellings and commercial uses, taxes may become so high that owners choose to sell and move elsewhere. Since the change to a higher-yield use is usually accompanied by a rise in land values, the owner's grief at moving may be assuaged by the profit from the sale.

4. Since World War II, urban and suburban sprawl in the United States have been encouraged by the ready availability of credit. Individuals can buy homes with minimal down payments—as little as $99 in many instances— and "the balance like rent." As a result, much agricultural land in the vicinity of cities has been taken over by housing developments. Without this availability of credit for the purchase of single-family dwellings, it is probable that urban landscapes in the United States and Canada would contain more large multiple-family structures such as are found in Europe, where the ownership of single-family homes is far less widespread.

8.6.3 Political Factors

At present, land use planning and zoning are important factors in designating the uses to which a given parcel of land may be put. Once planners have assigned an area to a given category, any new structure in that area can be used only for those activities permitted in that category. Although variances may be granted to allow noncomforming uses, this action tends to nullify the overall purpose of planning. The values of those responsible for the drafting and adoption of a plan are reflected in the plan. It can readily be seen whether economic benefits to individual developers have come first, or whether community needs for parks, schools, and public housing have also been taken into account. An adequate plan provides for separation of incompatible land uses, as well as propinquity of those uses which benefit from nearness to each other.

8.6.4 Social Factors

The value systems of individuals and shared values of individuals within a community are important in all land uses. Since what is *in* today may be *out* tomorrow, we should be aware of the values prevailing when the use of a given parcel is determined or changed. As Hoyt observed, in the United States higher-class residential areas tend to be located near high ground, open country, trading centers or other existing nuclei, and with convenient access to fast transportation to the city center. The presence of amenities such as schools, parks, and other recreational areas is also taken into consideration. Nearness to a particular ethnic group may be thought of as either desirable or undesirable, depending on the individual's and society's evaluation of that group. The desire to be separated from a particular group or groups leads to residential segregation and the development of ghettos.

Social values often provide criteria for choosing between competing land uses. If economic values are primary, then the decision rests mainly upon the cost-yield ratio. Social welfare, the good of the community as a whole or of certain groups with little economic and political power, and other noneconomic values are taken into account to various degrees in different places. Studies of cost-yield ratios, called cost-benefit studies, have usually been based primarily on economic considerations, although some attempts have been made to quantify noneconomic factors so that they can also be taken into account.

8.6.5 Technology

As with nonurban land uses, technology helps to determine the spatial structure of urban land use. Over the past century, technological developments have profoundly influenced transportation, increasing the distance which can be traveled in a given time and lengthening the distance of the journey to work while holding the time required relatively constant. Greater intensity of land use has been made possible by the development of techniques for constructing taller buildings. Improvements in communications have made nearness to the CBD less of an advantage, so that the disadvantages of its congestion are often sufficient to bring about decentralization of activities formerly located there. Automation has decreased the demand for unskilled and semiskilled workers, and increased that for professional and technical workers. Consequently, a new automated plant may be built in a suburban location, close to the homes of these workers. It may be anticipated that the continuing rapid rate of technological change will bring about more changes in both urban and rural land uses in the future, in ways which can be discerned only dimly at present.

This listing of factors related to urban land use is far from complete, and simply suggests some of those which have been found to be most significant. It is useful because it provides a framework for explaining the location of any given land use. For each use, certain factors may be more important, and others less. By considering each factor for any given land use, it is likely that a satisfactory explanation of its location can be achieved.

8.7 MODELS FOR EXPLAINING LAND USE

Once factors related to land use have been identified, they may be combined and manipulated in different ways to explain selected dependent variables. It is possible to formulate numerous empirical hypotheses about the relationships between variables. Several of these have already been suggested implicitly. For example:

1. Within a given urbanized area, high-value residential land use tends to be located in areas of higher elevation.
2. Commercial land uses tend to be located near a point of minimum aggregate time-distance-cost of travel for potential consumers.
3. When two users are competing for the same parcel of land, the higher-value use is more likely to be selected.

These hypotheses have been derived inductively by examination of data, and represent tentative generalizations about relationships between variables. They are low-level abstractions, which subsume small amounts of information. Ideally, we would like to have a general theory of land use from which a large number of hypotheses about many different aspects of land use could be derived deductively. Since, however, such a general theory is still far from realization, we shall consider instead some of the existing theories about land use. It should be recalled, from our earlier discussion of theories (Chapter 4, Section 4.3.5) that theories are arrived at inductively. In order to be considered as theories, however, they must be of a level of abstraction such that hypotheses can be derived from them deductively. Empirical tests of these hypotheses will then provide information needed for revision of the theory.

8.7.1 Definition and Elements of Models

Models are being used increasingly in the natural and social sciences. It is not surprising that much confusion has arisen as to what a model is. Some writers use the term as synonymous with *theory*, while others reserve it for complex mathematical formulations. Most simply and generally, a *model* may be defined as a simplified representation of some part of the real world. Maps and globes, for example, are models of certain selected aspects of the earth's surface. Models may be expressed in verbal, pictorial, graphic, diagrammatic, mathematical, or other forms. They can often be translated from one form to another; for example, from mathematical to verbal or graphic form.

Since models are simplified representations of reality, they are not expected to duplicate it exactly. A model is useful to the extent that it aids in conceptualization of the way in which the real world is ordered. Assumptions are often made in order to simplify the model conceptually. Although in its early formulations a model may obviously be far from the reality it is supposed to represent, by continued testing and reformulation it will come increasingly closer to explaining the observed data. As the early assumptions are relaxed and more variables fitted into the model, each reformulation achieves a closer approximation of the workings of the corresponding system in the real world. What is essential is that a model be logically consistent internally, so that when the operations of mathematics and logic are performed a logical truth will result. Unless a model is logically consistent, the deductions from it cannot be accepted as valid.

Because of the variation in the types of formulations which are considered to be models, it is difficult to specify what a model should contain. One of the most important elements, delimitation of the system within which the operation of the model is assumed to be valid, is often assumed implicitly rather than stated explicity. Such an error leads to the making of generalizations which are unjustified by the original formulation. When conditions are specified, even in terms such as *a technologically advanced society*, or *an urbanized area in the United States or Canada*, there is some basis for tentatively extending the findings to other situations.

Certain additional specifications of mathematical models may be suggested. To be fully operational, a model must contain *variables*, and *operations*. It may also contain certain *parameters*.

Variables are operationally defined, quantitative factors. Values of the independent variables are determined outside the model, and are used as data inputs. Values of the dependent variables are obtained as output, by operation of the model on the independent variables.

Operations are the mathematical or logical processes by which one quantity is derived from others. They include the familiar operations of arithmetic and algebra (addition, subtraction, multiplication, division, and exponentiation), as well as those of other branches of mathematics and formal logic.

Parameters are operationally defined quantities which are used as constants in any given run of a model, but which may vary for different runs. For example, a given land use may have one set of values for the parameters included in a model, whereas a different land use would have different values. For any land use, however, they would be constants. Parameter is also used in statistics with a different, but related meaning. A parameter, in this context, is a value, such as the mean or standard deviation, of a distribution which is for the entire population, whereas a statistic is the value for a particular sample.

8.7.2 Von Thünen's Model of Agricultural Land Use in an Isolated State

Von Thünen's (1826) model of agricultural land use combined verbal and diagrammatic forms. Recently, other theorists have modified it in different respects and translated some aspects into mathematical terms.

In constructing a model to explain rural land use, von Thünen made several simplifying assumptions, which enabled him to predict land use under conditions which were less complex than those of the real world. In later analyses, he relaxed certain of these assumptions and considered how each change would alter the land use predicted in the simple model. He considered as given the presence of a single isolated city situated in a uniform plain, all of which had the same climate and soil fertility. This city was the only market for goods produced in the area surrounding it. All goods were transported to market by horse-drawn wagon, carried by man, or, in the case of livestock, driven on foot. He implicitly accepted the assumptions of classical economics: a state of free competition among sellers in the market, maximization of profit as the farmers' sole motivation, and complete knowledge of the market price of all commodities by all farmers.

Given these original conditions and assumptions, he asked, "How will agricultural production and land use develop?" and "How will variations in distance from the city market affect land use?"

Since he had practical farming experience in northern Germany, he had data about costs, the analysis of which formed the basis for his conclusions. He reasoned that agricultural land use would develop in the form of six concentric rings around the city, each ring containing different land uses. He thought of the borders between the rings not as being sharply defined, but as merging gradually from one zone to another. Land uses in the zones he identified were: (Fig. 8.6)

Zone 1. Gardens, truck crops, stall-fed milk cows, and laying hens,

Zone 2. Forest products,

Zone 3. More intensively cultivated field crops; bulky crops such as potatoes, root crops and hay; and grain grown in rotation with these crops,

THEORETICAL

Fig. 8.6.   Theoretical land use zones in the von Thünen model.

Zone 4. Cereal crops and fallow or pastures,

Zone 5. Grazing, with sheep and cattle being driven to market, and

Zone 6. Undeveloped wilderness area.

Although these particular combinations were applicable primarily to the conditions existing at the time and place von Thünen lived, his generalizations have far wider validity. In more general terms, he reasoned that the land nearest the market would be used for goods which were perishable, bulky, or difficult to transport, since transportation costs of these items are high relative to their value. Forests were placed in the second zone because wood, the major fuel used at that time, was essential and yet heavy and bulky to transport.

He concluded that economic rent, or the profit to be derived from a parcel of land as net return above costs, was a controlling factor in land use. Land would not be used for growing a crop which brought less than the costs; the use selected for a particular piece of land would be one which maximized the net return. When the uses of several pieces of land were to be determined, each would be put to its most profitable use, so that the farmer's total profit would be maximized.

Von Thünen then relaxed some of his original assumptions and considered how certain changes might affect the model. He added another means of transportation by positing that a navigable river, on which the city was located, flowed through the area. He reasoned that, since transportation costs were less by river than by wagon and goods could be transported a greater distance to market from land located on or near the river for the same cost, the zones would be roughly elliptical, with the river as the long axis of the ellipse (Fig. 8.7).

In a similar manner, he considered the cases of multiple markets, different crop combinations, and variations in the cost of products. Although he recognized that soil fertility was not uniform, he did not deal with this problem explicitly.

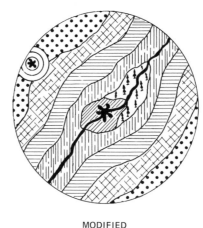

MODIFIED

Fig. 8.7. Modified land use zones in the von Thünen model—navigable river and additional market.

8.7.3 Later Modifications of the von Thünen Model

A verbal model such as von Thünen's, even when supplemented with diagrams, has certain shortcomings. The reasoning is intuitive and not strictly reproducible, even though logical. Translation of the terms of the model into mathematical symbols has the advantages of being both more precise and more general; that is, it can be applied to a wider variety of circumstances.

Lösch (1943) and Dunn (1954) have suggested a mathematical statement of the von Thünen model:

$$R = Y(P - C) - YFD,$$

where:

R = rent per unit of land (economic rent),
Y = yield (in dollars) per unit of land,
P = market price of commodity per unit of the commodity,
C = production cost of commodity per unit of the commodity,
F = transport cost (freight rate) per unit of commodity, and
D = distance from farm to market.

It is assumed that, for any given commodity at any given time and place, the values for Y, P, C and F may be taken as constant and are therefore parameters. D then becomes the independent variable which determines the value of R. The result is a linear equation of negative slope, in the general form $y = a - bx$. This may be represented graphically (Fig. 8.8).

From this graph it can be seen that economic rent is greatest at $x = 0$, and decreases to 0 at d_1 (the x-intercept). According to the von Thünen model, this crop would be grown only from distance 0 to distance d_1 from the market.

In this form the model is operational; that is, each of the terms in the equation has been operationally defined, so that numbers can be substituted into the equation and values of R calculated for corresponding values of D.

This model may also be extended to the consideration of two competing land

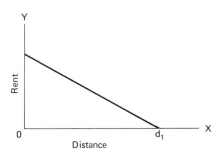

Fig. 8.8. Relationship between distance from a market and rent.

Table 8.5 Hypothetical values for yield, market price, production cost, and freight cost for two land uses

Land use	Yield	Market price	Production cost	Freight rate
1	125	1.65	1.50	0.005
2	150	1.00	0.60	0.03

uses. At the moment we shall assume hypothetical values for the constants, or parameters, in the equation for each of two crops (Table 8.5). We then calculate a few of the corresponding values of R and D and draw lines to represent the expected rent from each crop, when grown at a distance D from the market (Fig. 8.9).

PQ represents these relationships for crop or land use L_1, and ST the relationships for L_2. It can readily be seen that at a distance between 0 and d_1 from the market, L_1 will be more profitable, but that from d_1 to d_2, L_2 will be more profitable.

When this same approach is applied to more than two competing land uses, the relationships for each use may be diagrammed, and the most profitable distance from market determined for each use (Fig. 8.10). Practical application is, however, limited because many variables which determine land use are not considered in the model.

McCarty and Lindberg (1966) have further modified this formulation by introducing the concepts that : (1) there are, at any given time and place, physical, and areal limits within which a given crop can be grown economically, and (2) for each crop, there are optimal combinations of certain factors which produce the

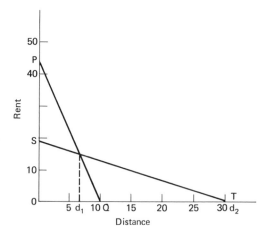

Fig. 8.9. Relationship between distance and rent for two competing land uses shown by using hypothetical data.

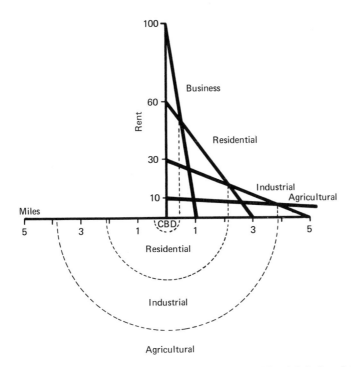

Fig. 8.10. Competition among four land uses: business, residential, industrial, and agricultural.

maximum yield. These limiting factors include physical requirements of crops such as minimum or maximum heat and moisture and particular combinations of soil nutrients. These are subject to change with technology, as new strains are introduced which are more tolerant to lack of moisture or resistant to insect pests and diseases. Economic limits exist when anticipated costs equal anticipated returns; that is, when $R = 0$. Thus, a less profitable crop may be grown nearer its limits, because it is displaced from its optimal location by a more profitable crop (Fig. 8.11).

8.7.4 Linear Programming

Linear programming techniques can be applied when it is desired to determine optimum production at a given number of sources, to be delivered to specific markets. In this respect, models using these techniques may be considered as extensions of von Thünen's search for a pattern of land use based on economic rent. Essentially, linear programming provides techniques for an orderly search to the solution to the problem of minimizing costs and maximizing profits in a complex situation. It has been applied widely to consideration of the optimum location of agricultural production. Although these agricultural applications are too over-

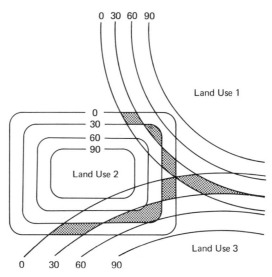

Fig. 8.11. Competition among three types of land use. Values represent rent per unit area. Shaded areas are zones of indifference where individuals have no economic preference between land uses. Adapted from Harold H. McCarty and James B. Lindberg, *A Preface to Economic Geography*, © 1966, Reprinted by permission of Prentice-Hall, Inc. Englewood Cliffs, N. J.

simplified to be of practical value to individual farmers at the present time, linear programming is being used extensively in industry to determine the optimum use of production facilities.

Hertsgaard (1964) applied linear programming to determination of the optimum location for the production of selected agricultural products, to be consumed over the entire United States. As he describes the analysis,

> In this study, the nation was divided into four consuming regions. Each of these regions was assumed to consume specified quantities of fed beef, pork, turkey, broilers, and eggs. Each of these consuming regions was assumed to be able to procure all or part of each of these products from any of fifteen producing regions in the nation. The amount of livestock and poultry which could be produced by each producing region was assumed to be limited by its feed grain supply. The analysis indicates the producing regions from which consuming regions can obtain these products at the least cost. The solution of the problem required estimates of consumption levels in each consuming region, of the feed supplies and typical production costs in each producing region, and of transportation costs for the end products among regions. These estimates were incorporated in a linear programming framework for solution of the problem. (p. 3)*

Certain limitations of the analysis were recognized. For example, the num-

---

*Reprinted by permission from T. A. Hertsgaard.

bers of producing and consuming regions were limited, and feed supplies were considered as the only production restraints.

Many aspects of the pattern of production resulting from the analysis were consistent with the actual situation. Pork production, for example, was concentrated in the Corn Belt. Other aspects were different: The analysis suggested specialized production of eggs in the Plains States, broiler production in California and the northeast, and a high level of cattle feeding in states west of the Corn Belt, sufficient to supply the entire market in the West.

8.7.5 Incorporating Noneconomic Variables into Models

In our discussion of the use of models, we have considered only the effects of economic variables, with maximization of profit and minimization of costs as the sole motivation. The techniques of carrying out cost-benefit analysis for different alternatives, using dollar costs and benefits alone, are well advanced. Although the importance of noneconomic factors is recognized, to date no satisfactory way has been devised to convert noneconomic values to units which may be used in comparing different factors with each other and with economic values. It is difficult to estimate the value of a sunset, a park, or a wilderness area.

Some progress has been made, however. One approach in estimating the value people place on certain amenities is to ask how much additional they would be willing to pay for a house located close to a park or with a view. Examination of spatial variations in land values reveals the importance of such features. The presence or absence of such amenities has been included in some analyses; Chapin and Weiss (1962), for example, used the presence of amenities such as paved streets, sewers, parks, schools, and general neighborhood appearance.

Another approach to estimating the value attached to noneconomic benefits, not by individuals, but by policy-making groups in a community, is to observe the results of planning for the city as a whole. For example, do zoning regulations require developers of large parcels of land to set aside a certain proportion of the area for parks and schools, and to put in amenities such as sidewalks and sewers? When the city council decides between two competing land uses, does it decide more often in favor of private profit than of the general welfare?

Often the relative advantages to be gained from two competing uses cannot be measured in any comparable way. For example, a given site may be considered by a company as prime industrial land. At the same time, its location, scenic values, and botanical interest make it ideal for park development. The park supporters contend that the scarcity of land for parks and the outstanding features of the site should outweigh its industrial potential. In the end, the decision often rests on the fact that an industry has money to purchase the site, whereas the governmental unit concerned does not, and economic competition alone determines the use.

8.7.6 A Simple Mathematical Model of Land Use

We have already briefly discussed linear programming, which is one mathematical model used in the study of land use. Other models which have been used include correlation-regression analysis, game theory, and simulation techniques. These differ conceptually, their main feature in common being that the factors involved are expressed in mathematical terms, and rules are given for the operations on these factors which produce the final results.

We can construct a simple mathematical model of land use by selecting some of the factors discussed above and designating these as the independent variables $X_1, X_2, \ldots, X_n$. We can then say that any given land use, Y_i will be some mathematical function of these variables. Expressed symbolically:

$$Y_i = f(X_1, X_2, \ldots X_n),$$

where:

        X_1 is an accessibility factor,

        X_2 is an elevation factor,

        $\vdots$

        X_n is a land cost factor.

This model is not operational; although it names the variables, it does not specify how the data for each variable are to be put into the form needed for use as input. Moreover, it says only that land use is some function of these variables, and does not specify the operations to be performed in order to obtain the dependent variable as output.

8.7.7 Correlation-Regression Analysis

One type of relationship among variables may be investigated by the use of correlation-regression analysis. This technique reveals how closely any two variables are related, by simple correlation; and how much of a change in any X_1, or independent variable is, on the average, associated with a corresponding change in Y, the dependent variable, by computation of a regression equation. The coefficient of simple correlation, r, measures of the relationship between any two variables; its square, r^2, indicates the proportion of the total variation in the dependent variable which is explained by the independent variable. Similarly, the coefficient of multiple correlation, R, indicates the relationship between the dependent variable and all the independent variables; its square, R^2, indicates the proportion of the total variation in Y which is explained by use of all the X_i variables considered simultaneously.

Chapin and Weiss (1962) used this technique as the first step in developing a simulation model of residential land use, in order to isolate factors which were related to certain elements of urban land use. Regression analyses were carried out for three urban centers in North Carolina: Greensboro, Winston-Salem, and Lexington. Two dependent variables were selected and defined operationally: Y_1, total land in urban use, and Y_2, dwelling density in 1960. We are concerned here only with Y_1. Thirty-seven independent variables were selected and defined operationally. These included: acessibility to major streets and to the high-value corner at the city center, measured both by distance and by travel time; accessibility to work areas; proximity to non-white areas; zoning protection; and assessed value. Different combinations of the variables were tried until a set of variables which met the researchers' criteria for acceptance was selected. In Lexington, 64.2 percent of the total land in urban use was accounted for by 11 independent variables ($R = 0.801$, $R^2 = 0.642$). In Winston-Salem, 50.3 percent explanation was obtained with 12 variables ($R = 0.709$, $R^2 = 0.503$). In Greensboro, 66.7 percent of the variation was explained by 14 variables ($R = 0.817$, $R^2 = 0.667$). The authors state that they believe these values are close to the maximum explanation which can be achieved at present by use of multiple linear correlation-regression analysis.

8.7.8 Decisions and Game Theory

An approach such as that of von Thünen is often termed behavioral, in that it is based on the behavior of individuals under specified conditions. The overall pattern of land use which evolves in an area is seen as the result of the summation of decisions of individual landowners, each of whom is bidding against others for a valuable commodity which will yield maximum profits for him. Land with desired site characteristics such as nearness to transportation, location within the central business district, or desirability for high-value residential purposes is a scarce and, therefore, economically valuable commodity. Since its price is determined by the economic interaction of supply and demand, the upper limit of the price which individuals will be willing to pay is set by its economic rent.

A system of two linear equations based on the von Thünen model and various modifications of it is one conceptualization of the way in which individuals may choose between two competing land uses. As has been pointed out, however, the model is so oversimplified that it is of more theoretical than practical interest. A major difficulty is that many of the basic assumptions of classical economics do not, in fact, hold. Even if an individual should act as if profit maximization were his sole motive, he does not have the complete information necessary for making decisions. Prices and costs fluctuate, and profits must be guessed at rather than being known as certainties. Decisions are based on best guesses rather than complete knowledge of the necessary factors involved. In short, the actual situation is probabilistic rather than deterministic.

Viewed in this way, a decision resembles a game of chance. One can guess at the probability that a given event will occur, and place his bet in the way which is most likely to win for him in the long run. A game may be played either by two persons against each other, or by one person against nature as an opponent. When two opponents are playing a game of dice or poker, for example, they have some idea of the long-range probability of obtaining doubles or a full house, and of the relative payoff they can expect if their bets are correct. Bets are based on these probabilities. The exact probabilities can, of course, be calculated mathematically. If the players are skillful and experienced, they place their bets so that they win more than they lose in the long run, even though they experience some wins and some losses. Similarly, a wealthy investor who plays the stock market, buying and selling speculative stocks, expects to lose money on some and to gain on others, but to make money in the long run.

Game theory provides a framework within which the best strategy can be chosen to resolve conflict situations, given knowledge about odds and the payoff matrix. Gould's (1963) experimentation with the application of game theory to land use in Africa suggests some of the possibilities of these techniques. At present, it represents a hypothetical formulation of risks and payoffs.

Gould describes the Barren Middle Zone of Ghana as a sparsely populated region in which farming is difficult because torrential rains are often followed by drying winds from the Sahara. The precipitation is so variable that it is difficult for farmers to plan what crops to plant. Over the years, they have learned through experience to plant a combination of crops with different resistance to dry conditions: yams, maize, cassava, millet, and hill rice (Table 8.6). Then, whatever the weather, they will have some food from their crops—more rice in dry years, more yams in wet years. To put the problem in a game-theory framework, the problem to be solved is: What is the optimum combination of any two crops which will give the greatest long-run yield, given the known proportions of wet and dry years?

In order to simplify the problem, only two extremes of precipitation are considered—wet years and dry years. These assumptions are recognized as being unrealistic. The average yield of each crop under the two extreme conditions may be represented in a payoff matrix as follows:

Table 8.6 Crop yields under two climatic conditions

Crops	Crop yield per unit of land*	
	Wet years	Dry years
Yams	82	11
Maize	61	49
Cassava	12	38
Millet	43	32
Hill rice	30	71

Source: Gould, 1963. Reprinted by permission from the *Annals* of the Association of American Geographers, Volume 53 (1963).
*Expressed in some comparable unit, such as calories; values are hypothetical.

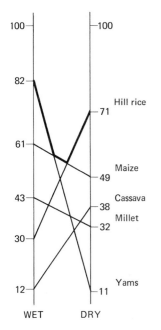

Fig. 8.12. Graphic solution for assigning critical pair of strategies in two-person-five-strategy-zero-sum game for Ghana example. Source: Gould, 1963. Reproduced by permission from the *Annals* of the Association of American Geographers, Volume 53 (1963).

The simplest way of selecting the two crops that will yield the maximum payoff is by drawing a graph (Fig. 8.12). The two crops that will yield greatest returns in the long run are selected at the lowest point of intersection of the lines forming the upper boundary—in this case, maize and hill rice. The next problem is to determine what relative proportions of these crops will give the greatest yield in the long run. Data are set up in a 2 × 2 matrix (Table 8.7), which is then solved to find the odds for the two strategies. These are converted to percentages.

Following the rules for determining odds, with which we need not be concerned here, the strategy for hill rice is found by subtracting the payoffs for maize, and taking the absolute value of the difference: $61 - 49 = |12|$. Repeating the process for maize, $30 - 71 = |41|$. The two crops should then be planted in

Table 8.7   Data for computing optimum strategy

	Wet years	Dry years
Maize	61	49
Hill rice	30	71

Source: Gould 1963. Reprinted by permission from the *Annals* of the Association of American Geographers, Volume 53 (1963).

the ratio of 41 maize to 12 hill rice. Converting this to percentages gives us maize, $41/(41 + 12) = 41/53 = 77.4$ percent; and hill rice, $12/53 = 22.6$ percent. Either 77.4 percent of the land could be planted to hill rice and 22.6 percent to maize every year or a different percentage could be chosen each year which would result in these percentages over a period of time; it would not make any difference in the long run.

Gould notes that since this model is based on hypothetical data, its applicability to a practical situation would not be known without empirical study. He suggests, as a possibility for further study, that a payoff matrix based on actual data be used to predict the proportions of each crop grown, and results compared with land use practices of farmers in the area.

8.7.9 Simulation Models of Urban Land Use

The approaches discussed above share certain disadvantages. They are cross-sectional and static; they represent the situation at any given point in time, under conditions of equilibrium. The development of computer technology and techniques of systems analysis have opened the way for dynamic study of human social systems. Although simulation models of urban land use now being developed represent only crude approaches to reality, much like the early attempts to understand such phenomena as planetary motion within the solar system and other laws of physics, it is hoped that further experimentation will lead to the development of more accurate models.

Some probability concepts used in simulation models. In discussing mathematical models, the attempt has been made to explain their main features, using as few mathematical terms as possible. Our intention is not to explain how to carry out the relevant analyses, but rather to point out the kinds of situations to which each model can be applied and the way in which it can be used to test hypotheses. Since many mathematical models are based on probability theory and other branches of higher mathematics, the actual techniques involved are beyond the scope of the present text. With some elementary knowledge of certain concepts, however, it is possible to understand some of the basic principles involved. Students with extensive mathematical backgrounds are engouraged to investigate the references for more detailed information.

In trying to understand models based on probability theory, called stochastic models, such as the two simulation models discussed below, two concepts are important: probability and randomness. *Probability* may be defined as the mathematical expression of the likelihood that a given event will occur. For example, a coin tossed into the air will come down either heads or tails. Since these are the only two possibilities, we can say that if it is a fair, or unbiased, coin, the probability of heads is $\frac{1}{2}$ or 0.5, and of tails also 0.5. The combined probabilities must always equal 1.0. We say that an event is *random* when the probabilities for each of the possible outcomes are equal. The outcome of a toss of a coin is random, as is the selection of a number in a bingo game. A selection may be *biased* by assigning unequal probabilities to different outcomes, as is done in the simulation models. Although the selection of any particular outcome remains probabilitistic, the probabilities assigned to each event are no longer equal. Such a technique is sometimes referred to as *biased randomization*. The method by which simulation is carried out is called the Monte Carlo method.

Simulation of urban growth patterns: Chapin and Weiss

Chapin and Weiss (1962) studied the expansion of urban land use in three North Carolina cities. They wished to develop a model which would simulate residential development on the urban fringes of these cities. The first phase of their investigation has been discussed above (Section 8.7.7). In a series of multiple correlation-regression analyses, the relationships between selected factors related to land use and the percentage of total land in urban use were determined. Eight variables were then selected for use in a simulation model of urban land growth. As ranked in order of importance in explaining the total amount of variation, they were: (1) marginal land not in urban use—that is, land available for urban development; (2) accessibility to work areas; (3) assessed value; (4) travel distance to nearest major street; (5) residential amenity—general upkeep and urban facilities, measured by trained observers using a standard scoring method; (6) distance to nearest available elementary school; (7) availability of sewerage; and (8) zoning protection. Although many of these variables are noneconomic, the economic ones related to transportation or time-distance-cost were among the ones which contributed most to the explanation.

For simplification, the study area was considered as being topographically uniform, with no hills or rivers, and with the first settlement already established. From this base, they wished to synthesize a new city, using the factors above to determine what kind of development would occur, and where. The area was divided into a grid, each cell of which was 23 acres, a reasonable size for a subdivision. Such a grid may be portrayed on a computer as a matrix, with each cell being locatable by its two-point (x, y) coordinates, much as a city may be located on a map by its latitude and longitude.

The total number of household units to be constructed within a given period was derived from economic and population forecasts, and the number of units to be distributed in each iterative period, or run of the model, was decided upon and fed into the model. On the basis of the existing pattern of development, each square was assigned a measure of attractiveness which combined the eight factors. The probability that a given cell would be selected for development was then expressed as a function of these combined factors.

On each run of the model, a predetermined number of housing units was distributed over the available space. At the end of the run, adjustments were introduced according to rules established in the program. For example, new roads were added, schools were built or the sewer system was extended. Because these improvements increased the attractiveness of nearby cells, the probabilities were readjusted before the next run was carried out.

Because simulation techniques are based on probability theory, the resulting pattern is not expected to correspond exactly to the observed one; it is intended only to resemble the pattern of actual development in certain respects. For this reason, it is difficult to test the correspondence of the model with reality.

A later simulation experiment: Morrill

Morrill (1965) reports on a simulation experiment of the growth of one area on the urban-rural fringe of Seattle. He conceived of urban growth as a spatial diffusion process, certain elements of which were considered to occur at random. The selection of a given parcel of land for development then becomes a biased random procedure, in which parcels with more of certain desirable features have a higher probability of being selected than those with less of the desirable features. Building on the work of others (Hägerstrand, 1953 and 1965; Chapin and Weiss, 1962), he selected those factors which he thought to be relevant in the area being studied. Probabilities were calculated so that the attractiveness of a given parcel of land varied inversely with distance from existing development and directly as to variations in site characteristics and neighborhood quality. More specifically, the variables included in the model were: (1) open land available for development, (2) distance to major arterials, schools and shopping centers, and (3) proximity to existing residential development. Since the whole area is equally inaccessible to exployment and of fairly homogeneous quality, these factors were not included.

Morrill chose to deal with existing parcels of land as units. A grid pattern superimposed on the map of the area made it possible to specify points for selection by means of two coordinates.

He describes the simulation model as a series of screening processes, or individual decisions, which result in the final decision as to whether to develop and, if so, what type of development will take place. A parcel is first selected for consideration by a random process. Two random numbers are drawn which give the x and y coordinates. The parcel of land on which this point is located is then put through the decision process specified in the model. If the site is already occupied, it is removed from further consideration.

The first screen takes into account access via arterials to two major centers in the area. Probabilities are established for a number of discrete distances. These probabilities decrease as distance increases. A property adjacent to a major development, for example, is assigned a probability of 0.70 of being developed, whereas one 25 or more blocks away has a probability of only 0.10. A random number from 0 to 99 is drawn to determine if the property will be developed. If the assigned probability is 0.10, for example, the property is developed only if a number from 0 to 9 is drawn, and not developed if the number drawn is between 10 and 99.

At the next screen, site quality is considered. In this model, only one variation in site quality is taken into account. If a piece of swampy land has been selected, it has a probability of 0.5 of being developed. Morrill suggests that other features of site quality could also be included, as could the effect of proximity to mixed uses or blight, and overall neighborhood amenity, both of which were included in the Chapin and Weiss model but omitted here because of the homogeneity of the area with respect to these factors.

If the parcel remains as a candidate for development, two decisions remain: the kind and the size of the development. Although the kind of development is restricted by zoning regulations, it has been found that not all parcels in an area are developed to the highest-yield use permitted there. If the parcel lies in an area zoned for single-family dwellings, this would be the use selected by the program, since other uses are not permitted in such an area. If, on the other hand, it were zoned for multiple-family or commercial use, another decision would be made. By study of the area, it was determined that in areas zoned for commercial use, 0.5 of the land is used for commercial purposes, 0.3 for multiple-family residences and 0.2 for single-family dwellings. Corresponding probabilities were therefore assigned to each of these possibilities, so that the distribution in the simulation model would follow the existing pattern of development. Similarly, in an area zoned for multiple-family dwellings, the probability of an apartment being built is 0.6, and of a house 0.4. These probabilities are used to determine the type of development, given the existing zoning.

The other decision to be made is whether the property, if larger than needed for a building, will be bought as a unit and subdivided by the buyer, or whether the present owner will sell it as individual lots. After this decision is made, the density of development is assigned according to the existing distribution of lot sizes in the area.

Morrill suggests that other factors could be taken into account, including the probability of vacancy in existing structures and a succession of uses. Although locations of schools and shopping centers are considered as given in the model, the selection of sites for such developments could be built into the model, as was done by Chapin and Weiss.

The closeness of the pattern resulting from operation of the model to that which actually developed during the period from 1957–1962 was tested statistically by examining the cumulative distributions of three factors: size of developments, and distances of larger developments to both major existing developments and major arterials. No statistically significant differences were found between the actual and simulated patterns in these respects.

Summary notes on simulation models

In spite of oversimplification in these models, an important feature is that the incremental nature of the process of urban growth is simulated. Beginning with an existing settlement, new growth takes place in relation to its features such as streets, schools, and shopping centers. As more houses are added to the area, demand for more streets, schools, and shopping centers builds up, and more of these are added. In these early simulation attempts, many of the features of urban growth were fed into the system from outside. For example, a decision might be made to build a new park or a major shopping center. Knowledge of the patterns of urban growth is sufficiently advanced, however, that factors such as these may be included in later models. Disadvantages include the fact that it is difficult to know what time period is covered by a single run of the model, as well as that, for any but the simplest models, a great deal of computer time is required.

8.8 SUMMARY

In this chapter we have changed scale from a macroscopic examination of land uses over the entire earth, based often on almost nonexistent data and guesswork, to consideration of some of the models which are being explored in the attempt to explain and predict patterns of land use in small areas. We have studied not only land use classes, but also some of the more recent approaches to explanation of the location of different land uses. In an introductory text, it is possible to consider but a few of the many aspects of land use which merit geographic study and which are dealt with in greater detail in courses such as urban geography and location theory.

We have discussed some of the variables which have been found to be related to land use. It would be desirable to have some way of quantifying all these variables, and of assigning weights to them. We might anticipate that these weights would vary for different land uses at a given time and place, as well as over time and space. Although some of the recent simulation models deal with change over time, most of the present explanations are essentially static, and explain a particular pattern of land use at a given time and place. With growing interest in systems analysis, however, it is to be hoped that more adequate explanations of processes of change may be achieved, since it is evident that many questions about land use remain unanswered.

REVIEW YOUR UNDERSTANDING OF THESE CONCEPTS

land use	misuse of land
intensive and extensive land use	spatial structure of urban land use
amount of technology used in farming	model
scale of a map	elements of models: variables,
parcel of land	operations, and parameters
standard land use coding	Von Thünen model
factors used for explaining a	$R = Y(P\text{-}C) - Y F D$
distribution	uniform plain

assumptions   optima and limits
game theory   linear programming
simulation   cost-benefit analysis
probability $Y_i = f(X_1, X_2, \ldots, X_n)$
distinction between random and biased

SUGGESTED ACTIVITIES

1. Map the distribution of a single land use within a city or a portion of it. Try to account for this distribution, first testing the relevant hypotheses proposed in the chapter. It may be possible to obtain a map of land use from the planning department of the city.

2. Map all the land uses in an area extending from both sides of the city limits, i.e. to some distance both inside and outside the city. Attempt to explain the observed distribution of land uses.

3. a) Construct a map of a hypothetical city having a uniform physical base. For simplicity, assume a population of 10,000 to 50,000. Locate the land uses described in the chapter and justify their locations.

   b) Draw another map of the same city, showing the differences in the location of land uses which might result if the physical base were not uniform, i.e. if a river flowed through the area, hilly land were present, and the like.

4. Map the locations of new areas of any land use in your city within the past 5–10 years. Try to account for the locations using von Thünen's model.

5. Consider the agricultural land uses in counties in your area. Give examples of the ways in which soils, climate, accessibility, or other relevant variables are related to the crops grown.

REFERENCES

Bartholomew, Harland (1955), *Land Uses in American Cities.* Cambridge: Harvard University Press.

Burgess, Ernest W. (1925), "The growth of the city," in Robert E. Park, Ernest W. Burgess, and Roderick D. McKenzie, eds., *The City.* Chicago: University of Chicago Press, pp. 47–62.

Burgess, Ernest W. (1929), "Urban areas," in T. V. Smith and L. D. White, eds., *Chicago: An Experiment in Social Science Research.* Chicago: University of Chicago Press, pp. 113–138.

Chapin, F. Stuart, Jr. and Shirley F. Weiss (1962), *Factors Influencing Land Development.* Chapel Hill and Washington, D.C.: Institute for Research in the Social Sciences, University of North Carolina and United States Bureau of Public Roads.

Clawson, Marion with Charles L. Stewart (1965), *Land Use Information: A Critical Survey of U.S. Statistics Including Possibilities for Greater Uniformity.* Washington, D.C.: Resources for the Future.

Dunn, Edgar S., Jr. (1954), *The Location of Agricultural Production.* Gainesville: University of Florida Press.

Firey, Walter (1947), *Land Use in Central Boston.* Cambridge: Harvard University Press.

Food and Agriculture Organization of the United Nations (1958 to date), *Production Yearbook.* Rome: United Nations.

Frey, M. Thomas, Orville E. Krause, and Clifford Dickason (1968), *Major Uses of Land and Water in the United States with Special Reference to Agriculture, Summary for 1964,* Agricultural Economic Report No. 149. Washington D.C.: U.S. Department of Agriculture.

Ginsburg, Norton S. (1965), "Urban geography and 'non-western' areas," in Leo F. Schnore and Philip M. Hauser. eds., *The Study of Urbanization.* New York: Wiley, pp. 311–346.

Gould, Peter (1963), "Man against his environment: a game theoretic framework," *Annals* of the Association of American Geographers **53**, 290–297.

Hägerstrand, Torsten (1953), *Innovationsförloppet ur Korologisk Synpunkt,* Lund, cf. Torsten Hägerstrand, "Quantitative techniques for analysis of the spread of information and technology," in C. Arnold Anderson and Mary Jean Bowman, eds., 1965, *Education and Economic Development.* Chicago: Aldine.

Hägerstrand, Torsten (1965), "A Monte Carlo approach to diffusion," *European Journal of Sociology* **6**, 43–67, reprinted in Brian J. L. Berry and Duane F. Marble, eds., 1968, *Spatial Analysis: A Reader in Statistical Geography.* Englewood Cliffs: Prentice-Hall.

Harris, Chauncy D. and Edward L. Ullman (1945), "The nature of cities," *The Annals of the American Academy of Political and Social Sciences* **242**, 7–17.

Hertsgaard, Thor A. (1964), *Optimum Patterns of Production and Distribution of Livestock and Poultry Products,* Technical Paper No. 10. Minneapolis: Upper Midwest Economic Study, University of Minnesota.

Hoyt, Homer (1939), *The Structure and Growth of Residential Neighborhoods in American Cities.* Washington, D.C.: Federal Housing Administration.

Lösch, August (1943), *Die räumliche Ordnung der Wirtschaft,* Jena, translated by William H. Woglom and Wolfgang Stolper, *The Economics of Location.* New Haven: Yale University Press, 1954, and New York: Wiley, 1967.

Marschner, Francis J. (1959), *Land Use and Its Patterns in the United States,* Agriculture Handbook No. 153. Washington, D.C.: Agricultural Research Section, U.S. Department of Agriculture.

McCarty, Harold H. and James B. Lindberg (1966), *A Preface to Economic Geography.* Englewood Cliffs: Prentice-Hall.

Morrill, Richard L. (1965), "Expansion of the urban fringe: a simulation experiment," *Papers,* Regional Science Association **15**, 185–199.

Niedercorn, John H. and Edward F. R. Hearle (1964), "Recent land-use trends in forty-eight large American cities," *Land Economics* **40**, 105–110.

Schnore, Leo F. (1965), "On the spatial structure of cities in the two Americas," in Leo F. Schnore and Philip M. Hauser, eds., 1965, *The Study of Urbanization*. New York: Wiley, pp. 347–398.

U.S. Housing and Finance Agency and Department of Commerce (1965), *Standard Land Use Coding Manual*. Washington, D.C.: Housing and Home Finance Agency and U.S. Department of Commerce.

Von Thünen, Johann H. (1826), *Der isolierte Staat in Beziehung auf Landwirtschaft und Nationalökonomie*, 3 volumes, Rostock, in Peter Hall, ed., 1966, *Von Thünen's Isolated State*, translated by Carla M. Wartenberg. New York: Pergamon Press.

Whittlesey, Derwent (1936), "Major agricultural regions of the earth," *Annals* of the Association of American Geographers **26**, 199–240.

Wingo, Lowdon, Jr. (1963), "The use of urban land," in Howard W. Ottoson, ed., *Land Use Policy and Problems in the United States*. Lincoln: University of Nebraska Press.

Additional Readings

Alonso, William (1964), "The form of cities in developing countries," *Papers*, Regional Science Association **13**, 165–173.

Birch, J. W. (1963), "Rural land use and location theory: a review," *Economic Geography* **39**, 273–276.

Brown, Alfred John, H. M. Sherrard, and J. H. Shaw (1969), *An Introduction to Town and Country Planning*, 2d rev. ed. Sydney: Angus and Robertson.

Chapin, F. Stuart, Jr. (1965), *Urban Land Use Planning*. Urbana: University of Illinois Press.

Chisholm, Michael (1962), *Rural Settlement and Land Use*. London: Hutchinson.

Committee for the World Atlas of Agriculture (1969), *World Atlas of Agriculture*. Novara, Italy: Instituto Geografico de Agostini.

Dorfman, Robert D., ed. (1965), *Measuring Benefits of Government Investments*. Washington, D.C.: The Brookings Institute.

Eisen, Edna E. (1948), *Educational Land Use in Lake County, Ohio*, Department of Geography Research Paper No. 2. Chicago: University of Chicago Press.

Garrison, William L. and Marion E. Marts (1958), *Influence of Highway Improvements on Urban Land: A Graphic Summary*, The Department of Geography and the Department of Civil Engineering. Seattle: University of Washington Press.

Getis, Arthur (1969), "Residential location and the journey from work," *Proceedings* of the Association of American Geographers **1**, 55–59.

Gould, Peter R. (1966), "Wheat on Kilimanjaro: the perception of choice within game and learning model frameworks," *General Systems Yearbook* **10**, 157–166.

Grigg, David (1969), "The agricultural regions of the world: review of reflections," *Economic Geography* **45**, 95–132.

Hoyt, Homer (1964), "Recent distortions of the classical models of urban structure," *Land Economics* **40**, 199–212.

Institute of British Geographers (1968), *Land Use and Resources: Studies in Applied Geography*, Special Publication No. 1. London: Institute of British Geographers.

Kostrowicki, Jerzy, ed. (1965), Land utilization in east-central Europe: case studies, *Geographia Polonica* 5.

Langham, Max R. (1963), "Game theory applied to a policy problem of rice farmers," *Journal of Farm Economics* 45, 151–162.

Mayer, Harold M. (1964), "Politics and land use: the Indiana shoreline of Lake Michigan," *Annals* of the Association of American Geographers 54, 508–523.

Neutze, Mas (1968), *The Suburban Apartment Boom: Case Study of a Land Use Problem.* Washington, D.C.: Resources for the Future.

Osborn, Frederic J. and Arnold Whittick (1963), *The New Towns: The Answer to Megalopolis.* New York: McGraw-Hill.

Pendleton, William C. (1965), "An empirical study of changes in land use at freeway interchanges," *Traffic Quarterly* 19, No. 1, 89–93.

Perloff, Harvey S., ed. (1969), *The Quality of the Urban Environment*, Washington. D.C.: Resources for the Future.

Sewell, W. R. D., John Davis, A. D. Scott, and D. W. Ross (1962), *A Guide to Benefit-Cost Analysis*, Ottawa: Queen's Printer.

Prest, A. R. and R. Turvey (1965), "Cost-benefit analysis: a survey," *The Economic Journal* 75, 683–735.

Simmons, James W. and Victor H. Huebert (1970), "The location of land for public use in urban areas," *The Canadian Geographer* 14, 45–56.

Sinclair, Robert, (1967), "Von Thünen and urban sprawl," *Annals* of the Association of American Geographers 57, 72–87.

Stamp, L. Dudley (1950), *The Land of Britain: Its Use and Misuse.* London: Longmans, Green.

Stein, Clarence S. (1957), *Toward New Towns for America.* Cambridge: The Massachusetts Institute of Technology Press.

Stein, Martin M. (1969), "Highway interchange area development: some recent findings," *Public Roads* 35, 241–250, 264.

Thorne, Wynne, ed. (1963), *Land and Water Use*, Publication No. 73. Washington, D.C.: American Association for the Advancement of Science.

United States Outdoor Recreation Resources Review Commission (1962), *Study Reports*, Vol. 1–17. Washington, D.C.: U.S. Government Printing Office.

CHAPTER 9
SETTLEMENT

9.1 INTRODUCTION

Geographers have studied phenomena associated with the settlement of areas, focusing both on the process whereby an area is occupied by men on a permanent rather than a transient basis and on the artifacts which result from this process—that is, on settlements as places. We shall be concerned here, however, with only a portion of the entire scope of settlement geography. As in previous chapters, in these explorations we shall first define and classify certain portions of this topic in order to organize our observations. We shall then explore certain spatial aspects both of settlements as places and of the process of settlement, and attempt to explain them.

9.2 DEFINITION AND CLASSIFICATION OF SETTLEMENTS

9.2.1 Ways of Classifying Settlements

As we have already learned, it is helpful to organize observations about a phenomenon such as settlements in a way that will help us answer the questions we have raised. Some geographers who have studied settlements have been concerned with contrasting urban and rural areas, others with identifying different types of rural settlements, and still others with distinguishing between different types of cities. Because different classifications are needed for each of these purposes, a number of different ways of classifying settlements have developed.

9.2.2 Morphological Classifications

Classifications based on morphology, or shape, have been of special interest to historical geographers studying European settlements, who concentrated on changes in the patterns of the settlements over time. (See especially Houston, 1953.) They considered both the shape of the settlement as a whole and the internal arrangement of its components, and identified various shapes such as circular, rectangular, and along crossroads. As yet, however, because no such scheme adapted to the classification of all settlements has been developed, this approach is not too helpful for comparing settlements in different areas. It is possible that, in the future, mathematical measures of shape (Bunge, 1966, Chap. 3) might be applied to the study of settlements and a more objective and universally applicable classification scheme developed.

9.2.3 Classification Based on Legal Definition

A variety of legal definitions of different types of settlements has been adopted not only in the United States but also in different countries throughout the world. Regardless of the number of people living in an area, it must usually be incorporated to qualify as a town, village, or city. Usually an area with a population of 25,000 or more is considered as a city, although in some cases the residents prefer not to incorporate and the area remains officially a village or simply an incorporated area. Since legal definitions vary from state to state and country to country, they are not too useful in studies of different political areas for which comparable data are required.

9.2.4 Classifications Based on Predominant Functions or Activities

A number of classifications based on the predominant functions of cities have been developed. These have differed as to the number of classes delineated, the criteria used, and the statistical areas classified. In general, work with classifications of this type has been limited to cities of 10,000 or more within the United States.

Harris (1943) pioneered in developing one such classification. His work was based on data of the 1930's, at which time employment and occupation data were the best variables related to functions of cities for which comparable data were available in the United States. He used employment in an activity as the primary criterion and the occupational structure of the inhabitants as a secondary one to determine the relative importance of different activities in an area.

He established criteria for each classification; for example, a city was considered to be a manufacturing city if employment in manufacturing constituted sixty percent or more of the total, and a retail center if employment in retailing was at least fifty percent of the total. He identified eight major classes: manufacturing cities, retail centers, diversified cities, wholesale centers, transportation and communication centers, mining towns, university towns, and resort and retirement towns. Although he recognized that all cities have more than one function, he assigned each city to a single class according to its most important activity. Those in which no one activity predominated were assigned to the class of diversified cities.

Aided by the availability of more and better data in subsequent censuses, later writers have developed additional functional classifications, of which Nelson's (1955) is probably the most widely used. A set of maps showing the distribution of cities in each class is available. Using 1950 census data, Nelson classified 897 urban

areas and urban places with populations of 10,000 or more. He placed each observation into one of ten classes, according to explicitly stated and objectively determined criteria. He first identified nine classes of activity which predominated in
urban areas. These were based on census classifications, but some classes such as
agriculture and construction were omitted and others were combined. The categories used were: mining, manufacturing, transportation and communication,
wholesale trade, retail trade, finance, insurance and real estate, personal service,
professional service, and public administration.

In order to place each city in one and only one class, he constructed a frequency distribution for each activity which showed the percentage of employment
in that activity for each of the 897 observations. Those cities which fell one or
more standard deviations above the mean of a particular activity were considered
to be specialized in that activity. Cities which did not fall into any one of the
nine classes were considered to be diversified. Three degrees of specialization of
cities within each class were identified: cities lying between one and two standard
deviations above the mean, cities lying between two and three standard deviations
above the mean, and cities more than three standard deviations above the mean.

Although this scheme has the advantage of being replicable because the
classes are objectively rather than subjectively determined, two major difficulties
are associated with its use. Because the frequency distributions of the different
activities are skewed rather than normal, the degrees of specialization identified
for different activities are not completely comparable. This difficulty could be
overcome, however, by normalizing all the distributions before delineating the
classes. Another more serious problem is that if another researcher wished to
replicate Nelson's work for a different area or time period, he would have to repeat
the entire process of classification. Since his results would be based on frequency
distributions derived from different data, they probably would not be fully comparable with Nelson's. It might, however, be possible to use a process similar to
Nelson's to establish criteria for degrees of specialization in different activities
and then to use these criteria for different studies, so that there would be greater
comparability among the findings. Factor analysis, a mathematical technique,
has also been used to group cities in accordance with activities and other variables.

9.2.5 Central and Noncentral Places

Christaller's (1933) theory about the location of central places, which will be
discussed in Section 9.4, has stimulated many recent geographic studies. In pro-
posing this theory, he suggests a functional classification which distinguishes between urban places serving the needs of the agricultural population around them,
which are called central places, and other urban places having more specialized
functions, such as mining, university or resort towns. He recognizes that in actuality, however, even such specialized communities have some central place functions for people living in the surrounding area.

9.2.6 Population Size

Because data are available for most areas, the criterion of population size is the one most frequently used not only to distinguish between urban and rural areas, but also to classify cities. A number of terms denoting differences among settlements have been widely used. Although the population size associated with each term is not always specified, a generally acceptable scheme for North America would be:

Type of settlement	Population size
Hamlet	less than 150
Village	150–1,000
Town	1,000–2,500
City	2,500–500,000
Metropolis	500,000 or more

There has been much discussion among urban geographers as to whether these categories constitute discrete size classes or whether they merely represent arbitrary divisions of a continuous variable. Considering the variety of classifications used, it would be difficult to defend the idea of discrete size classes. For example, the minimum population required for an area to be classified as urban varies from 250 in Denmark to 1,000 in Canada, 2,500 in the United States, and 30,000 in Japan. If, therefore, one were using data on "percent of population urban" from these countries, he would be dealing with areas with minimum populations of from 250 to 30,000, which would be difficult to defend as falling within the same classification, whatever criteria were used. In general, whenever raw data are available, it is better not to divide them into arbitrary classes. A minimum population size suited to the purposes of the research may be adopted; for example, the percentage of the population living in cities of 10,000 or more.

9.2.7 Census Definitions of Urban

The use of any one criterion for defining urban areas is not fully satisfactory, since any one alone often fails to include areas which are obviously urbanized even though they do not meet the specifications of that definition. The United States Census Bureau, therefore, has adopted definitions of the terms *urban population* and *urbanized area* which use a number of criteria. For example, urban population comprises all people living in places of 2,500 inhabitants or more incorporated as cities, villages, and towns (except towns in New England, New York, and Wisconsin). In addition, it is recognized that many people live in urbanized areas which are not incorporated. Certain additional criteria for defining such urban fringe areas have been adopted, any one of which qualifies an area as urban: (1) density of 1,000 or more inhabitants or 100 dwelling units or more per square mile, (2) incorporated places with less than 2,500 inhabitants (when contiguous to an urban area), and (3) towns in New England, townships in New Jersey and Pennsylvania which have either 25,000 inhabitants or more or a population of 2,500 to 25,000 and a density of 1,500 persons or more per square mile. An operational definition of these terms is achieved by thus combining the criteria of legal definition, population size, and population density.

It can easily be seen that the concept of a corporate city which is a political unit is seldom adequate for delimiting an urbanized area. In order to consider a central city and the surrounding area which was functionally associated with it as a unit, the *standard metropolitan statistical area* (SMSA) was adopted as a census classification. The criteria for an SMSA are applied to an entire county or counties. Although population size is most important, other factors are also taken into account*.

We should remember that since there are so many different ways of classifying settlements, it is important to know how terms such as city, urbanized area, or urban population have been used in a given study.

9.3 THE LOCATION OF URBAN PLACES

9.3.1 Questions to be Answered

We can ask many questions about settlements of different size. Where are they located? How many are in an area, and how are they distributed? What is the relative size of different settlements, and how are settlements of different sizes spaced and distributed? One way of answering these questions would be to carry out an empirical study and derive generalizations from observations of cities in different areas. Another might be to gain a background of empirical knowledge and then attempt to construct an idealized model of how settlements might be located, given an area with certain assumed conditions. Although both these approaches have been used, because the second, or theoretical, approach has been more heuristic or productive, we shall discuss it in greater detail.

9.3.2 Empirical Generalizations

Geographers have observed that settlements tend to be located at certain kinds of places. Many cities are found at or near junctions of rivers: St. Louis, Belgrade, and Frankfurt are examples. Cities are located on or near the coast where there are good ports, often at the mouths of rivers: Vancouver, Rio de Janeiro, Lisbon, Sydney, Osaka, and Leningrad are all port cities. Cities are often found where plains and mountains meet, as are Salt Lake City, Calgary, and Tehran. In arid

---

*Precise definitions of and specific criteria for these terms may be found in the introductory material of the *Census of Population.*

areas, cities are usually located at oases, sometimes near the base of alluvial fans: Phoenix, Ashkhabad, and Samarkand are at oases. Some cities are located at or near sites of resources such as coal, metallic ores, or hydroelectric power dam sites: Sudbury, Sverdlovsk, and Baku are all located in such places. Agricultural land must also be considered a natural resource, and cities are usually located at centers of agriculturally productive land, as are Des Moines, Regina, Rosario, Bucharest, and Delhi.

Wherever there are large numbers of people there are usually some means of transportation by which both people and goods can be moved into or out of the area. Sometimes cities are established along existing transportation routes such as caravan routes, railroad lines, highways, or rivers; at other times cities are established for a particular purpose such as mining or the development of atomic power, and transportation to the area is improved at the same time the city is established.

Usually more than one factor is related to the location of a particular city, and several factors must be considered simultaneously in attempting to account for its location.

9.3.3 A Theoretical Approach to Explaining the Location of Urban Places

These empirical generalizations have answered only our first question: In what kinds of places do cities tend to be located? They have not shed any light upon how many cities of different sizes would be found in an area and how they would be distributed relative to each other. In order to focus on this problem, Walter Christaller (1933), a German geographer, formulated what has been called central place theory, building upon the work of other European scholars such as Kohl, von Thünen, Weber, and Englander. Although a few scholars in the United States, notably Galpin and Kolb, were also working independently on more limited aspects of the problem, most of the original work was done by Europeans. Since Christaller's explanation of the theory and its derivation requires an entire book, we can touch on only the major points of his argument, especially those related to the location of cities.

Christaller wanted to find a general explanation for the size, number, and distribution of towns, and to discover laws related to these characteristics. He believed that the location of different types of cities was related to different factors, and was concerned primarily with those cities which could be classified as central places, that is, cities located in the centers of agricultural regions which existed mainly to serve the needs of farmers in the surrounding area. He noted that in many areas there were few cities of the largest size class, and that in each successively smaller size class there was a much greater number of cities than in the preceding class. He also observed that there was some regularity in the relative distribution of cities in all size classes. He wished to discover how regularities in the distribution of cities in different size classes might be explained by the workings of the market, under the assumption of the classical economists that individuals tend to behave in such a way as to maximize their economic gains.

In order to simplify the system he was considering, he assumed that the area in which cities were to be located was a limitless plain which was an agricultural region with a uniform physical base, making all parts of it equally attractive for settlement. In this region, population was homogeneously distributed, and each person had the same purchasing power and wants. All points were completely accessible to transportation in all directions, and there were no governmental policies affecting land use.

He identified seven classes of centers, ranging from the metropolis, with a population of over 1,000,000, to small towns, with populations of from 2,000 to 20,000, and still smaller towns, with populations under 2,000. He believed that these were distinct classes which could be clearly identified, and that cities in each size class had definite characteristics which distinguished them from all others. He emphasized as distinguishing features the number and types of so-called central functions; larger places offered a wider variety and larger number of central goods and services than smaller places.

In working out where cities would be located on the hypothetical plain he had defined, he first considered the location of a city with a population of about 30,000, which he called a G-place, after the German *Gaustadt*, a small state capital. This city offered the complete range of goods and services needed by the agricultural population and was in turn dependent upon consumers in the surrounding area for income, rather than upon internal markets. This notion of the interdependence of the central place and its surrounding agricultural region was basic to the theory. Christaller reasoned that a specific distance existed for each good beyond which people would not travel to obtain that good because of cost, time required, or other factors. He also assumed that people would buy a given good, by which he meant any thing purchased by individuals, including both goods and services, at the nearest location where it was available. Since some goods were needed infrequently or by few people, they would be available only in the largest centers, where the population of the city and its surrounding region provided sufficient demand for the good to support the person offering it. The minimum number of people needed to support one individual or establishment offering a particular good was termed the *threshold population* for that good. Those goods for which the threshold population was highest and which people were willing to travel farthest to obtain were termed *highest-order* goods. In order to determine the range for these goods, which in turn relates to the distance between centers, he recognized that the amount of any good consumed decreases with distance from the central place, since the cost to the consumer increases as part of the amount available for purchasing the good is used to cover not only direct transportation costs but also incidental expenses such as lunch or overnight lodging. Eventually a distance is reached beyond which the good either is no longer consumed by

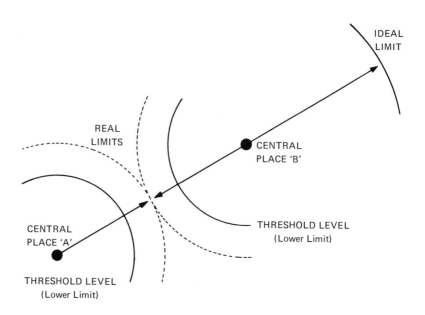

Fig. 9.1. The range of a good, showing the ideal or economic limit, real or actual limit, and lower limit or threshold level. Adapted from Getis and Getis, 1966. Reprinted by permission from the authors and *The Journal of Geography*.

that purchaser, or is obtained from another center. When discussing the range of a good, Christaller calls this maximum distance the *ideal limit*; it corresponds to what we have referred in Section 8.7 as the *economic limit*. The *real limit* is the distance which people actually travel to obtain the good, and the *lower limit* is the radius of the circle enclosing the threshold population, since the good will not be available in a given center if the population is lower than the threshold. These limits are illustrated in Fig. 9.1.

People who live near the economic limits for a particular good travel to the city only to purchase that good or similar ones. They purchase other, lower-order goods there only when they are already making the trip to buy the higher-order goods obtained only in the larger center. They travel shorter distances to smaller centers for the majority of their lower-order purchases. Consequently, the smallest centers, which offer only the lower-order goods, will be spaced at the shortest distances from each other or another larger center; cities in the next largest size class will be farther apart, and so on, up to cities of the largest size class. There will, therefore, be the largest number of places of the smallest size class and fewer of each successive larger class.

In order to determine where cities of different size classes would be located, he first considered the trade area of the central places with populations of about 30,000, G-places. He calculated that people would travel 36 km (22.4 mi) to such cities to obtain the highest-order goods available there. This distance was a reasonable one in southern Germany at the time Christaller was developing his theory; the actual value is not too important, as it varies from area to area and changes over time. If all people in the area were to live no more than 36 km from such a G-place, the G-places would have to be less than 72 km apart since, as shown in Fig. 9.2, tangent circles do not cover the entire area, and people in the shaded areas

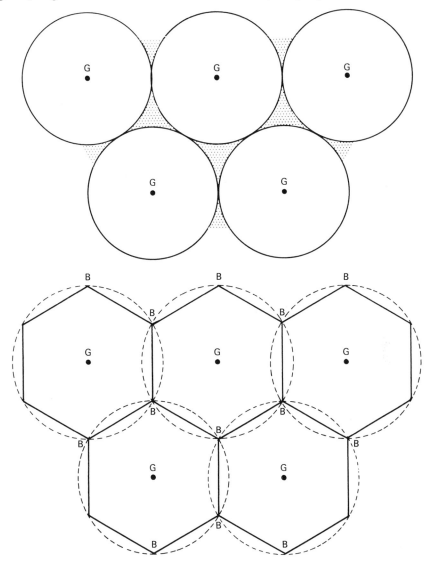

Fig. 9.2 Formation of hexagonal trading areas. Top: tangent circles with areas unserved, showing G-centers. Bottom: overlapping circles with areas of overlap eliminated by hexagons, showing G- and B-centers.

would be more than 36 km away. If, however, the cities were slightly closer together, so that their trading areas overlapped somewhat, no place would be more than 36 km away. If we follow Christaller's assumption that people will obtain a particular good at the closest place where it is available, we can see that persons living within the areas of overlap will travel to the nearer of the two cities. The

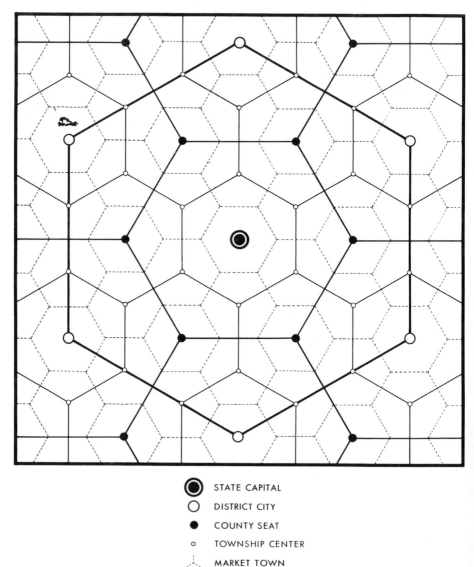

◎	STATE CAPITAL
○	DISTRICT CITY
●	COUNTY SEAT
○	TOWNSHIP CENTER
⋏	MARKET TOWN

Fig. 9.3. Theoretical central place pattern according to the marketing principle.

resulting trading areas defined by bisecting each of the overlapping areas will be regular hexagons inscribed in the circular trading area. From plane geometry, we know that the length of each side of this hexagon is equal to the radius of the circle, and we can calculate the shortest distance from the city to the edge of the hexagon to be $18 \sqrt{3} \approx 31.2$ km (19.5 mi). The entire area can be conceived of as being filled with these regular hexagons, with a G-place at the center of each.

The next smallest cities, or B-places, from the German *Bezirksstadt*, a district center, will be located at the vertices of the hexagons, equidistant from each other and from the G-place. Their hexagonal trade areas may again be determined by first constructing overlapping circles. Using geometry, we can calculate the radius of the circle whose center is a B-place as $12 \sqrt{3} \approx 20.7$ km (12.9 mi). Repeating this process for each smaller size class, we end up with a pattern of hexagons within hexagons, with every city located equidistant from three of a larger size class and from six of the next smaller size class, as shown in Fig. 9.3. The number of places in each class, the population size of a typical city in that class, and the range of its trading area are shown in Table 9.1. As can be seen, the progression of the number of places by size is: 1 of the largest, or L-places, not considered in the system; 2 P-places, also not considered; and from there on by multiples of three for each successive size class: 6 G-places, 18 B-places, 54 K-places, 162 A-places, and 486 M-places or market towns, the smallest considered.

Table 9.1   The number, population size, and range of trading areas of cities in a central place system

	Type of place		Number of places	Typical population	Range of region (km)	(mi)
M	Marktort	Market town	486	1,000	4.0	2.5
A	Amtsort	Township center	162	2,000	6.9	4.3
K	Kreisstadt	County seat	54	4,000	12.0	7.5
B	Bezirksstadt	District city	18	10,000	20.7	12.9
G	Gaustadt	State capital	6	35,000	36.0	22.4
P	Provinzhauptstadt	Provincial head city	2	100,000	62.1	38.6
L	Landeshauptstadt	Regional capital city	1	500,000	108.0	67.1

Source: Walter Cristaller, *Central Places in Southern Germany*, translated by Carlisle W. Baskin, © 1966. Reprinted by permission of Prentice-Hall, Inc., Englewood Cliffs, N.J.

Thus, beginning with simplifying assumptions which reduce the number of factors affecting the location of cities, and considering distance as the only variable related to where people will travel to obtain different goods, the end result is a neat geometric model for the location, number, and spacing of cities in all size classes considered.

9.3.4 Consideration of Additional Factors

This model is so orderly that it appears not to be relevant to conditions in the real world. Christaller recognized that factors other than distance to market, including differential access to transportation and the importance of non-central

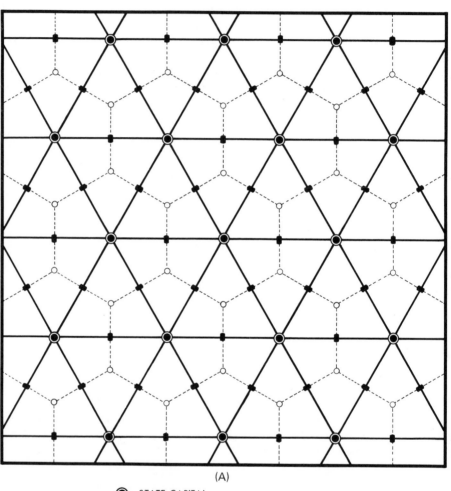

(A)

⊙ STATE CAPITAL
○ DISTRICT CITY: MARKETING PRINCIPLE
◗ DISTRICT CITY: TRANSPORTATION PRINCIPLE
• DISTRICT CITY: ADMINISTRATIVE PRINCIPLE
〜 ADMINISTRATIVE BOUNDARY

Fig. 9.4. Theoretical central place pattern according to (A) the transportation principle and (B) the administrative principle. Adapted from Berry and Pred, 1965. Reprinted by permission.

place functions, were also important. He therefore suggested two additional principles, which we would call factors or variables, which he believed were related to the location of cities: the transportation principle, and the administrative principle.

Looking at the pattern of cities resulting from application of the marketing

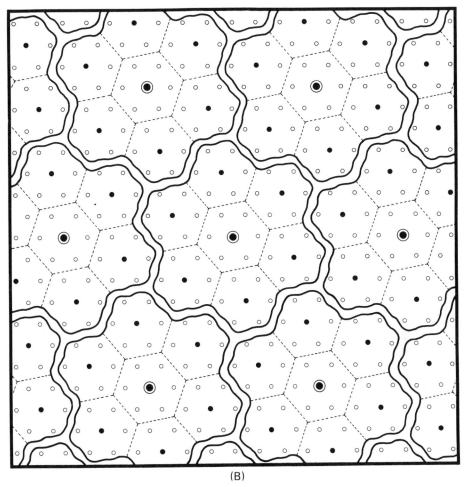

(B)

◉   STATE CAPITAL
O   DISTRICT CITY: MARKETING PRINCIPLE
▬   DISTRICT CITY: TRANSPORTATION PRINCIPLE
•   DISTRICT CITY: ADMINISTRATIVE PRINCIPLE
〜   ADMINISTRATIVE BOUNDARY

principle, as shown in Fig. 9.3, we can see that if transportation routes connected the cities of the system, in order to travel between cities of the same size class it would be necessary to zig-zag back and forth. Christaller decided that if cities were located according to the transportation principle, smaller places would be on the line directly connecting the larger cities. Thus, instead of a B-place being located equidistant from three G-places, it would be on the line connecting them, and midway between them, as shown in Fig. 9.4A. Changing the location of B-places would also involve a rearrangement of the entire system, and reallocation of market areas to different central places, according to the easiest access to transportation.

He also noted that, especially in those areas located near the boundary of an administrative district or county, people would tend to travel to the major center of that administrative district even though it might be farther from them than a center of comparable size in a different administrative district. He suggested that in such a case market areas would be organized into groups of seven, as shown in Fig. 9.4B.

Although Christaller did not interrelate these three principles in the theoretical part of his work, he did show in the empirical part how each might apply to the location of specific cities.

9.3.5 Relationship to Reality of Central Place Theory

Christaller analyzed the actual pattern of central places around the four largest centers in southern Germany: Munich, Stuttgart, Frankfurt, and Nürnberg (Fig. 9.5). He noted that although most places were located according to the marketing principle, many places, especially along major roads leading into the larger cities, were located according to the transportation principle, and still others were located according to the administrative principle. He found that there was definite correspondence between what was predicted by his theory and what was actually found, although it was closer in some areas than others.

Had Christaller written his book twenty-five or thirty years later, he might have expressed his ideas in terms with which we are more familiar. In order to create his model, it was necessary for him to adopt a set of simplifying assumptions which he recognized did not correspond with conditions in the real world. As we stated above, he postulated that the cities were to be located on a uniform plain with no variations in soil fertility, type of agriculture practiced, topography, distribution of population, and location of transportation routes; that there were no governmental regulations influencing the location of cities; and that all cities were central places. These conditions apply less to southern Germany than to parts of North America, such as Iowa, the central valley of California, or the settled portion of the Canadian Prairie Provinces; consequently, the pattern of central places in Germany is less like that predicted by the theory than it is in these areas. In addition, as has been noted in Section 8.7.1, any model describes the general case and is not expected to be accurate for every area.

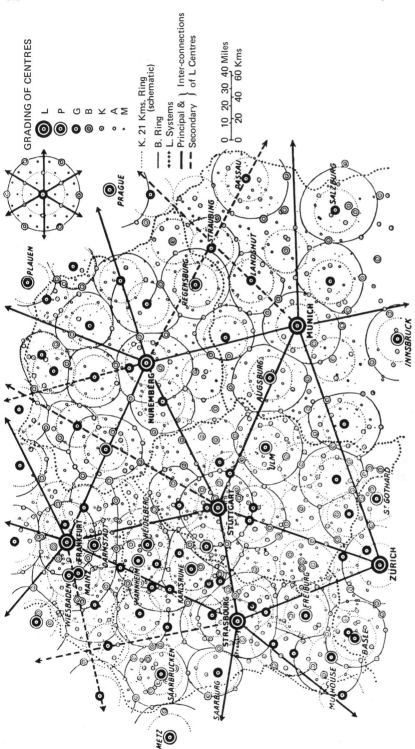

Fig. 9.5. The distribution of towns as central places in southern Germany. Service centers are graded from the Landeshauptstadt to the Marktort (see Table 9.2). Service areas are shown as follows: (1) K-centers are given a schematic radius of 21 km. (2) B-centers are given actual radius of influence (schematically it is 36 km). (3) Boundaries of the L-system. (4 and 5) Principal and secondary inter-connections of L-centers. Source: Walter Christaller, *Central Place in Southern Germany*, translated by Carlisle W. Baskin, © 1966 and Robert E. Dickinson (1964), *City and Religion*. Reprinted by permission of Prentice-Hall, Inc., Englewood Cliffs. N.J., Routledge Kegan Paul, and Humanities Press.

9.3.6 Christaller's Contribution

How, then, can we evaluate Christaller's contribution? We must emphasize that more of what he said has been omitted than has been included. He looked not only at the static aspects of the system, which we have summarized briefly here, but also at the dynamics. He considered, for example, differences in purchasing power of the population, variations in prices, and changes which would occur with changes in such factors as total population, supply of goods, production and transportation costs, range of goods, and technology. Even when all this has been said, it is probable that Christaller's greatest contribution lies not in the extent to which his theory corresponds with reality, but rather in the fact that he proposed it at all. Although he originally derived many of his ideas from knowledge of the region in which he lived and the principles of classical economics, he organized them in the form of a deductive theory. He showed that cities and towns were located in an orderly fashion with relation not only to external physical factors but also to each other. Perhaps most important, however, is the fact that this theory subsumes a number of concepts under one generalized explanation, in that it treats the location of cities as one aspect of economic theory. In addition, it has generated a large number of studies, and has introduced concepts which have been used not only in settlement geography, but even more widely in urban geography. Researchers have become interested in defining the trade area of a town, or of a shopping center within a city, by finding out the range of the goods offered there.

9.3.7 The Distribution of Cities According to Lösch

Lösch (1943) investigated the location of economic activities of all types, not just central place functions. As one aspect of his work, he considered the location of cities and the relationship between city size and trade area. He began with assumptions similar to those of Christaller, including the existence of a basic network of villages and their corresponding hexagonal trade areas. Rather than starting his analysis by considering the largest city first, however, he began by considering the trade areas of the smallest villages and the threshold population which would be required to sustain entrepreneurs offering different goods and services. He reasoned that when the threshold population for a particular good exceeded the size of the village and its surrounding trade area, that good would not be offered there but would be available in the next largest place, and so on up to the goods which were offered only in the largest city. He then mathematically rotated the networks composed of cities in each different size class about a central city until there were six so-called city-rich and six city-poor regions (Fig. 9.6). He noted that the city-rich regions were adjacent to lines connecting the metropolis to the vertices of the large hexagon defining its trade area, which corresponded to major transportation routes, and that the city-poor areas lay farthest from the transportation routes. This arrangement appeared to him to conform more closely to reality than the evenly-spaced network of Christaller (Fig. 9.3).

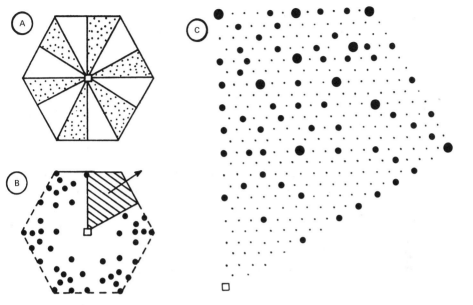

Fig. 9.6. City-rich and city-poor portion of one sector of a Löschian landscape. Source: Lösch, 1943. Reprinted by permission from Gustav Fischer Verlag.

9.3.8 Relative Sizes of Cities in an Area

In attempting to answer our question about the relative numbers of cities of different sizes in an area, we have already noted Christaller's conclusions. According to his theory, when cities are located according to the marketing principle, there will be one metropolis in a region, two other major centers, and then increasing numbers of each size class, in the progression 6, 18, 54, 162, 486. He assumed that the size classes were discrete and recognizable, with cities in each class having characteristics which distinguished them from cities in all other classes. This type of mathematical distribution is called a step-function.

Other writers have noted other types of distributions. Jefferson (1939) observed that in many countries there is one major city which is "disproportionately large" not merely in size but also in national influence. Examples of such primate cities are Mexico City, Vienna, Montevideo, Bangkok, and Madrid. In the countries in which they are located there are many small cities but relatively few of intermediate size.

Zipf (1941) suggested that a rank-size rule applied in many countries. He observed that when cities in these areas are ranked according to population size, the population of a given city multiplied by its rank equals a constant. Stated as an equation,

$$P_r \times r = k, \tag{9.1}$$

where P_r is the population of the city with rank r. This constant, k, is the population of the largest city, P_1, multiplied by its rank, 1. Thus, we can also express this equation in the form,

$$P_r = P_1/r. \tag{9.2}$$

If desired, an exponent may be assigned to the r value empirically; in practice, this exponent has been found to be so close to unity that it may be omitted. Equation 9.2 may be expressed in logarithmic form:

$$\log P_r = \log P_1 - \log r, \tag{9.3}$$

the graph of which is a straight line. The same line, with a slope of -1, results when the raw data are plotted on double logarithmic paper. Application of the rank-size rule, therefore, results in a continuous smooth curve rather than the step-function assumed in Christaller's theory. It appears to fit reality quite well in certain countries. The rank and size of cities in the United States for various years from 1790 to 1950 is shown in Fig. 9.7. As can be seen, the curves correspond fairly closely to what would be predicted from the application of the rank-size rule.

Berry (1961) investigated the relationship between types of city size distribution and both relative economic development and degree of urbanization in different countries. The three types he considered were: primate, rank-size (lognormal), and intermediate. He concluded that no relationship existed for either independent variable. At present, therefore, these three types of city size distributions must be considered as empirical generalizations for which no explanation has yet been found. Moreover, the findings of these and other studies do not give conclusive evidence as to which of the proposed orderings comes closest to fitting the observed data, since the findings are interpreted differently by different researchers.

9.3.9 Changes in the Spatial Distribution of Cities Over Time

Morrill (1963, 1965) was interested in changes in the spatial distribution of towns and cities over time. Unlike Christaller, he was concerned not only with central place functions, but also with the importance of non-central place functions, especially manufacturing, and of transportation. He saw these three factors as being closely related to migration, which in turn effected changes in the distribution of population and the size and location of towns. He decided that a simulation model was a good technique for reproducing changes based on these factors and operating over a period of time. As we have noted in Section 8.7, by means of a simulation model it is possible to reproduce interaction between variables over time, taking into account the effect of feedback on later developments. Morrill selected a portion of southern Sweden as his study area, partly because a variety of data covering many years were available with which to test the results of the simulation incorporating his ideas.

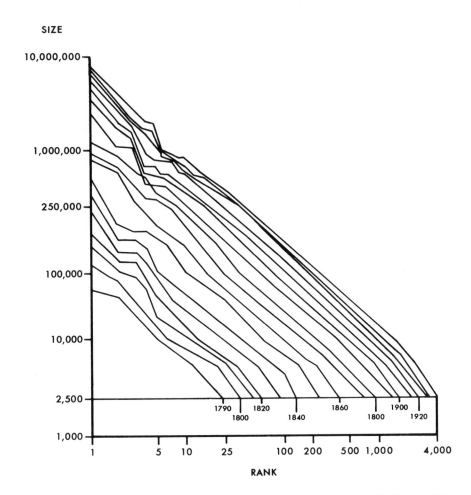

Fig. 9.7. Rank and size of cities in the United States from 1790 to 1950. Source: Brian J. L. Berry, *Geography of Market Centers and Retail Distribution,* © 1967. Reprinted by permission of Prentice-Hall, Inc., Englewood Cliffs, N. J.

The sequence for one run of the model began with the pattern existing at a given time. New transport links were assigned to the area according to certain predetermined conditions and probabilities as to which one of a number of eligible possibilities would be chosen. New factories and new central places were then located, taking the new transportation routes into account. On the basis of this revised pattern, the expected increase in urban population was distributed among the areas, forming new patterns with which to begin the second run of the model.

Simulation was carried out for a hundred-year period, from 1860 to 1960. Morrill used several evaluative criteria to determine how closely certain aspects of his model conformed with reality. By using various statistical tests, he found that (1) the simulated number of places in the different size classes corresponded closely to the actual number, (2) the number of central places, both actual and simulated, was greater than the maximum possible if all central places had been located strictly according to the threshold conditions for different goods, (3) there was a tendency toward uniform spacing of cities of the same size class in the simulated and actual conditions, in both 1900 and 1960, the only years for which this characteristic was tested, (4) tests as to the direction in which growth took place—that is, whether in sectors, as predicted by Lösch, or uniformly throughout the area, as predicted by Christaller—were inconclusive, although both patterns exhibited some tendency toward a hexagonal structure, and (5) early decisions about the locations of railways, towns, and manufacturers had lasting effects on both actual and simulated patterns. Although Morrill also tested several aspects related to migration and the redistribution of population, we are not concerned with them here.

This study is interesting in that it takes into account factors thought to be related to the number, size, and distribution of cities, which were derived both empirically and theoretically. It also gives a picture of how these factors interact over time to produce the effects which may be noted at a particular time. Comparisons were made of a number of different criteria in the actual and simulated situations, and some were found to correspond more closely than others. These discrepancies suggested areas for further investigation which might lead to closer correspondence between the actual and simulated patterns in future trials.

9.3.10 Possible Applications of These Theories

These theories may appear to be so abstract as to be irrelevant to practical considerations. This conclusion is not necessarily valid, however, since the need sometimes arises to plan the pattern of cities—relative size, spacing, and goods and services available in different places—in an area being opened for settlement. Two studies illustrate the way in which the ideas of Christaller and others might be applied in concrete situations.

Takes' (1960) study concerns size and spacing of towns in the Netherlands, where 225,000 hectares (about 562,500 acres) have been opened to settlement since 1930 by means of reclamation of land from the Zuider Zee. When the first polder, the Wieringermeer, was drained in 1930, little thought was given to its overall planning and many errors were made. Villages were located at the three most important crossroads; one of these became the seat of local government, another the main business center, and the third was a less important community. The inhabitants found it inconvenient to have to visit one village to transact legal and governmental business and another to purchase needed goods.

Consequently, before the northeast polder was opened in 1930, an overall plan was drawn up. The largest town was planned as an administrative, business, financial, and cultural center which would ultimately have about 8,000 to 10,000 inhabitants. Six smaller villages were located about 7 to 9 km ($4\frac{1}{4}$ to $5\frac{1}{2}$ mi) apart, about three times the distance between existing villages in older areas. This number of villages was later increased to ten, so that people would not have to travel more than 3 to 4 km from their farms to the village center for church and social activities. The farm owners lived on or near their farms, while the rest of the farm laborers lived in the village. As plans for future polders have been drawn up, however, it has been decided that more farmers will live on or near their farms, and that villages will be larger and farther apart, serving mainly as service centers for the agricultural population, or central places, rather than for housing farm laborers as well.

The Columbia Basin project of eastern Washington (Fig. 9.8) offers another example of government-sponsored settlement located fairly close to existing settled land. The land was made available for agricultural use by the construction of irrigation projects associated with Grand Coulee Dam on the Columbia River. Most of the land used for irrigated crops had been submarginal for dry farming of wheat. As people moved into the area, one new town was established and existing ones increased in population. In addition, some industry has located in these towns.

Before land was opened for settlement a survey was carried out to determine the optimum spacing of different sized towns. A study, reported in U.S. Bureau of Reclamation (1941) was made of the trade areas of towns in the Yakima Valley of Washington. It was found that 1,000 farm families were required to support a local shopping center, a town with a population of at least 1,500. The outer boundary of its trade area would be about ten miles from the town. Small rural service centers, consisting usually of a combined service station and grocery store and possibly providing a few other goods, would be located about four miles apart but no less than six miles from the town. The total population of the town and its trade area would be around 8,000: 4,000 living on farms (1,000 families with an average of four persons), 1,000 rural non-farm, and 3,000 living in or near the town.

These findings were never used for the purpose of locating towns in the Columbia Basin. Instead, existing town became shopping centers for the new population, since most people lived within thirty miles of a shopping center. One new town, Royal City, was established to serve those people who lived more than thirty miles from a town. Because most farm families are willing to travel about an hour by car to do their shopping, towns may now be located farther apart than they were in the days when people traveled by horse and wagon.

9.4 PATTERNS OF SETTLEMENT

9.4.1 Abstracting Patterns of Settlement

Although many geographers have concentrated on studying settlements and the process of settlement specific areas, other have abstracted the pattern of distribu-

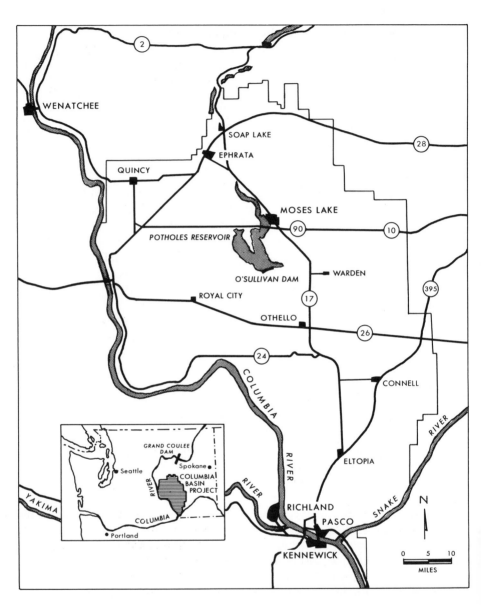

Fig. 9.8. The Columbia Basin Project and its location in the state of Washington.

tion of settlements. In studying settlement patterns, they have usually considered whether settlements are concentrated or dispersed within a given area, although this is only one of many possible abstract elements of distribution which could be considered.

9.4.2 The Location of Dispersed and Agglomerated Settlements

In some countries farmers tend to live in villages and go out from their homes to work their land in the surrounding areas; the pattern of settlement in such a country is termed agglomerated. In other areas, homes are located on the farms themselves; such a pattern of rural settlement is termed dispersed. Dispersed rural settlement patterns are found in the United States, Canada, Australia, New Zealand, the Scandinavian countries, parts of the U.S.S.R., the British Isles, western France, southern Portugal, highland areas of central Europe, Argentina, Uruguay, northern Japan, northern Manchuria, Szechwan province of China, and small areas in the highlands of Mexico, Costa Rica, and western Panama, and low-lands of Venezuela and Colombia.

Agglomerated patterns of rural settlement predominate in Latin America, most of Asia, and the U.S.S.R., with the exceptions noted above. A mixture of the two types is found in Europe. Agglomerated settlement patterns are found in very few areas of the United States and Canada, primarily in the Mormon villages in Utah, communal settlements such as those of the Amana colonies in Iowa and the Hutterite colonies in North Dakota, Manitoba, Saskatchewan, and Alberta, and French settlements in the lowland.

9.4.3 Proposed Explanations for Patterns of Rural Settlement

Although many people have studied rural settlement patterns, too little systematic study of their distribution has yet been done to achieve a clear explanation. Demangeon (1927) tried to explain why rural settlements were dispersed or agglomerated. Drawing upon European examples, he identified three main groups of factors which were associated with concentration or dispersal: natural factors in the physical environment, social factors, and the state of the agricultural economy.

Considering the natural environment first, he concluded that on plains, settlements tended to be concentrated, whereas in rugged or broken areas, dispersed settlements were more common. He noted certain exceptions; for example, dispersion exists in certain plains, as in Flanders, and villages exist in mountains, as in central Italy. His consideration of soil conditions—dry and solid versus boggy and soft—was inconclusive. Availability of water appeared to him to be relatively unimportant except in irrigated areas, where settlers tended to congregate around wells or other available water supplies.

In considering social factors he was more speculative. He believed that man had an original tendency towards concentration, but that the development of agriculture led to increasing dispersion. He also pointed out that although certain ethnic groups had adopted one form or the other and tended to perpetuate this form when they migrated, there was still the need to explain why they had adopted one form or the other. He also considered such conditions as the need for defense, which favors agglomeration, and type of social organization, which can support either pattern.

His category of agricultural economy includes a number of factors such as type of farming practiced, social organization, and the amount of technology in an area. He concluded that modern agricultural practices, with larger areas being farmed by a single family, led to increasing dispersal.

Because of the lack of systematic studies of settlement patterns, it is difficult to draw reliable conclusions. On the basis of existing knowledge, however, it appears that physical factors are less important than others. In general, in rugged areas where the amount of contiguous arable land is small, people tend to live in villages. We find this pattern, for example, in mountainous areas of Switzerland, southern Germany, southwestern Poland, eastern Czechoslovakia, Yugoslavia, and Japan. On the other hand, where there are large contiguous areas of arable land and the size of individual farms is large, as in the United States, Canada, Australia, and New Zealand, settlements tend to be dispersed.

The amount of technology in an area appears to be an important factor, because in an area with a large amount of technology only large farms are economically viable, except for certain specialized types of farming requiring intensive land use. Therefore, with increasing specialization and commercialization of farming, there tends to be increased dispersion.

In some areas, ideological considerations appear to be primary in determining whether settlement is aggregated or dispersed. Political, religious, or military considerations are often uppermost. For example, Israeli Kibbutzim, communal farms of Russia and other Communist countries, and settlements of religious groups such as the Mormons, Mennonites, and Hutterites, have all been established for primarily ideological rather than economic reasons.

In general, we also find that the pattern of concentrated settlement in villages was more common in previous centuries, but that in more recently settled areas, especially where large amounts of relatively inexpensive land have been available, dispersed settlement patterns predominate.

9.4.4 The Technique of Nearest Neighbor Analysis: An Objective Measure of Clustering and Dispersion

One reason for the difficulty encountered in drawing reliable conclusions from different studies of settlement patterns is that each investigator has relied on his own notion of what constitutes aggregated or dispersed settlement patterns. Fig. 9.9 illustrates aggregated, random, and uniform, or dispersed, patterns. In order to have an objective measure of these terms, the technique of nearest neighbor analysis, originally developed by plant ecologists, has been used by geographers concerned with studying patterns of distribution of various phenomena. In this technique, a statistic, R, is computed, which measures the deviations of point patterns from a random distribution in the direction of either dispersion or clustering.

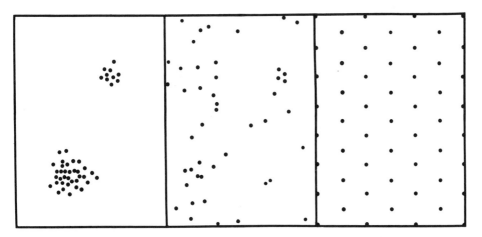

Fig. 9.9. Aggregated, or cluster; random; and uniform, or dispersed patterns (hypothetical).

It has been shown mathematically that, if points are randomly distributed in a given area, the expected mean distance between each point and its nearest neighbor can be calculated for any specified number of points within a specific area. This number then acts as a reference point: If the mean distance is the same as would be expected, the ratio between the observed and the expected mean distance is 1, and the distribution of points is said to be random. It has also been shown that if points are more aggregated, the observed mean distance is less than the expected, and the ratio of the two is less than 1. When the points are uniformly or evenly distributed, the observed mean distance is greatest, and the ratio therefore greater than 1. As Clark and Evans (1954) explain the interpretation of the R statistic.

> The ratio $R = \bar{r}_A/\bar{r}_E$ of observed [or actual] to expected mean distance provides a measure of the degree to which the distribution pattern of the observed population deviates from random expectation. This ratio is less than, equal to, or greater than 1 according to whether the distribution pattern of the individuals in the population is more aggregated, the same as, or more uniform than would be expected in an infinitely large random distribution of the same density (p. 451).*

In calculating R, the density of points in a given area is computed. Given this density, the actual mean distance separating these points in an observed distribution $\bar{r}_A$, is compared with what the mean spacing of the points would be if they were distributed randomly at the same density and within the same area $\bar{r}_E$. This calculation yields values of R ranging from 0, which represents a completely clustered or aggregated distribution with all observations located at a single point; through 1, representing a random distribution of observations, to 2.1491; representing a

---

*Reprinted by permission from *Ecology*, Volume 35 (1954).

distribution in which points are as widely and evenly spaced as possible for the given density.

9.4.5 Studies of Settlement Pattern Using the Technique of Nearest Neighbor Analysis

King (1962) studied the pattern of urban places in twenty sample areas in the United States. He found that in two of these areas the pattern tended toward aggregation, in twelve it tended more toward uniformity, and in the other four the distribution was random. He suggested three factors which were related to the type of distribution found: percent of the area in cropland, percent of the land area in farms, and percent of the total population classed as rural farm. There was a tendency toward uniform spacing in areas in which the value of these variables was high, with increasing aggregation as they decreased. There was more uniformity in areas with uniform relief, in which the original subdivision of land was based on the quarter section and in which there was a rectangular road pattern. Clustering was found only in two irrigated valleys in Washington and Utah.

In summary, we can see that, as has been noted in Section 9.4.3, the spacing tends to be more uniform in those areas where there are relatively large contiguous areas of arable land under cultivation. All the measures which King found to be associated with uniform spacing tend to be high in such areas, typical of the midwestern United States where the sample areas with the most uniform spacing were located.

Birch (1967) studied patterns of the distribution of farmsteads in a sample of thirty-one townships within the Corn Belt of the United States. He used both nearest neighbor analysis and the quadrat method to determine the type of distribution. In the quadrat method, each area is divided into quadrats, or squares, and the number of points in each quadrat counted. The observed number of points, rather than the distance between them, is then compared with the number that would be expected if the distribution were random. If the number is the same as would be expected in a random distribution, the distribution is random; if it is smaller, the distribution is more toward agglomerated; and if it is greater, the distribution is more toward uniform. The interpretation is thus similar to that of the nearest neighbor statistic. He found that results from application of the two techniques were similar, so that either one can be used to help determine the type of distribution.

He noted that in areas of rougher topography and lower road density, which were found in the southern Corn Belt, the distribution was either random or tended toward agglomeration. Conversely, in areas with greater topographic uniformity, such as those in the prairie townships of the central, western, and northern Corn Belt, there was a tendency toward uniformity in the distribution of of farmsteads. These results agree with those of King (1962).

In a study of the distribution of urban places in Alberta (Fig. 9.10), defined

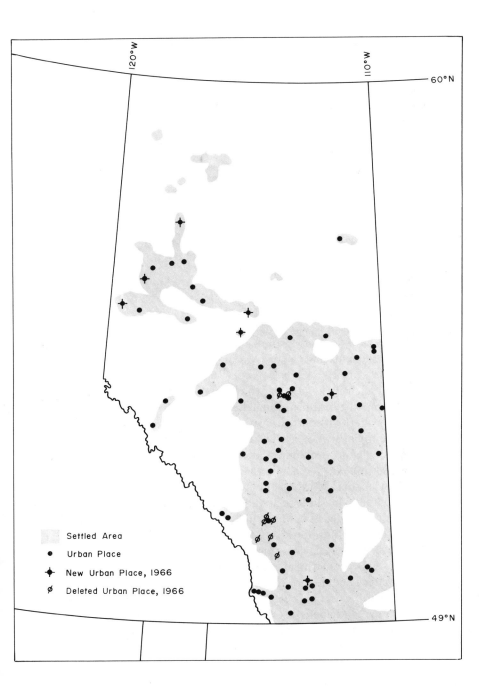

Fig. 9.10. Distribution of urban places in Alberta for 1961 and 1966. Source: Kariel, 1970.

by the Canada Census as places with 1,000 or more inhabitants, Kariel (1970) used nearest neighbor analysis. He found that in the settled area of the province, composed primarily of rolling prairie and having a relatively uniform agricultural-economic base, the spacing of urban places tended toward a uniform distribution. This tendency also is in keeping with the predictions which would be made on the basis of central place theory.

9.4.6 Extensions of Pattern Analysis

It is possible to analyze the patterns not only of farmsteads, settlements, and urban places, but also of other spatially-distributed phenomena such as schools, residences of church members, seating in a cafeteria, or accidents in a city. Quantitative techniques such as nearest neighbor analysis help to make terms such as concentrated or clustered and dispersed or scattered less ambiguous. They facilitate the testing of hypotheses by providing a means of operationalizing these notions so that they can be used as variables.

9.5 THE PROCESS OF SETTLEMENT

9.5.1 Definitions of Settled Area and Settlement

In studies of settlements and the process of settlement, the terms *settled area* and *settlement* are not always clearly defined. We shall begin, therefore, as we have done before, by identifying criteria which can be and have been employed either explicitly or implicitly. In approaching the definition of settled area in this manner, we can first consider two contrasting areas, one of which is obviously settled and one of which is obviously not settled. The contrast between the two should be sufficient that there is no problem of deciding where the boundary line between settled and unsettled lies. We can therefore think of a large city and contrast it with an area of the Canadian North or the Australian outback. In the city we find large numbers of people living in a relatively small area; that is, there is both a large population and high density. Many people reside or work in the city, and it is occupied all the time. Most of the land area has been put to some specific use such as residential, commercial, governmental, or recreational uses. Let us contrast such a closely settled area with an unsettled area. Nobody lives there permanently, although people may come through from time to time hunting, prospecting for oil, or traveling to another area. There are no permanent structures built by man, and the land is not presently being exploited by men for any purpose.

In contrasting these two areas, then, we have succeeded in identifying several criteria which might be used for distinguishing between settled and unsettled areas: the number and density of people in the area, the permanence of their occupation, and the activity to which the land is put. We have implied that the area which we are considering should be large enough to warrant consideration, which would rule out a few acres of abandoned farmland. Some difficulties will obviously arise when we attempt to apply all of these criteria to determining whether a specific area is settled or not. For example, a large ranch in the western United States might be used primarily for grazing cattle, which removes it from the natural state. On the other hand, there might be few, if any, people living there permanently. It is obviously used by man although not densely settled.

We can regard the settlement process as one in which one or more of these criteria would increase; that is, more people would come to an area, the population density would increase, permanent structures would be built, and the land would be exploited by man rather than being left in its natural state.

9.5.2 Examples of Areas Which Have Been Settled Within the Past 50–75 Years

From the seventeenth to the early twentieth centuries, the greatest unsettled frontier existed in North and South America. By now, most of the accessible areas of these continents have been settled, and the unsettled areas remaining are more remote and less hospitable for human habitation. The most recently settled areas in North America are primarily those which have been opened up for agriculture, such as the Matanuska Valley in Alaska, the Peace River area in Alberta and British Columbia, and parts of Manitoba. Similarly, areas in the mountains of Costa Rica and in southern Chile have recently been settled. In addition, settlements have been established for exploiting mineral resources. At Kitimat, British Columbia, a new city was built in a remote, unsettled area to process aluminum. Inuvik was established as a governmental center for the eastern portion of the Northwest Territories.

Besides these more remote areas, others have been opened up to agriculture by the establishment of irrigation projects. Although these may be found throughout the western United States, the largest are in parts of Arizona, along the Snake River in Idaho, and in conjunction with the Columbia Basin project in central Washington.

Governmental action has been important in encouraging settlement of parts of Siberia, developing new land for agriculture in the Netherlands on land reclaimed from the Zuider Zee and the delta of the Rhine River, in resettling parts of Israel which had once been used for agriculture and then virtually abandoned for centuries, and in opening up new areas for settlement in northern Finland and Sweden, as well as in the Australian interior.

9.5.3 Studies of the Settlement of Areas

Bowman (1931, 1937) and his co-workers, such as Joerg (1932) studied pioneer areas in order to determine the conditions under which settlement was successful. They were interested primarily in practical considerations, and hoped to draw conclusions which would be helpful in guiding settlement into new areas in such a way as to avoid the social and economic waste which often accompanies unregulated and uninformed migration. Their findings are similar to those of more recent studies, which are discussed below.

Adams (1956) found that a number of factors were related to the settlement of Oregon from 1840 until about 1900. She suggested that although many sites were available for settlement, people first migrated to an area which was known, the Willamette Valley. Following early settlement of the Willamette Valley, settlers first occupied adjoining hills and valleys, then migrated southward into other valleys and over the Coast Range to the coastal plain. Later they began to settle east of the Cascades in scattered valleys where irrigation water was available. Many parts of the state were unsuitable for settlement because of physical features such as mountains and deserts which made agriculture difficult or impossible; the eastern portion of the state remains sparsely settled today, primarily because of these features. She also noted that settlement tended to follow lines of transportation: water transportation routes and pioneer wagon trials at first, the railroad later. Discovery of gold and other minerals opened up land to agricultural settlement; Indian uprisings retarded it.

Wonders (1960) surveyed the entire history of settlement in the Mackenzie Valley area of northwestern Canada, using both published information and his personal knowledge. He, too, was trying to find what factors were related to settlement of different parts of the area, and what some of the major incentives had been. He found that trading posts to serve the fur trade were first. Next came Anglican and Roman Catholic missions, followed later by governmental installations such as Northwest Mounted Police (later the Royal Canadian Mounted Police) detachment, and weather and radio stations. In the 1930's extraction of radium, silver, gold, petroleum, natural gas, and, in 1944 uranium were of greatest importance.

Early settlement appeared to be concentrated around rivers and lakes, which served as transportation arteries for the fur trade. Later settlement was located at mining sites, for which airplanes were the main source of transportation. Products marketed outside the area had to be of high quality or in great demand in order to compensate for the high cost of transporting them. As the population of the area increased, so did local demand for goods and services, also imported at high cost.

Eidt's (1962) study of settlement in the Montaña of eastern Peru is a descriptive and historical discussion of different agencies encouraging settlement, and the conditions under which settlements were successful. It covers the time from the Spanish conquistadors in the sixteenth century to the present. He defined settlements as any taking up of new land and populating it, and/or establishing a village or other settlement. He found that the settlement of the area had been sporadic over the centuries, and that the same pattern continues today. The principal agencies which encouraged settlement included the Roman Catholic Church, different government agencies, and private organizations. Mission-sponsored settlements of Indians in the area were earliest. Later the government encouraged settlement by the construction of railroads and roads, passage of laws concerning land ownership, and the sale or granting of land to new settlers. Other governmental agencies such as the military, the Agrarian Development Bank, and the *Decree* (Plan) *Peruvia* were also involved. Private corporations also sponsored settlement schemes, as did the National University of Huamanga.

Eidt identified several factors which increased the probability of successful settlements. They were usually located at elevations above 1,000 feet where the climate was cooler, more comfortable, and there were fewer problems than in the lowlands with pests and diseases such as malaria. A safe water supply was desirable. Factors favoring agriculture included level land, productive soil, some dry season, and freedom from flooding. Nearness to markets for the agricultural products was also helpful. The presence of mineral resources and the possibility of producing goods from the agricultural products, such as rubber and Brazil nuts, also encouraged settlement. Safety from attacks by the indigenous population, sometimes due to the presence of the military, was found to encourage settlement as was accessibility by means of water, roads, railroads, or air strips. Often financial support was given in the form of free or subsidized passage, additional grants for land clearing and needed supplies, and fringe benefits such as free education, medical care, and various twentieth-century amenities such as modern housing, electricity, and stores. Stability of support was greater with private than with government-support schemes. Settlers who were relatively well educated and experienced in the type of agriculture they were undertaking, and who had clear title to the land granted to them so that they did not have to contend with squatters, were also more successful than those who had little education and no previous experience.

An applied study such as this one has many practical implications. For example, settlement schemes are often suggested as means of assisting people with little education and low incomes to better their status in life. It would appear, however, that unless an area has first been settled by a few experienced people and ways of farming developed which can be taught to inexperienced newcomers, the percentage of successful settlers will in all probability be extremely low, and the expense of the project out of proportion to the returns from it either to the individual settlers or to the government or other agency involved.

9.5.4 Conclusions About Characteristics of Areas Settled

Although the areas studied vary widely in character, many findings recur in several studies. Probably the most important motivation for individuals to settle in a new area is the hope for economic gain from agriculture, mining, or other pursuits. Where agriculture is the chief occupation, the areas settled tend to be those suited for agriculture; that is, they are not too rough, have a gentle slope, productive soil with good drainage, and no outstanding climatic handicaps such as too much or too little water, too short a growing season, or extreme of temperature which make both agriculture and human existence more difficult. They are relatively accessible by means of roads, rivers, or other routes of transportation. In some areas, the possibility of obtaining outside work until a farm becomes self-supporting had helped. Support by some agency, governmental or private, in the form of transportation, land, irrigation water, or the provision of amenities acts as an added inducement and increases the probability of successful settlement.

9.5.5 Changes in the Location of Settlement

McDermott (1961) examined the changing frontier of agricultural settlement in the Great Clay Belt of Ontario and Quebec. He collected data by means of field study, examination of census material, and consideration of governmental policies. He found that although there were areas of advance and retreat of the frontier in both provinces, most of the retreat, as indicated by abandonment of farms, occurred in Ontario, whereas most of the advance, or new settlement, took place in Quebec. He concluded that retreat of the frontier occurred in areas (1) in which individuals received low financial returns in proportion to the labor expended, (2) where other employment opportunities, such as employment at an asbestos mine, were available, (3) where settlers were unfamiliar with forestry or agriculture, or (4) which were located at the ends of roads or on peripheral roads, away from existing settlements.

In contrast, advance of the frontier occurred in areas (1) in which there was presettlement planning in the form of soil surveys, the withholding of land which needed major improvement from settlement, and overall planning of the location of roads, farm lots, houses, and parish centers, (2) where financial assistance was available for clearing and plowing, the purchase of livestock and farm equipment, construction of a house and barn, well drilling, and living expenses while the farmer was becoming established, (3) where technical assistance was provided by specialists such as drainage engineers, foresters, agronomists, building engineers, and business management consultants, and (4) where the church contributed additional enthusiasm and skill, taking an interest in individual settlers.

Similarly, Klimm (1954) studied the distribution of empty areas in the northeastern United States. Although we generally think of this region as being one of the most densely populated in the country, he was interested in why certain parts had been bypassed or abandoned. He defined an empty area as

> ... one (1) containing no used structures ... ; (2) containing no land used for agriculture ... or for industry; and (3) having a minimum dimension of at least one mile but not approaching a used structure nearer than a quarter of a mile.

The largest of these empty areas was in the northern and eastern two-thirds of Maine, the White Mountains of New Hampshire, the southern Green Mountains of Vermont, northeastern New York, and northern Pennsylvania. Throughout the rest of the northeastern United States the empty areas were smaller and more scattered. He found that most of these empty areas were used primarily for forestry and recreation, although some were brush and abandoned farmland.

In attempting to explain their distribution, he found certain physical factors: steep slope, inadequate drainage, poor soil, and climatic handicap, associated with the presence of more empty areas. He also noted that many of these areas were isolated, and remote from lines of through traffic. They were located at a distance from centers of population and economic activity, so that even if items could be produced in them, the increased transportation costs would make their production unprofitable.

By comparing the conclusions about the abandonment of settled areas and settlement of new areas, we can see that many of the same factors which account for the location of new areas also help to account for the location of areas being abandoned. Where a larger amount of a variable, such as financial return, is related to the settlement of an area, a smaller amount of it is related to the abandoning of settled land.

9.6. TOWARDS A MORE GENERALIZED EXPLANATION OF THE PROCESS OF SETTLEMENT

9.6.1 Settlement Considered as a Land Use

Since our aim is to achieve explanations which are at the same time more precise and generalizable to more phenomena, if we can relate settlement to other phenomena we have studied in some way, then we should be able to come up with a more general explanation of it. Because one aspect of the process of settlement involves progressive changes in the way land is used by man, from being totally unexploited by him to being very intensively used, as in a large city, we are justified in considering settlement as a type of land use or a combination of a number of types, as the term land use was defined in Section 8.1.1. We should, therefore, be able to draw upon the explanations for changes in land use which were discussed in Section 8.

9.6.2 Settlement as a Case of the Von Thünen Model

As we learned in Section 8.7, according to the von Thünen model and its later modifications, the type of land use found at a particular site can be explained by the returns, or economic rent, obtained from that use at that site in relation to the returns which might be obtained from other possible uses; that is, by the notion of land use competition, illustrated in Fig. 8.9. As can be seen, the slope of the agricultural land use curve is negative and of small magnitude. We also learned how the returns from each activity at a given site are related to the physical and economic optima and limits for that activity. If we consider new agricultrual settlement as occupying one part of the rent-distance from market curve for agricultural land use shown in Fig. 8.9, it would be located at the point where the curve approaches the X-axis; that is, where the rent is close to zero and the distance from market relatively great. For settlement, as for other land uses, the generalizations derived from the application of such models hold only to the extent that the simplified assumptions of the model are valid which, in the real world, they seldom are. It is, nevertheless, helpful as a conceptual framework because even though many factors have not been included, in principle it should be possible to add them to the model so that the total effect of all variables taken together could be calculated.

Most new land which is settled is used either for agriculture or mineral extraction; the areas being settled at a given time are those in which settlers believe that they can gain something, usually in an economic sense, but sometimes also in terms of what they consider as a better way of life, freedom from repression, or other personal advantages. Within a larger area, the land settled first for agricultural purposes is usually the most productive agriculturally and most accessible. Economic return from the land may be augmented by subsidies of various types which encourage settlers to take the risk of moving to a new area. The presence of settlers in itself tends to encourage additional settlement, as the area becomes known to more people.

Newly settled land, however, tends to be less productive than land already settled; that is, it is closer to the physical and economic limits of profitability. It may be almost too cold or hot, dry or wet for agriculture, soils may be unfavorable, and it is often more distant from markets. Such land is termed marginal, since the production from it, when marketed at existing prices, barely covers the cost of production. With changes in technology, such as the development of new hybrids, machinery, and farming methods, the lowering of transportation costs, or rising prices for goods produced, the land may yield higher returns and no longer be considered marginal.

9.6.3 The Importance of Noneconomic Factors

We have seen, however, that economic factors, although important, are not the only ones related to the settlement of new land; various studies which we have reviewed have pointed out the importance of other factors such as the availability of technical help, personal interest in settlers, and certain amenities of established areas such as stores, schools, and recreational facilities. In studies of settlement in Sweden, Enequist (1959) noted that ". . . even favorable natural and geographic conditions have not always attracted settlement. . . ," and Bylund (1960) observed that,

> . . . some good land close to established settlements and well suited for colonization may remain unsettled. On the contrary, other localities in remote districts and with inferior natural conditions may have been cultivated surprisingly early. (p. 225)

One possible approach to a more adequate explanation would be to add independent variables to the von Thünen model: both these social factors suggested by different writers, and others dealing with the behavior of individuals. Another would be to attempt to simulate the actual process of settlement, taking all variables into account in setting up the simulation model. This was the approach used by Morrill (Section 8.7.9) in his study of the expansion of residential land use in one part of the urban fringe of Seattle.

Bylund (1960) has used a simulation approach to studying the colonization of northern Sweden, considering a special case in which a few settlers came to the area originally, and expansion of settlement was carried on by their descendants rather than by other migrants. He first considered some of the ways in which settlement might spread. He assumed that all land in the area was equally desirable with respect to physical features, although he recognized that characteristics such as good soil and favorable climate were related to the choice of areas to be settled. He then considered other factors such as distance from the road, church, and market place, freedom from competition from existing settlements, and some variations in physical factors, such as the presence of swamps, which made certain areas unfit for agricultural settlement.

The first possibility, which he called the A model (Fig. 9.11) was that settle-

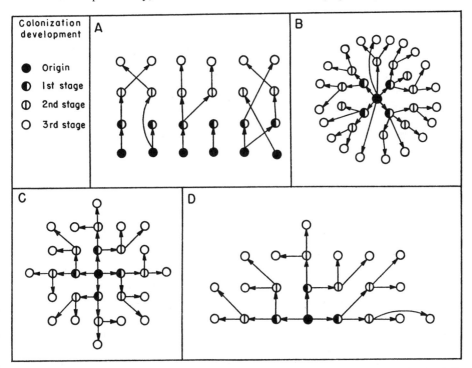

Fig. 9.11. Hypothetical models of settlement diffusion. Adapted from Bylund, 1960. Used by permission.

ment might take place more or less in a straight line along on advancing frontier. The second, or B model, involved circular spread from a single original settlement outwards in all directions, like the wave which spreads from a stone dropped into water. He rejected both of these as not conforming with the observed settlement pattern. In constructing his final model, he started with three original settlements from which the descendants spread out. Using a simulation process based on his assumptions, he ended up with a diagram which indicated that settlement was not completely even, but that some areas with equally desirable characteristics were skipped over and others farther from the original settlements were taken up first. As we found with Morrill's model, it is difficult to evaluate the correspondence of such a model to the observed pattern; Bylund (pp. 137–138) himself states that the similarity between the two models ". . . cannot be said to be immediately striking as regards the formation of the pattern." He concludes that the model nevertheless illustrates the influence of other than physical factors upon the development of the settlement pattern.

9.7 SUMMARY AND CONCLUSION

In our explorations in this chapter we have considered selected spatial aspects of settlements as places and the process of settlement. We have noted that settlements have been classified in many different ways, each of which serves a different purpose. With changes in geography, less emphasis tends to be placed on classification and more on explanation. We have therefore surveyed empirical and theoretical approaches to explaining the location of cities, and cited examples of applications of the proposed theories. We have next considered patterns of settlement, seeking an objective measure of the extent to which they are dispersed or agglomerated, and proposed explanations of differences in these patterns. Finally, in looking at the process of settlement, we have attempted to find factors associated with increases and decreases in settlement of frontier areas over time. We have then considered theoretical explanations for changes in settlement patterns and the use of simulation to test these notions.

Geographers studying settlement have also considered aspects other than those we have selected, especially the buildings associated with settlements, which we discussed in Chapter 2. It appears that some of the phenomena formerly studied as part of settlement geography are being incorporated into other topical specialties. With increased knowledge and greater specialization among geographers, the phenomena studied are being organized differently. For example, study of the location of cities has been incorporated into urban-economic geography. As geographers become increasingly concerned with explaining phenomena and developing theories to subsume many different phenomena, some of the traditional boundaries between topical specialties are changing. Thus, rather than studying patterns of the distribution of settlements, they are concerned with analysis of the distributional patterns of many phenomena. Moving from concrete study of the settlement of areas, they perceive the spread of people as part of the study of migration or movement of people and, more generally, as a specific instance of the diffusion process. It is likely, therefore, that future studies of some of the topics we have considered may take place outside the field of settlement geography as it is now known.

REVIEW YOUR UNDERSTANDING OF THESE CONCEPTS

settlements as places
morphology of settlements
legal definition of settlements
functional classification of settlements
central places and noncentral places
distinction between rural and urban
empirical and theoretical approaches
    to explaining locations

central place theory
relationships between size and
    number of cities
abstract patterns of settlement
nearest neighbor analysis
process of settlement
settlement as a case of the von Thünen
    model

SUGGESTED ACTIVITIES

1. Cite some areas in any country where future agricultural settlements might be located. Justify your selection, taking into account both the notion of land use competition and what settlers want in the way of economic returns and amenities of life.

2. Obtain data regarding the sizes of cities in an area such as a state and rank them. Plot them on graph paper, with population size on the Y-axis and the rank (1st, 2nd, 3rd, . . .) on the X-axis. Determine how closely they correspond to the rank-size rule.

3. Trace the spatial pattern of settlement in a state or province, or portion thereof, over a period of time. Attempt to explain changes in the observed pattern by using the generalizations discussed in this chapter.

4. Plot the cities in a selected area on a map, using a convenient set of size classes. How closely does the pattern you observe correspond to that of the models postulated by Christaller or Lösch? Attempt to explain deviations of the observed pattern from the theoretical, and make suggestions for revising the theoretical model to make it conform more closely to reality in the area you have studied.

5. A. Draw three squares or rectangles the same size to represent three different areas. Within each, place a convenient number of points—about 10 to 20. In one of the rectangles concentrate these points in a small area. In one, distribute them randomly; and in the third, space them uniformly, attempting to maximize the distance between them. Use the simplified

computational formula to calculate the nearest neighbor statistic R for each of these distributions

$$R = 2\overline{D}\sqrt{N/A},$$

where:

$\overline{D}$ = the mean distance between each point and its nearest neighbor,

N = the total number of points, and

A = the area of the rectangle, in the same units as were used to measure the distances between points.

B. Trace the settlement pattern from a map of a county or part of a state or province. Compute the value of R for this pattern. What relationship has the value obtained to what you might have expected from observation of the pattern. Does it confirm your evaluation of it as being clustered, uniform, or random?

REFERENCES

Adams, Georgia E. (1956), "Two isochronic maps of settlement in Oregon," *Yearbook of the Association of Pacific Coast Geographers* **18**, 36–41.

Berry, Brian, J. L. (1961), "City size distributions and economic development," *Economic Development and Cultural Change* **9**, 573–588.

Berry, Brian J. L. (1967), *Geography of Market Centers and Retail Distribution*. Englewood Cliffs: Prentice-Hall.

Berry, Brian J. L. and Allen Pred (1965), *Central Place Studies: A Bibliography of Theory and Applications*, Bibliography Series No. 1, with supplement. Philadelphia: Regional Science Research Institute.

Birch, B. P. (1967), "The measurement of dispersed patterns of settlement," *Tijdschrift voor Economische en Sociale Geografie* **58**, 68–75.

Bowman, Isaiah (1931), *The Pioneer Fringe*. New York: American Geographical Society.

Bowman, Isaiah, ed. (1937), *Limits of Land Settlement*. New York: Council on Foreign Relations.

Bunge, William (1966), *Theoretical Geography*, 2nd rev. ed., Lund Studies in Geography, Series C, No. 1. Lund: C. W. K. Gleerup.

Bylund, E. (1960), "Theoretical considerations regarding the distribution of settlement in inner North Sweden," *Geografiska Annaler* **42**, 225–231.

Christaller, Walter (1933), *Central Places in Southern Germany*, translated by C. W. Baskin, 1966. Englewood Cliffs: Prentice-Hall.

Clark, Philip J. and Francis C. Evans (1954), "Distance to nearest neighbor as a measure of spatial relationships in populations," *Ecology* **35**, 445–452.

Demangeon, Albert (1927), "The origins and causes of settlement types," in Philip

L. Wagner and Marvin W. Mikesell, eds., 1962, *Readings in Cultural Geography*. Chicago: University of Chicago Press, pp. 506–516.

Dickinson, Robert E. (1964), *City and Region: A Geographical Interpretation*. London: Routledge & Kegan Paul.

Eidt, Robert C. (1962), "Pioneer settlement in eastern Peru," *Annals* of the Association of American Geographers **52**, 255–278.

Enequist, Gerd (1959), *Geographical Changes of Rural Settlement in Northwestern Sweden Since 1523*, Uppsala Universitets Årsskrift. Uppsala: Almqvist and Wiksells.

Getis, Arthur and Judith Getis, 1966, "Christaller's central place theory," *Journal of Geography* **65**, 220–226.

Harris, Chauncy D. (1943), "A functional classification of cities in the United States," *Geographical Review* **33**, 86–99.

Houston, James M. (1953), *A Social Geography of Europe*. London: Duckworth.

Jefferson, Mark (1939) , "The law of the primate city," *Geographical Review* **29**, 226–232.

Joerg, W. L. G., ed. (1932), *Pioneer Settlement*. New York: American Geographical Society.

Kariel, Herbert G. (1970), "Analysis of the Alberta settlement pattern for 1961 and 1966 by nearest neighbor analysis," *Geografiska Annaler* **52** B, 124–130.

King, Leslie J. (1962), "A quantitative expression of the pattern of urban settlements in selected areas of the United States," *Tijdschrift voor Economische en Sociale Geografie* **53**, 1–7.

Klimm, Lester E. (1954), "The empty areas of the northeastern United States," *Geographical Review* **44**, 325–345.

Lösch, August (1943), *The Economics of Location*, translated by William H. Woglom and Wolfgang F. Stolper, 1954. New Haven: Yale University Press and 1967, New York: Wiley.

McDermott, George L. (1961), "Frontiers of settlement in the great clay belt, Ontario and Quebec," *Annals* of the Association of American Geographers **51**, 261–273.

Morrill, Richard L. (1963), "The development of spatial distribution of towns in Sweden: an historical-predictive approach," *Annals* of the Association of American Geographers **53**, 1–14.

Morrill, Richard L. (1965), *Migration and the Spread and Growth of Urban Settlement*, Lund Studies in Geography, Series B, No. 26. Lund: C. W. K. Gleerup.

Nelson, Howard J. (1955), "A service classification of American cities," *Economic Geography* **31**, 189–210.

Takes, Charles A. P. (1960), "The settlement pattern in the Dutch Zuiderzee reclamation scheme," *Tijdschrift van het Koninklijk Nederlandsch Aardrijkskundig Genootschap* **77**, 347–353.

U.S. Bureau of Reclamation (1941), *Columbia Basin Joint Investigations, Character and Scope*. Washington, D.C.: U.S. Government Printing Office.

Wonders, William C. (1960), "Postwar settlement trends in the Mackenzie Valley area," *Geografiska Annaler* **42**, 333–338.

Zipf, George K. (1941), *National Unity and Disunity*. Bloomington: Principia Press.

Additional Readings

Armstrong, Terence (1965), *Russian Settlement in the North*. Cambridge: Cambridge University Press.

Beckmann, Martin J. (1958), "City hierarchies and the distribution of city size," *Economic Development and Cultural Change* **6**, 243–248.

Berry, Brian J. L. and William L. Garrison (1958), "Alternate explanations of urban rank-size relationships," *Annals* of the Association of American Geographers **48**, 83–91.

Brush, John E. (1953), "The hierarchy of central places in southwestern Wisconsin," *Geographical Review* **43**, 380–402.

Brush, John E. and Howard E. Bracey (1955), "Rural service centers in southwestern Wisconsin and southern England," *Geographical Review* **45**, 559–569.

Change, K. C., ed (1968), *Settlement Archaeology*. Palo Alto: National Press Books.

Chisholm, Michael (1962), *Rural Settlement and Land Use: An Essay in Location*. London: Hutchinson University Library.

Dacey, Michael F. (1968), "An empirical study of the areal distribution of houses in Puerto Rico," *Transactions Institute of British Geographers* **45**, 51–69.

Dickinson, Robert E. (1949), "Rural settlements in German lands," *Annals* of the Association of American Geographers **39**, 239–263.

Dickinson, Robert E. (1956), "Dispersed settlement in southern Italy," *Erdkunde* **10**, 282–297.

Doxiadis, Constantinos A. (1968), *Ekistics: An Introduction to the Science of Human Settlements*. New York: Oxford University Press.

El-Sayed, El-Bushra (1967), "*The factors affecting settlement distribution in the Sudan,*" *Geografiska Annaler* **49** B, 10–24.

Enequist, Gerd (1960), "Advance and retreated of rural settlement in northwestern Sweden," *Geografiska Annaler* **42**, 211–219.

Gentilcore, Louis R. (1961), "Mission and mission lands of Alta, California," *Annals* of the Association of American Geographers **51**, 46–72.

Getis, Arthur (1964), "Temporal land-use patterns analysis with the use of nearest neighbor and quadrat methods," *Annals* of the Association of American Geographers **54**, 391–399.

Haggett, Peter (1966), *Locational Analysis in Human Geography*. New York: St. Martin's Press.

Hautamäki, Lauri (1967), "Development of settlement in some rural communes in western Finland since 1920," *Fennia* **96**, No. 2, 1–98.

Hoffman, George W. (1964), "Transformation of rural settlement in Bulgaria," *Annals* of the Association of American Geographers **54**, 45–64.

Hudson, John C. (1969), "A location theory for rural settlement," *Annals* of the Association of American Geographers **59**, 365–381.

Johnson, Hildegard Binder (1951), "The location of German immigrants in the Middle West," *Annals* of the Association of American Geographers **41**, 1–41.

Johnson, Hildegard Binder (1957), "Rational and ecological aspects of the quarter section: an example from Minnesota," *Geographical Review* 47, 330–348.

Johnson, James H. (1958), "Studies of Irish rural settlement," *Geographical Review* 48, 554–565.

Kallbrunner, Hermann (1957), "Farms and villages: the European pattern," *Landscape* 6, No. 3, 13–17.

Kersten, Earl W., Jr. (1964), "The early settlements of Aurora, Nevada and nearby mining camps," *Annals* of the Association of American Geographers 54, 490–507.

King, Leslie J. (1969), "Analysis of spatial form and its relation to geographic theory," *Annals* of the Association of American Geographers 59, 573–595.

Macinko, George (1963), "The Columbia Basin project: expectations, realizations, implications," *Geographical Review* 53, 185–199.

Matui, Isamu (1932), "Statistical study of the distribution of scattered villages in two regions of the Tonami Plain, Toyama Prefecture," *Japanese Journal of Geology and Geography* 9, 251–256, also in Brian J. L. Berry and Duane F. Marble, 1968, *Spatial Analysis: A Reader in Statistical Geography*. Englewood Cliffs: Prentice-Hall.

Maxwell, J. W. (1965), "The functional structure of Canadian cities: a classification of cities," *Geographical Bulletin* 9, 79–104.

Meitzen, August (1895), *Siedelung und agrarwesen der Westgermanen und Ostgermanen, der Kelten, Römer, Finnen und Slawen*, 3 vols. and atlas. Berlin: W. Hertz.

Meyer, Alfred H. (1954, 1956), "Circulation and settlement patterns of the Calumet region of northwest Indiana and northeast Illinois," First Stage, *Annals* of the Association of American Geographers 44, 245–274; Second Stage, *Annals* of the Association of American Geographers 46, 321–356.

Michelson, William H. (1970), *Man and his Urban Environment: A Sociological Approach*. Reading, Mass.: Addison-Wesley.

Miller, Elbert E. (1956), "Economic and social changes in the Columbia Basin, Washington," *Land Economics* 41, 335–346.

National Research Council (1956), *Rural Settlement Patterns in the United States as Illustrated on one Hundred Topographic Quadrangle Maps*. Washington, D.C.: National Academy of Sciences.

Olsson, Gunnar (1968), "Complementary models: a study of colonization maps," *Geografiska Annaler* 50 B, 115–132.

Ottoson, Howard W. and others (1966), *Land and People in the Northern Plains Transition Area*. Lincoln: University of Nebraska Press.

Rushton, Gerard (1971), "Postulates of central-place theory and properties of central-place systems," *Geographical Analysis* 3, 140–156.

Schwarz, Gabriele (1966), *Allgemeine Siedlungsgeographie*. Berlin: de Gruyter.

Skinner, G. William (1964–1965), "Marketing and social structure in rural China," Parts I, II, and III, *The Journal of Asian Studies* 24, 3–43, 195–228, and 363–399.

Stevens, Rayfred L. (1967), "European settlement ventures in the tropical lowlands of Mexico," *Erdkunde* 21, 258–277.

Stewart, Charles, Jr. (1958), "The size and spacing of cities," *Geographical Review* **48**, 222–245.

Stewart, Norman R. (1965), "Migration and settlement in the Peruvian Montana: the Apurimac Valley," *Geographical Review* **55**, 143–147.

Stone, Kirk H. (1962), "Swedish fringes of settlement," *Annals* of the Association of American Geographers **52**, 373–393.

Stone, Kirk H. (1966), "Finnish fringe of settlement zones," *Tijdschrift voor Economische en Sociale Geografie* **57**, 222–232.

Udo, R. K. (1965), "Disintegration of nucleated settlement in eastern Nigeria," *Geographical Review* **55**, 53–67.

U.S. Bureau of Reclamation (1947), *Towns and Villages*, Columbia Basin Joint Investigations, Columbia Basin Project, Problem No. 18. Washington, D.C.: U.S. Department of the Interior.

Vanderhill, Burke, G. (1962), "The decline of land settlement in Manitoba and Saskatchewan," *Economic Geography* **38**, 270–277.

Vanderhill, Burke G. and David E. Christensen (1963), "The settlement of New Iceland," *Annals* of the Association of American Geographers **53**, 350–363.

von Böventer, Edwin (1969), "Walter Christaller's central places and peripheral areas: the central place theory in retrospect," *Journal of Regional Science* **9**, 117–124.

CHAPTER 10
TECHNOLOGY

10.1 TECHNOLOGY AS A UNIFYING PRINCIPLE

The theme of technology has recurred throughout these explorations as an independent variable which has helped to explain spatial aspects of almost all the phenomena we have explored. In Chapter 2 we noted that the amount of technology in an area limits building materials and construction methods. Exploring dietary patterns in Chapter 5, we demonstrated a relationship between the amount of technology, measured as total energy consumption per capita, and calories consumed per capita per day. Our exploration of the geography of language, in Chapter 6, disclosed that as technology increases, there is increased interaction among speakers of different languages and dialects, and some provision is made for mutual intelligibility. We also saw that the development of computer technology has been accompanied by the development of many different languages for man-machine communication. In Chapter 7 we found that spatial variation in literacy was related to technology, industrialization, urbanization, and the amount of circulation of people and ideas in an area.

Exploring patterns of land use in Chapter 8, we saw that changes in agricultural technology in the form of hybrids, new and improved tools and machinery, fertilizer, and irrigation and drainage methods, have helped to alter the optima and limits for different crops, and therefore the crops which could economically be grown in an area. We also learned that technology affects land use within cities in many ways. Transportation technology is related to urban spatial structure; as transportation has become faster, more and more people live farther from work, and there is progressive decentralization of residential areas. At the same time, new building methods permit higher structures and consequently greater concentration in central business districts.

Finally, studying the location of settlements in Chapter 9, we found that transportation technology was related to the location of cities, which for thousands of years have been at the junction of transportation routes. As additional types of transportation are developed, new cities are located with respect to them. Central place patterns are also affected; as there is more technology in an area, the speed of transportation increases, so that people can travel farther in the same time. With time remaining constant, distance traveled increases, and central places tend to be located farther apart. Small towns diminish in size and may finally disappear as people travel to larger centers to shop.

We can see, then, that technology helps to explain both variations in the distribution of many different phenomena at any given time and changes in their distribution in a given area over time. As a concept which helps to interrelate many phenomena, it deserves careful consideration in its own right.

In this chapter we shall consider, therefore, technology as a dependent variable, remembering that whether a particular variable is designated as dependent or independent is determined by the question being asked. Following the pattern of previous chapters, we shall seek to explain its observed spatial distribution. In order to obtain data regarding this distribution, we shall adopt an operational definition, since we have been using the term without defining it precisely. Having done this, we shall attempt to find a number of independent variables which help to explain variations in the spatial distribution of technology, and determine how much of the variation is explained by the use of these variables. After this, we shall examine the interrelationships among some of the phenomena we have already studied, some additional phenomena, and technology, considering all these variables as elements within a dynamic system. In this way, it will be possible to explain variations from area to area at a particular time, changes within a given area over time, and the influence of areas upon each other as technology and related elements spread over space and time.

10.2 DEFINITION OF TECHNOLOGY

10.2.1 Identifying the Problem

As has been true of many variables used in these explorations, no one generally accepted definition of technology exists. Almost everyone has some idea of what it means; the mere fact of living with an accelerating rate of technological change, manifested by growing industrialization, urbanization, and automation, constantly reminds us of it. We constantly hear about such agricultural inventions as new hybrids with higher yields, mechanical picking machines to replace stoop laborers; developments in the space program which include communications satellites, manned and unmanned moon landings, and flights to the planets; and medical breakthroughs such as new drugs and heart transplants. Men are beginning to realize that not all the effects of technology are desirable; they are becoming aware of the many intricate interrelationships between man's activities on the earth and their effect on the total environment. Thus such conveniences as automobiles, freeways, automated factories, computerized accounting systems, and supersonic airplanes have both positive and negative impacts on the total life system of the earth, the biosphere. Technology as such, however, is value-free. A particular technological advance may be judged as being helpful or harmful in different ways by different people, depending on their points of view. Often the full impact of invention may not be known or recognized for many years, as happened with DDT.

Understanding of technology and technological change is complicated by the fact that a number of terms are often used interchangeably with technological change. These terms include: development, economic development, economic growth, technological development, technological growth, advancement, industrialization, and modernization.

10.2.2 A Conceptual Definition

To use this concept analytically it is necessary to sort out some of the ideas involved in order to specify those aspects in which we are interested. Trying to separate technology from economics, we can see that, in its more restricted sense, the term applies to the application of knowledge to the making of tools, machinery, and other devices which increase man's ability to produce goods and services and to manipulate his natural environment. In a broader sense, however, it refers also to the knowledge and human organization needed to create and maintain these devices. In this broader sense, technology includes everything which assists man to live in, compensate for, influence, pollute, or destroy his environment.

10.2.3 An Operational Definition

If we accept this broader meaning, it is clear that because technology is an abstract concept with many concrete manifestations, it is difficult to define operationally, using a single variable. It is, nevertheless, necessary to use some quantitative measure if we are to carry out analyses to help answer questions about relationships between technology and other variables. Since it is usually easier to deal with a single variable than an index employing several variables, we would like to find one which appears to be a valid indicator of the amount of technology in an area.

In order to choose such a variable, we first think of some areas which we would consider as having large amounts of technology and others which have very little, as we have done previously. We next identify some phenomena which differ in quantity between the two groups and which might therefore serve as measures of the amounts of technology present in them. One of the most frequently used in studies of development is gross national product (GNP) per capita. This variable has the advantages of recognized validity and data availability, but certain disadvantages make it desirable to use a different variable if we can find one which is equally valid. One problem is that GNP per capita is an economic variable; another is that a high GNP per capita is more logically thought of as the result of effective use of large amounts of technology than as a measure of technology itself. Many writers, including White (1949, 1959),

Cottrell (1955), and Guyol (1960) have pointed out that increases in technology involve substitution of other energy sources for human energy in performing productive work. It is not difficult to see that energy consumption per capita is intimately related to the level of technology prevailing in an area. When there is very little technology, humans do all the work, and wood or other fuel may be burned as a source of heat for cooking and warmth; the amount of energy consumed per capita is low. As technology increases, domesticated animals provide additional energy for work. With the development of machinery which transforms other forms of energy to work, increasing amounts of energy are used both for production of goods and services and for heating, cooking, lighting, and running household appliances. In high-consumption areas such as the United States and Canada, the amount of energy used from all sources is extremely high. If these sources, which include natural gas, electric power, and petroleum products, were cut off, it would be difficult for residents of these areas to survive for even a short time, as has been shown during prolonged power failures in some areas.

Among other variables which have been suggested are steel consumption per capita; paper consumption per capita; the amount of agricultural technology, measured by the use of fertilizer or mechanized equipment; use of computers; and chemical consumption. In order to select one variable which could be used as a measure of technology separate from economic development, the authors carried out a study (Kariel and Kariel, 1970). Three possibilities were considered: energy consumption per capita, steel consumption per capita, and paper consumption per capita. These variables were found to be closely interrelated. Table 10.1 shows similar relationships among these variables, using more recent data. In addition, all of them were closely related to a number of independent variables, most of which are discussed in the analysis of Section 10.4.2. Energy consumption per capita was selected because it is most closely related to almost all of the independent variables, can be logically justified, and is validated by its high correlation with GNP per capita.

Table 10.1 Coefficients of correlation between three possible measures of technology

	Y_1	Y_2	Y_3
Y_1 Energy consumption per capita	1.000	0.928	0.859
	(144)*	(71)	(130)
Y_2 Steel consumption per capita		1.000	0.851
		(71)	(71)
Y_3 Printing and writing paper consumption per capita			1.000
			(131)

Calculated on the basis of data for 1965 taken from United Nations Statistical Office, *Statistical Yearbook.*

*Number in paraentheses indicated the number of countries on which the coefficient of correlation is based.

All variables were transformed to common logarithms.

Table 10.2　Energy consumption per capita in 1965 (Kilograms of coal equivalent)

Area	Amount	Area	Amount
Nepal	8	Kenya	124
Ethiopia	10	Paraguay	126
Upper Volta	10	Senegal	145
Burundi	12	Congo	148
Niger	13	Honduras	151
Chad	15	Ivory Coast	152
Rwanda	15	Morocco	153
Mali	21	El Salvador	168
Afghanistan	25	India	172
Somalia	27	Mauritius	179
Dahomey	30	Guatemala	182
Haiti	33	Bolivia	185
Central African Rep.	38	Dominican Republic	194
Gambia	39	Tunisia	200
Togo	41	Philippines	209
Malagasy	42	Ecuador	212
Malawi	42	Nicaragua	234
Uganda	42	Gabon	240
Laos	43	Liberia	259
Nigeria	44	Macao	268
Cambodia	45	Sabah	285
Burma	47	Jordan	291
Mauritania	48	Algeria	300
Tanzania	55	United Arab Republic	301
Portuguese Guinea	57	Syria	303
Sierra Leone	68	Costa Rica	306
Sudan	69	Saudi Arabia	311
Cameroun	71	Libya	327
South Vietnam	73	Western Malaysia	338
Dem. Rep. of the Congo	83	Albania	347
Pakistan	90	Brazil	347
Guinea	98	Turkey	348
Western Samoa	102	Fiji	351
Cape Verde Islands	103	Iran	391
Ghana	104	British Honduras	396
Mozambique	106	Barbados	422
Thailand	110	Ryukyu Islands	431
Indonesia	111	French Guiana	444
Ceylon	114	South Korea	445
Angola	117	Zambia	487

(cont.)

Table 10.2   (cont.)

Area	Amount	Area	Amount
Portugal	521	Brunei	2178
Colombia	532	Israel	2239
Singapore	578	Ireland	2284
Iraq	581	Romania	2305
Sarawak	581	New Zealand	2530
Peru	588	Bulgaria	2571
Hong Kong	603	Austria	2630
Southern Rhodesia	651	Switzerland	2668
China (Taiwan)	654		
French Polynesia	708	Finland	2679
		South Africa	2716
Malta	727	Hungary	2812
Lebanon	747	France	2951
Greece	784	Venezuela	2974
Guyana	811	American Samoa	3000
Jamaica	887	Bahrain	3214
Cyprus	916	Netherlands	3271
Uruguay	916	Trinidad and Tobago	3482
Cuba	950	Norway	3588
Mexico	977		
Spain	1023	U.S.S.R.	3611
		Iceland	3963
Chile	1089	Denmark	4172
Panama	1115	West Germany	4234
Surinam	1128	Sweden	4506
Yugoslavia	1192	Belgium	4724
Gibraltar	1333	Australia	4795
Argentina	1341	United Kingdom	5151
Bahamas	1610	East Germany	5461
Japan	1783	Poland	5505
Italy	1787		
Bermuda	1833	Czechoslovakia	5676
		New Caledonia	5769
Guam	1948	Canada	7653
Puerto Rico	2125	United States	9201

Source: United Nations Statistical Office, *Statistical Yearbook* 1967, or *World Energy Supplies*; 1963–1966, Series J., No. 11, Copyright United Nations 1968. Reproduced by permission.

A rough approximation of its validity as a measure of technology may be further assessed by examining Table 10.2, showing energy consumption per capita in 144 countries, and the map of this distribution, Fig. 10.1. In order to portray the data, on the map, values were transformed to logarithms and the mean and

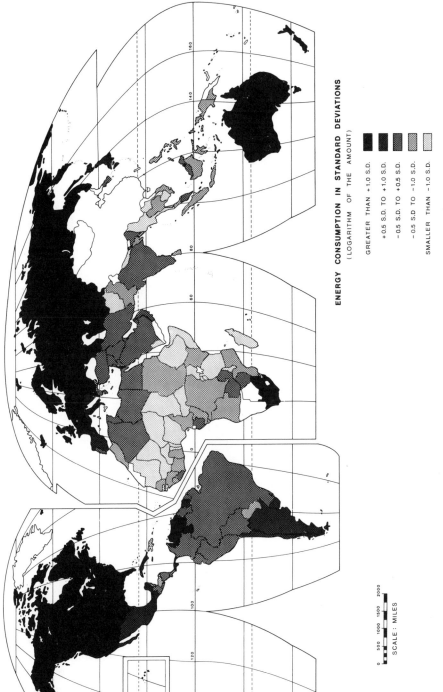

Fig. 10.1. Energy consumption per capita in kilograms of coal equivalent for 1965. Data from: *U.N. Statistical Yearbook* or United Nations Statistical office, *World Energy Supplies*, Series J. Goode's base map © copyright, University of Chicago. Used by permission of the University of Chicago Press.

ENERGY CONSUMPTION IN STANDARD DEVIATIONS
(LOGARITHM OF THE AMOUNT)

GREATER THAN +1.0 S.D.
+0.5 S.D. TO +1.0 S.D.
-0.5 S.D. TO +0.5 S.D.
-0.5 S.D. TO -1.0 S.D.
SMALLER THAN -1.0 S.D.

0 500 1000 1500 2000
SCALE : MILES

standard deviation of the distribution computed. Intervals are based on standard deviation units of the logarithmic data. It can be seen that the amount of energy consumed per capita in different areas appears to correspond reasonably well to what we think of as the relative amounts of technology in those countries. Further reasons for using it will be discussed in Section 10.5, where a systems framework is suggested.

10.2.4 Comments about Data

The availability of data often limits the choice of variables in a study, especially on a world scale. Since it is virtually impossible for an individual researcher to collect reliable data about phenomena such as energy, steel, or paper consumption for all countries of the world, investigators rely on data provided by private organizations, governmental bodies such as the United States Department of Agriculture, and international organizations such as various United Nations agencies. Even these data, although the most accurate and complete available, have certain deficiencies. Comparable data for a given variable, which are based on the same operational definition and cover the same time period, are often not available for all countries. Data for most of the Communist countries are of unknown accuracy and may not be comparable with those of other countries. Data for countries with less technology are often either grossly inaccurate or totally lacking. In general, data for fewer variables are available, and they are less reliable as the amount of technology decreases. Sometimes those which exist are for different time periods, so that their comparability is questionable. The choice of variables will therefore be restricted to those for which reasonably accurate data are available for a large number of countries.

Bearing all these problems in mind, our aim is to find the best possible data and use them with discretion, so that generalizations based on them are justified. This being the case, it should be recognized that countries with less technology and some of the Communist countries will tend to be underrepresented.

10.3 THE SPATIAL DISTRIBUTION OF TECHNOLOGY

Discrepancies between less and more developed countries in the distribution of technology, resources, and consumer goods are often pointed out. In 1963, for example, the United States and Canada, with 10.1 percent of the world's population, produced 46.9 percent of its GNP. While the per capita GNP of these two countries was almost $3,000 U.S., that of thirty African and Asian countries was under $100. It was estimated that only 36.2 percent of the world's population received an adequate diet, while that of the remaining 63.8 percent was nutritionally deficient. In the United States and Canada in 1969, 82.1 percent of the population aged 5–19 was enrolled in school; in Latin America the figure was 43.3 percent, in Asia 38.0 percent, and in Africa, 24.8 percent. Many other contrasts could be cited, all of which would point out the gap that exists between rich and poor, more and less developed nations.

These discrepancies can be seen by referring to Table 10.2. Although it is difficult to obtain estimates of the amount of animate energy consumed, data for the consumption of energy from inaminate sources such as coal, natural gas, electricity, and atomic energy are reasonably accurate. These estimates are all converted to a single unit, coal equivalents, although other units, such as mega-watt hours, are used elsewhere. Conversion factors have been calculated; for example, 198 U.S. gallons of gasoline or 800 kilowatt hours of electricity derived from hydro, nuclear, or geothermal sources are equivalent to one metric ton of coal (1,000 kilograms). The amount of energy consumed on a per capita basis is more useful for comparing the amounts of technology among areal units of different population sizes than total energy consumption. Since the same reasoning extends to other variables, all variables will be expressed in terms of units of population.

Returning to the table, it can be seen that in the highest ranking country, the United States, the equivalent of 9201 kilograms of coal is consumed per capita; in the lowest ranking one, Mongolia, only 8 kilograms are used, less than 1/1000th of that consumed in the United States. When the value of each observation is plotted on the Y-axis against its rank on the X-axis and a curve drawn connecting these points, a concave J-shaped curve results (Fig. 10.2). Its shape indicates that

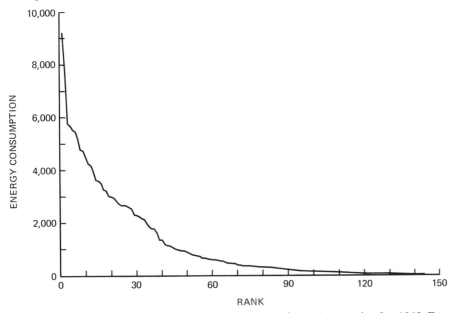

Fig. 10.2. Rank and amount of energy consumption for 144 countries for 1965. Data from: *U.N. Statistical Yearbook* or United Nations Statistical Office, *World Energy Supplies,* Series J.

although a few countries are very high in energy consumption, many are very low. Since there are no apparent breaks or discontinuities in this distribution of the ranked data which would suggest boundaries between groups or classes, the phenomenon may best be treated as a continuum rather than as a number of discrete classes.

Examining Table 10.2 in conjunction with the world map, Fig. 10.1, we can see that most observations rank about where we would expect to find them. Countries with the highest per capita energy consumption include the United States and Canada, northern European countries, Australia, New Zealand, and South Africa. Countries with the lowest per capita energy consumption are located primarily in Asia and sub-Saharan Africa. In the middle range are a few southern European countries and most of Latin America and the Middle East.

10.4 EXPLANATION OF THE SPATIAL DISTRIBUTION

10.4.1 Independent Variables

Eight independent variables were selected to help explain the spatial distribution of technology. The major source of data was the United Nations *Statistical Yearbook*, but supplementary sources were used for some variables and some countries. Data for 1965 were used whenever possible. If none were available, either data for the closest year to 1965 were used, or interpolations were made between two years to approximate 1965 values.

These variables, the phenomena which they measure, and the abbreviations which we shall use in discussing them are:

1. Level of health and medical care
   - a. Calorie consumption per capita per day   CALCNS
   - b. Number of inhabitants per physician   POPPHS

2. Communication within areas
   - a. Newspaper circulation per 1000 population   NWSCRC
   - b. Domestic mail flow per capita   MLFLOW
   - c. Radio receivers per 1000 population   RADPOP

3. Education
   - a. Percent of population illiterate   ILLITR
   - b. Percent of eligible population attending
     first and second level school   SCHNRL

4. Specialization of the labor force
   - a. Percent of economically active population
     in agriculture   AGRPOP

The abbreviation ENRCNS will be used for energy consumption per capita.

10.4.2 Relationships among the Variables

We would like to answer two questions about the relationships among these variables: (1) How closely is each variable related to each of the others, and (2) how much of the variation in energy consumption per capita, the dependent variable, can be explained by variation in the independent variables?

The technique of linear correlation analysis was used to determine the relationships among the variables. In applying this technique it is assumed, among other things, that each variable is normally distributed and that the relationship between every pair of variables is linear. Since neither of these assumptions was valid for all the data, transformations were carried out where necessary to bring the data more closely into line with them. The logarithm (base 10) of the actual data was satisfactory for most variables, but other transformations were used for some. Each coefficient of simple correlations (r) was computed using all observations for which data were present for both variables; this number (N) ranges from 72 to 144.

The matrix of coefficients of simple correlation, which also shows the N for each value, is given in Table 10.3. It can be seen that these intercorrelations range in absolute value from 0.634 to 0.894. These figures can be more easily interpreted if we recall, from Section 8.7.7, that the total variation about the mean of one variable which can be explained by the second variable is determined by calculating r^2. We can then see that the lowest value of r explains 0.634^2, or 40.2 percent of the variation, while the highest explains 0.894^2, or 79.8 percent. ENRCNS is most closely related to POPPHS and least closely to CALCNS.

We were also interested in predicting the amount of technology in an area by using the stepwise regression technique. Whereas in the usual multiple correlavariables for all observations, we chose a combination which yielded the highest coefficient or multiple correlation (R) while including as many observations as possible. Four independent variables for which data were present for the same 135 observations were selected; data for these same observations were also available for ENRCNS. A multiple correlation-regression analysis was carried out using the stepwise regression technique. Whereas in the usual multiple correlation-regression analysis all variables are used simultaneously to compute R, in a stepwise analysis the independent variable most closely related to the dependent variable is selected first, and others are added one at a time until the amount of additional variation explained is no longer statistically significant at some desired level. The four variables used were: POPPHS, SCHNRL, ILLITR, and AGRPOP. The R obtained was 0.930; $R^2 = 0.865$. Since the first variable, POPPHS, alone explains 81.1 percent of the variation in ENRCNS, an additional 5.4 percent is added by the other three combined.

The multiple regression equation expresses mathematically the average relationships of the independent variables with the dependent. From it a value for Y, Y_c, can be computed for any actual or hypothetical observation by substituting

Table 10.3 Matrix of simple correlation coefficients between energy consumption and eight other variables

	ENRCNS	CALCNS	POPPHS	NWSCRC	MLFLOW	RADPOP	ILLITR	SCHNRL	AGRPOP
Transformation	log	—	log	log	log	square root	arcsine	—	—
ENRCNS	1.000 (144)*	0.758 (99)	−0.894 (144)	0.840 (135)	0.821 (93)	0.796 (141)	−0.801 (144)	0.820 (144)	−0.873 (135)
CALCNS		1.000 (99)	−0.751 (99)	0.775 (94)	0.724 (72)	0.634 (98)	−0.696 (99)	0.645 (99)	−0.680 (99)
POPPHS			1.000 (148)	−0.878 (138)	−0.721 (94)	−0.741 (144)	0.869 (148)	−0.807 (148)	0.831 (137)
NWSCRC				1.000 (138)	0.751 (89)	0.722 (136)	−0.876 (138)	0.791 (138)	−0.827 (129)
MLFLOW					1.000 (94)	0.659 (92)	−0.666 (94)	0.699 (94)	−0.745 (90)
RADPOP						1.000 (144)	−0.687 (144)	0.683 (133)	−0.822 (133)
ILLITR							1.000 (148)	−0.861 (148)	0.795 (137)
SCHNRL								1.000 (148)	−0.810 (137)
AGRPOP									1.000 (137)

*Number in parentheses indicates the number of countries on which the coefficient of correlation is based.

the values of each independent variable for that observation into the equation. Y_c is also called the expected, theoretical, or predicted Y-value. The regression equation for these data is:

$$Y_c = -0.708\,X_1 - 0.0103\,X_2 + 0.00454\,X_3 + 0.260\,X_4,$$

where:

$X_1 = \log_{10}$ POPPHS,

$X_2 =$ AGRPOP,

$X_3 =$ SCHNRL, and

$X_4 =$ arcsin ILLITR.

Residuals from regression are calculated by subtracting the values of Y_c for each observation from the observed or actual value; that is,

Residual $= Y_o - Y_c$.

If R were equal to 1.0, the calculated value of Y for each observation, Y_c, would correspond exactly to the observed value, Y_o, and all residuals would equal zero. The smaller the value of R, the greater is the overall discrepancy between calculated and observed values. By studying the observations with the largest residuals, where the calculated values deviate most widely from the observed, it is sometimes possible to discern some consistent reason for these deviations and thereby improve upon the original explanation in future analyses.

Figure 10.3 shows those observations which were either under- or overpredicted more than one and one-half standard errors. In areas of overprediction, the actual energy consumption per capita was less than would have been predicted from the independent variables; in areas of underprediction it was greater. It is difficult to discern any consistent pattern among these residuals which would help in obtaining a better explanation. Some of these deviant cases may be the result of data inaccuracy, but most appear to be explainable only by conditions unique to each area.

10.5 A SYSTEMS APPROACH

10.5.1 The Concept of System

We saw from the correlation matrix (Table 10.3) that all variables included in the analysis are closely interrelated. We know, therefore, that for most areas, when all observations are drawn from the same time period, the value of any one variable can be predicted fairly closely from the value of at least one other variable. What we do not know is how each variable changes over time, and how changes in one or more variables affect others. The next problem, therefore, is to find an approach which will help us to predict, for example, what the effect of an increase in the

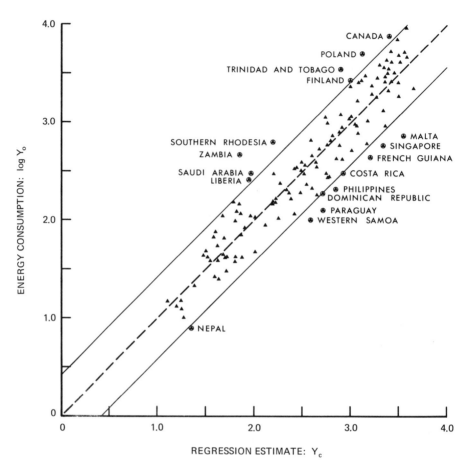

Fig. 10.3. Relationship between the regression estimate and the observed value of the dependent variable. Observations over– and under–predicted by more than one and one-half standard error unit by use of the regression equation.

amount of technology in a given area might be upon newspaper circulation, or how an increase in literacy might affect education and medical care.

One way of doing this is to consider a set of interrelated phenomena as constituting a system. The concept of a system as a set of interrelated objects or selected attributes of these objects has long been employed by physical scientists. The bodies of the solar system, properties of gases under specified conditions, and reactions among combinations of chemicals can all be described and analyzed as systems. Biologists also study systems ranging in size from the ecosystem of the entire biosphere to intracellular organelles. More recently, social scientists have become interested in the analysis of social systems.

A system may be defined by specifying (1) its physical and temporal boundaries; (2) the objects and their attributes to be included, which comprise the elements of the system; and (3) known or hypothesized interrelationships among these elements. If it is considered desirable to apply mathematical techniques used in systems analysis, a more rigorous specification of certain concepts is required. The elements must be operationally defined so that they can be used as variables, and relationships among them stated in mathematical terms. If enough is known about a particular system and all variables and relationships are operationally defined, it can be represented by a set of equations such that if the value of all but one of the variables is given, the remaining one can be computed.

The general gas laws of physics and chemistry serve as a familiar example of a physical system, which is composed of a specified amount of gas confined within a defined physical space. The elements, that is the properties of this gas, included in the system are temperature, pressure, and volume; its color, smell, or possible poisonous nature are not of concern. It is known that, for a specified weight of gas in any such system,

Pressure × Volume/Temperature = a known constant.

From this basic equation it can be deduced that if any one variable changes either one or both of the other two will also change; if two variables change by a known amount, the change in the third can be computed.

A system may be either open or closed. In a closed system there are no influences from the outside; neither matter nor energy is gained or lost. In an open system, on the other hand, there is interchange between the system and its surroundings. In any system which is performing work, either physical or biological, energy is continually being used. Some of it is used to perform work and the remainder leaves as heat. According to the second law of thermodynamics, although the total amount of energy in the universe remains constant, the amount of usable energy decreases as various forms of energy are degraded and converted to unusable heat energy.

It is now possible to see an additional reason for selecting energy consumption as a measure of technology. Since a system requires a continuous supply of energy if work is to be performed, there must be some source of this energy. By analogy, social systems utilize energy for various purposes; we have seen that the greater the amount of technology in a system, the greater the energy consumption. Thus we can think of technology, and the various forms of energy associated with it, as supplying the energy to power the system. In making such a comparison, however, it is important to remember that the concepts related to physical and biological systems are helpful primarily as analogies which suggest ways of analyzing social systems. They should not, therefore, be adopted indiscriminately, but rather used as sources of hypotheses to be examined and tested. With a change of scale, level of abstraction, or type of phenomena, all of which differ among physical, biological, and social systems, different principles or laws may well be found to apply.

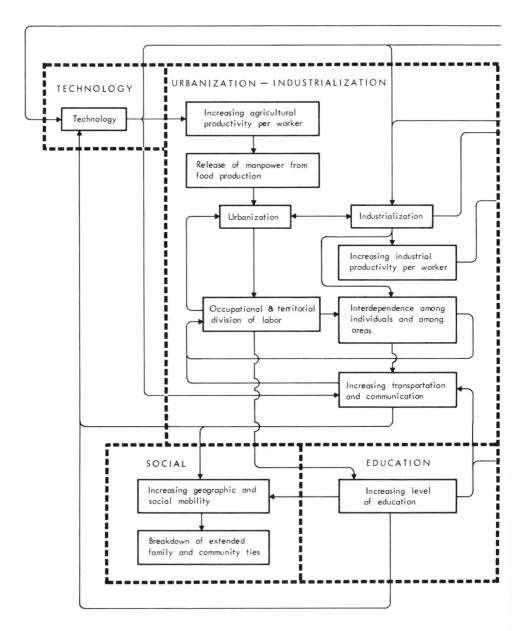

10.5.2 A System Model of Technological Change

Having considered briefly some of the concepts associated with systems, we shall now look at a model showing the relationships among a number of phenomena which have been found to be related to technology and technological change.

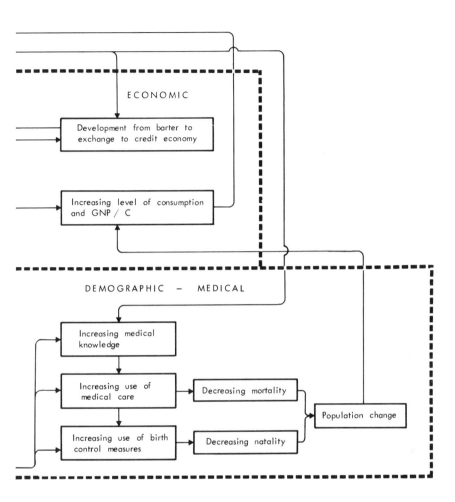

Fig. 10.4. Schematic model of selected elements related to technological change indicating major flows and subsystems.

Although the analysis of social systems, broadly defined as systems incorporating primarily social variables, has not yet attained the same degree of precision as that of physical and biological ones, in principle it should be possible to develop a systems model of some of the factors related to technology and its spatial extent, following the procedure outlined above.

The boundaries of the system are set as being those of any country, in order to make the scheme general. The elements to be considered included some of the phenomena operationalized as variables in the analysis of Section 10.4, and others which have been found to be related to technology. Tentative hypotheses about the interrelationships among these elements are then formulated. For simplicity at present and for purposes of mathematical analysis, should this be desired in the future, we shall establish a starting point for the system. From there, further interrelationships may be drawn in, and feedback loops included. The system must eventually be closed by one or more such loops, much like an electrical circuit, if it is to be operational.

Figure 10.4 shows a simplified systems model of various phenomena related to technology, and some of the relationships among them. Because it represents interactions within relatively large areas such as entire countries, it is on a macroscopic scale. The system which it represents is conceived of as an open system, since it is recognized that external inputs can be added to any variable at any time. Although a closed system would be easier to work with, an open system is more realistic, as it helps to show internal relationships among the elements, while allowing for external influences such as crop failures, wars, and the diffusion of innovations or foreign capital from other areas. Each of the boxes represents a complete subsystem, only part of which is shown in detail; the size of each box is related only to the amount of writing in it, not to its importance to the system as a whole. The economic subsystem, for example, has been sketched out by economists, and we are interested here only in the end products of it rather than the workings within it involving such items as capital formation, savings, and consumer expenditures. Similarly, educational and medical subsystems, for example, could be worked out, and many suggestions have been made as to demographic subsystems, relating such factors as medical care, food supply, and use of birth control measures. In addition, an environmental subsystem could have been included. It is known that the greater the amount of technology in an area, the greater is man's impact on his environment. Resources are used more rapidly, and there is more pollution of air, land, and water by the byproducts and wastes of technology such as automobile exhaust and industrial smoke and effluents. Since, however, the purpose of the model is to give an overall picture of the interrelationships among a few factors in each of the subsystems, none is sketched out in detail.

Having established the boundaries of the system and selected the elements upon which we wish to concentrate, we next turn to relationships among them. The lines or paths connecting various elements indicate that they are related and suggest the direction in which influence operates, or the direction of flow through the system. At this point, they do not show the magnitude of the flows. Returning to the electrical circuit analogy, we can see that these lines are analogous to wires connecting points in a circuit. Each has a different resistance to the flow of current, so that in some parts of the system the flow may be relatively unimpeded, and a change in one variable will bring about a rapid and almost equally large change in another. In other parts the resistance may be very high, so that there is little influence of one variable on the other. Resistance to change is present in all social systems, as are factors encouraging change; the amount varies over space and time. These resistances come from many sources: economic, such as shortage of capital; political, related to all the factors underlying decision making and allocation of the nation's resources among different sectors; and social, including a preference for the comfort of what is known over the less sure new and unknown. They are, therefore, related to the values, goals, and cultural biases of the people living in a particular area in a given time as implemented in decision making. Although we are aware of their existence, our knowledge is insufficient to measure them in order to incorporate them into the model mathematically. By keeping them in mind, however, we can understand why changes vary from area to area.

The starting point, technology, is taken as an external input which is considered as given and does not have to be explained. The value of this variable and all others are set at the values existing at an arbitrary initial time, t_0. The model can then be used as a device to suggest what relationships to look for among the elements, and what changes to anticipate as changes take place in one or more variables, either from the internal workings of the system or influences of external inputs. It points out only what these changes might be, and which phenomena influence what others, rather than how changes are brought about. Urbanization, for example, appears to be necessary for industrialization, but it does not follow that if urbanization increases industrialization will also increase. In that sense, the model is descriptive rather than explanatory. It depicts what has happened in many areas rather than attempting to explain why the chain of events has occurred in that particular manner.

10.5.3 An Illustration of the Working of the Model

In Section 8.7.1 a model was defined as "a simplified representation of some part of the real world." The model presented here helps us to visualize some of the complex interactions among a few of the many phenomena related to technology, and so to predict some of the changes which might take place in a given area over time as technology changes. Although based primarily on European culture, it also applies to others if we take into account a different set of resistances to change for each area. On a world-wide basis, even though each situation is unique, there are many similarities among areas. It has been observed in many areas, for example, that industrialization requires urbanization and that with urbanization come increased geographic and social mobility which in turn tend to break down extended family ties.

Let us consider as an example some changes which have occurred within some hypothetical area within the European tradition. At some time t_0, thousands of years ago, when we begin looking at it, the area has little technology. The value of this and the other variables are very low in comparison with what they are today. Most of the technology is applied to obtaining food. As it becomes easier, more time and energy are available for devising additional ways of obtaining food more efficiently. In time, fewer and fewer people need to devote most of their time and energy to this pursuit, and human energy is freed for other activities. Occupational specialization gradually develops and, with it, territorial specialization with the concomitant exchange of increasing amounts of goods with people in other areas. These changes make possible the development of cities, whose people depend upon food grown by agricultural specialists in other areas and provide goods and services to the farmers in exchange.

As specialization increases so do communication and transportation; goods and people move from one area to another. As more goods are moved, the demand for transportation increases; as transportation facilities increase, specialization increases further. People in one area can subsist by specializing in growing rubber, mining coal, or producing aluminum only if their other needs are supplied from external sources. With increasing transportation and communication comes increasing interaction among people living in different areas and an increase in the rate of diffusion of many different phenomena: not only goods, but also non-material ones such as languages, religions, and architectural styles. As occupational specialization grows, parents can no longer teach their children everything they need to know as adults, and formal education becomes more important. In the operation of the political decision-making process resources are allocated for education. Growth in this sector creates further demand for education both because of the need for teachers and the growing acceptance of education as a desired end in itself.

Although urbanization-industrialization is thought of as one of the most important trends in contemporary society, industrialization was a comparative latecomer. It was preceded by the development of an exchange economy and a commerical banking system which made possible the accumulation of enough capital to support large-scale enterprises. At this point technological and economic developments converged to enable the growth of industries, which in turn gave added impetus to urbanization. In some of the less industrialized countries today, capital and technology are largely external inputs, and change is far more rapid than it would be if the system were closed.

Changes in technology appear to operate upon social organization primarily through the industrialization-urbanization complex, with its associated increase in geographic and social mobility. Changes in family structure and function include breakdown of the extended family system with corresponding increase in the importance of the conjugal family.

Although the demographic-food medical care subsystem has merely been sketched in, its effects are well known. We are seeing in some countries the "green revolution," an improvement in crop yields which is helping to hold the dismal prophecies of Malthus at bay, hopefully until the combination of increased education, communication, and use of contraceptives can stem population growth.

These and other factors not included operate to produce as an end result the total output of goods and services in a country—its GNP. In principle, the more technology there is in an area, the higher the productivity per individual and, therefore, the higher the GNP per capita. This hypothesis is confirmed by the high correlation between energy consumption and GNP per capita: $r = 0.88$.

10.6 TECHNOLOGICAL CHANGE AT A MICROSCALE

10.6.1 Introduction

Variations in spatial aspects of most phenomena exist within countries and even smaller areas. In most cases these variations are less than those between countries, but occasionally large regional disparities are present. The greater the homogeneity, the more difficult it is to measure differences. For example, in Section 7.4 we saw that the rate of literacy is generally so high throughout the United States that a different variable, median school years completed, must be used to detect variations in educational level within the country. Although the model discussed in the previous section was designed for analysis on a macroscopic, or worldwide, scale, it should prove helpful in providing a theoretical framework for suggesting variables and relationships among them, together with factors which either facilitate or impede change over time.

10.6.2 Quebec as an Example of an Area with less Technology

Areas with less technology than that prevailing in the rest of the country exist almost everywhere. In the United States, Appalachia is one of these areas; the South has been, but is rapidly increasing in technology. In Canada, areas such as Newfoundland, the Arctic regions, and Quebec have historically had less technology than others. Although we shall consider Quebec as an example of such an area, it seems reasonable that many of the same variables would be involved and similar relationships exist in other similar areas.

Quebec, in which about one third of Canada's population lives, has always been relatively backward with respect to the rest of Canada. By considering some historical factors and analyzing these in terms of our model, we may be able to understand better the interrelationships among the variables and see how change has been slowed down or accelerated at different times. (Hughes, 1943; Cook, 1966.)

In order to encourage agricultural settlement in pre-Revolutionary New France, the French established the seigneural system, a quasi-feudal arrangement in which the seigneur agreed to provide protection and certain services, such as a flour mill, to the *habitants* in exchange for a fixed proportion of their produce. This social system controlled many important aspects of life, including social roles, stratification, and government. The resulting society was one with relatively few persons in the upper and middle classes and many in the lower class, almost peasants. Each farm was relatively self-sufficient, and there was relatively little transportation and communication among them. Out-migration began when no additional land was available for settlement, since by French law only the eldest son inherited the land. Many younger people moved to cities in Quebec, Ontario, and New England.

In this closely knit, ethnically and spatially circumscribed village existence, the clergy exercised almost complete control. Only elementary education was free, and it was usually an inadequate preparation for secondary education. Because of their low educational level and lack of knowledge of English, most rural French Canadians who moved to cities were able to participate in the economy only as factory workers or unskilled laborers. Because the Church provided an avenue of upward mobility, in most families at least one son entered the clergy and girls often joined religious orders.

Although changes gradually took place in rural areas, the amount of agricultural technology, such as types and amounts of farm machinery used, remained less than in other areas of Canada. Transportation and communication within the province improved slowly, so that rural residents remained isolated from the cities. During and after World War II the premier, Maurice Duplessis, continued to oppose change. He worked with the religious establishment to try to keep Quebec predominantly rural and the population at a low educational level. Nevertheless, as more jobs became available in the cities, more rural residents migrated to them. Although these migrants had relatively little contact with the dominant English-speaking culture, radio and television helped them to realize that they were being deprived of many economic, political, and social opportunities enjoyed by other Canadians. The Catholic clergy tried to retain their control of the people by urging them to return to their villages, but this effort was unsuccessful. They then built larger institutions within cities and extended their control over labor unions, education, and social organizations. For a time these attempts were moderately successful because of Duplessis' support, but after his death in 1959 change became almost inevitable.

During the 1960's there were major changes in the economy as well as the educational and political systems. By 1962 the government had gained financial control of energy production by nationalizing eleven private hydro-electric companies. Expansion of the economy was due in part to massive governmental investment. Spending on education increased rapidly. Change in control from church to state occurred over a period of several years; not until 1964 did Quebec have a full-fledged provincial Ministry of Education. Free education was extended through the secondary level and many new vocational and technical training institutions were established.

More recently, in part as a result of the report of the Royal Commission on Bilingualism and Biculturalism, French has become a working language of more jobs, especially in government offices. This change has opened up avenues of social mobility into the middle class, although upper executive jobs are still held primarily by English-speaking Canadians.

We can see from this example how many of the phenomena included in the model, as well as additional ones, were interrelated as changes took place. In Quebec, certain values in the social subsystem tended to operate against change, but demographic factors, a high birth rate with corresponding rapid population increase, and lack of economic opportunity worked to push residents out of rural areas into cities. Increased contact with people in urban areas with higher educational levels and greater technology led eventually to improved transportation and communication, in turn decreasing rural isolation and resistance to change. New political leadership instituted extremely rapid change, primarily by means of governmental policy and expenditures.

10.7 RELATIONSHIPS TO OTHER RESEARCH AND THEORY

10.7.1 Empirical Research Findings

Similar changes have occurred in other parts of the world; this process is usually called development or modernization. Many empirical studies of development have been made, mostly for relatively small areas. The model suggested here seems to apply in general, although the importance of the interactions among different subsystems varies, and resistances differ. All the variables tend to increase over time, but at an uneven rate, and at different rates in different areas.

Studies of technological change and economic development are of two major types: case studies describing changes within relatively small areas, and studies in which generalizations have been derived. Since different case studies often do not include the same variables or consider the topic in ways which make the findings comparable from study to study, they are useful primarily for suggesting relevant variables and shedding light upon the manner in which these phenomena may be related to technological change.

Studies in the second category confirm relationships between technology and phenomena related to education (Anderson, 1965; Harbison, 1963, 1964), political phenomena (Russet and others, 1964), energy consumption (Guyol, 1960), income (Ogburn and Allen, 1959) and a number of economic and demographic variables (Berry, 1960).

10.7.2 Theories of Technological Change and Economic Development

Different explanations of the way in which technological change and economic development occur have been proposed. According to the evolutionary approach, cultures tend to pass through certain stages as they become technologically more sophisticated. A classification of these stages based on agricultural methods, often used by geographers and anthropologists, includes categories such as: hunting and gathering; migratory agriculture, including both shifting cultivation and pastoral nomadism; and sedentary agriculture, which developed from use of the hoe or digging stick in primitive subsistence methods of tillage through the simple human- or animal-drawn plow to the present highly mechanized forms of commercial agriculture. Although the particular terms used may vary from writer to writer, the general sequence is similar. Classes such as these are useful for description, but do not lead to a model of technological change and economic development.

Rostow (1960) emphasizes economic development as a process culminating in a level of high mass consumption such as that prevailing in the United States and Canada, Western Europe, Australia, and New Zealand. He identifies five stages: traditional society, preconditions, takeoff, the drive to maturity, and high mass consumption. He perceives traditional society as being in a state of equilibrium at a low level of productivity. During the preconditions stage, slow changes occur which set the scene for takeoff. Changes in attitudes make possible some steps toward development, such as improvement of transport and increases in occupational, geographic, and social mobility. During the takeoff stage development is more rapid, and the rate of investment jumps from about five percent of GNP to more than ten percent. Following takeoff, development spreads to all sectors of the economy and growth becomes continuous, until the stage of high mass consumption is attained. Rostow hypothesizes that further increases in technology would further increase income.

Galbraith's (1964) analysis of economic development and the technological changes accompanying it parallels Rostow's in many respects but differs from it in others. He sees development as a continuous process rather than a series of stages. Because different conditions exist in areas in the early phases of development than those in later ones, the inputs needed to initiate and maintain development will vary from place to place. In areas where political organization is primarily at a tribal or local level, corresponding roughly to Rostow's traditional stage, effective government and administrative machinery and an educated elite are essential if development is to begin. Large inputs of technology, capital, or popular education will be not only ineffective but actually harmful. Capital or other money poured into the economy may primarily enrich persons in power and create inflation, since mechanisms for using it productively are lacking. At best, it may provide short-term employment in construction for a few individuals.

To the preconditions for development stated by Rostow, Galbraith adds the need for personal incentives to farmers for increasing production. Given an effective administrative structure, a trained and educated elite concerned more with the welfare of the country than with power and self-enrichment, the potential for increasing agricultural productivity, a basic transportation and communications system, the stage is set. At this point popular education is needed, beginning with a goal of primary schooling for every child and basic literacy instruction for adults. Development workers have learned that a certain minimum of schooling is essential to both the acceptance of new ideas accompanying the development process and the provision of a labor force ready to be trained in basic skills needed in a more developed economy. Communications and transport must also continue to be improved.

Capital and technology become useful at this point. The establishment of chemical industries to produce fertilizer, the building of dams to provide hydro-electric power and water for irrigation, and the provision of technological assistance to farmers can work together to increase agricultural production per unit of land and per man hour.

In order for further development to occur, essential inputs include capital, a labor force with a basic education and capable of learning a variety of specialized skills, technology in the form of machinery and specialized knowledge which can be applied to problems of the area, and skilled management with autonomous authority, the factor which combines all others into an effectively functioning mechanism. By introducing the idea of the need for different inputs at different points along the development continuum, Galbraith provides a framework for a model of the development process and suggests lines for further inquiry.

Both Rostow and Galbraith recognize that the stages they have suggested are not clearly demarcated, but are convenient for discussion purposes. As we have seen from the data on the worldwide distribution of technology, Table 10.2, it would be difficult to separate countries into classes on other than a purely arbitrary basis. For this reason, we prefer to consider technology as a continuous phenomenon.

10.8 THE SPREAD OF TECHNOLOGY

We have looked primarily at changes in technology within areas and only secondarily at the spread of technology. This process by which people, goods, and ideas move from one area to another is often termed spatial diffusion. It will be explored in Chapter 12, but we shall consider here some aspects of the diffusion of technology as it relates to the systems model.

Returning to the analogy of a physical system, we know that, according to the second law of thermodynamics, energy flows from areas of higher to lower energy, and that particles of substances flow from areas of greater to lesser concentration, with a resulting tendency towards equilibrium within the system. Similarly, in human societies we usually find that technology, for example, diffuses from areas where greater amounts are present to areas with lesser amounts. If there were no resistance to the acceptance of innovations in an area, as soon as a new product or idea was introduced at any location it would rapidly spread over the entire area. We know, however, that there are many resistances to change, among them custom, habit, expense, failure to recognize that benefit might accrue from adoption of the innovation, and poor transportation and communication.

Just as physical systems tend toward equilibrium, biological systems tend to maintain a state of dynamic equilibrium, usually termed homeostasis, by continual expenditure of energy. Although some sociologists claim that a similar tendency toward equilibrium is also found in social systems, others believe that this claim is not valid. There does, however, seem to be a certain range within which the values of different variables must fall in order for a system to operate adequately. Consequently, as Galbraith stated, a very large input of any one variable such as technology, capital, or education can create extreme dislocations throughout a system, whereas smaller amounts can usually be absorbed and utilized.

Findings of various empirical studies of development or modernization indicate that the spatial spread of technology is similar to that of diffusion of other phenomena. In general, it tends to occur along lines of personal communication, so that proximity and accessibility to major cities affects the extent to which people are exposed to and transformed by the processes of change. Mass media appear to be most effective in making people aware of new ideas or products, whereas personal influence and example tend to operate at the level of actual decision to try out the idea or product.

10.9 IMPLICATIONS FOR THE FUTURE

Most writers about development or modernization fail to specify long-range goals. There seems to be a generally accepted but implicit assumption that the aim is to change the presently underdeveloped countries so that they will more closely resemble the developed ones; that is, to continue along the lines portrayed in the model of Section 10.4. Rostow, for example, considers the stage of high mass consumption as the final product of the development process. People are beginning to realize, however, that technological expansion with its wasteful use of natural and human resources cannot continue indefinitely along present lines. In order to minimize some of the undesirable consequences of technology, new methods of waste disposal and recycling of resources must be developed, and thought must be given to curbing unlimited increases in energy consumption, use of private vehicles, and other conveniences.

The situation is especially acute in developing countries, where too rapid change and the introduction of foreign values have often created extreme dislocations. It is impossible for the millions of people in India and China together, for example, to sustain a level of consumption equal to that of the United States, Canada, and Western Europe. Iron reserves would be exhausted long before the same automobiles per person ratio was achieved, and not enough gasoline would be available to fuel the cars even if they could be built. Similarly, there would seem to be limits to the extent to which inanimate energy can be substituted for animate energy, or capital for labor. In India, for example, millions of agricultural laborers have been deprived of a livelihood by the introduction of tractors. These people move to the cities, compounding the already grave problems of housing, feeding, and providing amenities to the population. Planners are being forced to recognize that it may be necessary to provide subsidized jobs, if necessary, in rural areas in order to keep from compounding urban problems while providing rural residents with an adequate standard of living. Some of these problems are discussed in the excerpt that follows (Weatherall, 1970).*

But it is difficult to persuade people to give up voluntarily comforts and conveniences once they have experienced them or even seen others with them, so that they have developed a desire for them. We must somehow change from considering our world as an open system with an endless supply of resources and unlimited ability to absorb wastes to recognizing that it is a closed system providing limited resources which, if wisely used and recycled in order to minimize waste, can sustain a reasonable population at a comfortable level of existence. How this change is to be brought about is a challenge for the future.

The Tragic Plight of India's Landless

Each day, an average of 100 people drift into Bombay, India's second-largest city. They come without money, shelter, or a trade. All they bring is the hope for some kind of work.

Slums are so overcrowded that sleeping space on the sidewalk is limited. And so the migrants build shacks outside the city in swamps and sewer drains.

Calcutta, India's most populous and industrialized city, has slums called by social workers from all over the world, the worst they have seen. Nobody knows how many families in search of work drift into the decaying city from rural areas of West Bengal. The population of Calcutta has grown beyond the ability of the municipal authorities to serve it. Sources of fresh water have been exhausted, and slums spread an urban blight so rapidly it threatens to overwhelm the city.

Nor have India's other cities escaped the social ills of an overconcentrated population. Large-scale migration from the rural areas has also descended on New Delhi, India's capital. Thousands of shacks called "juggis" have sprung up on all available space within the capital. As quickly as police evacuate juggi colonies, more shacks spring up elsewhere.

The alarming aspect of this migration is that it is just a tiny fraction of what it may become in the future. As tractors and other machines begin to replace the landless rural workers, these workers will be forced to turn to the cities as a last hope of survival.

---

*Weatherall, 1970. Excerpted by permission from *The Christian Science Monitor* © 1970. The Christian Science Publishing Society. All rights reserved.

The United States experienced the same nagging problem on a much smaller scale when illiterate sharecroppers were forced off the land through a change in farm technology. They, too, drifted into the city, only to find that automation replaced untrained manpower.

Rural migrants, especially blacks, then found themselves trapped in ghettos and quickly became hard-core unemployed. America with all its wealth and resources has not been able to solve this problem completely. India, burdened by poverty, can only make brave attempts to keep the growing problem from becoming a disaster. . . .

It is too late to send the millions who have migrated to India's cities back to the rural areas. The government must improve conditions for the landless agricultural workers so they won't stream into the metropolitan areas.

Mohandas Gandhi knew well that, unlike the West, which could absorb its rural population in its cities when mechanization reached the land, India, with 80 percent of its population living in the rural areas, could not.

Gandhi was for setting up small cottage industries in India's villages so there would be employment for landless laborers, and eventually prosperity for the rural communities.

Sophisticated economists felt that the Gandhian concept did not belong in the 20th century, and planners contended that industries should be built in large metropolitan areas where there was an adequate labor force. But during the past two five-year plans; the Indian Government returned to the Gandhi philosophy.

Many public-sector plants were built in depressed areas to help ease the unemployment problem and also keep people out of the cities. Numbers of these plants have poor production records and are running at a great loss. Often the site was unsuitable, or the plant was tremendously overstaffed. But the plants have served the partial purpose of making jobs available to the rural population.

Unfortunately, the government cannot continue to use taxpayer's money to build unproductive plants to solve the rural unemployment problem. The country could soon become bankrupt.

Once the public-sector plants began making a return on the government's huge investment, more could be built. But at present many economists are urging New Delhi not to expand industry too rapidly until the present plants become profitable.

Prime Minister Indira Gandhi is also embarking on a land-reform program that will break up large holdings and distribute them to the landless peasants, who for generations have dreamed of owning a farm. This again is intended to keep people from drifting away from their rural communities once they own land.

As for land reform, there is a limit to fragmentation of large holdings. In many states the saturation point has already been reached. India has still not become self-sufficient in food and must import food grains from the United States and other countries.

As land is fragmented, the law of diminishing returns sets in, and the smaller farms produce less food.

However, the blunt fact is that there is not enough land in India to allot to the millions of landless laborers in the rural areas. . . .

The catalyst in the expected rural exodus will be the tractor. At the moment these machines are in short supply because the good harvests of the green revolution are bringing farmers money which they want to invest. As a result of the demand there is a lively black market in choice machines.

The government is even encouraging Indians living in the United Kingdom and other countries to make a gift of a tractor to their farmer-relatives in their homeland.

India's Fourth Plan envisages a demand of 80,000 to 90,000 tractors a year by 1973. The Ministry of Agriculture feels the demand will be higher. Some private sources put it at about 70,000. . . .

The mechanization of Indian farms will also cause a tremendous demand for fuel and oils—a demand which could become a major bottleneck since India is not self-sufficient in petroleum. The tire industry must be expanded to keep pace with the local production of tractors. Operators must be trained to run the machines and perform first-echelon maintenance, and spare parts must be available.

Landless agricultural workers are becoming aware of the machine that will some-day deprive them of their livelihood. As more and more tractors arrive in rural areas, farmers are telling laborers whose families have worked their land for generations that they are no longer needed.

Antitractor agitation has broken out in some areas. Rural workers have shouted slogans against the use of tractors, and in some cases have attempted to prevent the machines from being operated in the fields.

But their agitation could possibly be just as effective as that of French workers who during the industrial revolution smashed the newly arrived machinery with their wooden shoes, giving rise to the word "sabotage."

REVIEW YOUR UNDERSTANDING OF THESE CONCEPTS

technology as a unifying principle
conceptual and operational definition
 of technology
matrix of coefficients of correlation
multiple correlation-regression
 analysis
residuals from regression
systems and systems analysis
open and closed systems

homeostasis

systems model of technological
 change
theories of technological change
 and economic development
distinction between stages
 and a continuum
spread of technology

SUGGESTED ACTIVITIES

1. Compare Whittlesy's classification of agricultural land use, discussed in Section 8.2.1 with both Rostow's and Galbraith's discussions of the stages of economic growth.

2. Check through a number of articles and books on economic development and modernization. Find the terms in each source which are used to discuss development and modernization, and attempt to establish a definition for each term used. How consistent is the usage both within and between sources? The use of Venn diagrams or some similar device may be helpful in visualizing areas of overlap.

3. This activity is suggested as a way of investigating the spatial distribution of technology within a relatively small area. It might be carried out by a number of students, each studying a different time period or making a different transect of the same area at a given time.

   a. Select a study area such as a state, province, or small country. Obtain the data for some dependent variable Y_i which is related to technology, such as median family income, for which data are available. Use areal units which are of an appropriate size for showing spatial variations in this variable.

   b. Map the distribution of Y_i for each of a number of time periods for which comparable data are available. Describe and analyze changes in it over time.

   c. Take a series of transects through the area, being sure to include some urban centers. For each time period, plot the Y_i observations on the Y-axis against distance on the X-axis. Try to account for variations in Y_i in terms of distance from urban centers, transportation lines, or any other relevant factors. Compare these transects to determine whether there are any biases associated with either direction or distance, and what common factors appear to be related to Y_i in all transects.

REFERENCES

Anderson, C. Arnold and Mary Jean Bowman, eds. (1965), *Education and Economic Development*. Chicago: Aldine.

Berry, Brian J. L. (1969), "An inductive approach to the regionalization of economic development," in Norton Ginsburg, ed., *Essays on Geography and Economic Development*, Department of Geography Research Paper No. 62. Chicago: University of Chicago Press, pp. 78–107.

Cook, Ramsey (1966), *Canada and the French Canadian Question*. Toronto: Macmillan of Canada.

Cottrell, Fred (1955), *Energy and Society*. New York: McGraw-Hill.

Galbraith, John Kenneth (1964), *Economic Development*. Cambridge: Harvard University Press.

Guyol, Nathaniel B. (1961), "Energy consumption and economic development," in Norton Ginsburg, ed., *Essays on Geography and Economic Development*. Department of Geography Research Paper No. 62. Chicago: University of Chicago Press, pp. 65–77.

Harbison, Fredrick (1963), "Education for development," *Scientific American* **209**, No. 3, 140–147.

Harbison, Frederick and Charles A. Myers (1964), *Education, Manpower, and Economic Growth*. New York: McGraw-Hill.

Hughes, Everett C. (1963), *French Canada in Transition*, 2d ed. Chicago: University of Chicago Press.

Kariel, Herbert G. and Patricia E. Kariel (1970), "Toward an operational definition and measurement of technology," *The Annals of Regional Science* **4**, No. 2, 15–25.

Ogburn, William F. and Francis R. Allen (1959), "Technological development and per capita income," *The American Journal of Sociology* **65**, 127–131.

Rostow, W. W. (1960), *The Stages of Economic Growth*. Cambridge: Cambridge University Press.

Russett, Bruce M., Hayward R. Alker, Jr., Karl W. Deutsch and Harold D. Lasswell (1964), *World Handbook of Political and Social Indicators*. New Haven: Yale University Press.

Weatherall, Ernest (1970), "The tragic plight of India's landless," *The Christian Science Monitor* **62**, No. 262, 9.

White, Leslie A. (1949), *The Science of Culture*. New York: Farrar, Straus and Giroux.

White, Leslie A. (1959), *The Evolution of Culture*. New York: McGraw-Hill.

Additional Readings

Adelman, Irma and Cynthia T. Morris (1965), "A factor analysis of the interrelations between social and political variables and per capita GNP," *The Quarterly Journal of Economics* **79**, 555–578.

Asher, Robert E. and others (1962), *Development of the Emerging Countries: An Agenda for Research*. Washington, D.C.: The Brookings Institution.

Black, C. E. (1966), *The Dynamics of Modernization: A Study of Comparative History*. New York: Harper and Row.

Bobek, Hans (1959), "The main stages in socio-economic evolution from a geographical point of view," translation of "Die Hauptstufen der Gesellschafts- and Wirtschaftsent-faltung in Geographischer Sicht," *Die Erde: Zeitschrift der Gesellschaft für Erdkunde zu Berlin* **40**, 259–298, in Philip L. Wagner and Marvin W. Mikesell, eds., (1962), *Readings in Cultural Geography*. Chicago: University of Chicago Press, pp. 218–247.

Buchanan, R. A. (1965), *Technology and Social Progress*. Oxford: Pergamon Press.

Carol, Hans (1964), "Stages of technology and their impact upon the physical environment: a basic problem in cultural geography," *Canadian Geographer* **7**, 1–8.

Cook, Earl (1971), "The flow of energy in an industrial society," *Scientific American* **224**, No. 3, 135–144; also in *Energy and Power*, a Scientific American Book. San Francisco: W. H. Freeman.

DeGregorio, Thomas R. and Oriol Pi-Sunyer (1969), *Economic Development: The Cultural Context*. New York: Wiley.

de Vries, Egbert and José Medina Echavarría eds. (1963), *Social Aspects of Economic Development in Latin America*, Vol. I. Paris: UNESCO.

Echavarría, José Medina and Benjamin Higgins (1963), *Social Aspects of Economic Development in Latin America*, Vol. 11. Paris: UNESCO.

Epstein, Daniel M., "The Lapps: nomads in transition," *The Journal of Geography* **68**, 26–33.

Forbes, R. J. (1968), *The Conquest of Nature: Technology and its Consequences*. New York: Praeger.

Foster, George M. (1962), *Traditional Cultures and Impact of Technological Change*. New York: Harper and Row.

Friedman, John (1963), "Regional economic policy for developing areas," *Papers and Proceedings*, The Regional Science Association **11**, 41–61.

Ginsburg, Norton (1961), *Atlas of Economic Development*. Chicago: University of Chicago Press.

Gruber, W. H. and D. G. Marquis, eds. (1969), *Factors in the Transfer of Technology*. Cambridge: The Massachusetts Institute of Technology Press.

Hall, A. D. and R. E. Fagen (1956), "Definition of system," *General Systems Yearbook* **1**, 18–28.

Halpern, Joel M. (1967), *The Changing Village Community*. Englewood Cliffs: Prentice-Hall.

Hill, A. David (1964), *The Changing Landscape of a Mexican Municipio, Villa Las Rosas, Chiapas*, Department of Geography Research Paper No. 91. Chicago: University of Chicago Press.

Hoelscher, H. E. (1969), "Technology and social change," *Science* **166**, 68–72.

Hoselitz, Bert F., (1960), *Sociological Aspects of Economic Growth*. New York: The Free Press of Glencoe.

McIntire, Elliot G. (1971), "Changing patterns of Hopi Indian Settlement," *Annals* of the Association of American Geographers **61**, 510–521.

Moseman, Albert H., ed. (1964), *Agricultural Sciences for the Developing Nations*. Washington, D.C.: American Association for the Advancement of Science.

Nash, Manning (1958), "Machine age Maya: the industrialization of a Guatemalan community," *The American Anthropologist*, Memoir No. 87, Vol. 60, No. 2.

Nash, Manning (1966), *Primitive and Peasant Economic Systems*. San Francisco: Chandler.

Pant, Pitambar (1963), "The development of India," *Scientific American* **209**, No. 3, 189–206.

Riddell, J. Barry (1970), *The Spatial Dynamics of Modernization in Sierra Leone: Structure, Diffusion, and Response*. Evanston: Northwestern University Press.

Rodwin, Lloyd and Associates (1969), *Planning Urban Growth and Regional Development: The Experience of the Guayana Program of Venezuela*. Cambridge: The Massachusetts Institute of Technology Press.

Rogers, Everett M. and Lynne Svenning (1969), *Modernization Among Peasants*. New York: Holt, Rinehart and Winston.

Shannon, Lyle W. (1961), "Underdeveloped areas and their influence on personal development," *The Journal of Negro Education* **30**, 386–395.

Smith, T. Lynn (1967), *The Process of Rural Development in Latin America.* Gainesville: University of Florida Press.

Soja, Edward W. (1968), *The Geography of Modernization in Kenya: A Spatial Analysis of Social, Economic, and Political Change*, Syracuse Geographical Series No. 2. Syracuse: Syracuse University Press.

Southworth, Herman M. and Bruce F. Johnston, eds. (1967), *Agricultural Development and Economic Growth.* Ithaca: Cornell University Press.

Spencer, Joseph E. (1960), "The cultural factor in 'underdevelopment': the case of Malaya," in Norton Ginsburg, ed., *Essays on Geography and Economic Development*, Department of Geography Research Paper No. 62. Chicago: University of Chicago Press, pp. 35–48.

Steward, Julian H., ed. (1967), *Contemporary Change in Traditional Societies*, Vol. I, *Introduction and African Tribes*; Vol. II, *Asian Rural Societies*; Vol. III, *Mexican and Peruvian Communities.* Urbana: University of Illinois Press.

Stolper, Wolfgang F. (1963), "The development of Nigeria," *Scientific American* **209**, No. 3, 168–184.

Tremblay Marc-Adélard and Walton J. Anderson (1966), *Rural Canada in Transition: A Multi-dimensional Study of the Impact of Technology and Urbanization on Traditional Society.* Ottawa: Agricultural Economic Research Council of Canada.

U.S. Agency for International Development (1962–1963), *Science, Technology, and Development*, 12 volumes. Washington: D.C.: U.S. Government Printing Office.

CHAPTER 11
SPATIAL INTERACTION

11.1 INTRODUCTION

Up to this point in our explorations in social geography we have concentrated upon explaining the location of various phenomena at particular times and places; although we have sometimes been concerned with changes in their distribution over time, we have not considered them systematically. We have noted, however, that ideas and artifacts tend to spread from one area to others along established routes of travel, transportation, and communication, by means such as trade, migration, and military conquest. We have learned that study of relationships between variables is essentially a static approach, which helps us to learn what factors are areally related to the phenomenon we are studying at a given time. Although a series of such cross-sectional studies for different areas and time periods may suggest the way in which change occurs over time, it cannot substitute for longitudinal studies in revealing the process whereby change occurs.

In order to learn more about the process of change in spatial distributions, we shall survey some findings of studies which help us to understand some ways in which ideas and artifacts are spread; that is, the process of spatial diffusion. It is almost self-evident that diffusion requires communication between individuals, either in direct face-to-face contact or less directly, by telephone, letter, or some other means of transmitting ideas. Mass communications media, including radio, television, newspapers, and magazines also are used to transmit messages about items such as space exploits, riots, and deodorants. These messages can be effective in the spread of ideas only if enough members of the potential audience possess radios or television sets, or are able to read printed messages, and understand the language in which the messages are sent.

We shall begin our study of the diffusion of ideas and artifacts with a survey of the existing network by means of which people and ideas circulate, and consider some factors which influence the volume of contact and interaction between different areas. Then, building upon this knowledge, in the following chapter we shall look at some of the approaches which have been taken to studying the diffusion of innovations and the findings of some of the many studies which have been made. In so doing, we shall draw upon many of our previous explorations to see how such phenomena as religions, house types, languages, and technological change have spread over time and space. We may then be able to derive some generalizations about the diffusion of phenomena which will help us to predict how innovations might spread over a given area.

11.2 TRANSPORTATION AND COMMUNICATION

11.2.1 Definition of Terms

No single English word exists to denote the complex of flows of goods, people, and ideas from place to place over the entire world, by all modes of transportation and communication combined. The French geographer, Vidal de la Blache, used the word *circulation*; for this concept, this term may be translated as either circulation or traffic, neither of which is fully satisfactory. Awkward as it seems, the combined term transportation and communication is probably the clearest to use in English. The term spatial interaction is also used to refer to these flows of goods, people, or ideas from one area to another.

11.2.2 Historical Overview of Transportation and Communication

As we are constantly being reminded, the speed and ease of travel are increasing rapidly. From earliest prehistoric times, men have moved about the earth in search of food, water, and other necessities, as well as to obtain luxuries and for the pleasure of traveling. For a long time people and goods were transported only by human power; gradually domesticated animals were used to carry burdens and to pull wheeled vehicles. Other sources of power, such as wind, were used to propel ships. Not until the nineteenth century, however, were mechanical sources of power generally available. Steam engines drove ships and locomotives; with the introduction of internal combustion engines, cars and airplanes entered the picture. In addition, some goods were transported by conveyor belts, cable railways, and pipelines.

Early means of communications included personal carrying of verbal or written messages as well as the use of smoke signals, signal flags, lights, and drumbeats. With increases in technology, new ways of reproducing and delivering messages came into use. First printing; and then the telegraph, telephone, and radio increased the distance over which messages could be carried and the speed with which they traveled.

11.2.3 The Location of Different Networks of Transportation and Communication

In studying transportation and communication, we are concerned both with the routes along which flows occur and with their volume. Ideally, we would like to have some all-inclusive measure of circulation which would take all the different modes into account. Since, however, we lack not only the measure but also the data from which to construct one for the entire world, we shall examine some of the modes of transportation and communication. We may then hope to gain some idea of the relative accessibility of various parts of the world; that is, of the cost of reaching a given place from other places, as expressed in terms of time, distance, money, or effort.

Looking at a world map of railways, we can note that the densest network is located in western Europe, especially in Germany, France, Great Britain, Switzerland, Belgium, and the Netherlands. Then, approximately in decreasing order, come the eastern United States, Japan, southern Canada, eastern Europe, India, western U.S.S.R., eastern Argentina, and the western United States. In other areas local railway networks, often sparser, are present. These include southeastern Australia, New Zealand, Brazil, middle Chile, South Africa, and China. In addition, isolated spurs connect the interior of some land areas to the coast. Regardless of the density of railways in a country, however, we note that most major cities are located on or near a railway line.

The distribution of motorable roads is similar to that of railways, with two exceptions. First, the road network is denser, so that more roads than railroads are found in areas served by both; in some large areas almost no place is more than twenty-five miles from a motorable road. Second, some areas which have virtually no railroads are accessible by road, notably parts of Africa and central Asia. Areas with dense road networks include the eastern and central United States, southern Canada, most of Europe, Japan, much of India and Pakistan, southeastern Australia, New Zealand, South Africa, eastern Argentina, southern Brazil, and middle Chile.

Looking at the location of airlines in terms of traffic density rather than of routes, we find the pattern similar to those of railways and motorable roads. The heaviest traffic in western Europe is between major cities, including London, Paris, Rome, Berlin, and cities of the Ruhr industrial district. In South America, Rio de Janeiro, Sao Paulo, Buenos Aires, and Montevideo are major centers of air transportation. Centers in other parts of the world include Sydney, Melbourne, Tokyo, and Bangkok in the Pacific, and Khabarovsk, Omsk, Moscow, and Leningrad in the U.S.S.R. Some areas not served by railways or roads are accessible by air transport. These include much of Alaska, the Canadian North, and Australia, interior Brazil, Venezuela, Ecuador, and Colombia, as well as parts of Asia and Africa. Heaviest airline travel, however, is found in the United States, which has approximately 50 percent of the world's air cargo and 57 percent of its passenger traffic. Although most of the traffic is between larger cities, many smaller cities have airports served by feeder lines which channel through traffic to larger airports as well as providing local transportation.

Ocean shipping between major coastal ports accounts for the largest volume of waterborne traffic. Coastwise and intracoastal shipping are found on the Atlantic, Pacific, and Gulf coasts of the United States, as well as in the Mediterranean and some other areas. Inland waterways which are important trade arteries include the Great Lakes and St. Lawrence Seaway and the Mississippi and Ohio Rivers in North America; the Amazon in South America; the Rhone, Seine, Danube, Volga, and Dnieper in Europe and the U.S.S.R.; the Nile in North Africa, the Ganges in India, the Mekong in southeast Asia, and the Yangtze in China. Man-made features such as dams, locks, and canals make the rivers navigable, and canals connect major waterways and provide access to areas.

11.2.4 A Composite Picture of Routes of Transportation

From this brief survey it can be seen that, with few exceptions, those areas well served by any one mode of transportation tend also to have good access to other modes. Europe, the United States, and southern Canada, for example, are well served by all modes of transportation. In areas with less technology, however, such as parts of Asia and Africa, although there is less transportation of all kinds, often one or two kinds are dominant and another kind, such as railroads, may be lacking. In general, however, as we have observed in Section 10.5.2, there is a close relationship between the amount of technology in an area and the total amount of transportation, both internal and external.

11.2.5 Location of Communications

Although it would also be conceptually possible to make a composite map of communications networks over the world, it would be extremely difficult, at best, to do so in practice. Data are available for such items as the number of radio and television stations and receivers in various countries, newspaper circulation, and the volume of both domestic and international mail flows. As with transportation data, however, none of these items alone is an adequate measure of the total amount of communication within a country or between countries. Since, however, as we have noted in Section 10.4.2, there is a close relationship between technology and such phenomena as newspaper circulation and number of radios per 100 population, we would expect to find the communications network to be similar to that described for transportation.

11.2.6 The Notion of Accessibility

On an intuitive basis, we would expect those areas which are well served by transportation and communication to be more accessible than those areas which are less well served. Unfortunately, although the notion of accessibility has a certain appeal for descriptive purposes, attempts to define it precisely enough for analytic purposes generally have been unsuccessful. Some investigators have used the density of transportation networks as a measure. Essentially, we can define accessibility as some function of the time, distance, cost, or effort required to get people, goods, or messages from one place to another. Since this is so, it would seem to be more desirable to use one or more of these measures than to attempt to operationalize the notion of accessibility. We could use the time required by air, sea, or automobile, the air or road distance between points, or the cost of using one or more of these modes of transportation. In some cases these correlate highly and may be used interchangeably; in others, one may be the most desirable for a particular purpose. Time, distance, and cost have been used extensively by geographers studying transportation; effort, being more subjective, is little used. By considering each of the possibilities in light of the purpose of the questions to be answered in a particular study, it should be possible to select a suitable measure.

11.2.7 The Use of Graph Theory to Study Transportation Networks

Geographers interested in analyzing certain abstract properties of networks, especially those studying transportation, have drawn upon graph theory for measures of these properties. Graph theory is included in topology, a branch of mathematics in which sets of points and lines connecting them are the basic features studied. Each point is called a vertex, and the lines or curves connecting vertices are referred to as edges. Figure 11.1 includes a graph of a highway network. Various measures relating the numbers of vertices and edges have been developed to measure properties such as the connectivity, shape, and complexity of networks. These measures provide bases for empirical comparison of different networks and means for determining relationships between characteristics of networks and other variables. They are further discussed and applied in activity number 4 at the end of this chapter.

Graph theory has been applied to designing electrical networks, pipelines, and other phenomena where flows over a network are studied. Werner and others (1968) have suggested that it could be applied to determining a road network which would make all points in an area equally acessible to all other points or to designing a mass transportation system, such as a subway line, in such a way as to optimize flows among places, transporting individuals from one place to another with minimal delay.

Kansky (1963) calculated various graph theoretic measures of railway and highway networks in twenty-five countries, and correlated these with selected independent variables. Using the technological scale developed by Berry (1960), he found that countries which were high on that scale had railway networks (1) of high connectivity as measured by the β index; (2) such that the network diameter was a small portion of the total network length as measured by the π index; (3) with shorter average edges, the η index; (4) with a larger number of vertices; v; and (5) with a larger number of high order vertices or intersections, used in computation of the i index. The opposite was true of countries low on the technological scale. Results of analyses for the highway networks were similar. Although there were some significant relationships between each of the dependent variables, or indices,

A. MAP

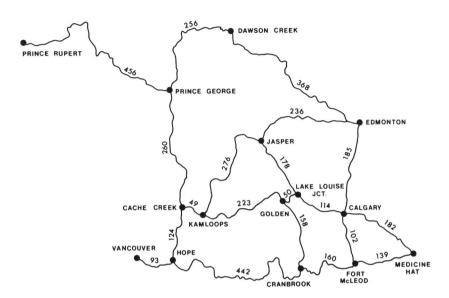

B. GRAPH

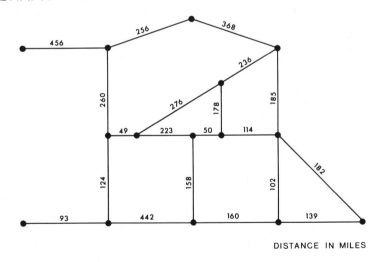

DISTANCE IN MILES

Fig. 11.1. Map and graph of a simplified highway network of parts of Alberta and British Columbia, Canada.

and the other independent variables—size, shape, and relief of countries—these were less consistent and of smaller magnitude. It is interesting to note that these findings are consistent with those of our explorations of transportation and communication and the relationship to the amount of technology in an area.

11.3 SPATIAL INTERACTION

11.3.1 Ways of Studying Spatial Interaction

In our study of spatial interaction we wish not only to learn the means by which people, goods, and ideas travel from one place to another, but also to derive laws about the amount of interaction which takes place between people in different locations. We recognize that there are wide variations in individuals' trip behavior; some people seldom, if ever, leave their home areas, whereas others spend much time traveling about the world. In general, however, we know that most people take the greatest number of trips over relatively short distances, and fewer trips over longer distances. They go to work, shop, or visit friends in the same city frequently; they go on longer business or vacation trips less frequently. We could either study the actual behavior of many individuals or question them as to how far they would be willing to travel to obtain a variety of goods and services. By using descriptive statistics we could then derive a pattern of individual trip behavior or arrive at some measures of individual space preferences.

Instead of studying the behavior or preferences of individuals for many types of trips, we could study the total volume of interactions of various types taking place between areas. We could, for example, investigate trips to different shopping centers, telephone calls, or enrollment at colleges and universities, all of which involve travel or communication between areas. To date, study of total interaction has been more heuristic, but studies of individual space preference are continuing in the hope of obtaining a better explanation of spatial interaction.

11.3.2 Study of the Volume of Interaction Between Areas

A subject can be approached by beginning either with theory, as Christaller did, or with empirical observations. Here we shall take the second approach, first looking at data relating the amount of interaction taking place between people to the distances which separate them from each other, and then deriving generalizations which suggest a law applicable to other sets of observations.

Let us look first at a set of data showing the amount of spatial interaction of a given phenomenon over varying distances. We are concerned not with the particular phenomenon, but with the amount of interaction as related to distance. Morrill and Pitts (1967) obtained data regarding the distance between residences of marriage partners in Seattle. From this set of data, presented in Table 11.1, we can see that the number of marriages tend to decrease with distance. Stated more generally, an inverse relationships exists between the amount of interaction and distance.

Table 11.1 Seattle marriage distances, 1962

Distance in miles	Number of marriages	Marriages per square mile
0– 1	47	15.00
1– 2	41	4.36
2– 3	30	1.91
3– 4	28	1.27
4– 5	20	0.71
5– 6	22	0.61
6– 7	22	0.54
7– 8	17	0.36
8– 9	14	0.26
9–10	10	0.17

Source: Morrill and Pitts, 1967. Reproduced by permission from the *Annals* of the Association of American Geographers, Volume 57 (1967).

In order to see whether this generalization might be applicable to other data, let us examine data first for this same phenomenon in a different area, and then for other phenomena. Table 11.2 shows the relationship between number of marriages and distance of residences of the marriage partners in Kagawa prefecture,

Table 11.2 Kagawa (Japan) marriage distances, 1951

Distance band (kilometers)	Marriages within band	Marriages per square kilometer
0.0– 0.5	43	78.48
0.5– 1.5	65	10.35
1.5– 2.5	63	5.01
2.5– 3.5	56	2.97
3.5– 4.5	60	2.39
4.5– 5.5	83	2.64
5.5– 6.5	56	1.49
6.5– 7.5	46	1.05
7.5– 8.5	34	0.68
8.5– 9.5	35	0.62
9.5–10.5	29	0.46
10.5–11.5	21	0.30
11.5–12.5	17	0.23
12.5–13.5	16	0.20
13.5–14.5	10	0.11
14.5–15.5	13	0.14

Source: Morrill and Pitts, 1967. Reproduced by permis- from the *Annals* of the Association of American Geographers, Volume 57 (1967).

Table 11.3   Migration distances Asby, Sweden, 1930–1939 and Cleveland, Ohio, 1933–1936

Distance band (kilometers)	Moving units	Units per sqaure kilometer	Ring center distance (miles)	Moving units	Units per square mile
0.0– 0.5	9	11.39	0.29	5,585	5,475.
0.5– 1.5	45	7.17	0.86	2,471	808
1.5– 2.5	45	3.58	1.43	1,313	263
2.5– 3.5	26	1.38	2.00	737	104
3.5– 4.5	28	1.11	2.57	431	47
4.5– 5.5	25	0.80	3.14	320	29
5.5– 6.5	20	0.53	3.71	217	16
6.5– 7.5	23	0.52	4.28	178	12
7.5– 8.5	18	0.36	4.85	172	10
8.5– 9.5	10	0.18	5.42	125	6.5
9.5–10.5	17	0.27	5.99	137	6.4
10.5–11.5	7	0.10	6.56	106	4.5
11.5–12.5	11	0.15	7.13	85	3.3
12.5–13.5	6	0.07	7.70	102	3.8
13.5–14.5	2	0.02	8.27	102	3.5
14.5–15.5	5	0.05	8.84	57	1.8
			9.41	30	0.9
			9.98	39	1.1

Source: Morrill and Pitts, 1967. Reproduced by permission from the *Annals* of the Association of American Geographers, Volume 57 (1967).

Japan. The same inverse relationship may be noted. Considering a different phenomenon, migration, in two different areas—Asby, Sweden and Cleveland, Ohio—we can note a similar relationship (Table 11.3).

As we have learned, there are many ways of portraying and testing relationships between variables. We can see, therefore, that a similar relationship is shown in the two scatter diagrams of Fig. 11.2. These depict the relationship between distance and two different phenomena at two different areal scales: truck trips around Chicago and railway shipments within the United States. The negative slope of the estimated regression lines indicates that inverse relationships exist between each pair of phenomena depicted.

Visual inspection of maps is also useful, since the spatial elements is emphasized by mapping a phenomenon. Figures 11.3 and 11.4, which are taken from a study by Helvig (1964), illustrate the number of trucks arriving in Chicago during a selected 24-hour period. The size of each circle is proportional to the number of trucks arriving from that area. As can be seen, although there is clearly some relationship between volume of interaction and distance, it is far from perfect. For example, more trucks originate in such areas as Rock Island, Terre Haute, Evansville, Indianapolis, and Detroit than might be anticipated if distance were the only relevant factor. Study of the map in light of general knowledge of the area helps to suggest at least two possibilities for additional explanatory variables. We can see that some areas with relatively large amounts of interaction in relation to distance contain large population centers. We might also guess that other areas of this sort are ones from which agricultural products are shipped to Chicago. The first observation is more strongly supported by the evidence than the second, although there is probably some support for that as well. The relationship between population size and interaction appears to be direct: the greater the population size, the greater the interaction.

11.3.3 The Gravity Model of Spatial Interaction

These two generalizations about the amount of interaction between areas may be combined into a single mathematical expression:

$$I_{ij} = f(P_i P_j / D_{ij}),$$ (11.1)

where:

I_{ij} = the interaction between area i and area j,
P_i = the population of area i,
P_j = the population of area j, and
D_{ij} = the distance between area i and area j.

In words, this expression says that the volume of interaction between any two areas i and j is some function of the population sizes of both areas and the inverse of the distance between them. This model does not, however, define the exact nature of the mathematical function. By looking at the scatter diagrams (Fig. 11.1) which have been plotted on a double logarithmic scale, we can see that there appears to be a linear relationship between the logarithms of the two variables: the amount of interaction, whether truck trips, railroad shipments, or ocean freight, and distance.

Since the general equation for a straight line is given by

$$Y = ax + b,$$ (11.2)

where:

a = the slope of the line, and
b = the Y-intercept, or value of Y when $X = 0$.

We can substitute the interaction variables to derive the equation for this line, which would then be written:

$$\text{Log } I_{ij} = a \log (P_i P_j / D_{ij}) + b.$$ (11.3)

Correlation regression analysis is used to fit a line which minimizes the total squares of the deviations of all observations from it.

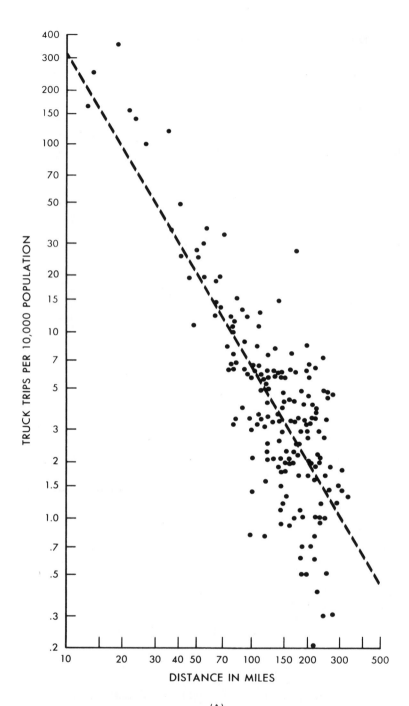

(A)

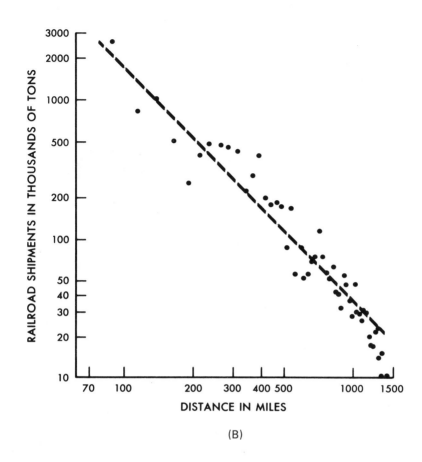

(B)

Fig. 11.2. Relationships between distance and movements or spatial interaction. (A) Truck trips around Chicago and (B) Railroad shipment within the United States. Source: Helvig, 1964 and Isard, 1956. (A) Reprinted by permission of the author and the University of Chicago Department of Geography. (B) Reprinted from Location and Space-Economy by Walter Isard by permission of the MIT Press, Cambridge, Mass. Copyright © 1956 by The Massachusetts Institute of Technology.

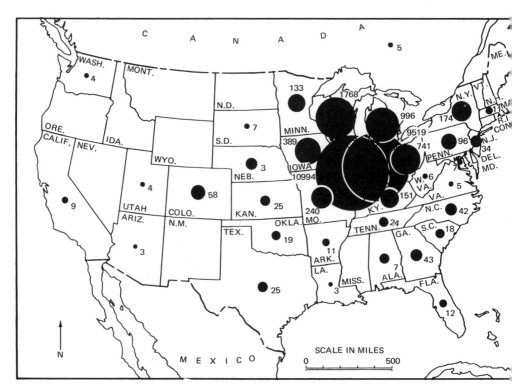

Fig. 11.3. Number of trucks traveling to the Chicago area on an average weekday in 1956 by state of origin. Source: Helvig, 1964. Reprinted by permission of the author and the University of Chicago Department of Geography.

Fig. 11.4. Number of daily truck trips to the Chicago Area by counties of origin in Illinois, Indiana, Wisconsin, and Michigan, 1956. Source: Helvig, 1964. Reprinted by permission of the author and the University of Chicago Department of Geography. ▶

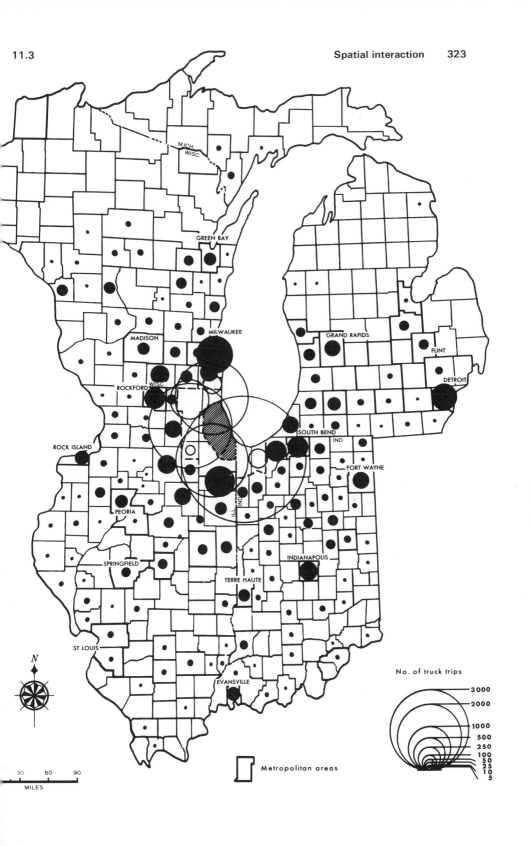

11.3.4 Theoretical Basis for Use of the Gravity Model

Since the use of this model was suggested by analogy to the gravity model of classical physics, gravitational force = $Mass_1 \times Mass_2 / Distance^2$, it is often called the gravity model of spatial interaction. Interaction is analogous to gravitational force, P_1 and P_2 to $Mass_1$ and $Mass_2$. Not only has it been found empirically useful in explaining and predicting interaction, but its use can also be justified by a line of reasoning based on our observations above.

With respect to the population, or P, components, it is reasonable to believe that there is an average probability p that one unit of the behavior being studied will be generated by a given number of units of the relevant population within a given time period. The greater value of P_i, therefore, the greater the number of units of the given behavior that will be generated at that particular point. Similarly, we can assume that the probability that one of these units of behavior will be directed toward another area j will be proportional to the population of that area. A concrete illustration may be helpful in clarifying this justification. Telephone calls are a form of spatial interaction, as defined above. We can see that areas with larger population size will both generate and receive more telephone calls than areas with smaller population size. If we assume that some average rate of sending and receiving telephone calls can be applied to all areas, then the number of telephone calls sent by each area will equal the population of the area times the average rate.

This last assumption is not completely valid; for some phenomena a relevant sending or receiving population may be identified. We might guess, for example, that a major commercial center would have a higher rate of sending and receiving calls than a rural agricultural area, or that areas in which median family incomes were higher would generate more calls than areas with lower median family incomes. We might, therefore, arrive at more accurate estimates of interaction by using some measure of the relevant population rather than total population size. A subset of the population with specified characteristics with respect to age, sex, or income, for example, might in such a case be used to estimate the generating population more accurately.

We have already discussed justification for including the distance variable. Empirically, we have observed that the amount of interaction between people in different areas tends to decrease as the distance between the areas increases. This decrease is also partly due to increased influence from competing centers, or intervening opportunities. As we shall discuss and illustrate more fully below, although many measures of distance may be used, airline and road distance are the two most frequently chosen.

11.3.5 Studies of Interaction Using the Gravity Model

Phenomena which have been studied using the gravity model include such apparently unrelated ones as migration (Hägerstrand, 1957; Olsson, 1965), newspaper circulation (Dahl, 1957), cinema attendance (Claeson, 1964), and telephone calls (Dahl, 1957; Mackay, 1958; Kariel, 1968). Values for the amount of spatial interaction predicted from the model have been found to correlate closely with observed values.

To cite one phenomenon, enrollment at colleges has been studied by different investigators. Stewart (1941) found that the number of students enrolled at Princeton from each state in the United States varied as predicted by the gravity model. Since he did not compute coefficients of correlation, his findings cannot be compared mathematically with those of later studies. McConnell (1965) reported that the number of students from each county in Ohio attending Bowling Green University was closely correlated with that predicted by use of the model. The computed r was 0.905, $r^2 = 0.819$, indicating that almost eighty-two percent of the spatial variation in student enrollment could be explained by the gravity model alone. Similarly, Kariel (1968) studied freshman enrollment at Western Washington State College in Bellingham (Fig. 11.5). He found that the correlation between

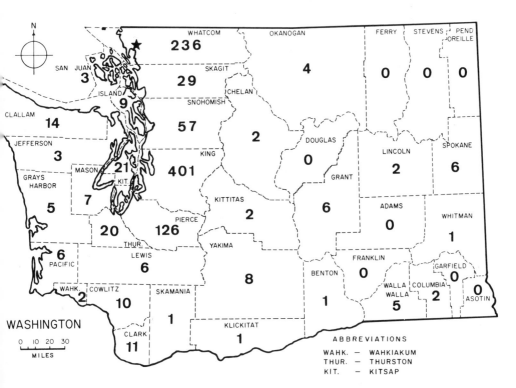

Fig. 11.5. Frequency of home residence of freshman enrolled at Western Washington State College by counties in Washington state, Fall 1962. ★Indicates site of Western Washington State College. Source: Kariel, 1968. Reprinted from *The Annals of Regional Science*, Volume II, 1968, with permission from the publisher. Copyrights *The Annals of Regional Science*, 1968.

the number of freshmen enrolled from each county of the state of Washington and predicted enrollment was $r = 0.989$, $r^2 = 0.979$.

Various investigators have modified the basic gravity model in different ways in the attempt to increase the value of the coefficient of correlation obtained, and thus to explain or predict more accurately. Both McConnell and Kariel tried several variations.

McConnell used six different combinations employing different values for the population component, P, and distance, D. Besides using total population as a measure of P, he also used population weighted by income (population × income). To the D-component, he applied an arbitrarily selected exponent, 2, so that he used the square of the actual distance. He also substituted a different measure of D, the number of intervening opportunities. An intervening opportunity is defined as a place which offers the good or service a person is seeking, but which lies nearer to him than the one under study. Since people are most likely to travel to the nearest place and decreasingly less likely to continue to the second or third place, or more distant ones, the number of students from any area attending a given college will be inversely related to the number of other colleges between their homes and the particular college, which represent intervening opportunities for a college education.

He then combined these two P-measures and three D-measures in various ways, devising six different formulations. When correlations between the observed enrollment and that predicted from each of these formulations were calculated, however, none of the values of r obtained was significantly different from that using the original gravity model.

Kariel approached the problem somewhat differently. Besides the simple gravity model, he used two variations: (1) changing the measure of P, using the population aged sixteen at the time of the 1960 census (P_{16}), from which most freshmen would be drawn two years later, when the sample was taken; and (2) adding another empirical measure of interaction, outgoing telephone calls from the location of Western Washington State College, Bellingham, to selected points in the state of Washington. He found that there were no significant differences between (1) the coefficients of simple correlation, r, computed using either P or P_{16}; and (2) the coefficients of multiple correlation, R, using either P or P_{16}; or by adding telephone calls as a second independent variable.

What conclusions can we draw by looking at the findings of these two studies? First, the gravity model predicted about 82 percent of the observed enrollment in one case and about 98 percent in the other. None of the different variations tried seemed any better than the original model. It is interesting to note an additional finding: in Kariel's study, the correlation between observed enrollment and telephone calls was $r = 0.917$, $r^2 = 0.841$, which indicates a close relationship between these two empirical measures of interaction. As might be expected, there was also a close relationship between P_j/D_{ij} and telephone calls: $r = 0.936$, $r^2 = 0.877$, showing that, for this set of data, the gravity model was also fairly accurate for predicting the number of telephone calls.

11.3.6   Modifications of the Gravity Model

As was noted in Section 4.3.3, scientific laws are often derived by starting from an observed relationship between two variables. This relationship may be stated mathematically and tested to determine how closely the mathematical statement conforms to the observations. This procedure was followed in the studies cited above; the linear relationship between the logarithms of the variables was noted, equations for the lines were calculated, and the closeness of the fit between the line and the observations was then tested by correlation analysis.

The next step in obtaining explanations and deriving laws often involves an educated trial-and-error approach, following hunches, in the hopes of finding something which will yield a closer correspondence between law and observation. We have discussed four major modifications of the basic gravity model in the preceding section. Let us now look at each of these modifications in more detail.

Some investigators have reasoned that the measure of P or D used should reflect as accurately as possible relevant features of the phenomenon being studied; that is, it should represent the particular population and the effective distance involved in that type of interaction. Besides the examples given above, variables such as retail sales (Dunn, 1956), number of registered cars (Cavanough, 1950), and commodity output (Warntz, 1959), have been used instead of total population in studies of economic phenomena. As to different measures of distance, those which have been used include airline and road distance, travel time, cost, or some combination of these. Psychological distance also may be considered as an important factor; that is, the prospective traveler's feelings about how far away another point is, and how much effort would be involved in going there.

Weighting of P or D, or both, has been tried by some investigators, who believe that weighting population by a measure such as income more accurately measures the probability of generating certain types of behavior. McConnell tried this approach in two formulations, because persons from higher-income families are more likely to attend college than those from lower-income families. Other investigators, such as Stewart (1947), have used empirically derived weights, trying several and selecting the one which results in the best coefficient of correlation. Although such an approach may be helpful in raising the coefficient of correlation, we would like to be able to have some independent, *a priori* way of assigning weights which would have some logical justification, as does the use of income.

Although exponents have been assigned to both P and D, more interest has been shown in the latter. If distance is considered to be analogous to friction, in that it slows down or decreases interaction as it is applied, then increasing the exponent is analogous to increasing the amount of friction, or the influence of distance upon the particular behavior being studied, and decreasing the exponent is analogous to decreasing the amount of friction and the effect of distance. It has been found that an exponent of 2, or the use of D^2, gives close results in Europe, whereas in most American studies, an exponent of 1 is closer. Haggett (1966) suggests that this difference may be related to the higher level of technology in the United States, with correspondingly easier circulation, so that distance has less effect on interaction.

Exponents have been calculated empirically by some researchers so that the resulting curve most closely fits their observations. They suggest that the exponent varies not only with the area but also with the phenomenon. Adults travel farther to work than children to school; people travel farther to buy specialized commodities such as fine china or furniture than everyday needs such as groceries. As yet, however, no regularities have been identified which permit prediction of exponents for particular phenomena.

11.3.7 Extension of the Gravity Model

The gravity model may also be extended to apply to more than one center of influence. Returning to the physical analogy, we know that as a space ship travels away from the earth toward the moon, for example, the gravitional pull of the earth on it decreases and that of the moon increases. At some point in the journey they become equal; from then on it falls toward the moon with no need for power to help it escape the earth's gravitational field. Similarly, if we consider two urban centres located a given distance apart, one larger than the other, we can imagine that the attraction of the larger city would be stronger than that of the smaller. People living somewhere between the two would be more likely to travel to the larger one as long as its attractiveness outweighed the disadvantage of distance to be traveled; at some point they would be about equally likely to go to one as to the other, and beyond that they would go to the smaller center most of the time.

The relative attractiveness of each center at any point between them can be. expressed in terms of probability, as suggested by Huff (1963). Assuming that an individual has only the two alternatives, if he were living at the point of indifference, as the point of equal attraction is called, he would be equally likely to go to one as to the other. The probability for each of the two areas would then be 0.5, summing to 1.0. Persons living nearer the smaller city, on the other hand, would have higher probabilities of going there and lower ones of going to the larger city, as suggested in Fig. 11.6.

These probabilities can be calculated by using attraction-distance ratios corresponding to each of the centers of attraction. The attraction-distance ratio is calculated for any point on the surface; these are then summed, and each ratio expressed as a proportion of that sum, with the total adding to 1.0. These proportions are expressions of the theoretical probability that an individual living at that particular point will travel to each of the centers considered. They can be calculated for a number of points, located by laying a grid over a map of the area. Isolines or probability contours can then be drawn connecting points with the same probability, as has been done in Fig. 11.6. It can be seen that when three

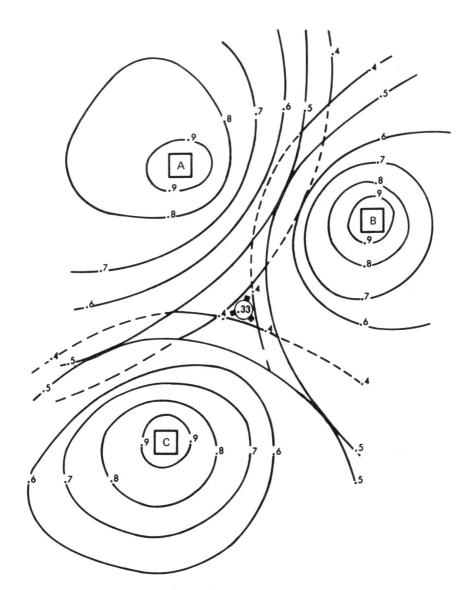

Fig. 11.6. Probability contours for three attractions. Source: Brian J. L. Berry, *Geography of Market Centers and Retail Distribution*, © 1967. Reprinted by permission of Prentice-Hall, Inc., Englewood Cliffs, N. J.

centers are considered, there is one point of equal attraction from all centers, with 0.33 probability of going to each. Dotted lines indicate that people are less likely to travel beyond the 0.5 probability point; this approach could, therefore, be used in determining theoretical trade areas for each of the centers.

The general form of the equation is

$$P\left(I_{ij}\right)=\frac{A_j/D^y{}_{ij}}{\sum\limits_{j=1}^{n}A_j/D^y{}_{ij}},\qquad\qquad(11.4)$$

where:

$P(I_{ij})$ = the probability of interaction taking place between place i and a point of attraction j,

A_j = the attraction of point j,

D_{ij} = the distance between point i and attraction j,

y = a parameter that reflects the effect of distance on various kinds of interactions, and

n = the number of attractions.

This formulation can be used to determine the probability of individuals' going to one of a number of attractions such as national or state parks, schools, or shopping centers. Both the attraction, A, and the distance D, can be weighted, as was discussed for the simple gravity model.

11.3.8 A More General Statement of Curve Fitting for Spatial Interaction

In Section 11.2.5 we reviewed two studies of spatial interaction in which gravity models were used. In these investigations linear regression analysis was used to fit a straight line to the data for two variables: P_iP_j/D_{ij} and the observed or actual interaction. The result was a regression equation from which the expected or theoretical interaction could be computed. Theoretical and actual values were then compared to determine how closely they corresponded; that is, how well the curve fitted the data from which it was derived.

In fitting a curve to a set of data, a researcher usually begins by selecting a curve which appears to conform to the pattern of the data as plotted on a scatter diagram. Through experience, and knowledge of the nature of the phenomenon with which he is dealing, he will probably have some idea as to the type of curve to be expected. Since linear regression analysis by the method of least squares is the simplest approach presently available, it is generally preferred when the relationship between the variables appears to be linear. When the scatter diagram does not suggest a linear relationship, however, data for one or both of the variables may be transformed, or expressed in a different form such as the common logarithm, so that a linear relationship results.

When a straight line does not give a good fit to either raw or transformed data, other methods of fitting varous mathematical curves may be used. Different investigators have experimented with the fitting of a variety of curves to data on spatial interaction. Morrill and Pitts (1967) found that the Pareto function ($Y = aD^{-b}$) exaggerated close-in frequencies. The log-normal function $[Y = ae^{(-b\ \log\ D)^2}]$

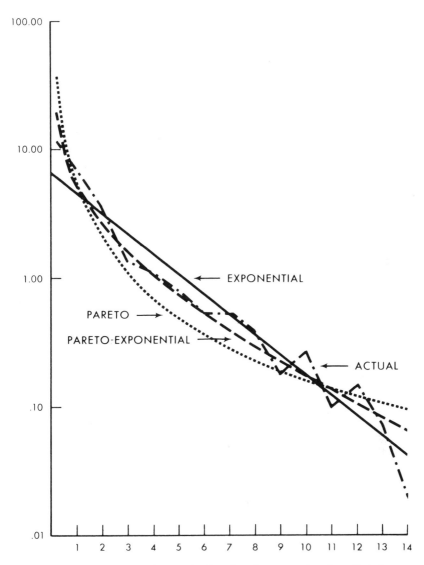

Fig. 11.7. Asby, Sweden, marriage and migration data: actual and predicted moves per square kilometer. Source: Morrill and Pitts, 1967. Reproduced by permission from the *Annals* of the Association of American Geographers, Volume 57 (1967).

was best for use in dealing with data representing repeated trips over the same path, such as trips to shopping or work. The exponential function ($Y = ae^{bD}$) was best for data in which there is some relationship between successive interactions. They concluded that since the Pareto function tended to overestimate close-in frequencies and the exponential function to underestimate them, a combination of the two, called the Pareto-exponential function ($Y = aD^{-b}e^{-cD}$), gave the best estimate for many phenomena. In constructing a simulation model discussed in Section 8.7.9, they used this curve to determine mean information fields, which represent sets of probabilities of interaction over specified distances. In Fig. 11.7, actual migration distances in Asby, Sweden (shown in Table 11.3) and those predicted by the three different curves are shown. By use of the Kolmogorov-Smirnov test, it was determined that the distribution represented by the actual curve did not differ significantly from that of any of the three mathematical curves, the Pareto, the exponential, or the Pareto-exponential. They concluded, therefore, that all three fitted the data equally well.

11.4 WHERE ARE WE NOW AND WHERE ARE WE GOING?

In this chapter we have discussed aspects of transportation and communication and indicated their conceptual link to the notion of interaction. We then traced the development of the application of the gravity model to the study of spatial interaction from the recognition by Stewart that a relationship existed between one type of interaction, college enrollment, and distance, to a more sophisticated measurement of the amount of change in the dependent variable, interaction, which was associated with a specified amount of change in the independent variable, distance. We have thus moved from specific observations, or sets of data, to more general statements about relationships between distance and a variety of phenomena which involve interaction over space. We have recognized that there is sound justification for the existence of these relationships.

We also recognize the limitations of the present state of knowledge; although we can derive mathematical functions from the data, we are unable to specify in advance what certain parameters will be. In computing the equation for a straight line, for example, we derive the slope and Y-intercept from the data by the method of least squares regression analysis. We would like, however, to understand enough about such questions as the effect of distance upon the amount of interaction for different phenomena that we could derive further generalizations about values such as to the coefficient representing the slope and the exponent to be applied to the distance.

As we have seen throughout our explorations and discussed in Section 4.3.3, scientific laws are often derived by starting from an observed relationship between two variables. Further study may then reveal some regularity which can be expressed mathematically, and tested to determine how closely the mathematical statement conforms to the observation. If the fit is not considered sufficiently close, various methods may be tried to improve the correspondence between observations and theory. We have shown how investigators attempted to improve upon the prediction obtained by use of the gravity model by using measures other than total population for P and actual distance for D, weighting of P or D, assigning exponents to P or D, and fitting a curve other than a straight line to the observations. Some studies of interaction have included other variables in addition to population and distance. They have found, however, that factors such as age, social class, and religion are relatively unimportant quantitatively; that distance and population together explain the largest amount of the spatial variation, and that other variables add relatively little. Physical, political, and social barriers to interaction, discussed in Section 12.5, also modify the effects of distance.

Some geographers are working to develop a better understanding of some of the factors underlying human spatial behavior, in hopes that further modification of existing models or possibly development of new ones will lead to both more precise and more general laws about spatial interaction. One approach is the study of individual space preference: how far people are willing to go to procure specified goods or services. Researchers taking this approach hope to learn whether factors such as age or income are related to space preference, and what the effect of distance is upon different people under different conditions. However, we recognize that although we have answered many questions, many more remain to be answered.

REVIEW YOUR UNDERSTANDING OF THESE CONCEPTS

spatial interaction

accessibility

transportation network

graph theory

individual space preference

gravity model

modifications of the gravity model

curve fitting

SUGGESTED ACTIVITIES

1. Carry out a study of spatial interaction using the gravity model for any one topic such as visitors at a national park, guests at a hotel, student enrollment at a college or university, newspaper circulation, destination or origin of letters received or sent by a group of individuals, or the destination of moving vans leaving a city or origin of vans arriving. Select a suitable time period and areal unit for compiling the data. After obtaining the required data, prepare a scatter diagram, plotting the actual interaction on the Y-axis and P/D on the X-axis. Calculate a line of best fit, or sketch one in. Compare the results obtained with those discussed in this chapter, and attempt to explain any differences.

2. Assume that you are responsible for advising a city council or state or provincial legislature on the location of a new facility. Select the location for a building or institution such as a new convention center, hospital, or university and justify your choice in terms of accessibility for clientele and employees.

3. Attempt to predict the changes in interaction between two or more areas which would occur with changes brought about by construction of a bridge where formerly there was a ferry, construction of a freeway to a suburban area of a city, establishment of a new feeder airline route, or other similar phenomena.

4. A. Select a transportation network of a state, province, or some other convenient area. Draw a map of this network and transform it into a graph as was done in Fig. 11.1. Compute some of the graph theoretic measures explained below. Remember that some of these measures refer to elements of a network, some to the network as a whole, and some to relationships between elements and the network.

   1) Cyclomatic number, μ: a measure of the degree of connectivity of the network; the higher the number, the more connected the network.

      $$\mu = e - v + p$$

      where:

         e = number of edges,

         v = number of vertices, and

         p = number of networks (one in this example.)

      For the example shown in Fig. 11.1, $\mu = 19 - 14 + 1 = 6$.

   2) Diameter, δ : the smallest number of edges between the furthest pair of vertices. In the example $\delta = 5$, the smallest number of edges between Prince Rupert and Medicine Hat.

   3) Associated number of a vertex: a measure of the accessibility of a place from other places in the network. It is the maximum number of edges between a vertex and any of the other vertices when the shortest route, that is the one using the fewest number of edges, is taken. In the example the associated number for Golden is 3, for Vancouver 4, for Lake Louise Junction 4, and for Prince Rupert 5. The maximum associated number is equal to the diameter of the network.

   4) Beta index, β : a measure of network connectivity. $\beta = e/v$. Beta index values less than one indicate disconnected networks, values of one indicate networks with only one circuit, and values greater than one have high connectivity, since they occur in networks with a large number of vertices. In the example $\beta = 19/14 = 1.35$.

   5) Gamma index γ: a measure of the complexity or the maximum possible complexity of a network $\gamma = e/3 (v\text{-}2)$.
      This index has a lower limit of 0 and an upper limit of 1. In the example, $\gamma = 19/3 (14–2) = 0.53$.

   6) Pi index, π : a measure of shape, so called because it is analogous to the geometric constant π, found by dividing the circumference of a circle by its diameter.

$$\pi = C/d$$

where:

C = the total length (mileage) of the network, and

d = the length of the diameter of the network.

In the example, $\pi = 4110/1450 = 2.83$.

7) Eta index, η : the average length of an edge. $\eta = C/e$. As the number of vertices along an edge increases, η decreases. In the example, $\eta = 4110/19 = 216.32$. If Banff, Trail, Grande Prairie or Penticton were added, η would be smaller.

8) Iota index, i: a measure of length in relation to some variable such as population, educational level, traffic flow, or the number of vertices from which a given vertex can receive goods or to which they can be shipped.

$$i = C/w$$

where:

w = the observed number of vertices, weighted by some variable. i was not computed for this example.

B. Answer the following questions:

1) Compare the values for the measure you have computed with those obtained by other students using different networks.

2) In what ways would these measures vary with differing levels of development or amount of technology?

3) What effect would the placement of a new link (edge) between two vertices not now connected have on places in the network and flows within the network?

4) In what ways could the measures be used in further research?

REFERENCES

Berry, Brian J. L. (1960), "An inductive approach to the regionalization of economic development," in Norton Ginsburg, ed., *Essays on Geography and Economic Development*, Department of Geography Research Paper No. 62. Chicago: University of Chicago Press.

Cavanough, Joseph A. (1950), "Formulation, analysis and testing of the interactance hypothesis," *American Sociological Review* **15**, 763–766.

Claeson, Claes-Fredrik (1964), "A regional chorological analysis of the cinema audience," *Geografiska Annaler* **46**, No. 4, 1–130.

Dahl, Sven (1957), "The contacts of Västerås with the rest of Sweden," in David Hannerberg, Torsten Hägerstrand, and Bruno Odeving, *Migration in Sweden: A Symposium*. Lund Studies in Geography, Series B, No. 13, pp. 206–243.

Dunn, Edgar S. (1956). "The market potential concept and the analysis of location,"

Papers, and Proceedings, Regional Science Association **2**, 183–194.

Hägerstrand, Torsten (1957), "Migration and area: survey of a sample of Swedish migration fields and hypothetical considerations on their Genesis," in David Hannerberg, Torsten Hägerstrand, and Bruno Odeving, *Migration in Sweden: A Symposium*. Lund Studies in Geography, Series B, No. 13, pp. 27–158.

Haggett, Peter (1966), *Locational Analysis in Human Geography*. New York: St. Martin's Press.

Helvig, Magne (1964), *Chicago's External Truck Movements: Spatial Interactions Between the Chicago Area and its Hinterland*, Department of Geography Research Paper No. 90. Chicago: University of Chicago Press.

Huff, David L. (1963), "A probability analysis of shopping center trading areas," *Land Economics* **39**, 81–90.

Isard, Walter (1956), *Location and Space Economy*. Cambridge: The Technology Press of Massachusetts Institute of Technology and New York: Wiley.

Kansky, Karyl J. (1963), *Structure of Transport Networks: Relations: Relationships Between Network Geometry and Regional Characteristics*, Department of Geography Research Paper No. 84. Chicago: University of Chicago Press.

Kariel, Herbert G. (1968), "Student enrollment and spatial interaction," *The Annals of Regional Science* **2**, No. 2, 114–127.

Mackay, J. Ross (1958), "The interactance hypothesis and boundaries in Canada," *The Canadian Geographer* **11**, 1–8.

McConnell, Harold (1965), "Spatial variability of college enrollment as a function of migration potential," *The Professional Geographer* **17**, No. 6, 29–37.

Morrill, Richard L. and Forrest R. Pitts (1967), "Marriage, migration, and the mean information field: a study in uniqueness and generality," *Annals* of the Association of American Geographers **57**, 401–422.

Olsson, Gunnar (1965), "Distance and human interaction: a migration study," *Geografiska Annaler* **47** B, 3–43.

Stewart, John Q. (1941), "The 'gravitation,' or geographical drawing power, of a college," *Bulletin of the American Association of University Professors* **27**, 70–75.

Stewart, John Q. (1947), "Empirical mathematical rules concerning the distribution and equilibrium of population," *Geographical Review* **37**, 461–485.

Warntz, William (1959), *Toward a Geography of Price*. Philadelphia: University of Pennsylvania Press.

Werner, Christian and others (1968), "A research seminar in theoretical transportation geography," in Frank Horton, ed., *Geographic Studies of Urban Transportation and Network Analysis*, pp. 128–170, Northwestern University Studies in Geography No. 16. Evanston: Department of Geography, Northwestern University.

Additional Readings

Ajo, R. (1953), *Contributions to Social Physics*. Lund Studies in Geography, Series B, No. 11.

Brown, Robert C. (1968), "Use and misuse of distance variables in land-use analysis," *Professional Geographer* **20**, 337–341.

Carrothers, Gerald A. P. (1956), "An historical appraisal of the gravity and potential concepts of human interaction," *Journal of the American Institute of Planners* **22**, 94–102.

Catton, William R., Jr. (1965), "The concept of 'mass' in the sociological version of gravitation," in Fred Massarik and Philburn Ratoosh, *Mathematical Explorations in Behavioral Science*. Homewood Ill.: Richard D. Irwin and The Dorsey Press.

Ellis, Jack B. and Carlton S. Van Doren (1966), "A comparative evaluation of gravity and system theory models for statewide recreational traffic flows," *Journal of Regional Science* **6**, 57–70.

Garrison, William, L. and others (1959), *Studies of Highway Development and Geographic Change*. Seattle: University of Washington Press.

Garrison, William L. (1960), "Connectivity of the interstate highway system," *Papers*, Regional Science Association **6,** 121–137.

Gossman, Charles S. and others (1967), *Migration of College and University Students: State of Washington*. Seattle: Washington State Census Board.

Haggett, Peter (1966), "Interaction models," pp. 31–40 "Network Models," pp. 61–86, *Locational Analysis in Human Geography*. New York: St. Martin's Press.

Haggett (1967), "Network models in geography," Ch. 15 in Richard J. Chorley and Peter Haggett, eds., *Models in Geography*. London: Methuen.

Hammer, C. and F. Ikle (1957), "Intercity telephone and airline traffic related to distance and the 'propensity to interact'," *Sociometry* **20**, 306–316.

Huff, David L. (1965), "The use of gravity models in social research," Ch. 19 in Fred Massarik and Philburn Ratoosh, *Mathematical Explorations in Behavioral Science*. Homewood Ill.: Richard D. Irwin and The Dorsey Press.

Isard, Walter (1960), "Gravity, potential, and spatial interaction model," Ch. 11 in *Methods of Regional Analysis: An Introduction to Regional science*. New York: Wiley.

Meinig, Donald W. (1962), "A comparative historical geography of two railnets: Columbia Basin and South Australia," *Annals* of the Association of American Geographers **52**, 394–413.

Ohlin, Bertil (1967), *Interregional and International Trade*, rev. ed. Cambridge: Harvard University Press.

Olsson, Gunnar (1965), *Distance and Human Interaction: A Review and Bibliography*. Philadelphia: Regional Science Research Institute.

Pitts, Forrest R. (1965), "A graph theoretic approach to historical geography," *The Professional Geographer* **17**, No. 5, 15–20.

Reed, Wallace E. (1967), *Areal Interaction in India: Commodity Flows of the Bengal-Bihar Industrial Area*, Department of Geography Research Paper No. 110. Chicago: University of Chicago Press.

Richmond, Samuel B. (1957), "Interspatial relationships affecting air travel," *Land Economcs* **33**, 65–73.

Rikkinen, Kalevi (1968), "Decline of railroad passenger traffic in Minnesota," *Acta Geographica* **19**, No. 3, 5–52.

Schneider, Morton (1959), "Gravity models and trip distribution theory," *Papers and Proceedings*, Regional Science Association **5**, 51–56.

Smith, David A. (1963), "Interaction within a fragmented state: the example of Hawaii," *Economic Geography* **39**, 234–244.

Stewart, J. Q. and William Warntz (1958), "Macrogeography and social science," *Geographical Review* **48**, 167–184.

Taaffe, Edward J., Richard L. Morrill, and Peter R. Gould (1963), "Transport expansion in underdeveloped countries: a comparative analysis," *Geographical Review* **53**, 503–529.

Ullman, Edward L. (1949), "The railroad pattern of the United States," *Geographical Review* **39**, 242–256.

Ullman, Edward L. (1956), "The role of transportation and the bases for interaction," in William L. Thomas, Jr., ed., *Man's Role in Changing the Face of the Earth*. Chicago: University of Chicago Press.

Ullman, Edward L. (1957), *American Commodity Flow: A Geographic Interpretation of Rail and Water Traffic Based on Principles of Spatial Interchange*. Seattle: The University of Washington Press.

Vidal de la Blache, Paul (1926), "Transportation and circulation," in *Principles of Human Geography*. New York: Holt, pp. 349–446.

Warntz, William (1958), "Transportation, social physics and the law of refraction," *Professional Geographer* **10**, 6–10.

Warntz, William (1961), "Transatlantic flights and pressures patterns," *Geographical Review* **51**, 187–212.

Wingo, Lowdon, Jr. (1961), *Transportation and Urban Land*. Washington, D.C: Resources for the Future.

Wolfe, Roy I. (1961), "Transportation and politics: the example of Canada," *Annals* of the Association of American Geographers **52**, 176–190.

Zipf, George K. (1949), *Human Behavior and the Principle of Least Effort: An Introduction to Human Ecology*. Reading, Mass.: Addison-Wesley.

CHAPTER 12
SPATIAL DIFFUSION

12.1 INTRODUCTION

In our explorations we have looked not only at the spatial distributions of phenomena at a given time and over a particular area, but also at the way these distributions changed over time; that is, their spatial diffusion. In our consideration of religion, especially as discussed in Section 3.5, we found that spread of different religions occurred by person-to-person contact, sometimes peaceful and other times forceful. The travels of missionaries and traders, military conquest, and migration of adherents all helped to disseminate various religions from their points of origin to other areas. In our exploration of languages we studied the development of language families, the differentiation of languages and dialects, and the gradual disappearance of local languages and dialects as contacts with speakers of the prevailing language increased. When studying changes in land use over time, we saw that both economic and social factors were important, and that these factors could be taken into account in Monte Carlo simulation models which helped to predict changes in land use within specific areas over a given period of time.

Numerous descriptions of the diffusion of people, plants, animals, diseases, ideas, and artifacts have been accumulated by scholars in many disciplines: physicians, biologists, historians, sociologists, anthropologists, and geographers. More recently, some investigators have been seeking out regularities in the diffusion of these diverse phenomena, hoping to discover general laws. By considering the spread of a wide variety of apparently dissimilar phenomena within the broad topic of diffusion it may be possible to derive a more general law or set of laws which subsumes a larger number of laws dealing with each of the individual phenomena—one of the goals of scientific study.

Although, as we have observed earlier, laws may be derived both by induction from observation and by deduction from theory, the former approach has generally been used in studying the diffusion process. From the description of the diffusion of many different phenomena, investigators were able to abstract certain similarities and to derive hypotheses about diffusion of other artifacts and ideas.

We shall look first, therefore, at a few of these descriptive studies, and then follow some of the lines of reasoning which led to the development of mathematical models of various types.

12.2 DESCRIPTION OF THE SPREAD OF SELECTED PHENOMENA

12.2.1 Agricultural Complexes

Carl Sauer (1952) devoted many years to his study *Agricultural Origins and Dispersals*. He used evidence obtained by archaeologists and anthropologists to locate the original nodes or foci from which various domesticated plants and animals, and agricultural practices spread over the world.

He proposed Southeast Asia as the area in which agriculture began in the Old World, where bananas, yams, taro, breadfruit, and citrus fruits were among the plants early cultivated by man. Since these plants are mainly sources of carbohydrates, it is assumed that the diet of the people cultivating them was supplemented by fish protein. Animals which were raised included dogs, pigs, chickens, ducks, and geese. This original complex of plants and animals was gradually dispersed in all directions away from the point of origin, and supplemented by other plants especially suited to the growing conditions of each area. Over a period of time, plants and animals in this agricultural complex were carried across the Arabian peninsula to tropical Africa, and thence to the Atlantic and northern Africa by way of the Mediterranean.

Similarly, another agricultural complex developed in tropical regions of the New World, clustered around the edges of the Caribbean Sea. As in the Old World, the principal plants served primarily as sources of carbohydrates, and included manioc, sweet potatoes, and the peach palm. Nonfood plants included sources of various narcotics as well as plants of the genus *Nicotiana*, from the leaves of which tobacco is made. Animal protein was presumably obtained by fishing and hunting, since few animals were domesticated in this area. Modifications of this complex developed in colder, mountainous areas: animals raised were the llama, alpaca, and guinea pig; while maize and potatoes were the major plants grown.

In North America, maize, beans, and squashes or pumpkins were raised from Mexico to Canada. These plants are thought to have originated in Central America whence they were spread northward and eastward over the continent. The turkey was the only animal domesticated. Other elements of culture—various forms of family and social organization, and artifacts and ceremonials associated with them—accompanied the agricultural complex.

12.2.2 Other Culture Traits

The rate at which these agricultural complexes spread in prehistoric times has been inferred from archaeological evidence. Edmonson (1961) analyzed the dates at which a number of culture traits were found in different areas. He considered the projectile point, the ground stone axe, pottery, domesticated plants, and alphabetic writing. He calculated the length of time required for each trait to travel a distance of a thousand miles from its estimated point of origin, and each additional thousand miles up to 8,000. The mean rate of diffusion found for all six traits was 1.15 miles per year, or 115 miles per century. Study of other traits indicated a similar rate.

12.2.3 Tobacco

Seig's (1963) study of the spread of tobacco is based on speculative evidence from the pre-Columbian period and historical documentation after the time of Columbus. Two main species have been used by man: *Nicotiana rustica* and *Nicotiana tabacum*. The former originated in what is now northern Peru, and spread during pre-Columbian times into Mexico and eastern North America; the latter originated in what is now Bolivia, and spread throughout South America and the Caribbean.

    N. rustica was taken from Florida to England in 1565; by 1600 it was used throughout northern Asia. *N. tabacum* was apparently more favored. In 1548 it was taken from Brazil and Cuba to Spain, Portugal, and France. By 1565 it was available throughout Europe, with the exception of Scandinavia. By 1600 it had been carried along established trade routes throughout Africa and the Near East. At the same time it reached the Philippines directly from Mexico, and other parts of Southeast Asia by sea from Europe. It did not get to Scandinavia until 1616, indicating that this area was at that time more isolated from the rest of Europe than were Indonesia, China, and India.

12.2.4 Covered Bridges

A study by Kniffen (1951) traces the diffusion of covered bridges in the United States. The American covered bridge was developed in New England from antecedents in Switzerland, northern Italy, and Scandinavia. Its extension from a focal area in southern and eastern New England, southeastern New York, and eastern Pennsylvania and New Jersey is shown in Fig. 12.1. As can be seen, diffusion occurred most rapidly towards the west, accompanying westward migration and settlement, and most slowly towards the north, in the heavily forested and less populated state of Maine. About 1850, the time of the furthest expansion into the Middle West and South, a new focus originated in the Willamette Valley of Oregon. The spread continued along the Pacific coast and west of the Cascade Mountains until 1890.

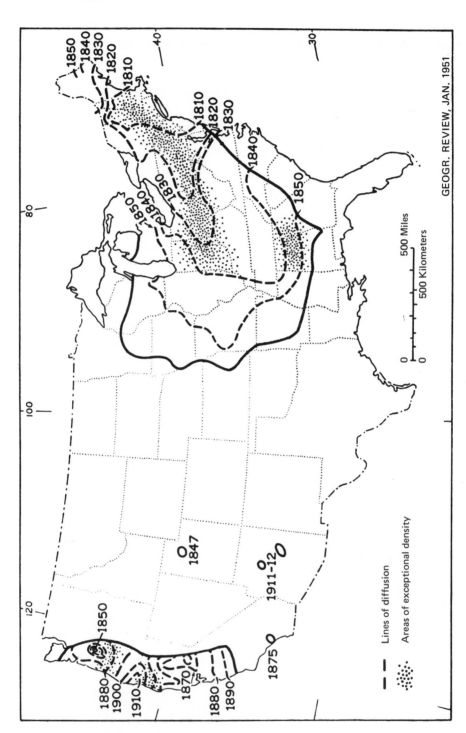

Fig. 12.1. Diffusion of the covered road bridge in the United States. Source: Kniffen, 1951. Reprinted by permission from the *Geographical Review*, Volume 41, 1951. Copyrighted by the American Geographical Society of New York.

12.3 GENERALIZED DESCRIPTION OF THE DIFFUSION PROCESS

12.3.1 Introduction

In studies of the spread of ideas, artifacts, and people, many regularities in the process of diffusion of different phenomena have been found which provide a basis for a generalized description of this process. All investigators have studied the spread of innovations; that is, ideas or artifacts which are newly introduced to a group of people or a given area. A considerable period of time often elapses between an invention or discovery, its introduction into different areas, and its spread within local areas; during this period of time the diffusion process is taking place.

Most of the recent empirical studies have been restricted to relatively small areas or groups of people. It is generally agreed, however, that new discoveries are most likely to take place in major centers—often, but not necessarily, large urban areas—from where they diffuse to secondary centers and then over the entire area. (Fig. 12.2.) Although some areas tend to serve as centers for the diffusion of many different types of innovations, there is some variation with the phenomena. For example, cities with large medical centers tend to act as innovation centers for medical developments such as organ transplants and the establishment of specialized units for the care of patients with heart disorders, whereas the state of Iowa is an innovation center for hybrid seed corn.

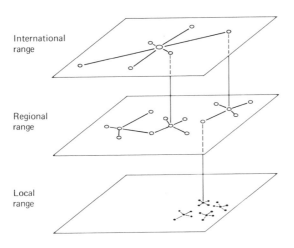

Fig. 12.2 Schema of social communication among and within three levels of ranges. Sources: Hägerstrand, 1953 and L. A. Brown, 1968. Reproduced by permission from the authors and C. W. K. Gleerup.

12.3.2 Aspatial Elements in the Diffusion Process

Rogers (1962) has reviewed and synthesized the findings of many studies. He states that knowledge about an innovation may be spread both by mass media such as newspapers, magazines, professional and trade journals, radio, and television, and by personal contact, such as seeing the innovation and talking with other persons about it; usually both means of spread are important. Within a given area and for a particular set of phenomena, certain people tend to act as innovators. They seek out new ideas by reading professional journals, attending meetings, and corresponding or talking directly with people who have information about new developments in their field of interest. They then introduce some of the innovations to the area in which they live and work, both adopting them themselves and telling others about them. For example, agriculture agents in the United States, who are professional innovators, have access to reports about new agricultural developments. They introduce these ideas to farmers who might use them by using the innovations in demonstration plots as well as by making speeches at meetings of farm organizations.

Once the innovation has been introduced, diffusion takes place along lines of communication established by friendship and personal contact. The decision to adopt is often based on an individual's evaluation of what his reference group thinks of it; that is, how he perceives that other people whom he considers to be like himself would behave.

The initial number of innovators for a particular phenomenon in a given area is usually small; the rate of adoption of the innovation is slow at first, but speeds up as more potential adopters become actual adopters. The first inflection point is often called the threshold. Then, as the percentage of actual adopters increases, that of potential adopters decreases, and the rate of adoption slows down until a ceiling, or saturation level, is reached. When the cumulative proportion of adoptions in an area is plotted against time, an S-shaped curve similar to that shown in

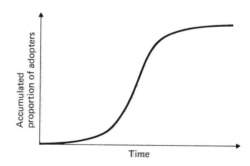

Fig. 12.3. Logistic growth curve showing accumulated proportion of adopters within an area over time.

Fig. 12.3 usually results. This resembles several mathematical curves, including one called the logistic growth curve or learning curve, discussed below.

Rogers suggests that although this adoption curve actually represents a continuum, it is often convenient to divide persons who adopt at different times into a number of discrete categories. He uses the terms innovators, early adopters, majority, late majority, and laggards to describe persons in each group. The innovators introduce the innovation to an area; a few early adopters, who are usually in close personal contact with the innovators, gradually try it out, and then the majority quite quickly take up the innovation. Late in the adoption period a few of the late majority become adopters, and finally the laggards accept it.

An individual's actual decision to adopt an innovation is seen as the final step in a process which may take varying periods of time, depending on the nature of the innovation and of the potential adopter. Before a decision can be made, an individual must first become aware of the innovation and recognize that it might benefit him to adopt it. Even after deciding to adopt it, he may not do so immediately, for reasons such as inconvenience or cost. It has been found that although information received from mass media may be important in making persons aware of the existence of an innovation, person-to-person discussion is the most important means of communicating information leading to the actual decision to adopt. A farmer, for example, may read about an innovation in a farm magazine or agricultural bulletin, or observe the results of its use as he drives past a demonstration plot. When his interest is aroused, he discusses the possibility of adoption with his friends or other persons he believes have relevant information, such as those farmers who are already using the innovation. Resistance to adoption may be related to a general hesitancy to try anything new, specific questions as to whether adoption of the innovation would be feasible for him, or concern about its cost. Since person-to-person contact is important in the spread of innovations, it is evident that the presence of barriers to such communication—social, political, or physical—will also slow down, channel, or otherwise influence the diffusion process.

Attempts have been made to identify characteristics of persons in each category. Although findings of various studies conflict, some generalizations can be made. Innovators and early adopters tend to be younger, better educated, and of higher socioeconomic status than the late majority and laggards. They obtain information from a variety of sources, including professionals who are involved in developing new practices or promoting their use, technical publications, and attendance at meetings, as well as by personal contact with friends and neighbors. Later adopters tend to rely more on personal contact alone. There is some support for the belief that innovativeness is a consistent characteristic; that is, that persons who are innovators from one practice tend also to be innovators for other practices.

Understanding of some of these nonspatial elements has helped geographers to explain some of the spatial elements.

12.3.3 Mathematical Models of Diffusion

Although verbal descriptions are often useful first steps in the development of theory, they are less precise, less general, and of less predictive value than mathematical models. It is not surprising, therefore, that researchers should have attempted to devise such models to assist them in understanding and predicting diffusion.

When geographers such as Hägerstrand (1953) and sociologists such as Coleman (1964) began trying to develop mathematical models for the diffusion of innovations, they noted similarities between this phenomenon and the spread of epidemics, for which mathematical models had been devised. The basic equation of the epidemiological model is:

$$dx/dt = kx, \tag{12.1}$$

where:

> $x =$ the number of people possessing the attribute (disease, information about an innovation) at any one time,
> $t =$ time,
> $dx/dt =$ the number of people acquiring the item per unit time, and
> $k =$ a constant of proportionality, usually determined empirically.

What this equation tells us is that change in the number of people acquiring the characteristic in a given time period is proportional to the number of people possessing it at that time. Since this differential equation deals with change over time, it can be integrated in order to determine the number of people who possess the characteristics at any given time; that is, to express x, the number of people, as a function of t, time. If we set $x = 1$ when $t = 0$, the integral of equation 12.1 is:

$$x = e^{kt}, \tag{12.2}$$

where:

> $e \approx 2.718$, the base of natural logarithms.

The resulting exponential function has been applied to such diverse phenomena as population growth and the decay of radioactive substances. It is, however, inadequate for describing diffusion among a population of limited size, since it considers only x and t, and fails to take into account the fact that some persons in the population have already acquired the attribute and thereby have been removed from the population of susceptibles. Consequently, if we consider a finite population of N persons, x of whom are removals who have already acquired the attribute, then $(N-x)$ do not possess it. We would then express the differential equation as:

$$dx/dt = kx (N - x), \tag{12.3}$$

where $N =$ the size of the population being studied.

This equation tells us that the change per unit time is proportional to the product of the number of people possessing the attribute, x, and the number of people not possessing it, $N-x$.

Integrating equation 12.3, again letting $x = 1$ at $t = 0$, we get

$$x = \frac{Ne^{kt}}{N-1 + e^{kt}}.$$

(12.4)

The graph of this equation is termed a logistic growth curve, or learning curve. We can see that it might be used to predict spread of a disease which is easily transmitted from person to person, such as measles, and for which the only factor determining whether a person acquired the disease is whether he had already developed immunity. It is necessary to assume free movement and contact among all members of the population, as might occur in a small town; no barriers to such movement, either social or geographic, would exist. In addition, it is assumed that every susceptible person will acquire the disease from one contact with a person who has it, termed an infective.

Although the epidemiological model based on the logistic growth curve has been found to correspond fairly closely to empirical findings in a number of diffusion studies such as Griliches' (1957, 1960) investigation of the diffusion of hybrid corn, the assumptions which must be made in order to apply a deterministic model are so restrictive that reality is not closely approximated for most phenomena. Perhaps the greatest difficulty arises from the assumption that an innovation will be accepted after a single contact, since we know that most people adopt only after several tellings. In order to modify this assumption it is necessary to adopt a probabilistic rather than a deterministic model, specifying the probability that a person will adopt an innovation if he comes into contact with a carrier of information about it. Another unrealistic assumption is that people intermix freely, whereas we know that networks of friendship and interpersonal relationships sharply limit contacts between people. In addition to these social barriers to interaction there are also physical barriers, which must also be considered if reality is to be more closely approximated by the model.

In order to take some of these many factors into account, various investigators have used a Monte Carlo simulation approach to the study of diffusion. Not only can a larger number of variables be considered by using this method, but each can also be assigned some probability value so that many of the variations among individuals and situations found in the real world can be included.

12.4 STUDIES OF SPATIAL DIFFUSION: FROM THE SIMPLER TO THE MORE SOPHISTICATED

12.4.1 Overview

Geographers began their research on diffusion by examining the spread of particular innovations over specified areas. The next step was to study empirical data with a view to deriving generalizations from which it then became possible to experiment with different mathematical models of diffusion, using concepts which had been identified in earlier studies. We have reviewed some descriptive studies in Section 12.2, and considered certain nonspatial aspects of diffusion, such as the importance of personal communication, which are relevant to spatial studies of diffusion. We shall now look at some studies representative of later developments.

12.4.2 A Deterministic Model of Diffusion

Griliches (1957, 1960) investigated the spread of hybrid seed corn in parts of the United States, considering both nonspatial and spatial aspects of diffusion and using many different approaches and analyses. The study of this phenomenon was facilitated by the availability of detailed data from the United States Department of Agriculture, by crop reporting districts. When he plotted the percentage of total corn acreage planted with the hybrid seed against time, for five states (Fig. 12.4), he found that all of the curves conformed to the S-shape of the logistic growth curve. The use of hybrid seed corn began earliest, increased fastest, and reached the highest level of adoption in Iowa. Although its use in Wisconsin began only slightly later, the rate of adoption was slower and began to level off at about 70 percent. Farmers in Kentucky, Texas, and Alabama began using hybrids later and adopted them more slowly, and the percentage of acres planted to them leveled off at a lower point.

In order to fit logistic growth curves to the empirical data it was necessary for

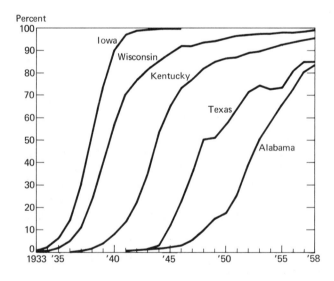

Fig. 12.4.   Percentage of all corn acreage planted to hybrid seed over time for five states. Source: Hybrid Corn and the Economics of Innovation. Griliches, Z., *Science*, Vol. 132, pp. 275–280, Fig. 1, 29 July 1960. Reproduced by permission from the author and the American Association for the Advancement of Science. Copyright 1960 by the American Association for the Advancement of Science.

Griliches to determine three different parameters: origin, ceiling, and rate of growth.* In equation 12.4 only one parameter, the slope k, corresponding to the rate of growth, had to be determined from the data, since the origin was arbitrarily set at $x = 0$ at time $t = 1$, and the ceiling at 1. After considerable thought and experimentation with different possible measures of the origin, he decided to set time $t = 1$ at the date at which 10 percent of the farmers in an area were using hybrids; that is, when x, expressed as a proportion, was equal to 0.1. This date seemed to represent the time at which hybrids passed beyond the experimental stage and were actually available to farmers. This date varied from area to area because it was necessary to develop specific hybrids for the growing conditions prevailing in different states. The value for the ceiling was arrived at by a trial-and-error process. The rate of growth was determined by graphing the data on logarithmic paper; the slope of the resulting graph became the exponent k.

These three values were computed for each of 132 crop-reporting districts in the 31 states which account for almost all of the corn grown in the United States. From them, logistic growth curves were calculated both by states and by crop-reporting districts. The coefficients of simple correlation, r, indicated close correspondence between the observed adoption curves and those computed from logistic growth curves based on the three parameters. The coefficients of determination, r^2, between observed and predicted values of the dependent variable, percentage of total corn acreage planted with hybrid seed corn, ranged from 0.89 to 0.99 for the five curves. These findings suggested that the actual values could be predicted reasonably accurately from the three parameters: origin, slope, and ceiling.

Griliches next considered the spatial variations of the three parameters. He noted that the rate of acceptance was highest in Iowa, and declined with distance from the Corn Belt. Similarly, the date at which the 10 percent level of acceptance was reached increased with distance from the Corn Belt and the ceiling decreased, although these relationships appeared to be less close. Additional analyses led him to conclude that the adoption of hybrid seed corn was related primarily to profitability, and could be explained adequately by economic variables alone, without recourse to notions of person-to-person contact or other social variables.

12.4.3 Development of a Probabilistic Model of Spatial Diffusion

Hägerstrand (1952) concentrated upon spatial aspects in his study of the diffusion of radios and automobiles in Scania, a district of southern Sweden. Figure 12.5 shows the central place system of this area, and Fig. 12.6 the cells used to study the diffusion of these phenomena. Because data were available beginning with the

---

*The details of the mathematics involved in fitting the data to the logistic growth curve and testing the fit are beyond the scope of the present text, but interested students are encouraged to refer to the original article.

date of introduction of these innovations to the area, their spread could be followed over a period of years.

Data concerning the ownership of automobiles from 1918 to 1930, by two-
year periods, was first mapped, using number of automobiles per 1,000 inhabitants
(Fig. 12.7). After studying these maps, he noted that: (1) areas including and surrounding towns appeared early as peaks in the distribution; (2) with one exception, diffusion occurred from west to east; (3) it did not take place along a boundary,
but through the urban hierarchy, beginning with larger centers and spreading to
smaller towns, with the areas between centers filling in more slowly; (4) although
the distribution tended to become more uniform over time, some areas remained
without cars as late as 1930.

Growth curves were drawn for selected districts within Scania. Three of these
are shown in Fig. 12.8. Malmö, in the cell labeled K-5, is the largest center; the

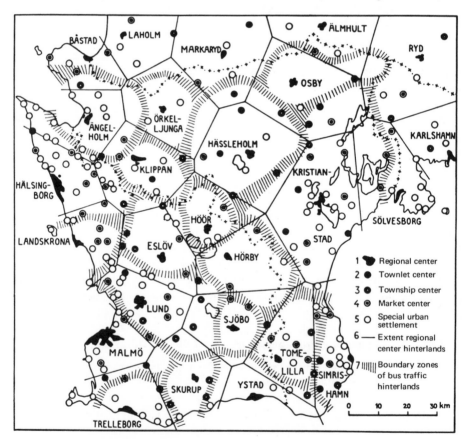

Fig. 12.5. Central place system of Scania, Southern Sweden. 1–4 represent centers in
order of rank and 5 represents special function settlements such as industrial villages,
fishing, and watering places. Source: Godlund, 1951. Reproduced by permission from the
author and C. W. K. Gleerup.

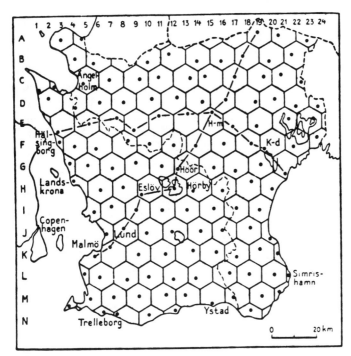

Fig. 12.6 The hexagonal unit areas used to study the diffusion of these phenomena. Dots show the position of the median population point in each cell. The broken lines from K 5 to A 19 and from E 3 to G 21 refer to the courses of profiles. Source: Hägerstrand, 1952. Reproduced by permission from the author and C. W. K. Gleerup.

cell I-ll is in central Scania; and A-21 is in northeastern Scania, the most remote district. The mean ratio of automobiles per 1,000 inhabitants is shown by the dashed line, M. This graph may be compared with Griliches' graph of the increase in the use of hybrid seed corn, Fig. 12.4. Although the shapes of curves in the two graphs are not comparable, because Hägerstrand used logarithms in graphing the ratios, whereas Griliches used the actual values, we can note similarities in the overall patterns. Malmö begins with a high ratio and continues so, followed by I-ll with a time lag of about three years and A-24 with a time lag of five years. All curves have approximately the same slope, taking the time lag into account. We can compare these curves with those for Iowa, Wisconsin, and Alabama.

Another approach to visualization of this process is the drawing of a profile, taking areas in order of their distance from Malmö. Hägerstrand notes that this profile (Fig. 12.9) shows that: (1) there is a continuous increase in the ratio of automobiles in all areas for all periods of time; and (2) the ratio tends to decline with distance from Malmö, although the larger centers represent peaks. This second observation appears to be more difficult to substantiate than the first.

A stronger effect of distance is shown by a similar graph of the number of radios per 1000 inhabitants, from 1925–1947, Fig. 12.10 A radio station was

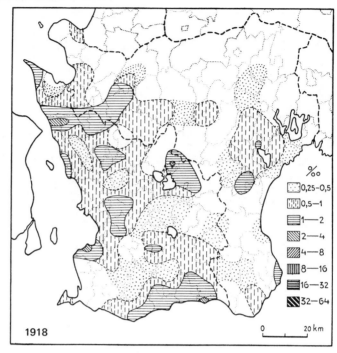

Fig. 12.7. Automobiles per 1000 inhabitants in Scania, biannually from 1918 to 1930. Source: Hägerstrand, 1952. Reproduced by permission from the author and C. W. K. Gleerup.

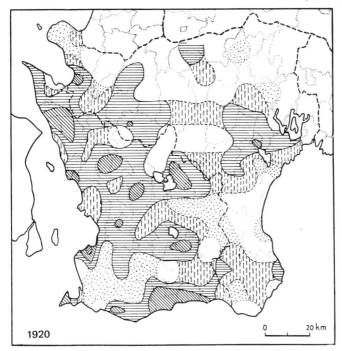

1920

0   20 km

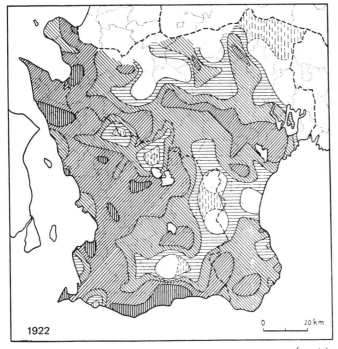

1922

0   20 km

(cont.)

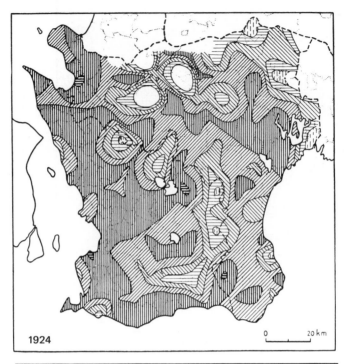

1924   0   20 km

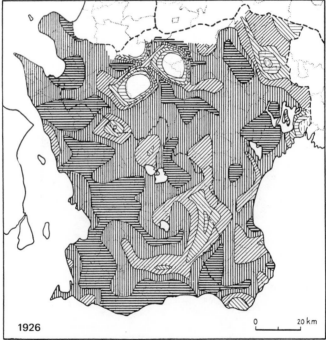

1926   0   20 km

Fig. 12.7   (cont.)

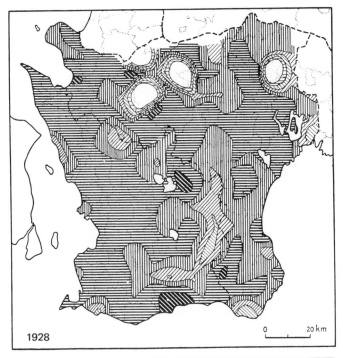

1928

0   20 km

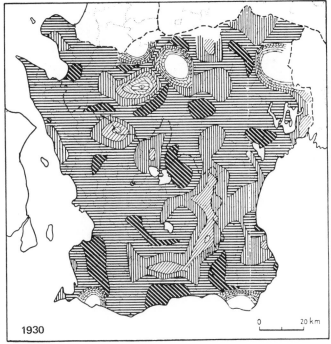

1930

0   20 km

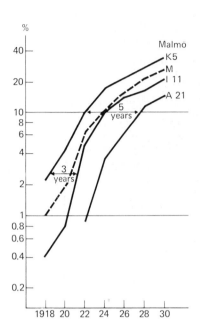

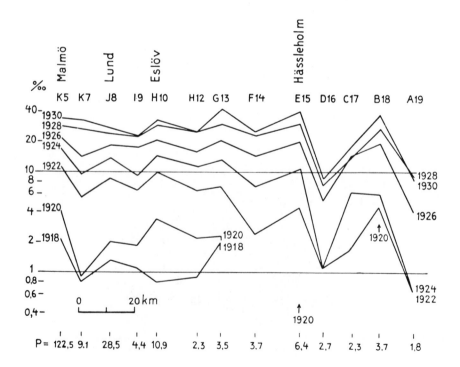

Fig. 12.8. Automobiles per 1000 inhabitants 1918–30 for Scania (dashed line *M*) and for the cells K 5 (Malmo), I 11, and A 21. Source: Hägerstrand, 1952. Reproduced by permission from the author and C. W. K. Gleerup.

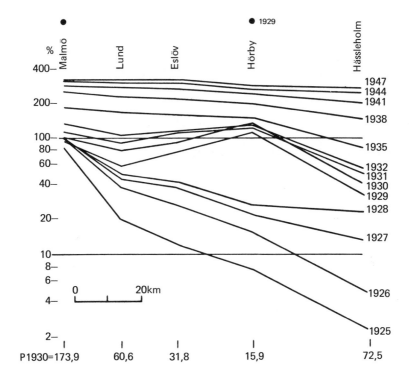

Fig. 12.10. Profile Malmo—Hassleholm. Radios per 1000 inhabitants 1925–1947. The two dots at the top indicate the location of the radio station. *P* denotes the population in thousands in 1930. Source: Hägerstrand, 1952. Reproduced by permission from the author and C. W. K. Gleerup.

Fig. 12.9. Profile K 5—A 19, Automobiles per 1000 inhabitants 1918–30 in logarithmic scale. In 1918 the cells F 14—A 19 contain no automobiles. In 1920 isolated peaks (the ◀arrows) appear in E 15 and B 18. Not until 1922 is the profile continuous. *P* denotes the population in thousands in 1930. Source: Hägerstrand, 1952. Reproduced by permission from the author and C. W. K. Gleerup.

present in Malmö before 1925; another one was started in Hörby in 1929. For the years 1925–1928, the ratio declined markedly with distance from Malmö. In 1929, however, a big jump occurred in the ratio in and near Hörby, which created a second peak. This peak was noticeable until about 1935, after which the curves tended to level off as the ownership of radios approached a saturation level.

These findings helped to confirm Hägerstrand's hypothesis that diffusion was channeled through the urban hierarchy; an innovation tended to be introduced in the larger centers, then spread to smaller centers, and more slowly disseminate to areas between centers, as each center acts as a new point from which diffusion occurs.

These and other empirical studies provided a background for subsequent attempts to construct mathematical models of the diffusion process. In working out such models, Hägerstrand began with the idea that knowledge of innovations was spread primarily by person-to-person contact, much as infectious diseases are transmitted in epidemics. He then considered some of the factors which might affect person-to-person transmission, and incorporated these into a Monte Carlo simulation model.

In Section 8.7.9 we discussed some of the principles underlying the use of such models. We noted that in order to construct any model it is usually necessary to make a set of assumptions which simplify reality; then, after the model is tested, these assumptions may gradually be modified so that reality is more closely approximated. These assumptions are needed because conditions in the real world are complex. By beginning with an admittedly oversimplified version of reality, as von Thünen and Christaller did, it is possible to consider and test a few elements at first, and then gradually to modify the assumptions in order to conform more closely to observations.

In developing a series of models of the diffusion process based on spread of information by means of person-to-person contact, Hägerstrand (1965) adopted the following conditions as his initial set of simplifying assumptions: (1) the innovation is spread from a single individual living at the center of the area. This area, referred to as the *model plane*, has an even population distribution and is an ideal transportation surface; (2) information is spread only by direct person-to-person contact. This assumption ignores the influence of mass media, group meetings, and other sources of information; (3) once told about an innovation, an individual adopts it immediately and becomes a carrier; that is, he transmits it to other individuals with whom he comes in contact; and (4) during one run of the model, all tellings occur at the same time.

In order to carry out a simulation such as this one, the model plane is divided in some manner, usually into rectangular cells. Each cell contains the same number of individuals. The probability of a carrier telling any other individual may be either random or biased by probabilities derived from various empirical data. In this instance, this probability was a function of distance between the sending and receiving areas, Fig. 12.11. In each, the address of a potential receiver was

.01	.02	.04	.02	.01
.02	.06	.10	.06	.02
.04	.10		.10	.04
.02	.06	.10	.06	.02
.01	.02	.04	.02	.01

(a)

1	2 – 3	4 – 7	8 – 9	10
11 – 12	13 – 18	19 – 28	29 – 34	35 – 36
37 – 40	41 – 50		51 – 60	61 – 64
65 – 66	67 – 72	73 – 82	83 – 88	89 – 90
91	92 – 93	94 – 97	98 – 99	100

(b)

Fig. 12.11. (a) A migration of diffusion field, giving the probabilities for each cell and (b) its transformation to a range of discrete numbers. Source: Morrill, 1965. Reprinted by permission from the author and C. W. K. Gleerup.

first drawn; the draw of a random number then determined whether the one carrier transmitted the information to that receiver, with the probability that sender and receiver would meet at a pairwise meeting being proportional to the distance between them. Because of this biased probability, although most of the early adopters were located close to the point of origin, when a person located at some distance away became a carrier, his address formed a focus for local spread from that area. This result conforms to findings of empirical studies of the spread of covered bridges and automobiles discussed in Sections 12.2.4 and 12.4.3.

When the simulation is run, the number of carriers increases rapidly at first, almost by a geometric progression. On successive runs of the model, however, as more receivers of information become carriers, the probability of a message being transmitted to someone who is already a carrier increases, so that the rate of spread of information slows down until the area becomes saturated with adopters. In the epidemic analogy, the proportion of the population which either already has had the disease or is immune rises high enough that the epidemic dies out.

A map showing one run of this model, Fig. 12.12, depicts the simulated pattern of spatial distribution over time. As previously stated, testing the correspondence of such a simulation model to actual situations is difficult. Because it is stochastic, or based on chance and the laws of probability, the probability that any two runs of the model will produce identical results is extremely small. One can primarily look for similarities in the patterns, even though we know that visual comparison involves subjective and not always accurate judgment. Nevertheless, if the phenomenon and area selected for comparison conform fairly closely to the assumptions of the model, it should be possible to note some correspondence between the observed pattern of diffusion and that resulting from the simulation.

Hägerstrand next compared the results from three runs of a modified model with the actual spread of the acceptance of subsidies for the improvement of pasture land (Figs. 12.13–12.16). He selected this phenomenon because he reasoned that, although the assumption of immediate adoption was obviously not valid for all innovations, acceptance of government subsidies should meet with

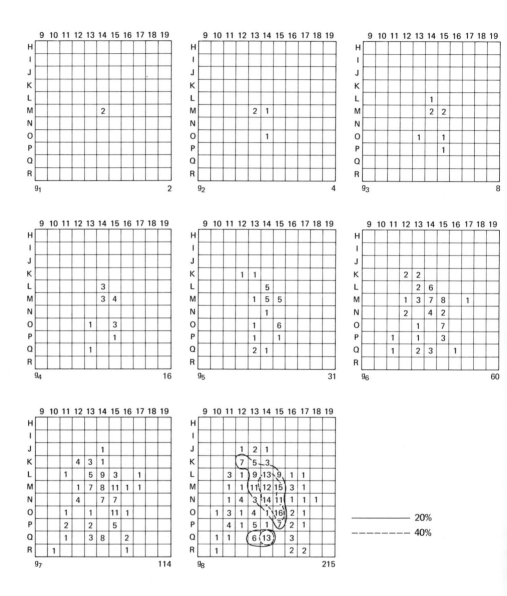

Fig. 12.12. Run of simulation under isotropic conditions, i.e., with an even distribution of potential adopters and no barriers to communication. For g_8 isolines indicate relation between adopters and potential adopters. Source: Hägerstrand, 1965. Reprinted by permission from the *European Journal of Sociology*, Volume VI (1965), 43–47.

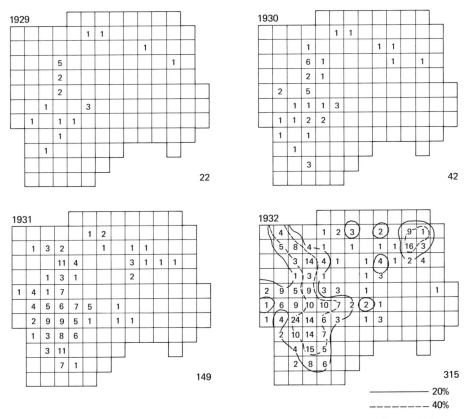

Fig. 12.13. Observed spread of subsidy for improved pasture on small farms. Cells are 5 × 5 km in size. Figures give the absolute number of adopters from the start up to the end of given years. Potential adopters have an approximately uniform distribution over the area. For 1932, isolines indicate relation between adopters and potential adopters. Source: Hägerstrand, 1965. Reprinted by permission from the *European Journal of Sociology*, Volume VI (1965), 43–47.

minimal resistance, and so come close to meeting this assumption. The strict assumptions of the original model were modified to conform more closely to conditions prevailing in that particular area for the phenomenon being studied. Three modifications were made: (1) the number of person in each cell was varied to conform to the situation in the area being studied; (2) the number of initial tellers was increased, and they were distributed in the same manner as the ones in the area; and (3) physical features such as highways, which served as communication channels, and lakes, which acted as barriers to communication, were taken into account. The simulation model, thus modified, was run three times.

Hägerstrand found many similarities between the actual and simulated diffusion processes, notably the outward spread not only from the original center but also from secondary ones established during the diffusion process. When he

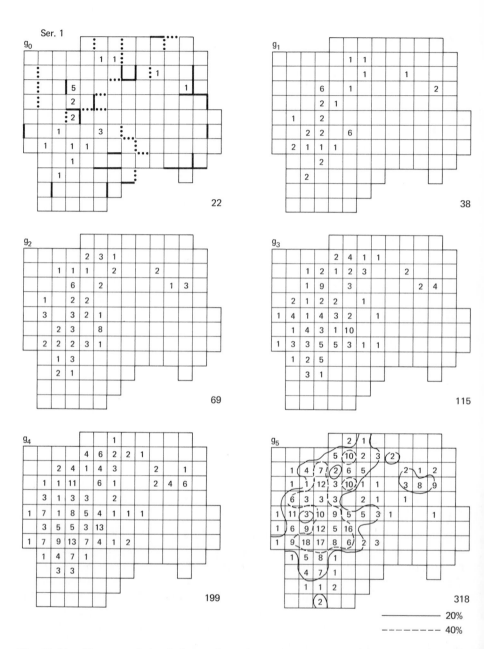

Fig. 12.14. First run of simulation under anisotropic conditions, i.e., potential adopters and barriers to communication as in actual area. Full line: no telling is allowed to pass. Dotted line: tellings reduced by factor two on the average, g_0 equals 1929 in the observed case (cf. Fig. 12.12). Source: Hägerstrand, 1965. Reprinted by permission from the *European Journal of Sociology*, Volume VI (1965), 43–47.

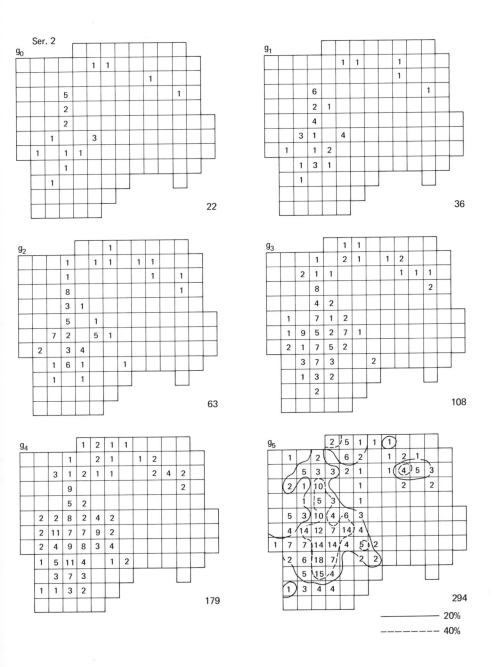

Fig. 12.15. Second run of simulation. Source: Hägerstrand, 1965. Reprinted by permission from the *European Journal of Sociology*, Volume VI (1965), 43–47.

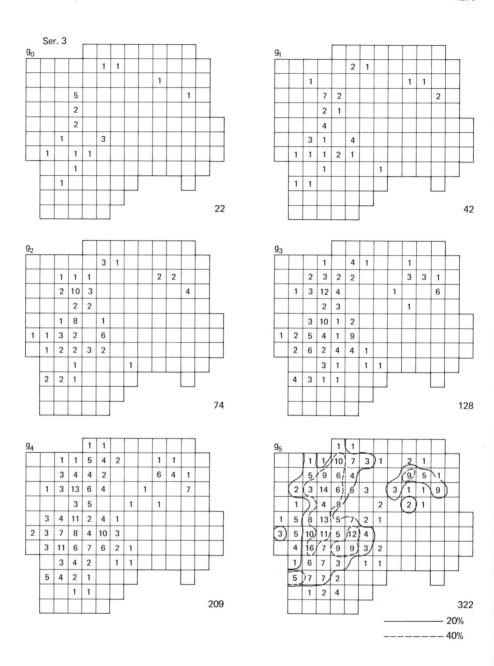

Fig. 12.16. Third run of simulation. Source: Hägerstrand, 1965. Reprinted by permission from the *European Journal of Sociology*, Volume VI (1965), 43–47.

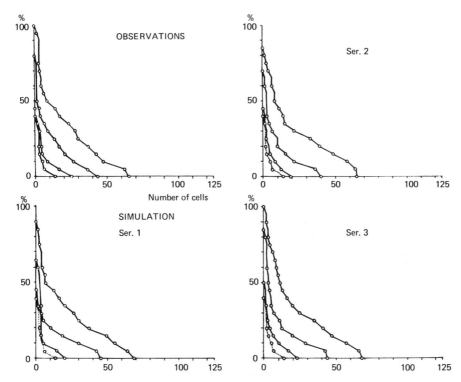

Fig. 12.17. Observations and simulations compared. Curves show number of cells which have reached above a certain percentage of adoptions at comparable stages of observations and simulations. The initial situation—short left curve in each graph—is everywhere the same as it represents input values. Source: Hägerstrand, 1965. Reprinted by permission from the *European Journal of Sociology*, Volume VI (1965), 43–47.

compared the percentages of adopters in different numbers of cells during both simulated and actual diffusion, he found that the number of empty cells was comparable at different stages, and the slopes of the adoption curves were similar. (Figs. 12.17, 12.18.) He therefore concluded that the results of the simulations conformed reasonably well to the observed data.

12.4.4 Additional Studies

Bowden (1965) studied the diffusion of the decision to irrigate in western Yuma County, Colorado. He selected an area in which irrigation was (1) physically possible; (2) economically gainful; (3) socially acceptable; and (4) legally permissible. He then asked the question: How does the decision to irrigate, as measured by the drilling of one or more irrigation wells, diffuse over an area? His simulation model followed Hägerstrand's basic model, using most of the same assumptions. Some modifications were made in order to approximate the actual situation; for ex-

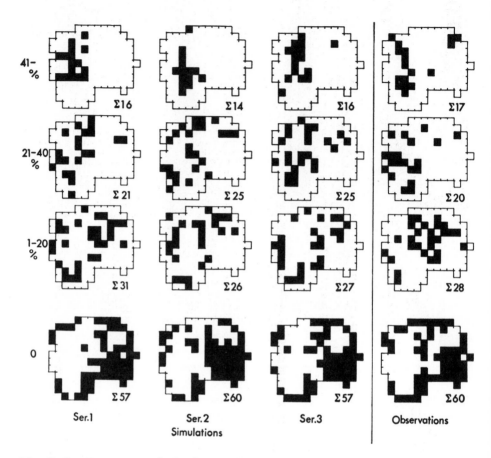

Fig. 12.18. Percentages of adoptions at the end-stages of simulations and observations split into levels as indicated at left. Source: Hägerstrand, 1965. Reprinted by permission from the *European Journal of Sociology*, Volume VI (1965), 43–47.

ample, a township was considered to be saturated when 16 wells had been located there, and no new wells could then be located in it. A mean information field, representing the network of interpersonal communications in the area, was derived from two sources of empirical data: attendance at a barbecue at Yuma and the number of long-distance telephone calls from Yuma to other centers in the area in a month. From these data, probabilities of contact between persons located at varying distances from each other were established.

When the results of ten simulation runs were compared with the actual location of wells up to 1962, they were found to be similar. In addition, the mean number of wells per township in the ten simulations corresponded closely to the actual number. Bowden suggested that additional runs of the model would aid in predicting the number and location of future wells, so that steps could be taken to ensure that the ground water level would not become depleted by drilling too many.

L. A. Brown (1968) studied the adoption of television receivers for 12 market areas in the Kristianstad-Hasselholm district in southern Sweden from 1960 through 1965. Because he was interesed in testing a number of general models against the actual adoptions, he took many factors into account in designing the exact models on which simulation was based. He stated that the probability that a resident of any given place, i, adopted an innovation during the time period $t + 1$ was a function of the combined probabilities that (1) adoption did not occur earlier; (2) individuals received sufficient information during the time period $t + 1$ by means of personal contact, or through the mass media, or by seeing the item in the market place; (3) he was not resistant to adoption; and (4) he came into contact with at least one distributor of the item. This formulation might be expressed in everyday language by saying that the probability of an individual's purchasing a given innovation depends upon whether he already owns the item, he has learned about it, he wishes to buy it, and finds a place where he can purchase it. Although these ideas do not seem profound in themselves, the problem of defining each variable operationally and fitting it into a model presents more difficulties. Brown obtained empirical values for some of the factors, including the number of retail distributors of television receivers for each market in the area, shopping trip behavior, newspaper circulation, and number of acquaintances. In the process of curve fitting, other parameters were estimated from actual adoptions.

He experimented with variations of each of three different simulation models: (1) a completely random model; (2) one incorporating "socio-structural" bias, or acquaintanceship, and (3) one which adds a social pressure effect. Model 1 is based on the probabilistic form of equation 12.4. In it, it is assumed that personal contacts within a particular area are completely random; that is, that each individual has an equal probability of contacting every other individual and telling him about the innovation if he has already adopted it. Only one parameter, S, representing the number of acquaintances contacted during a single time period, must be estimated from the observations in order to fit the curve. Brown found that predicted adoptions based on this model reached a peak sooner than did the actual adoptions (Fig. 12.19).

In Model 2, therefore, he added another parameter, which he termed socio-structural bias. He reasoned that the probability of a given individual's contacting any other individual was not random but based on his circle of acquaintances; any person is more likely to discuss an innovation with people he knows and with whom he has frequent contact, than with people he does not know. Although predictions based on this model, which required the estimation of a second parameter, were more accurate than those based on Model 1, they did not reach a peak soon enough (Fig. 12.20), suggesting that not enough information was reaching individuals.

In Model 3, an additional source of awareness, the sight of television aerials

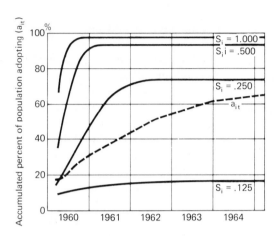

Fig. 12.19. Predicted percentages of adopters under case 1, the completely random model, for the central place Broby. Dashed line indicates observed percentages of adopters. Source: L. A. Brown, 1968. Reproduced by permission from the author and C. W. K. Gleerup.

on roofs, was added; it was considered by Brown to represent the effect of social pressure on the individual. Predictions based on this model corresponded most accurately to the data, as tested both by use of the Kolmogorov-Smirnov test and by visual inspection (Fig. 12.21). In concluding, he pointed out that although further modifications might result in still more accurate predictions for each individual area, there seemed to be little point in continuing to fit curves.

As we have seen in previous discussions, generality is lost in attempting to explain each individual observation more precisely. In addition, the results derived from Model 3 suggest that the major elements in the system have been taken

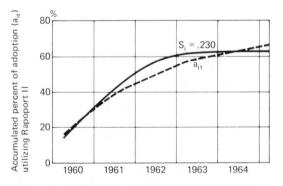

Fig. 12.20. Predicted percentages of adopters under case 2, the model with personal information component recognizing "socio-structural" bias, for the central place Broby. Dashed line indicates observed percentages of adopters. Source: L. A. Brown, 1968. Reproduced by permission from the author and C. W. K. Gleerup.

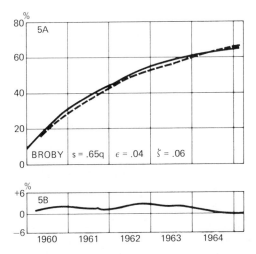

Fig. 12.21. Predicted percentages of adopters under case 3, the model including "social pressure," for the central place Broby. Solid line indicates observed percentages of adopters and dashed line indicates expected percentages. Source: L. A. Brown, 1968. Reproduced by permission from the author and C. W. K. Gleerup.

into account, since a large part of the variance has been explained. It is likely that each additional factor will result in a smaller amount of increase in the proportion of explained variance. Also there will undoubtedly always remain certain random elements of human behavior which will be unaccounted for in any model, and represent a residual error term.

12.5 BARRIERS TO DIFFUSION

We have considered that diffusion of innovations takes place primarily by person-to-person contact, even when other means of the spread of information, such as mass media, are taken into account. We have noted that some factors facilitate person-to-person contact, while others hinder it. Geographers have considered those factors which hinder such contact to be barriers to communication, and recognize that barriers may be physical—mountains, deserts, swamps, or oceans; social—occupation, education, ethnic origin, or age; political—boundaries between states and countries; or psychological. R. H. Brown (1948), Kniffen (1951), and Hägerstrand (1965) took physical barriers into account. Other geographers, including Mackay (1958) have considered the effects of political boundaries as barriers. Yuill (1965) concentrated upon certain abstract properties of barriers, without reference to specific situations.

R. H. Brown considered the effects of physical barriers such as the Appalachian Mountains and the forests of Maine upon travel by stagecoach in colonial days. When these barriers were included in a simulation model, the resulting pattern closely resembled that of the actual number of miles traveled in a day in different directions. In his study of covered bridges, Kniffen noted that the densely forested, sparsely populated state of Maine acted as a relative barrier to their diffusion, slowing their spread to the north. Similarly, Hägerstrand found that the location of highways and large lakes was related to the number of telephone calls between neighboring settlements in an area of southern Sweden. Some of the lakes appeared to act as complete barriers to interaction, whereas others simply reduced the number of contacts across them. Mackay found that less interaction, in the form of long-distance telephone calls, occurred between Montreal and cities in Ontario than between Montreal and cities in Quebec; the provincial boundary acted as a political and linguistic barrier to such communication.

Yuill considered some of the abstract properties of barriers. He recognized the difficulty of defining the term, since few barriers are absolute in that no flows occur across them. He also realized that what acts as a barrier for one phenomenon may not be a barrier to others. He suggested that barriers could be considered at one extreme as absolute, or reflecting, and at the other extreme as absorbing, in which case they would not be barriers. Since most barriers fall somewhere between these extremes, they might be classed as semipermeable. A percentage value of reflection could be assigned to each barrier which would in turn form the basis for assigning a probability that a message would be transmitted across it from a sender on one side to a receiver on the other. For example, a barrier which is 50 percent reflective would be assigned a 0.50 probability of blocking a message transmitted across it. This approach was used by Hägerstrand in considering lakes as barriers; probabilities were derived from the analysis of data on telephone calls between settlements.

Similar analyses of factors which facilitate interaction, such as good transportation routes, or friendship and acquaintanceship networks, would probably clarify further our present notions of the diffusion process.

12.6 DIRECTIONS FOR FUTURE WORK

In our exploration of the process by which innovations diffuse over time and space we have followed the development of knowledge from case studies to mathematical models. One of the most important steps in formulation of a general theory was the conceptualization of diffusion as an abstract construct which could itself be investigated, with conclusions applying to many different phenomena. As we have seen in earlier chapters, such abstraction and generalization are crucial to the development of laws and theories.

Even though our knowledge of this process is incomplete, if we know certain social and economic characteristics of an area we can predict with a fair degree of accuracy the way in which a particular phenomenon might spread. The work of Hägerstrand and others with both deterministic and probabilistic models has helped to point out areas in which further study should be carried out before our predictions can come closer to our observations. L. A. Brown, for example, found that he was unable to take into account accurately the effect of different information sources by using the measures of socio-cultural interaction which he had selected. It is likely, therefore, that further empirical work on the influence of social networks upon the flow of information would provide fresh insights. It is also possible that experimentation with different mathematical models and techniques might prove fruitful. It is most likely, however, that some combination of empirical and theoretical work will be required for a better understanding of the process.

REVIEW YOUR UNDERSTANDING OF THESE CONCEPTS

spatial diffusion
diffusion process
threshold
saturation
logistic growth curve

mathematical models of diffusion
epidemiological model
deterministic and probabilistic models
simulation of the diffusion process
barriers to diffusion

SUGGESTED ACTIVITIES

1. Interview a number of your instructors to find out where they obtain new ideas for their courses or research. Describe and alalyze the diffusion process of these ideas in order to discern some regularities and to derive a general pattern.

2. For a particular area, such as a state, province or a group of states or provinces, get the dates of establishment of institutions of higher education, either one type or several, e.g., state universities, private colleges, or junior colleges. Analyze and attempt to explain the diffusion of such institutions over the area.

3. Try to find out the pattern of spatial diffusion of a particular phenomenon from the innovation center to the present spatial distribution. In what ways is this pattern similar to the one described in this chapter? You might wish to study phenomena such as: an educational idea in a school system or within a country; student activism; billboards along a highway; medical practice, such as heart transplants or fluoridation; residential land use at the outskirts of a city; an agricultural practice, such as mechanical cherry pickers or a type of seed; popular songs; and new goods introduced for sale.

4. Describe any similarities which you might expect to find between the spatial diffusion of human phenomena and that of some non-human phenomena, such as animals or plants in an area.

5. Imagine that a new variety of grape is discovered which produces a better-quality wine than any existing variety. Hypothesize the origin and spread of this phenomenon, describing the diffusion process in some detail. Justify your hypothesis.

REFERENCES

Bowden, Leonard W. (1965), *Diffusion of the Decision to Irrigate*, Department of Geography Research Paper No. 97. Chicago: University of Chicago Press.

Brown, Lawrence A. (1968), *Diffusion Dynamics*, Lund Studies in Geography Series B, No. 29. Lund: C. W. K. Gleerup.

Brown, Ralph H. (1948), *Historical Geography of the United States*. New York: Harcourt, Brace.

Coleman, James S. (1964), *Introduction to Mathematical Sociology*. New York: The Free Press of Glencoe.

Edmonson, M. S. (1961), "Neolithic diffusion rates," *Current Anthropology* 2, 71–102.

Godlund, Sven (1951), "Bus services, hinterlands, and the location of urban settlements in Sweden, especially Scania," in *Studies in Rural-Urban Intereaction*, Lund Studies in Geography, Series B, No. 3. Lund: Carl Bloms Boktryckeri A.-B.

Griliches, Zvi (1957), "Hybrid corn: an exploration in the economics of technical change," *Econometrica* **25**, 501–522.

Griliches, Zvi (1960), "Hybrid corn and the economics of innovation," *Science* **132**, 275–280.

Hägerstrand, Torsten (1952), *The Propagation of Innovation Waves*, Lund Studies in Geography Series B, No. 4. Lund: C. W. K. Gleerup, also in Philip L. Wagner and Marvin W. Mikesell, eds., 1962, *Readings in Cultural Geography*. Chicago: University of Chicago Press, pp. 355–368.

Hägerstrand, Torsten (1953), *Innovationsförloppet ur korologisk synpunkt*. Lund: C. W. K. Gleerup, translated by Allan R. Pred as *Innovation Diffusion as a Spatial Process*. Chicago: University of Chicago Press, 1967.

Hägerstrand, Torsten (1965), "A Monte-Carlo approach to diffusion," *European Journal of Sociology* **6**, 43–67, reprinted in Brian J. L. Berry and Duane F. Marble, eds., 1968, *Spatial Analysis: A Reader in Statistical Geography*. Englewood Cliffs: Prentice-Hall. pp. 368–384.

Kniffen, Fred (1951), "The American covered bridge," *Geographical Review* **41**, 114–123.

Mackay, J. Ross (1958), "The interactance hypothesis and boundaries in Canada," *The Canadian Geographer* **11**, 1–8.

Morrill, Richard L. (1965), *Migration and the Spread and Growth of Urban Settlement*, Lund Studies in Geography, Series B, No. 26. Lund: C.W.K. Gleerup.

Rogers, Everett M. (1962), *Diffusion of Innovations*. New York: The Free Press of Glencoe.

Sauer, Carl O. (1952), *Agricultural Origins and Dispersals*. New York: The American Geographical Society.

Seig, Louis (1963), "The spread of tobacco: a study in cultural diffusion," *The Professional Geographer* **15**, No. 1, 17–20.

Yuill, Robert S. (1965), *A Simulation Study of Barrier Effect in Spatial Diffusion Problems*, Michigan Inter-University Community of Mathematical Geographers Discussion Paper No. 5. Ann Arbor: Department of Geography, University of Michigan.

Additional Readings

Anderson, C. Arnold (1965), "Patterns and variability in the distribution and diffusion of schooling," Ch. 17 in C. Arnold Anderson and Mary Jean Bowman, eds., *Education and Economic Development*. Chicago: Aldine.

Barrau, Jacques, ed. (1963), *Plants and the Migrations of Pacific Peoples*, Honolulu: Bishop Museum Press.

Brannen, Nancy, L. (1967), "The spatial pattern of enrollment at the University of Cincinnati: a case study concerning factors influencing the sphere of influence of a large university," unpublished M.A. thesis, University of Cincinnati.

Brown, Lawrence A. (1968), *Diffusion Processes and Location: A Conceptual Framework and Bibliography*. Philadelphia: Regional Science Research Institute.

Childe, Gordon V. (1937), *Independence, Convergence, and Borrowing in Institutions, Thought, and Art*. Cambridge: Harvard University Press, pp. 3–21, also in Philip L. Wagner and Marvin W. Mikesell, eds., 1962, *Readings in Cultural Geography*. Chicago: University of Chicago Press, pp. 209–217.

Cliff, Andrew D. (1968), "The neighbourbood effect in the diffusion of innovations," *Transactions Institute of British Geographers* **44**, 75–84.

Coleman, James S., Elihu Katz, and Herbert Menzel (1966), *Medical Innovation: A Diffusion Study*. New York: Bobbs-Merrill.

Colenutt, Robert J. (1969), "Linear diffusion in an urban setting," *Geographical Analysis* **1**, 106–114.

Fleming, Donald and Bernard Bailyn, 1969, *The Intellectual Migration: Europe and America 1930–1960*. Cambridge: Harvard University Press.

Hägerstrand, Torsten (1965), "Quantitative techniques for analysis of the spread of information and technology," in C. Arnold Anderson and Mary Jean Bowman, eds., *Education and Economic Development*. Chicago: Aldine.

Hägerstrand, Torsten (1966), "Aspects of the spatial structure of social communication and the diffusion of information," *Papers*, Regional Sciences Association **16**, 27–42.

Highet, Gilbert (1954), *The Migration of Ideas*. New York: Oxford University Press.

Hudson, John C. (1969), "Diffusion in a central place system," *Geographical Analysis* **1**, 45–58.

Kariel, Herbert G. (1969), "Spatial diffusion: the Alaskan camper unit in Washington State," *The Canadian Geographer* **12**, 63–72.

Kniffen, Fred (1965), "Folk housing: key to diffusion," *Annals* of the Association of American Geographers **55**, 549–577.

Morrill, Richard L. (1965), "The Negro ghetto: problems and alternatives," *Geographical Review* **55**, 339–361.

Morrill, Richard L. (1968), "Waves of spatial diffusion," *Journal of Regional Science* **8**, 1–18.

Murray, J. S. (1966), "Educational innovations," in W. E. Mann, ed., 1968, *Canada: A Sociological Profile*. The Copp Clark Publishing Co.

Nystuen, John D. (1967), "Boundary shapes and boundary problems," *Papers*, Peace Research Society (International) Papers **7**, 107–128.

Pitts, Forrest R. (1963), "Problems in computer simulation of diffusion," *Papers*, Regional Science Association **11**, 111–119.

Pred, Allan R. (1971), "Large-city interdependence and the preelectronic diffusion of innovations in the U.S.," *Geographical Analysis* **3**, 165–181.

Pred, Allan R. (1971), "Urban systems development and the long-distance flow of information through preelectronic U.S. newspapers," *Economic Geography* **47**, 498–524.

Pyle, G. F. (1969), "The diffusion of cholera in the United States in the Nineteenth century," *Geographical Analysis* **1**, 59–75.

Riley, Carroll L., J. Charles Kelley, Campbell W. Pennington, and Robert L. Rands (1971), *Man across the Sea: Problems of Pre-Columbian Contacts* Austin: University of Texas Press.

Stanislawski, Dan (1946), "The origin and spread of the grid-pattern town," *Geographical Review* **36**, 105–120.

Wolpert, Julian (1966), "A regional simulation model of information diffusion," *Public Opinion Quarterly* **30**, 597–608.

Zelinsky, Wilbur (1967), "Classical town names in the United States," *Geographical Review* **57**, 463–495.

CHAPTER 13
PERSPECTIVES

13.1 SCOPE OF CONTEMPORARY GEOGRAPHIC STUDY

Now that we have reached this point in our explorations it can be seen that this apparent end is actually only a beginning, since the few topics we have explored represent only a small sample of the many possible ones. All of them could be investigated further, and studies could be made of different areas and at various scales. In addition, persons concerned about current issues might wish to investigate spatial aspects of topics such as those suggested in Section 1.1: disease and medical care, pollution and other environmental problems, crime, housing conditions, residential choice, characteristics of the population, or urbanization. Because it is obviously not feasible or desirable to study all possible phenomena at all possible scales, investigators select topics which seem most relevant and interesting and which are considered to be either theoretically or socially significant, or both.

In the first chapter we pointed out that as man's knowledge increases, his view of the world and his relationship to it changes, and illustrated this idea by referring to the Hereford map, shown on the end papers. It is important to remember that the ideas of contemporary geography, some of which have been discussed in this book, are equally limited by our own knowledge and point of view, and subject to change and modification.

As we have seen, contemporary geography deals with the areal arrangement of phenomena on the earth and with abstract properties of these distributions. Its principal concern is with the attempt to discern order in the apparently haphazard distributional patterns of physical and cultural features. As with most disciplines, geographic study may be either basic or applied, or a mixture of the two. Basic geographic research arises out of intrinsic interest in finding answers to more abstract geographic questions, and is only incidentally concerned with the solution of practical problems. Applied geographic research, on the other hand, arises from the desire to use findings for solving human problems. The two types complement each other: Findings of basic research are often useful to persons engaged in solving practical problems, and findings which arise in the course of solving practical problems can provide insights helpful to persons engaged in basic research. Geographers might concern themselves with problems such as illiteracy, poverty, malnutrition, or poor housing in either of the two ways: They might try to answer questions about where these problems are concentrated and explain why, or they might apply knowledge about the location of the phenomena to alleviating the problems.

13.2 REGIONAL AND TOPICAL EMPHASES

Although geographers approach the study of phenomena in many different ways, two major emphases, which complement each other, can be discerned. Some geographers focus on the study of regions, while others are more interested in analyzing spatial aspects of various phenomena.

In regional studies emphasis is on describing the content of areas, both past and present. The dominant features and unique aspects of regions are characterized; the distribution, association, and functional interrelations of elements within an area which give it its distinctive character are investigated. Regions are identified and their boundaries delineated on the basis of similarities in any phenomenon or combination of phenomena such as climate, vegetation, agriculture, political control, income, and trade.

In topical geography, the focus is upon a phenomenon or group of phenomena to be studied rather than a region. Generally, physical geography deals with all non-human phenomena and involves analysis of the distribution of landforms, climates, water, plants, animals, soils, and minerals. Human geography is concerned with analysis of the distribution of man and his social, cultural, economic, and political activities. Its subdivisions include: (1) economic geography, study of the distribution of man's activities in the production and consumption of commodities and services; (2) political geography, study of spatial patterns of political units and organizations; (3) social and cultural geography, study of the distribution of people and their cultures, and elements of them; (4) settlement geography, study of rural settlements and the processes by which areas are settled; (5) urban geography, study of the distribution of cities and the location and distribution of phenomena within them; and (6) human ecology, study of the mutual interaction between man and his physical environment; the effect of man upon his environment and of the environment upon man.

Geographers concerned with spatial analysis of phenomena investigate their spatial aspects—location, spatial distribution, flows or movements, and diffusion —together with the interrelations among these aspects. They also attempt to identify and study certain abstract properties of spatial distributions and other spatial aspects of phenomena: densities, patterns, arrangements, and shapes. Both groups are interested in changes within regions over time and the processes of change which affect the spatial distribution of phenomena and other spatial aspects.

13.3 TECHNIQUES USED BY GEOGRAPHERS

Many of the techniques used by geographers are also used by other academic disciplines; for example, they collect data by means of interviews, library research, and field studies. Cartography, however, is generally thought to be uniquely and primarily geographic. Cartographers study ways of representing features of the earth's surface on maps and globes. They develop and use techniques for representing the location and spatial distribution of phenomena, flows from one area to another, and changes in spatial distributions which result from these flows. In common with researchers in other disciplines, geographers are becoming increasingly interested in using quantitative methods. They study ways of developing and using mathematical techniques for studying regions and for describing, analyzing, and explaining spatial aspects of phenomena quantitatively.

13.4 DISTINCTIVE CONTRIBUTIONS OF GEOGRAPHERS

Geographers make certain distinctive contributions to man's knowledge about the world in which he lives. They contribute knowledge and understanding of regional characteristics of the earth's surface, spatial aspects of phenomena, and properties of distributions. They provide cartographic, quantitative, and other techniques for describing, analyzing, and explaining spatial elements of phenomena. They offer theoretical models of interrelationships observed to exist among phenomena. And, finally, they can apply their knowledge to the solution of social problems such as facilitation of the spread of ideas, economic development of depressed areas, and land use planning.

13.5 SCIENCE AND VALUES

Throughout these explorations it has been emphasized that we are interested in both substantive knowledge of each topic—the geographic facts related to it—and the ways in which this knowledge has been accumulated and organized. The importance of learning to ask the right questions and to use various techniques to answer them have also been discussed. We have looked for relationships among facts which can be organized into patterns; generalizations which, when confirmed, become laws which, in turn, form the basis for more comprehensive theories. Through this cumulation of knowledge held together by a body of laws and theories, a mass of facts can gradually become organized so that generalizations derived from it are applicable beyond a given set of data. Each question answered opens up new ones. Thus, even though facts change, as they do in these times of exponentially expanding knowledge, an orientation to learning which teaches ways of using knowledge in the future should remain useful, since it prepares us to cope with change.

In these explorations we have concentrated upon understanding the phenomena we were studying; although applications of some of the findings were sometimes suggested, they were not of primary interest. Scientists are, nevertheless, often concerned about the relationship between science and immediate social problems. Should science be value-free, and should scientists keep themselves aloof from the problems of the world? This issue has long been debated but remains unsettled; opinions fluctuate with the tenor of the times. Some scientists believe that they cannot be truly scientific if they become advocates for a particular point of view; others are of the opinion that there is little justification for science which does not deal with real issues. These viewpoints represent the extremes, and most people would probably take a stand somewhere between them.

The distinguishing aspect of science is that laws are expressed in propositions of an if. . ., then . . . form, which tells us simply that if conditions A are present, we should also find B. These laws say nothing about the social desirability of either A or B, which is judged according to social and individual values. It is often important to be able to find out as objectively as possible what the probable consequences of a particular course of action are likely to be. If a dam is built, for example, what benefits are likely to accrue, and what problems might be expected to arise? If preconceptions and biases influence the results of a study aimed at answering these questions, the findings will not be likely to provide the basis for making a valid, informed decision. In a situation such as this a scientist can, if he wishes, contribute his approach which hopefully maximizes objectivity, make recommendations, and leave the final decision to others.

The findings of science may be applied by workers in many fields. For example, in Section 8.7.9 we considered interrelationships between changing land use and transportation patterns. These findings can be extrapolated to consider possible future effects of changes. We know from experience in many cities something about how the continued building of freeways and increasing use of private automobiles affects the environment. If more freeways are constructed, more automobiles will travel on them and the results will be more smog and traffic congestion rather than less. Under the existing value system in North America, personal comfort and convenience as well as profit for automobile manufacturers, oil companies, and freeway builders take precedence over the more diffuse general good. According to this set of values, more freeways and more cars are needed. On the other hand, people are beginning to realize that smog is not merely a nuisance, but a very real threat to life and health, and it appears that these values are beginning to change. The resulting decision may be to extend and improve mass transit in order to decrease use of private cars, but this will not be confirmed until substantial amounts of money are allocated for this purpose and deflected from building freeways. The authors believe that the scientist as scientist can make his greatest contribution by pointing out the probable consequences of different courses of action, rather than championing particular ones. As a citizen, however, he should advocate the course of action he deems best, and support his claim with professional knowledge.

Even though scientists try to be as objective as possible, scientific research is influenced by values of persons within a society through decisions which allocate money and resources. Money set aside for research may be used for such diverse purposes as raising the level of health care, improving education at all levels, developing more efficient means of mass transport, or inventing faster ways of killing more people. Although the output of knowledge from research is by no means exactly proportional to the input of resources, it is probable that fields which are relatively neglected will not produce much new knowledge.

Although in principle it should be possible to apply a law to any specific instance for which it is relevant, numerous limitations exist. Knowledge may be imperfect; although some generalizations about certain phenomena have been formulated, they are not yet well enough confirmed to be applied. In the social sciences laws are usually probabilistic rather than deterministic, so that it is possible to predict what the outcome is likely to be only for a large number of cases over a relatively long period of time, rather than for each individual occurrence of the event. Even when this handicap of imperfect or limited knowledge is not present, other limitations may hinder application of scientific laws to practical situations. These limitations may be technological, economic, social, political, or some combination of these and other factors. They are present whether the United States is trying to reach and explore the moon's surface or a city government wishes to build low-cost housing.

13.6 SOME CURRENT RESEARCH EMPHASES

Decisions to be made among alternative uses for a particular piece of land, or in determining the site for a library, school, or park are among the problems which form the basis of the geography of resource use, the environment and planning, and man-land relationships. For example, decisions must often be made about the use of forested areas. Various interest groups might desire to use a particular area for a number of different purposes: hunting, logging, mining, summer cottages, watershed protection, or a national park. Obviously not all these uses are compatible. Conservation groups might suggest that the area be preserved in its original state and only those uses allowed which were compatible with this decision. Other groups might emphasize the economic benefit to be gained from exploiting land for its mineral, timber, or other resources. It is usually possible to predict some, if not all of the possible outcomes from putting the land to each type of use or combination of uses. Ideally, the decision as to which ones should be allowed would then be based on which of the projected outcomes was most desirable. In practice, however, such a decision is likely to be based on the relative power of various pressure groups, and to reflect the dominant values of the society: personal or corporate profit, political expediency, or the long-run welfare of a larger group of people.

Some geographers wish to understand why and how certain alternatives are chosen and to have a better understanding of the process by which certain events have come about. There is, therefore, a growing interest in what is now termed the behavioral aspects of geography—that is, how and why people behave as they do with respect to spatially varying phenomena. They are not satisfied with the type of empirical laws derived from the gravity-potential model; they investigate the actual travel behavior of persons engaging in different activities and try to learn the motives behind them. They acknowledge that a certain mathematical curve often describes people's behavior, but ask the next question as to why this should be so. These geographers are concerned with such questions as how different people perceive their environment: what kind of mental maps they base their actions on, or their perceptions of natural hazards such as floods and droughts. Behavioral explanations often overlap into other fields of study such as economics, political science, psychology, social psychology, and sociology. By making increasing use of interdisciplinary studies, geographers and others should be able to apply existing knowledge in these fields to the study of spatial behavior, and to work towards a more nearly integrated science of human behavior.

By applying the approaches and techniques presented in this text to various phenomena of interest within a region, persons interested in regional study may arrive first at a description of what is there and then at some understanding of why the phenomena vary spatially and what interrelationships exist among their distributions. It might be desirable to develop a systems model incorporating these interrelationships. This approach is important in planning, for example, because it is no longer considered adequate to think about only one aspect of human life, such as transportation or housing, but it is necessary to take into account possible interactions among many aspects of the environment and how changes in one might influence others.

Further developments along these and other lines can be anticipated. By looking over geographical journals of the past 10 or 15 years, it is possible to see a trend toward increasing abstraction. In our exploration of diffusion in Chapter 12, for example, we saw that early studies concentrated on a particular phenomenon, such as the diffusion of hybrid seed corn. In later ones, attempts were made to construct models which were useful not only for describing the spread of a particular phenomenon but also for predicting in a more general way how other phenomena might spread from a point or points of origin. Hopefully new knowledge will be based on existing knowledge and used to help delineate areas of inquiry for additional studies. In this way, geographers may hope not simply to make bricks, each consisting of a few empirical generalizations little related to other knowledge, but to fit these bricks together to construct edifices, relating their findings to those of other investigators, as well as to theory. This accumulation of knowledge should, in turn, make possible more accurate prediction or anticipation of human spatial behavior in a variety of situations.

REVIEW YOUR UNDERSTANDING OF THESE CONCEPTS

constraints upon contemporary points of view
distinction between applied and basic research
distinction between regional and topical emphases
relationship between science and values

Additional Readings

Ackerman, Edward A. (1963), "Where is a research frontier?" *Annals* of the Association of American Geographers **53**, 429–440.

Ad hoc Committee on Geography (1965), *The Science of Geography*, Publication No. 1277. Washington, D.C.: National Academy of Sciences—National Research Council.

Brownowski, Jacob (1958), "Truth and value," in *The Common Sense of Science*. Cambridge: Harvard University Press, 120–137.

Brownowski, Jacob (1965), *Science and Human Values*. Harper Torchbooks.

Bunge, William (1966), *Theoretical Geography*, 2nd rev. ed., Lund Studies in Geography, Series C, No. 1. Lund: C.W.K. Gleerup.

Bunge, William (1969), *The First Years of the Detroit Geographical Expedition: A Personal Report*, The Detroit Geographical Expedition Discussion Paper No. 1, Detroit: The Society for Human Exploration.

Cox, Kevin R. and Reginald G. Golledge, eds. (1969), *Behavioral Problems in Geography: A Symposium*, Northwestern University Studies in Geography No. 17. Evanston: Department of Geography, Northwestern University.

Curry, Leslie (1966), "Chance and landscape," in J.W. House, ed., *Northern Geographical Essays in Honour of G.H.J. Daysh*. Newcastle-upon-Tyne: Oriel Press, 40–55.

Deutsch, Karl W. (1958), "Scientific and humanistic knowledge in the growth of civilization," in Brown, Harcourt, ed., *Science and the Creative Spirit*. 1–52.

James, Preston E. and Lorrin Kennamer, eds. (1966), *Geography as a Professional Field*, U.S. Department of Health, Education, and Welfare, Office of Education Bulletin 1966 No. 10, OE-26015. Washington D.C.: U.S. Government Printing Office.

Kates, Robert W. (1962), *Hazard and Choice Perception in Flood Plain Management*, Department of Geography Research Paper No. 78. Chicago: University of Chicago Press.

Kohn, Clyde F., (1970), "The 1960's: a decade of progress in geographical research and Instruction," *Annals* of the Association of American Geographers **60**, 211–219.

Krutch, Joseph Wood, 1953, 1954, "The idols of the laboratory," in *The Measure of Man*. Bobbs-Merrill, 77–93.

Mead, Margaret (1970), "The changing significance of food," *American Scientist* **58**, 176–181.

Muller, Herbert J. (1943), "The use and abuse of science," in *Science and Criticism*. New Haven: Yale University Press, 69–75.

Parsons, James J. (1969), "Toward a more humane geography, (Guest Editorial) *Economic Geography* **45**, 189.

Peet, Richard, ed. (1970), "The geography of American poverty," special issue of *Antipode: A Radical Journal of geography*, Vol. 2 No. 2.

Pred, Allan R. (1967, 1969), *Behavior and Location: Foundations for a Geographic and Dynamic Location Theory*, Parts I and II, Lund Studies in Geography Series B, No. 27 and No. 28. Lund: C.W.K. Gleerup.

Saarinen, Thomas F. (1969), *Perception of Environment*, Commission on College Geography Resource Paper No. 5. Washington, D.C.: Association of American Geographers.

Stace, W.T. (1948), "Man against darkness," *Atlantic Monthly* **182**, No. 3. 54–55.

Taaffe, Edward J., ed. (1970). *Geography, The Behavioral and Social Sciences Survey.* Englewood Cliffs: Prentice-Hall, Inc.

Thomas, William L., Jr., ed. (1956), *Man's Role in Changing the Face of the Earth.* Chicago: University of Chicago Press.

Warntz, William (1964), *Geographers and What They Do.* New York: Watts.

White, Gilbert F. (1965), "Rediscovering the earth," *American Education* **1**, No. 2, 8–11.

Wolpert, Julian (1964), "The decision process in spatial context," *Annals* of the Association of American Geographers **54**, 537–558.

Wolpert, Julian (1970), "Departures from the usual environment in locational analysis," *Annals* of the Association of American Geographers **60**, 220–229.

APPENDIX A
GUIDE FOR
ANALYZING ARTICLES

This guide gives a series of logical steps to follow in reading research. These steps are similar to those involved in analyzing a problem on which one proposes to do research. It is necessary first to know the purpose of the study: What is it that the researcher was attempting to find out? Next, how was the study carried out—what was done? What were the substantive findings of the study and do they confirm the hypotheses? The findings may be presented verbally or symbolically, and supplemented by maps, charts, graphs, or diagrams. There is usually a section in which the author discusses the findings and states their significance. Unfortunately, since many studies are not reported in such a clear-cut organizational pattern, it may be difficult to separate the writer's report of the substantive findings from his ideas as to the significance of these findings. If, however, the reader searches for this distinction, he will be rewarded by gaining a clearer view of the significance of the study. In conclusion, the reader may wish to make a brief evaluative summary.

A. *Definition of the problem:*
1. What is the general topic?
2. What is the general frame of reference?
3. In what ways is the study geographic?
4. What are the specific aspects upon which attention is focused?
5. How are the phenomena defined; are the definitions operational?
6. How does the study draw upon existing knowledge, observations, laws, or theories?
7. What are the underlying assumptions?
8. What hypotheses are stated? Are they explicit or implicit?
9. What spatial and temporal delimitations are made?
10. Are key concepts defined?

B. *Techniques used in problem analysis:*
1. What is the areal organization?
    a) Choice of scale of areal generalization.
    b) Choice of sample and/or universe.
2. How were data collected?
    a) Sources
    b) Validity
    c) Reliability
3. What type of data analysis was used?
    a) Descriptive
    b) Comparative
    c) Classificatory
    d) Statistical
    e) Mathematical

C. *Substantive findings:*
1. What were the findings?
2. How were they presented: maps, tables, diagrams, etc.?
3. Were the hypotheses confirmed?

D. *Conclusions:*
1. What explanation and discussion of the findings is given?
2. How do the findings relate to theory?
3. In what ways are the generalizations better than previous ones?
    a) Are they more precise?
    b) Do they have a higher probability of being valid?
    c) Are they more generally applicable, either spatially or temporally?
    d) Do they subsume more phenomena or laws?
4. How are residuals—those observations not fitting the general pattern—analysed?
5. Are the conclusions derived from and consistent with the findings?
6. Is the possible significance of the findings pointed out?
7. What suggestions for further research are made?

E. *Evaluation and importance to reviewer:*
1. How would you evaluate the study as to consistency and completeness?
2. What is the value of the methods, findings, and/or conclusions for other studies?
3. What, if any, criticisms of the conclusions would you make?
4. What alternative methods of dealing with the problem might there be?

APPENDIX B
SELECTED PERIODICALS
AND MONOGRAPHS*

Important English Language Journals and Monographs Dealing with Topics in Social Geography

Annals of the Association of American Geographers
A leading geographical journal, covering all topics and areas, but with emphasis on North America.

Australian Geographer
Deals with all topics; mainly, but not solely, on Australia.

Australian Geographical Studies
Deals with all topics; mainly, but not solely on Australia.

The Canadian Geographer
Leading professional geographical journal of Canada. Some of the articles are written in French, with English summaries; articles in English are summarized in French.

Economic Geography
A leading journal devoted to economic geography and related topics such as urban geography and methodology.

Geoforum: Journal of Physical, Human, and Regional Geosciences
A new international journal. Part of each issue typically devoted to a particular aspect of man-land relationships.

Geografiska Annaler, Series B, Human Geography
A leading international geographical journal, with articles published primarily in English, but also in German, Swedish, and French. This series deals entirely with human or social geography.

*Adapted with permission from: Harris, Chauncy D. (1971), *Annotated World List of Selected Current Geographical Serials in English, French, and German*, 3rd rev. ed., Department of Geography Research Paper No. 137. Chicago: University of Chicago Department of Geography.

Geographical Analysis
A journal of theoretical geography with emphasis on quantitive and theoretical approaches.

Geographical Review
Publishes articles on a variety of geographical topics, with emphasis on social geography.

Geography
A British journal which emphasizes geographic education, but also contains substantive articles.

Institute of British Geographers Transactions
Articles deal with all topics and areas, but with emphasis on Great Britain.

Journal of Geography
Emphasis on geographic education, but also contains substantive articles.

Journal of Tropical Geography
Articles on physical and social aspects of tropical areas, especially in Asia and Africa.

Lund Studies in Geography, Series B, Human Geography
Articles and monographs primarily in English dealing with important research frontiers in social, economic, and urban geography.

Lund Studies in Geography, Series C, General and Mathematical Geography
Quantitative, statistical, and air-photo methods in geographic research.

New Zealand Geographer
Deals with all topics within Oceania, with particular emphasis on New Zealand.

Northwestern University Studies in Geography
Primarily research monographs on a variety of geographical topics, mainly in social geography.

Proceedings, Association of American Geographers
Papers presented at annual meetings of the Association.

The Professional Geographer
Contains short articles and professional notes dealing with a wide variety of topics.

Soviet Geography: Review and Translation
Translation and reviews of articles appearing in Soviet journals.

Tijdschrift voor Economische en Sociale Geografie
A leading international journal in the field of social and economic geography, with world-wide coverage and authorship. Articles are primarily in English and Dutch.

University of Chicago, Department of Geography Research Papers
Primarily monographs on wide variety of geographical topics.

Important Canadian Journals Dealing with Topics in Social Geography with Articles in French

Cahiers de géographie de Québec
La Revue de géographie de Montréal

Regional Journals within the United States and Canada frequently containing articles of more general interest

Albertan Geographer
B.C. Geographical Series
California Geographer
Ecumene
East Lakes Geographer
Maryland Geographer
Ontario Geography
Pennsylvania Geography
Southeastern Geographer
Yearbook of the Association of Pacific Coast Geographers

Journals in Fields Related to Social Geography

American Anthropologist
American Behavioral Scientist
American Economic Review
American Journal of Sociology
American Sociological Review
Canadian Review of Sociology and Anthropology
Demography
Economic Development and Cultural Change
Ekistics
Human Organization
Journal of Developing Areas
Journal of Regional Science
Land Economics
Landscape
Papers of the Regional Science Association
Pacific Viewpoints
Population Studies
Regional Studies
The Review of Regional Studies
Rural Sociology
Town Planning Review
Urban Studies

NAME INDEX

SUBJECT INDEX

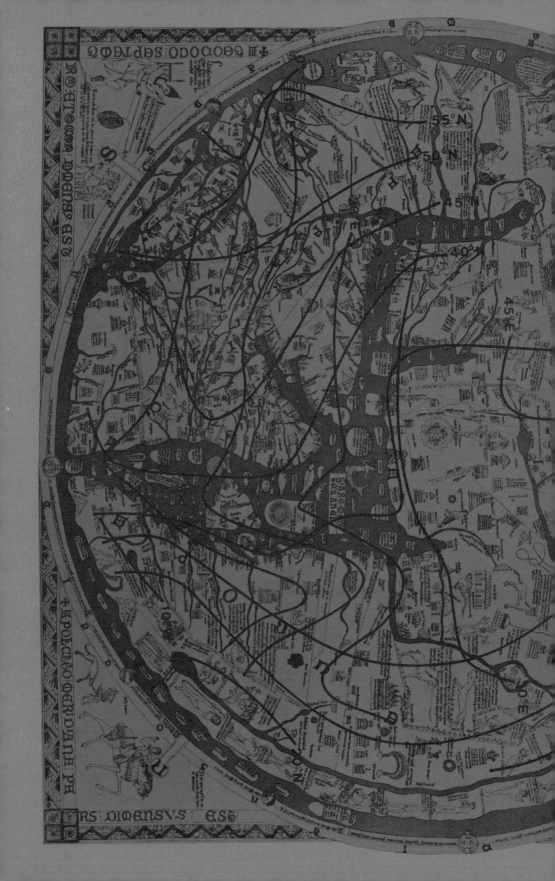

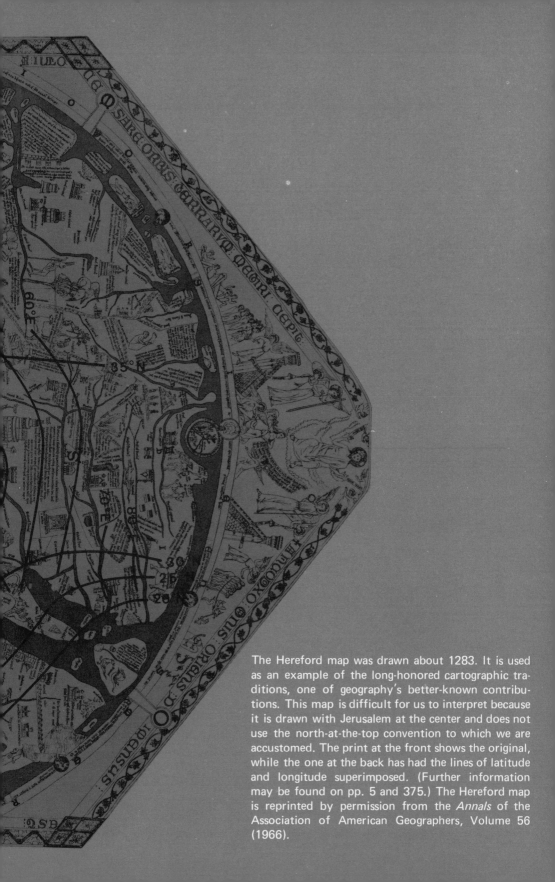

The Hereford map was drawn about 1283. It is used as an example of the long-honored cartographic traditions, one of geography's better-known contributions. This map is difficult for us to interpret because it is drawn with Jerusalem at the center and does not use the north-at-the-top convention to which we are accustomed. The print at the front shows the original, while the one at the back has had the lines of latitude and longitude superimposed. (Further information may be found on pp. 5 and 375.) The Hereford map is reprinted by permission from the *Annals* of the Association of American Geographers, Volume 56 (1966).